ARCTIC OCEAN

Franz Josef Land

New Siberian Islands

Novaya Zemlya

FINLAND

RUSSIAN FEDERATION
Asiatic Russia

ESTONIA
LATVIA
saw
LITHUANIA
LAND
BELARUS
• Minsk
• Moscow
Chelyabinsk •
Omsk •

European Russia

• Kiev
UKRAINE
IRKUTSK •

ROMANIA
HUNGARY
SLVK
KAZAKHSTAN
Astana •

SERBIA
BULGARIA
Ulan Bator •
MONGOLIA

ALB.
GEORGIA
• Istanbul
Bishkek •
N. KOREA

GREECE
TURKEY
AZERB.
Tashkent •
KYRGYZSTAN
The Great Wall of China • ○
Pyongyang •
JAPAN

Athens •
SYRIA
TURKMEN.
UZBEKISTAN
Forbidden City • ○
Beijing •
Seoul •
Nikko • ○ Tosho-gu Shrine

at Mosque
LEBANON
○ Krak des Chevaliers
Tehrán •
The Registan
• Dushanbe
Temple of Heaven • ○
S. KOREA
• Tokyo

ISRAEL
IRAQ
Ashgabat •
TAJIKISTAN
Nara •

Masada ○
• Jerusalem
IRAN
• Kabul
CHINA
○ Todai-ji Temple

Cairo •
○ Dome of the Rock
AFGHANI-
Islamabad •
Amritsar •
• The Golden Temple
Shanghai •

Petra ○
○ Church of the Holy Sepulcher
STAN
Delhi •
PACIFIC
OCEAN

t Pyramid ○
JORDAN
PAKISTAN
Fatehpur • Taj Mahal
○ Potala Palace

BYA
EGYPT
Riyadh •
Sikri
Dhaka •
Taipei •

Abu Simbel ○
SAUDI ARABIA
The Great Stupa • ○ • Sanchi
BANGLADESH
TAIWAN

CHAD
SUDAN
OMAN
MYANMAR
• Hong Kong

YEMEN
Abu Dhabi •
Mumbai •
INDIA
LAOS
• Hanoi

Khartoum •
ERITREA
Rangoon •
THAILAND
• Manila

DJIBOUTI
Chennai •
Bangkok •
• Angkor Wat
PHILIPPINES

Northern
Mariana
Islands
(to US)

Wake Island
(to US)

Addis Ababa •
ETHIOPIA
Grand Palace and Wat Phra Kaeo ○ • Phnom Penh
Guam
(to US)

MARSHALL
ISLANDS

C.A.R.
SOMALIA
Wat Arun ○
CAMBODIA
VIETNAM

ndé
UGANDA
SRI LANKA
Colombo •
MICRONESIA

ngo
DEM. REP.
CONGO
KENYA
• Nairobi
Kuala Lumpur •
MALAYSIA
PALAU

Kinshasa •
RWANDA
BURUNDI
MALDIVES
SINGAPORE
NAURU

TANZANIA
• Dodoma
British Indian
Ocean Territory
(to UK)
INDONESIA
PAPUA
NEW GUINEA
TUVALU

SEYCHELLES
Jakarta •
○ Borobodur Temple
• Port Moresby
SOLOMON
ISLANDS

GOLA
ZAMBIA
COMOROS
Java
Pura Ulun Danu Batur
EAST TIMOR

MALAWI
Bali
VANUATU

• Lilongwe
Mayotte (to France)
INDIAN

MBIA
ZIMBABWE
Harare •
MOZAMBIQUE
Antananarivo •
MAURITIUS
New
Caledonia
(to France)
FIJI

BOTSWANA
OCEAN
AUSTRALIA

• Gaborone
MADAGASCAR
Reunion
(to France)
• Brisbane

SOUTH
AFRICA
• Maputo
SWAZILAND

WITHDRAWN
○ Sydney Opera House

LESOTHO
• Sydney
Canberra •

n ○ Castle of Good Hope
• Melbourne

Tasmania
• Wellington
NEW ZEALAND

French Southern
& Antarctic Territories
(to France)
Dunedin Railway Station

Prince Edward Islands
(to South Africa)

SOUTHERN OCEAN

THE WORLD'S MUST-SEE PLACES

Content previously published as
200 of the World's Most Beautiful Places

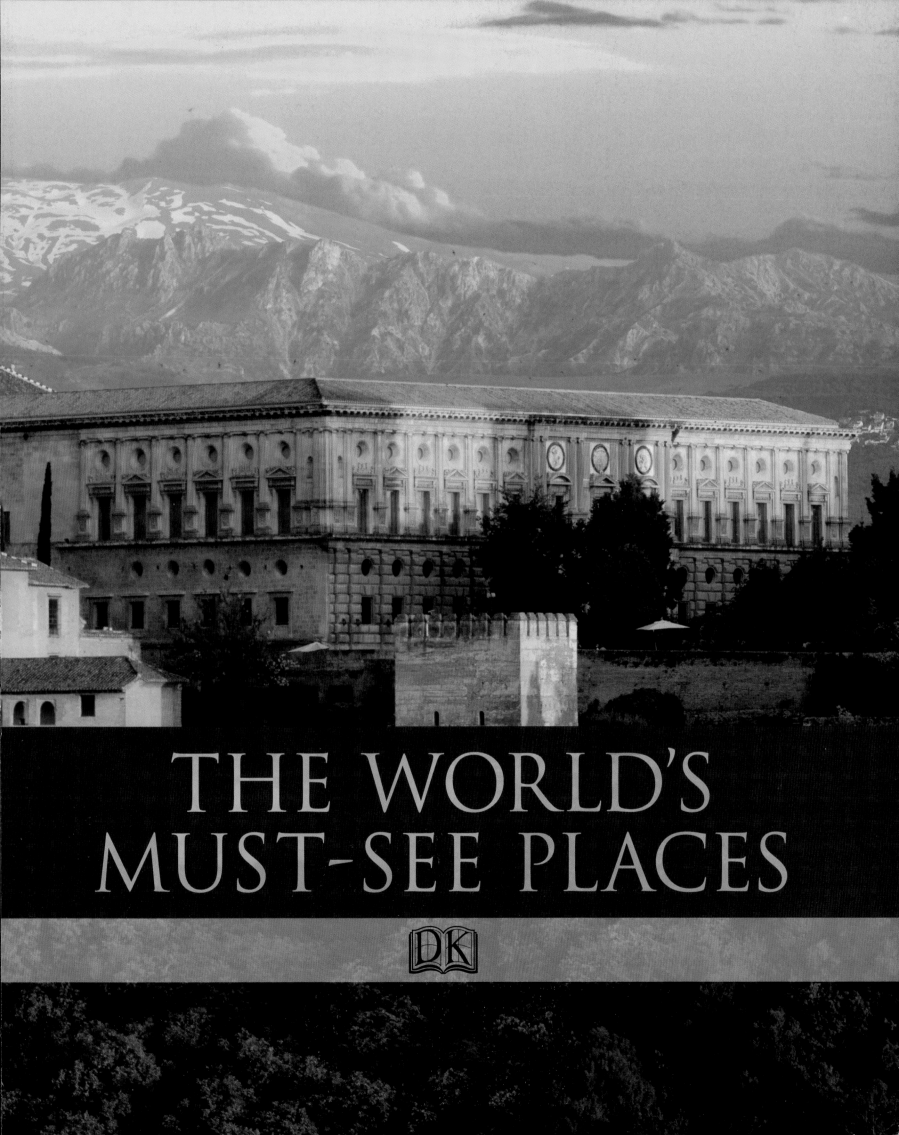

THE WORLD'S
MUST-SEE PLACES

DK

LONDON, NEW YORK, MELBOURNE, MUNICH AND DELHI

PUBLISHER Douglas Amrine
LIST MANAGER Julie Oughton
DESIGN MANAGER Mabel Chan
PROJECT EDITOR Alexandra Whittleton
CARTOGRAPHER Casper Morris
SENIOR DTP DESIGNER Jason Little
PRODUCTION CONTROLLER Erika Pepe

Produced for Dorling Kindersley by
ART EDITOR Sunita Gahir
PROJECT EDITOR Debra Wolter
US EDITOR Margaret Parrish

2005 edition
PUBLISHER Douglas Amrine
PUBLISHING MANAGER Kate Poole
MANAGING EDITOR Anna Streiffert
PROJECT EDITOR Lucinda Cooke
SENIOR ART EDITOR Marisa Renzullo
SENIOR DESIGNER Tessa Bindloss
DESIGNER Maite Lantaron
SENIOR DTP DESIGNER Jason Little
DTP DESIGNER Conrad Van Dyk
SENIOR MAP COORDINATOR Casper Morris
EDITORS Sherry Collins, Vandana Mohindra,
Mani Ramaswarmy
PRODUCTION Joanna Bull, Sarah Dodd
PICTURE RESEARCH Taiyaba Khatoon, Ellen Root

First American Edition, 2005
This edition, 2011

Published in the United States by
DK Publishing
375 Hudson Street
New York, New York 10014

11 12 13 14 10 9 8 7 6 5 4 3 2 1

001—178878—Oct/2011

A catalog record for this book is available from
the Library of Congress.

ISBN 978-0-7566-8382-5

DK books are available at special discounts
when purchased in bulk for sales promotions,
premiums, fund-raising, or educational use. For
details, contact: DK Publishing Special Markets,
375 Hudson Street, New York, New York 10014
or SpecialSales@dk.com.

Color reproduction by Media Development
Printing Ltd, UK
Printed and bound in Singapore by Star Standard

Discover more at
www.dk.com

Half title image: Sagrada Família, Barcelona, Spain
Title page image: The Alhambra, Granada, Spain

CONTENTS

▼ Ruins of Machu Picchu, Peru

▼ Fresco by Giotto, Basilica of St. Francis, Assisi, Italy

▼ Château de Chenonceau, France

Sydney Opera House, Australia ►

Introduction

Ancient Greek and Roman travelers, whose idea of enjoyment was probably little different from our own, had few sights to visit. It was therefore not difficult for Greek writers to list the seven best and call them the "wonders of the world." Civilizations have come a long way since then, the world has shrunk with high-speed travel, and there has been no let-up in the desire to build. These days, it would be hard to pinpoint the seven most wondrous buildings in the world, but here are 103 sights that should not be missed.

◄ **St. Basil's Cathedral in Moscow, crowned with colorful domes**

CREATED for people of vision and flair to glorify themselves, their gods, and their power, these sights are landmarks that tell us about the past, where we have come from, and what we are capable of achieving. Each one needs close inspection to appreciate its setting, structure, style, and ornament. Palaces, castles, religious houses, and places of entertainment have been handed to artists and artisans to embellish. Around and within these walls, masons, carpenters, wood carvers, ceramicists, sculptors, glassmakers, painters, metalworkers, cabinet makers, embroiderers, tapestry makers, and landscape gardeners have all sought some kind of perfection. Some of these craftsmen are well known, but most were journeymen whose names were never meant to be remembered. In the creation of these buildings, they captured the glory of their age for all the world to see forever.

It is astonishing that some of these buildings have lasted for so long. With a few exceptions, such as Norway's stave churches and the Todai-ji Temple in Japan, most wooden structures have not survived. Even stone buildings have frequently come to grief in earthquakes, wars, fires, and floods. As a result, many are like palimpsests, written over again and again. In Europe, a single building can have within it the marks of half a dozen cultures dating back more than 2,000 years. Also, the use of a building can change, from castle to palace, church to fort, and many flourish today as museums.

UNESCO WORLD HERITAGE SITES

The Great Pyramid at Giza in Egypt is the only surviving wonder of the ancient world. In 1979, it was inscribed as a World Heritage Site by the United Nations Educational, Scientific, and Cultural Organization (UNESCO), an agency of the United Nations set up in 1945. The idea of a fund to preserve the world's cultural and natural heritage was sparked in 1959 when the temples at Abu Simbel in Egypt were in danger of being submerged in Lake Nasser by the building of the Aswan High Dam. Following an appeal from the governments of Egypt and Sudan, UNESCO raised $80 million to move the temples of Ramses II and Nefertari more than 200 ft (60 m) out of harm's way. The work was completed in 1968, and as a result of this success, UNESCO, with the International Council on Monuments and Sites (ICOMOS), went on to draft a new convention. Joined by ideas from the International Union for the Conservation of Nature (IUCN), proposals for safeguarding both cultural and natural sites were formally adopted by UNESCO's General Conference in 1972.

Today, there are some 800 UNESCO World Heritage Sites around the world, more than 600 of them cultural, as opposed to natural, sites. Italy and Spain have the most, followed by France and Germany. Each year, a dozen or more sites are added to the list. Proposals for sites can come from any one of the member countries, which each give one percent of their UNESCO dues to the fund. With voluntary contributions, the fund receives around $3.5 million a year. The money goes toward preserving the sites, while some is set aside for those currently deemed at risk through man-made or natural calamities.

▲ **The imposing façade of Edinburgh Castle, Scotland**

Cambodia's spectacular Angkor Wat temple, built in the 12th century by the Khmer empire ►

▲ The Great Wall of China, a major tourist attraction and a powerful symbol of China

▼ Cartouche at Abu Simbel, Egypt

▲ The Patio de los Leones in Spain's Alhambra is typical of the sensual architecture of the Moors

◄ The White House, Washington, D.C., the official residence of the president of the United States

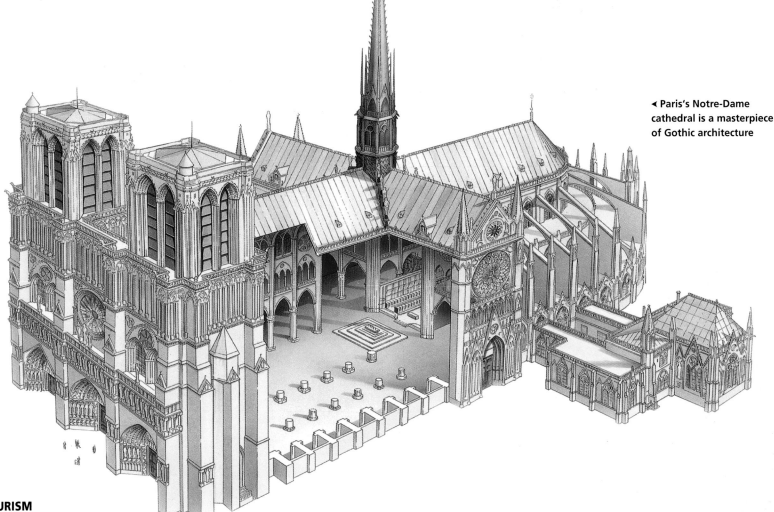

◄ Paris's Notre-Dame cathedral is a masterpiece of Gothic architecture

TOURISM

The feet of thousands of visitors also put sights at risk, and many have had to restrict access because of this. However, tourism can help preserve sights by providing an income from entrance fees.

We now have a chance to see inside the world's most spectacular sights—to wander their corridors and squares—and our curiosity is unbounded. Many of the sights in this book are only a weekend break away. Some of them provide exhibitions, talks, conferences, or concerts, while others are the upholders of colorful rituals and traditions. Not all of the sights are so easily accessible, however. Religious devotees often sought remote places for their contemplations and some sights are remote for strategic reasons, for example, the Inca estate of Machu Picchu in Peru, so hard to find that it was lost to the world for centuries.

Many ancient and prehistoric sites were oriented in alignment with the movements of the Sun, the Moon, the planets, and stars, and being there at dawn or at a solstice is to feel their potent magic. Other sights also have their special times: when choirs and music fill the churches; when a festival recalls a building's heyday; when a full Moon hovers over the Taj Mahal, the Sun sets on San Francisco's Golden Gate Bridge, or when the snow is snug around St. Petersburg's Winter Palace. Some museums are free on a particular day, and visiting a sight early in the morning is always a good way of avoiding the crowds. Rainy or baking-hot seasons should be avoided, and sometimes, buildings,

or parts of them, are closed for renovation. However, you might want to visit Mali in the spring to watch the renovation of Djenné Mosque, when around 4,000 townspeople gather to replaster the mud-brick building in a splendid festival.

MEN AND MATERIALS

Conservation requires skilled craftspeople. A stone-mason these days may be as much in demand as one in the Middle Ages. The right materials are important, too. They are not only required to be authentic, but they must also work within their limitations. Stone can only reach a certain height and it wasn't until the 19th century that the 482-ft (147-m) high Great Pyramid at Giza was surpassed.

Discoveries pepper the 19th century, a time when steam power made travel easier and artifacts from sights were waiting to be uncovered. Ideas were revived, too, and the century saw the rebirth of many styles. France's Arc de Triomphe revisited the Classical style, while Budapest's Parliament revived the Gothic style. Castle building was spectacularly revived in King Ludwig's fantasy, Neuschwanstein, in Germany, and in Portugal's Palace of Pena, where various styles were incorporated into the stately pile.

In the 20th century, new shapes became possible through the use of reinforced concrete, notable in the structures of Oscar Neimeyer's Brasília and in Frank Lloyd Wright's Solomon R. Guggenheim Museum,

completed in 1959, the year that Jørn Utzon's Sydney Opera House was begun. These were among the first buildings to make use of computer technology. Less than 50 years later, this technology helped produce marvels such as the titanium waves of Frank O. Ghery's Guggenheim Museum in Bilbao, Spain.

Buildings are monuments to patrons and architects and through them their names have been handed down to us. At ancient sites, the archeologists are also remembered, men driven by the desire to be the first to uncover treasures lost for millennia: imagine the delight of the explorer who first sighted Egypt's Abu Simbel.

Buildings have become emblems of whole nations: the Statue of Liberty, the Registan, Angkor Wat, the Taj Mahal. Romantic, exotic, seductive, the names speak volumes. By the same token, churches, monasteries, mosques, temples, and shrines have become defining symbols of different faiths, and their spaces may produce an inner peace. More modestly, buildings help to conjure up the lives of their former occupants, be they the homes of artists such as Rubens in Antwerp, or palaces for rulers, like the Forbidden City in Beijing, home to emperors of dynastic China.

Whatever a building's form and function, and whatever its age and condition, it always has many stories to tell. In these pages, walls are peeled back and the layers of history are revealed to provide an oppor-tunity to step inside and let the imagination roam.

The magnificent Apollo fountain in the gardens of Château de Versailles

EUROPE

Borgund Stave Church, Norway

The only stave church to have remained unchanged since the Middle Ages is Borgund Stavkirke at Lærdal in western Norway. Dedicated to the apostle St. Andrew, it dates from around 1150 and is built from almost 2,000 carefully crafted pieces of wood. The interior is very simple: there are no pews or decorations, and the lighting is limited to a few small openings high up on the walls. The exterior is richly decorated with carvings: dragonlike animals in life-and-death struggles, dragonheads, and runic inscriptions. There is a 16th-century pulpit and a free-standing belfry with a medieval bell.

CONSTRUCTION METHODS

The earliest stave churches, built in the 11th century, had wooden wall columns that were set directly into the ground. These churches lasted no more than 100 years, since moisture in the ground caused the column bases to rot away. As construction techniques developed, it became customary to set the wooden framework on sills that rested on a stone foundation. This raised the entire wooden skeleton above ground level, protecting it from humidity. This method proved so effective that churches built in the 12th century are still standing today.

STAVE CHURCH DESIGN

Borgund Stave Church is one of the largest and most ornately designed of the almost 30 remaining stave churches in Norway. Usually stave churches were simple, relatively small structures with a **nave** and a narrow chancel. Borgund's chancel also has a distinctive semicircular apse. Stave posts mark a division between the two. The interior is dark, since light can only filter through from small round openings (**windows**) under the three-tiered roof, which is crowned by a turret. An **external gallery** often encircles stave churches.

ORNAMENTATION

The introduction of Christianity to Norway around the year 1000 saw the merging of pagan and Christian cultures and beliefs. Most stave churches were erected on the sites of old temples that were destroyed in the wake of Christianity. The impact of this can be seen in the richly decorated carvings in stave churches, which unite pre-Christian and Christian symbolism. Pagan gods were represented in disguise alongside medieval Christian saints. The door frame designs (**West Door**) are particularly elaborate and demonstrate the skill of the carpenters who embellished them from top to bottom with intricate carvings. Wood from pine trees was commonly used, since this was most readily available. Branches and bark were removed from the trees, which were then left to dry out before being chopped down. This method meant that the wood was more weather-resistant and durable.

Stave Church Location ▶
Many of the surviving stave churches are in remote locations. High, exposed sites that were noticeable and remarkable were generally chosen to create a dramatic visual effect.

▼ **Nave**

▲ **Intricate framework of the main roof**

▲ **West Door**
The exterior of the church is richly adorned. The decorations on the Romanesque West Door feature vinelike ornamentation and depictions of dragon battles.

KEY DATES			
c. 1150	**1300s**	**1500–1620**	**1870**
Borgund Stave Church is built to replace the rotting existing church.	A chancel and an apse are added to the building.	The pulpit is constructed and the altarpiece added.	The church goes out of regular service when a larger church is constructed nearby.

KING OLAV THE HOLY

Olav Haraldsson became king of a united Norway in 1016 and went on to convert the country to Christianity. Pagan statues were torn down and stave churches built. He died in battle in 1030. A year later, his body was exhumed and he was declared a saint.

King Olav the Holy

Spire
This sits atop the three-tiered roof.

Central Tower
There are three tiers on the roof of this tower. The first tier is decorated with dragonheads on the gables, similar to those on the main roof. These were meant to cleanse the air, purging it of the evil spirits of unlawful pagan worship.

Windows
Simple, circular openings in the outer walls let in a small amount of light.

◢ Main Roof
This, along with the other roofs, is clad in pine shingles.

◢ Nave
Twelve posts (staves) around the central part of the nave support the roof. Disappearing into the semidarkness of the roof, they give an increased sense of height.

Crosses
The gables above the doorways and apse tower are decorated with plain crosses.

▲ Altarpiece
The interior of Borgund Church contains no ornate embellishment, only a simple pulpit and altar. This altarpiece dates from 1654.

Crosses of St. Andrew
The central nave is bordered by crosses in the shape of the letter "X."

External gallery

Entrance

◢ West Door

VIKING HERITAGE

Rich ornamentation in stave churches is evidence of Norway's Viking era, when skilled carving techniques were developed to combine art and woodworking in construction. The depiction of animals such as dragons and serpents in these carvings is thought to derive from Viking art.

Vasa Museum, Stockholm

Sweden's most popular museum enshrines the royal warship *Vasa*, which capsized on its maiden voyage of just 4,265 ft (1,300 m) in calm weather, on August 10, 1628, in Stockholm's harbor. About 50 people went down with what was designed to be the pride of the Swedish Navy. Guns were all that was salvaged from the vessel during the 17th century, and it was not until 1956 that a marine archeologist's persistent search led to the rediscovery of *Vasa*. After a complex salvage operation, followed by a 17-year conservation program, the Vasa Museum was opened in June 1990, less than a nautical mile from the scene of the disaster.

▼ Lion Figurehead
King Gustav II Adolf, who commissioned *Vasa*, was known as the Lion of the North, so a springing lion was the obvious choice for the 13-ft (4-m) figurehead.

▲ Upper Deck
◀ Gun-Port Lion

▲ Gun Ports
◀ Bronze Cannon

◀ Emperor Titus
Carvings of 20 Roman emperors stand on parade on *Vasa*.

▲ Upper Gun Deck
Visitors cannot enter the warship itself, but a full-size replica of the upper gun deck, with carved wooden dummies of sailors, is on view, giving a good idea of conditions on board.

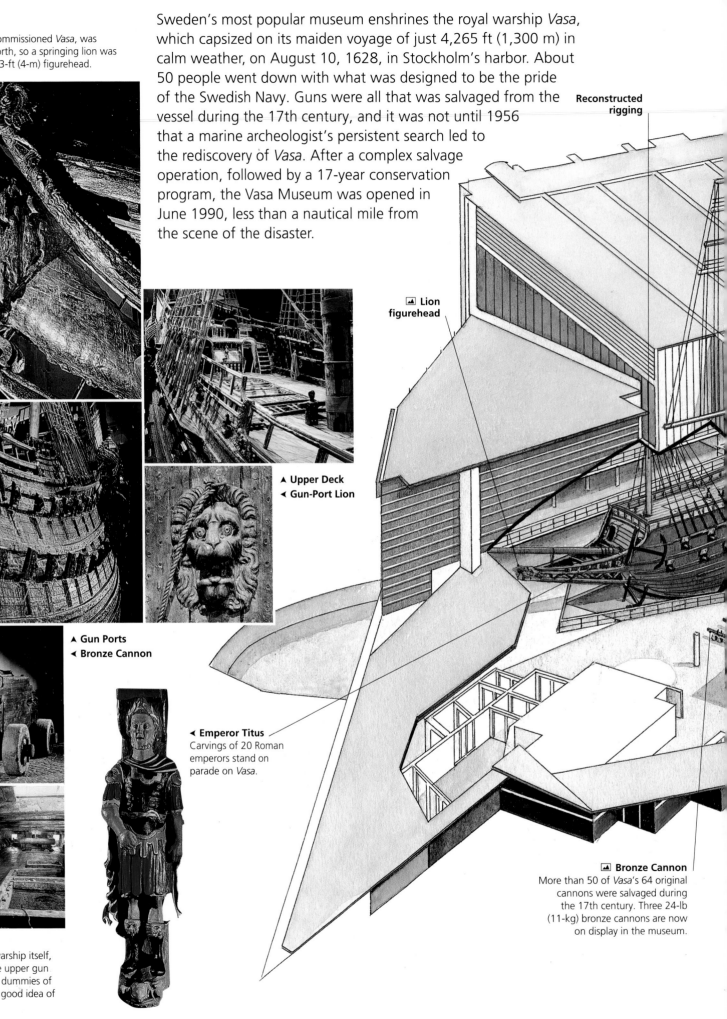

Reconstructed rigging

◪ Lion figurehead

◪ Bronze Cannon
More than 50 of *Vasa*'s 64 original cannons were salvaged during the 17th century. Three 24-lb (11-kg) bronze cannons are now on display in the museum.

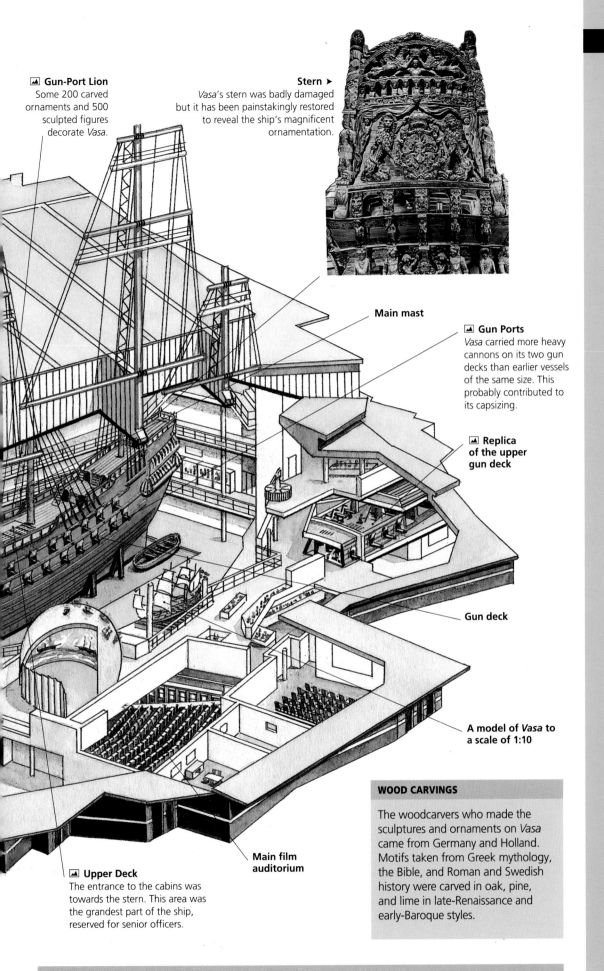

⚑ Gun-Port Lion
Some 200 carved ornaments and 500 sculpted figures decorate *Vasa*.

Stern ▶
Vasa's stern was badly damaged but it has been painstakingly restored to reveal the ship's magnificent ornamentation.

Main mast

⚑ Gun Ports
Vasa carried more heavy cannons on its two gun decks than earlier vessels of the same size. This probably contributed to its capsizing.

⚑ Replica of the upper gun deck

Gun deck

A model of *Vasa* to a scale of 1:10

Main film auditorium

⚑ Upper Deck
The entrance to the cabins was towards the stern. This area was the grandest part of the ship, reserved for senior officers.

WOOD CARVINGS

The woodcarvers who made the sculptures and ornaments on *Vasa* came from Germany and Holland. Motifs taken from Greek mythology, the Bible, and Roman and Swedish history were carved in oak, pine, and lime in late-Renaissance and early-Baroque styles.

THE SHIP

Vasa was built as a symbol of Swedish might by King Gustav II Adolf, who was steadily increasing Swedish influence over the Baltic region during the 1620s, through war with Poland. *Vasa* was the largest vessel in the history of the Swedish fleet and was capable of carrying 64 cannons and more than 445 crew. From its 170-ft (52-m) high **stern** it would have been possible to fire down upon smaller ships. *Vasa* was equipped for both traditional close combat and artillery battles. The musketeers had shooting galleries for training, and on the **upper deck** were so-called "storm pieces," erected as protection against musketry fire.

LIFE ON BOARD

Vasa's intended destination on its maiden voyage was the Älvsnabben naval base in the southern Stockholm archipelago, where more soldiers were to embark. Each man's life on the ship would have been determined by his rank. The officers would have slept in bunks and the admiral in his cabin. Officers also ate better food than the crew, whose meals were very basic, and consisted of beans, porridge, salted fish, and beer. The decks would have been very crowded—the small space between every two guns was the living and sleeping quarters for seven men (**gun deck**). There was no fresh food, so many of the crew would have had scurvy and died from deficiency diseases before they reached battle.

THE SALVAGE OPERATION

The marine archeologist Andérs Franzen had been looking for *Vasa* for many years. On August 25, 1956, his patience was rewarded when he brought up a piece of blackened oak on his plumb line from *Vasa*, located 100 ft (30 m) beneath the surface. From the autumn of 1957, it took divers two years to clear tunnels under the hull for the lifting cables. The first lift with six cables was a success, after which *Vasa* was lifted in 16 stages into shallower water. Thousands of plugs were then inserted into holes left by rusted iron bolts. The final lift started on the morning of April 24, 1961, and on May 4, *Vasa* was finally towed into dry dock after 333 years under water.

KEY DATES

1625	1628	1956	1961	1990
King Gustav II Adolf orders new warships, including *Vasa*.	*Vasa* is ready for its maiden voyage, but it capsizes in Stockholm's harbor.	Archeologist Andérs Franzen locates *Vasa* and participates in its salvage.	*Vasa* is raised to the surface after 333 years on the seabed.	The Vasa Museum opens as a permanent museum, showing the restored *Vasa* and its treasures.

TARA AND ITS KINGS

A site of mythical importance, Tara was the political and spiritual center of Celtic Ireland and the seat of the High Kings until the 11th century. Whoever ruled Tara could claim supremacy over the country. It is thought that many of Tara's kings were buried in pagan ceremonies at Newgrange. Tara's importance as a spiritual center diminished as Christianity flourished. Legend says that Tara's most famous king, Cormac Mac Art, who ruled in the 3rd century, did not want to be buried at Newgrange among pagan kings. His kinsmen, disregarding his wish, tried to cross the Boyne River to Newgrange but failed due to the huge waves and so he was buried elsewhere.

WINTER SOLSTICE AT NEWGRANGE

The shortest day and the longest night occurs each year on December 21 and is known as the winter solstice. At Newgrange, on the morning of December 21, rays of sunlight shine into the roof box of the passage grave and light up the **passage**, illuminating the north recess of the cruciform burial **chamber**. At all other times of the year, the tomb is shrouded in darkness. Newgrange is the only passage grave currently excavated that has this characteristic—temples tend to be the usual locations for this type of event. Many believe that because of this, Newgrange was originally used as a place of worship, and only later as a burial ground for pagan kings.

DOWTH AND KNOWTH

Described as the "cradle of Irish civilization," the Boyne valley contains two other prehistoric burial sites not far from Newgrange. The closest is Knowth, which is just 1 mile (1.6 km) away. Excavation of this site began in 1962 and it was found to contain two tomb passages and the greatest concentration of megalithic art in Europe. Archeologists also found evidence that the site was occupied from the Neolithic period and was used for habitation as well as for burials up until about 1400. Dowth, another passage grave 2 miles (3 km) from Newgrange, is less spectacular. Its tombs are smaller and most of its artifacts were stolen by Victorian souvenir hunters.

Newgrange

Tri-spiral carving on stone in chamber

The origins of Newgrange, one of the most important passage graves in Europe, are steeped in mystery. According to Celtic lore, the legendary kings of Tara were buried here, but Newgrange predates them. The grave was left untouched by all invaders except the Danish, who raided its burial chambers in the 9th century. In 1699, it was rediscovered by a local landowner, Charles Campbell Scott. When it was excavated in the 1960s, archeologist Professor M. J. O'Kelly discovered that on the winter solstice, December 21, rays of sunlight enter the tomb and light up the burial chamber—making it the world's oldest solar observatory.

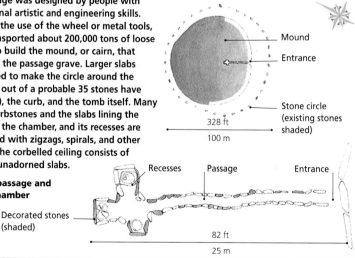

Burial Chamber Ceiling
The burial chamber's intricate corbelled ceiling, which reaches a height of 20 ft (6 m) above the floor, has survived intact. The overlapping slabs form a conical hollow, topped by a single capstone.

Burial Chamber
There are three recesses, or side chambers: the north recess is the one struck by sunlight on the winter solstice.

Basin Stone
The chiseled stones found in each recess would once have contained funerary offerings and the bones of the dead.

Standing Stones
The passage contains slabs of slate, which would have been collected locally.

CONSTRUCTION OF NEWGRANGE

Newgrange was designed by people with exceptional artistic and engineering skills. Without the use of the wheel or metal tools, they transported about 200,000 tons of loose stones to build the mound, or cairn, that pro-tects the passage grave. Larger slabs were used to make the circle around the cairn (12 out of a probable 35 stones have survived), the curb, and the tomb itself. Many of the curbstones and the slabs lining the passage, the chamber, and its recesses are decorated with zigzags, spirals, and other motifs. The corbelled ceiling consists of smaller, unadorned slabs.

Plan of passage and burial chamber

Mound

Entrance

Stone circle (existing stones shaded)

328 ft

100 m

Recesses   Passage   Entrance

Decorated stones (shaded)

82 ft

25 m

KEY DATES

c. 3200 BC	c. 860	c. 1140	1962–75	1967	1993
Construction of the tomb at Newgrange by Neolithic farmers.	Danish invaders raid the burial chamber and remove most of its treasures.	Newgrange is used as farmland for grazing cattle until the 14th century.	Newgrange is restored and the roof box is discovered.	Archeologists learn that rays of sunlight shine up the chamber on the winter solstice, December 21.	Newgrange is listed as a UNESCO World Heritage Site.

▲ **Megalithic motifs adorning the walls of Newgrange**

▲ **Restoration of Newgrange**
Located on a low ridge north of the Boyne River, Newgrange took more than 70 years to build. Between 1962 and 1975, the passage grave and mound were restored as closely as possible to their original state.

▼ **Burial Chamber Ceiling**

Passage ➤
At dawn on December 21, a beam of sunlight shines through the roof box (a feature unique to Newgrange), travels along the 62-ft (19-m) passage and hits the central recess in the burial chamber.

Basin Stone ➤

Entrance ➤
The opening was originally blocked by the stone standing to its right. Newgrange's most elaborately carved curbstone is in front, part of the curb of huge slabs around the cairn.

Retaining Wall
White quartz and granite stones found scattered around the site during excavations were used to rebuild this wall around the front of the cairn.

Roof box

MYTHOLOGICAL TALE

In Irish mythology, Aenghus Mac Og was the God of Love, who tricked his way into owning Newgrange. It is said that he was away when the magical places of Ireland were being divided up. On his return, he asked to borrow Newgrange for the day and night, but refused to give it back, claiming it was his, since all of time can be divided by day and night.

Trinity College, Dublin

Queen Elizabeth I founded Trinity College, Dublin's oldest and most famous educational institution, in 1592. Originally a Protestant college, it only began to take Catholics in large numbers after 1970, when the Catholic Church relaxed its opposition to them attending. Among Trinity's many famous students were the playwrights Oliver Goldsmith and Samuel Beckett, and the political writer Edmund Burke. The college's lawns and cobbled quads provide a pleasant haven in the heart of the city. The major attractions are the Old Library and the *Book of Kells*, housed in its treasury.

Trinity College coat of arms

THE BOOK OF KELLS

The most richly decorated of Ireland's medieval illuminated manuscripts, the *Book of Kells* may have been the work of monks from the island of Iona in Scotland, who fled to Kells in County Meath in 806 after a Viking raid. The book, which was moved to Trinity College (**Old Library Treasury**) in the 17th century, contains the four Gospels in Latin. The scribes who copied the texts embellished their calligraphy with intricate, interlacing spirals, as well as human figures and animals. Some of the dyes used in the manuscript were imported from as far away as the Middle East. The monogram page is the most elaborate page in the book, and contains the first three words of St. Matthew's account of the birth of Christ.

FAMOUS ALUMNI

Since its foundation, Trinity has cultivated many distinguished writers and historical figures. Their time here had a discernable impact on their lives. Among the most outstanding graduates are the writers and dramatists Jonathan Swift, Oliver Goldsmith, Oscar Wilde, Bram Stoker, William Congreve, and Samuel Beckett; the philosopher George Berkeley; the statesman and political philosopher Edmund Burke; Nobel prizewinning physicist Ernest Walton; Ireland's first president, Douglas Hyde; and Ireland's first female president, Mary Robinson. Statues of its famous scholars stand throughout the college.

PARLIAMENT SQUARE

Trinity College stands on what was once part of the grounds of All Hallows monastery. The wood-tiled archway at the main entrance leads to Trinity's main quadrangle (**Parliament Square**). Fine green lawns and an array of splendid 18th- and 19th-century buildings characterize the cobbled square. An imposing centerpiece (**Campanile**) marks the original site of the monastery. The chapel was designed by Sir William Chambers in 1798. Beside it is the **Dining Hall**, built by Richard Castle in 1742, where Trinity's students eat. This building has been considerably altered over the past 250 years, particularly after a fire in 1984 that caused severe damage. Its walls are hung with huge portraits of college dignitaries.

THE DOUGLAS HYDE GALLERY

Situated in the Trinity College grounds, this is one of Ireland's leading contemporary arts venues. Exhibits feature film, painting, installation, and sculpture work by emerging as well as recognized artists.

Campanile
The 100-ft (30-m) bell tower was built in 1853 by Sir Charles Lanyon, architect of Queen's University in Belfast.

Reclining Connected Forms (1969) by Henry Moore

Library Square

Dining Hall

Chapel
This was the first university chapel in the Republic to accept all denominations. The painted window above the altar is from 1867.

Statue of Edmund Burke (1868) by John Foley

Parliament Square

Main entrance

Statue of Oliver Goldsmith (1864) by John Foley

Examination Hall

◄ **Old Library Treasury**
This detail is from the 7th-century *Book of Durrow*, one of the other magnificent illuminated manuscripts housed in the Old Library's treasury, along with the celebrated *Book of Kells*.

Provost's House (c.1760)

▲ Examination Hall

▲ Chapel Window

Museum Building
Completed in 1857, this is notable for its Venetian exterior, and its magnificent multicolored hall and double-domed roof.

▲ Library Square
The red-brick building (known as the Rubrics) on the east side of Library Square was built around 1700 and is the oldest surviving part of the college.

▲ Old Library

Campanile ►

Entrance to the Old Library

New Square

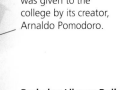

Sphere within Sphere
This sculpture (1982) was given to the college by its creator, Arnaldo Pomodoro.

Marble bust of the author Jonathan Swift in the Old Library ►

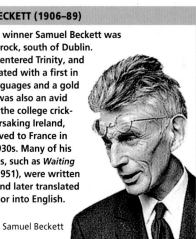

Berkeley Library Building (1967) by Paul Koralek

Fellows' Square

Douglas Hyde Gallery
This was built in the 1970s to house temporary art exhibitions.

SAMUEL BECKETT (1906–89)

Nobel prize winner Samuel Beckett was born at Foxrock, south of Dublin. In 1923, he entered Trinity, and later graduated with a first in modern languages and a gold medal. He was also an avid member of the college cricket team. Forsaking Ireland, Beckett moved to France in the early 1930s. Many of his major works, such as *Waiting for Godot* (1951), were written in French, and later translated by the author into English.

Samuel Beckett

Entrance from Nassau Street

▲ Old Library
The library's main chamber, the splendid Long Room (1732), measures 210 ft (64 m). It houses 200,000 antiquarian texts, marble busts of scholars, and Ireland's oldest harp.

KEY DATES

1592	c. 1661	1689	1712–61	1793	1853	1987
Trinity College is founded on the site of All Hallows monastery.	The medieval *Book of Kells* is given to Trinity by the Bishop of Meath.	The college is temporarily turned into a barracks.	A building drive results in the creation of the Old Library and the Dining Hall.	Religious restrictions on entry are abolished.	The Campanile is erected and becomes a symbol of Trinity College.	Restoration of the Dining Hall, damaged during a fire in 1984, takes place.

Rock of Cashel

A symbol of royal and priestly power for over 1,000 years, this is one of Ireland's most spectacular archeological sites. From the 5th century, it was the seat of the kings of Munster, whose kingdom extended over much of southern Ireland. In 1101, they handed Cashel over to the Church, and it flourished as a religious center until a siege by English troops in 1647 culminated in the massacre of its 3,000 occupants. The cathedral was finally abandoned in the late 18th century. A good proportion of the medieval complex is still standing, and Cormac's Chapel is one of Ireland's most outstanding examples of Romanesque architecture (*Romanesque Style, see p.122*).

Angel corbel in the Hall of the Vicars Choral

CASHEL MUSEUM

The 15th-century, two-story **Hall of the Vicars Choral** was once the residential quarters of the cathedral choristers and today displays copies of medieval artifacts and furnishings. Its lower level houses the **Cashel Museum**, which exhibits rare silverware, stone carvings and **St. Patrick's Cross**, a 12th-century crutched cross with a crucifixion scene on one side and animals on the other. The cross stands on a supporting coronation stone dating from the 4th century. Tradition held that the kings of Cashel were crowned at the base of the cross.

CORMAC'S CHAPEL

The king of Munster, Cormac MacCarthy, donated this chapel to the Church in 1134, because it had helped to protect the Rock of Cashel from being invaded by the Eoghanachta clan. Romanesque in style, the chapel was constructed in sandstone with a stone roof and two towers on either side of the nave and chancel. The interior is decorated with various motifs, some showing dragons and human heads. At the west end of the chapel is a stone sarcophagus embellished with serpent carvings. This is thought to have once contained the body of Cormac MacCarthy. The chancel is decorated with the only surviving Romanesque frescoes in Ireland, which include a depiction of the baptism of Christ.

LIFE OF ST. PATRICK

Born in Wales in 385, St. Patrick lived his early life as a pagan. At the age of 16, he was captured and sold as a slave to work in Ireland. During his captivity, he converted to Christianity and dedicated his life to God. He escaped and traveled to France, where he entered St. Martin's monastery to study the scriptures, under the guidance of St. Germain of Auxerre. He was appointed Bishop to Ireland in 432 and went on to found some 300 churches and baptize more than 120,000 people, including King Aenghus, when he visited Cashel in 450. Today, the life of St. Patrick, Ireland's patron saint, is celebrated on March 17 all over the world with special religious services and the wearing of shamrocks—the three-tipped clover leaf that is the national emblem of Ireland.

ROCK OF CASHEL GUIDE

KEY

☐ 12th Century

4 St. Patrick's Cross (replica)
12 Cormac's Chapel
13 Round Tower

☐ 13th Century

6 Cathedral porch
7 Nave
8 Crossing
9 South transept
10 Choir
11 North transept

☐ 15th Century

1 Ticket office
2 Hall of the Vicars Choral (museum)
3 Dormitory
5 Castle

▲ **Cormac's Chapel**
Superb Romanesque carving adorns this chapel—the jewel of Cashel. The tympanum over the north door shows a centaur in a helmet aiming his bow and arrow at a lion.

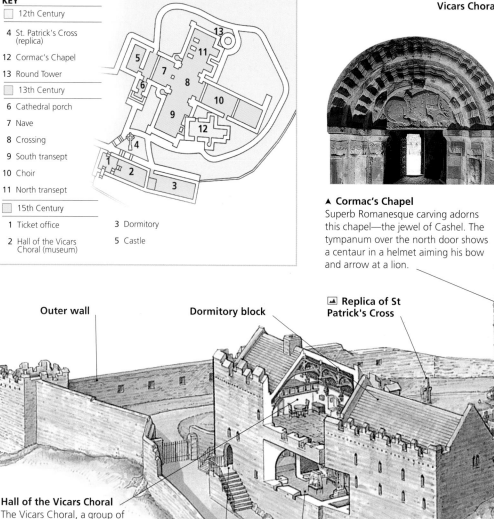

Outer wall

Dormitory block

▲ **Replica of St Patrick's Cross**

Hall of the Vicars Choral
The Vicars Choral, a group of men appointed to sing during services, were housed in this building. The ceiling, a modern reconstruction based on medieval designs, features several decorative corbels.

Entrance

Cashel Museum
Stone carvings and religious artifacts are displayed in this museum in the hall's lower level, or undercroft.

▲ North Transept
There are three 16th-century tombs here, decorated with remarkably fresh and intricate carvings. This one, against the north wall, features a vine-leaf design and strange stylized beasts.

ST. PATRICK AND KING AENGHUS

During the baptism ceremony of King Aenghus, St. Patrick accidentally stabbed him in the foot with his crozier and the king, thinking it was part of the initiation, bore the pain without complaint.

▲ Replica of the 12th-century St. Patrick's Cross; the original is in the museum

Round Tower ➤
The Rock's oldest surviving building, this 92-ft (28-m) free-standing bell tower enabled the inhabitants to scour the surrounding plain for potential attackers.

St Patrick's Cathedral ➤

Crossing

🖼 Round tower

Choir
The 17th-century tomb of Miler Magrath—who caused a scandal by being both a Protestant and a Catholic archbishop at the same time—is located here.

O'Scully Monument
This ornate memorial, erected in 1870 by a local landowning family, suffered damage during a storm in 1976.

Graveyard

🖼 North transept

Limestone rock

🖼 **St. Patrick's Cathedral**
The roofless Gothic cathedral has thick walls riddled with hidden passages; in the north transept these are seen emerging at the base of the windows.

KEY DATES

450	1101	1127–1134	1230–1270	1647	1975
St. Patrick visits Cashel and converts King Aenghus to Christianity.	Cashel is handed over to the Church by King Muircheatach O'Brien.	King Cormac MacCarthy builds Cormac's Chapel as a gift to the Church.	The large, aisleless, cruciform St. Patrick's Cathedral is built.	Cashel is invaded and besieged by an English army under Lord Inchiquin.	The Hall of the Vicars Choral undergoes restoration work.

Stirling Castle

▲ *Stirling Castle in the Times of the Stuarts,* painted by Johannes Vorsetermann (1643–99)

Rising high on a rocky crag, this magnificent castle was prominent in Scottish history for centuries and remains one of the finest examples of Renaissance architecture in Britain (*Renaissance Style, see p.131*). Legend has it that King Arthur wrested the original castle from the Saxons, but there is no historical evidence of a castle at this location before 1124. The present building dates from the 15th and 16th centuries and was last defended in 1746 against the Jacobites, who were mainly Catholic Highlanders wishing to restore the Stuart monarchy to the throne. Between 1881 and 1964, the castle was used as a depot for recruits into the Argyll and Sutherland Highlanders, although it serves no military function today.

THE EARL OF DOUGLAS

The eighth Earl of Douglas was suspected of treachery and murdered in 1452 by James II, who threw his tortured body out of a window into the gardens below. These are now known as the Douglas Gardens.

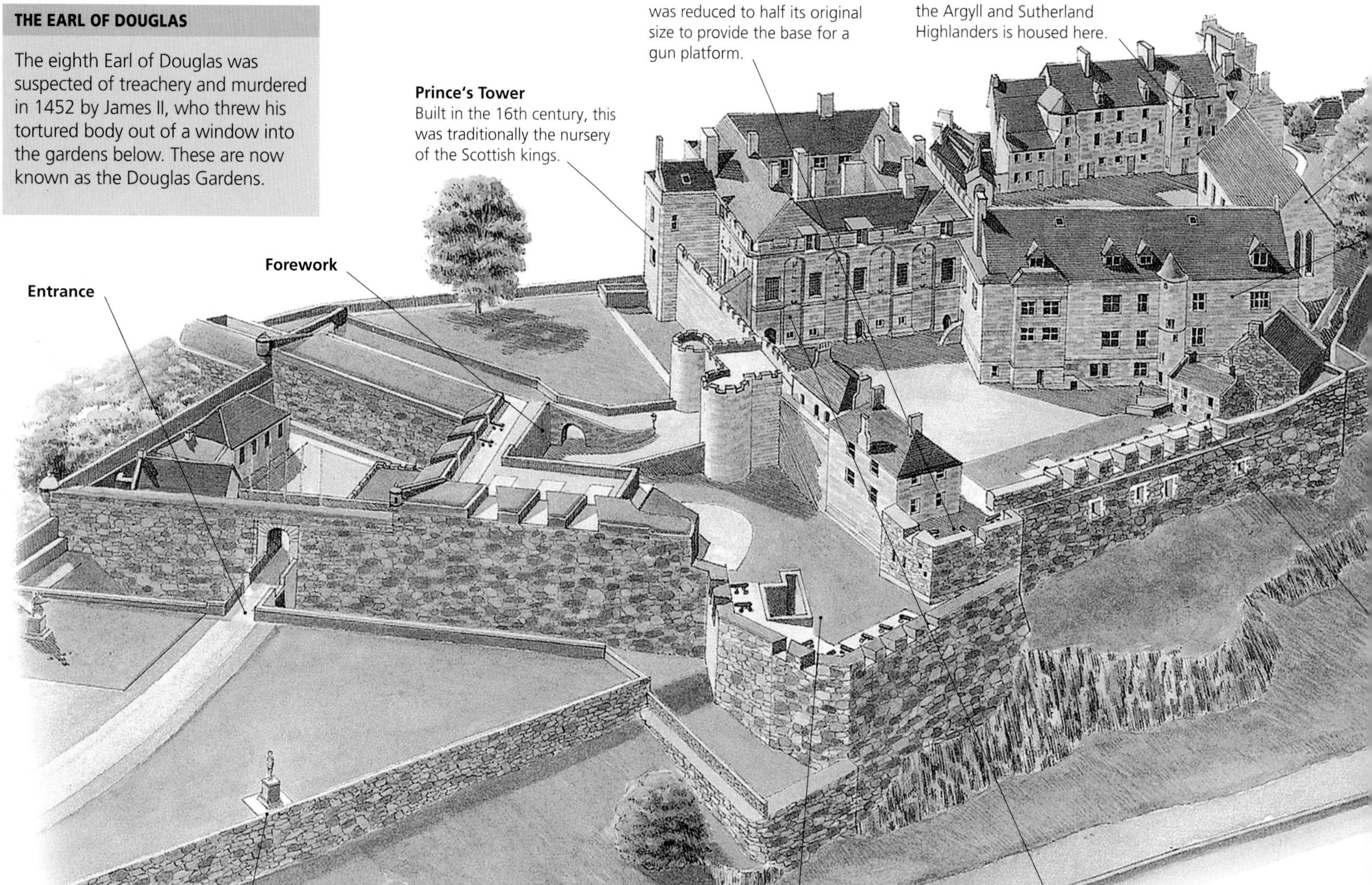

Elphinstone Tower
In 1689, this defensive tower was reduced to half its original size to provide the base for a gun platform.

King's Old Building
The Regimental Museum of the Argyll and Sutherland Highlanders is housed here.

Prince's Tower
Built in the 16th century, this was traditionally the nursery of the Scottish kings.

Forework

Entrance

Palace
The otherwise sparse interiors of the royal apartments contain the Stirling Heads (*right*). These Renaissance-era roundels depict 38 figures, thought to be contemporary members of the royal court.

 **Robert the Bruce Statue**
This modern statue in the esplanade shows Robert the Bruce sheathing his sword after the Scottish victory at the Battle of Bannockburn in 1314.

French Spur
In the mid-16th century, a new line of defenses, including this artillery spur, was constructed to protect the castle against enemies equipped with modern weaponry.

▲ Gargoyle on castle wall

▲ Grand Battery

Chapel Royal ▲
Seventeenth-century frescoes by Valentine Jenkins adorn this rectangular chapel, which was built in 1594.

🔲 Chapel Royal

Great Hall
The royal hall has been carefully restored to appear as it would have in the early 1500s.

Nether Bailey

Robert the Bruce Statue ▲

🔲 **Grand Battery**
Seven guns stand on this parapet overlooking the town of Stirling. They were built in 1708 during a strengthening of the defenses.

STIRLING BATTLES

At the highest navigable point of the Forth, and holding the pass to the Highlands, Stirling occupied a key position in Scotland's struggles for independence. Seven battlefields can be seen from the castle; the Wallace Monument at Abbey Craig recalls William Wallace's defeat of the English at Stirling Bridge in 1297, fore-shadowing Robert the Bruce's victory in 1314.

The Victorian Wallace Monument

THE BATTLE OF BANNOCKBURN

Stirling Castle was strategically vital to Scotland's military resistance to the English, and was frequently under siege as a result. In 1296, Edward I of England led a devastating invasion that defeated the Scots, but William Wallace organized a revolt, recapturing the castle in 1297, only to lose it again the following year. On June 23, 1314, Scotland, led by Robert the Bruce, won back its independence at the Battle of Bannockburn. However, the wars with England continued for another 300 years. The castle's last military use was against an attack by the Jacobite army in 1746, after which the English army set up barracks here until 1964.

THE GREAT HALL

This splendid royal hall, the largest ever built in Scotland, was erected by James IV between 1501 and 1504 to host lavish state events and banquets. When the focus of the monarchy shifted to London after the Union of the Crowns in 1603—when King James VI of Scotland became King James I of England—the **Great Hall** was no longer required for state occasions. Changes were made to the hall in the 18th century to reinforce the castle's defenses and to create space for military barracks. After more than 30 years' work, the Great Hall, restored as closely as possible to its original condition, was reopened by Queen Elizabeth II on November 30, 1999.

THE KING'S OLD BUILDING

Built for James IV around 1496 as his private residence in the castle, the **King's Old Building** stands on the highest point of the volcanic castle rock and commands long, wide views. Following the completion of the **Palace** in the 1540s, the King's Old Building was no longer the ruling monarch's residence and so was put to a variety of uses. Additional floors and walls were added in the 1790s to provide accommodation for a military garrison. It was also rebuilt after fire damage in the mid-19th century. The building now serves as the regimental home and museum of the Argyll and Sutherland Highlanders and contains a collection of memorabilia that includes medals, uniforms, and weapons.

KEY DATES

1296	1297	1314	1496	1501	1503	1855	1964
Edward I captures Stirling Castle.	The castle yields to the Scots after the Battle of Stirling Bridge.	Robert the Bruce defeats the English at the Battle of Bannockburn.	James IV begins extensive construction.	Work begins on the Great Hall.	Building work starts on the forework.	The King's Old Building is badly damaged by fire.	The army leaves the castle barracks.

STONE OF DESTINY

The origins of this famous stone are steeped in myth and legend. It is said to have been Jacob's pillow when he dreamed that the angels of God were descending to Earth from heaven. Scottish kings, from Kenneth I in 847, sat on the stone during coronation ceremonies. It was kept in Scone, Perthshire, which is why it is sometimes called The Stone of Scone. The stone was seized on Edward I's invasion of Scotland in 1296 and taken to Westminster Abbey, where it was kept for 700 years. The 1326 Treaty of Northampton promised the return of the stone, but this was not honored until 1996, when a handover ceremony took place at the English-Scottish border and the stone was transported to Edinburgh Castle, where it remains today.

VOLCANIC GEOLOGY

Edinburgh Castle is set in the Midland valley of Scotland. The rocky volcanic outcrops of Arthur's Seat (823 ft/251 m) and Salisbury Crags (400 ft/122 m) dominate Edinburgh's skyline. Salisbury Crags are igneous rocks exposed by the tilting of local rock and erosion by glaciers. Arthur's Seat is the remnant of a Carboniferous volcano, partly eroded by glacial activity. Edinburgh Castle sits on a rock that plugs a vent of this volcano. The "crag" of basalt on which it stands was resistant to glacial erosion in the last Ice Age. This left a "tail" of soft sedimentary rock lying behind it, which forms Edinburgh's main street, the Royal Mile.

THE MILITARY TATTOO

Since 1947, for three weeks over the summer, Edinburgh has hosted one of the world's most important arts festivals, with every available venue overflowing with international artists and performers (from theaters to street corners). The festival is an exciting fusion of film, music, theater, dance, comedy, and literature. The most popular event is the Edinburgh Military Tattoo, held every night on the **Esplanade**. The finest military bands perform, with bagpipers and drummers from Scottish regiments in full regalia. The music and marching, set against the backdrop of the illuminated Edinburgh Castle, make for a marvelous spectacle.

Edinburgh Castle

Standing on the basalt core of an extinct volcano, Edinburgh Castle is a remarkable assemblage of buildings dating from the 12th to the 20th centuries, reflecting its changing role as fortress, royal palace, military garrison, and state prison. There is evidence of Bronze Age occupation of the site, which takes its name from Dun Eidin, a Celtic fortress captured by King Oswald of Northumbria in the 7th century. The castle was a favorite royal residence until the Union of the Crowns in 1603, after which the king resided in England. After the Union of Parliaments in 1707, the Scottish regalia (Crown Jewels) were walled up in the palace for more than 100 years. The castle is now the zealous possessor of the so-called Stone of Destiny, a relic of ancient Scottish kings that was seized by the English and not returned until 1996.

Beam support in the Great Hall

◄ **Scottish Crown**
Now on display in the Palace, the crown was restyled by James V of Scotland in 1540.

▣ **Govenor's House**
Complete with Flemish-style crow-stepped gables, this mid-18th-century building now serves as the officers' mess for the castle garrison.

Military prison

STOLEN STONE

In 1950, long before the Stone of Destiny was returned to Scotland, a group of Scottish students stole the stone from Westminster Abbey. A search was mounted by the British, but it was not found until a year later in Scotland's Arbroath Abbey.

▣ **Prison Vaults**
French prisoners were held here during the wars with France in the 18th and 19th centuries. Their graffiti can still be seen, along with the objects they made.

▣ **Great Hall**

▲ **Edinburgh Castle viewed from Princes Street**

◄ **Palace**
Mary, Queen of Scots (1542–87) gave birth to James VI in this 15th-century palace, where the Scottish regalia are on display.

▼ **Argyle Battery**

🔳 **Argyle Battery**
The castle's northern defense commands spectacular views of Edinburgh's New Town.

🔳 **Mons Meg**

MONS MEG

The siege gun Mons Meg, near St. Margaret's Chapel, was made in 1449 for the duke of Burgundy, who subsequently gave it to his nephew, James II of Scotland (r. 1437–60), in 1457. It was used by James IV (r. 1488–1513) against Norham Castle in England in 1497. After exploding during a salute to the duke of York in 1682, the gun was kept in the Tower of London before being returned to Edinburgh in 1829.

▲ **Graffiti in the Prison Vaults**

Great Hall ►
With its restored open-timber roof, the hall dates from the 15th century and was the meeting place of the Scottish parliament until 1639.

🔳 **Palace**

The Royal Mile ⟶

▲ **Govenor's House**

Esplanade
The Military Tattoo is held here.

Entrance

Half Moon Battery
This was built in the 1570s as a platform for the artillery defending the castle's northeastern wing.

◄ **St. Margaret's Chapel**
This stained-glass window depicts Malcolm III's saintly queen, to whom the chapel is dedicated. Probably built by her son, David I, in the early 12th century, the chapel is the castle's oldest surviving building.

KEY DATES

638	1296	1496–1511	1573	1650	1995
King Oswald of Northumbria's army captures the site and builds a fortress.	Edward I takes the castle after an eight-day siege and installs a garrison of 347 men.	James I adds more buildings to the castle, including the Palace.	After a failed siege by Mary, Queen of Scots, the castle is modified and the Half Moon Battery is built.	The castle is fortified with barracks, officers' quarters, and storehouses.	Edinburgh and its castle are inscribed as a UNESCO World Heritage Site.

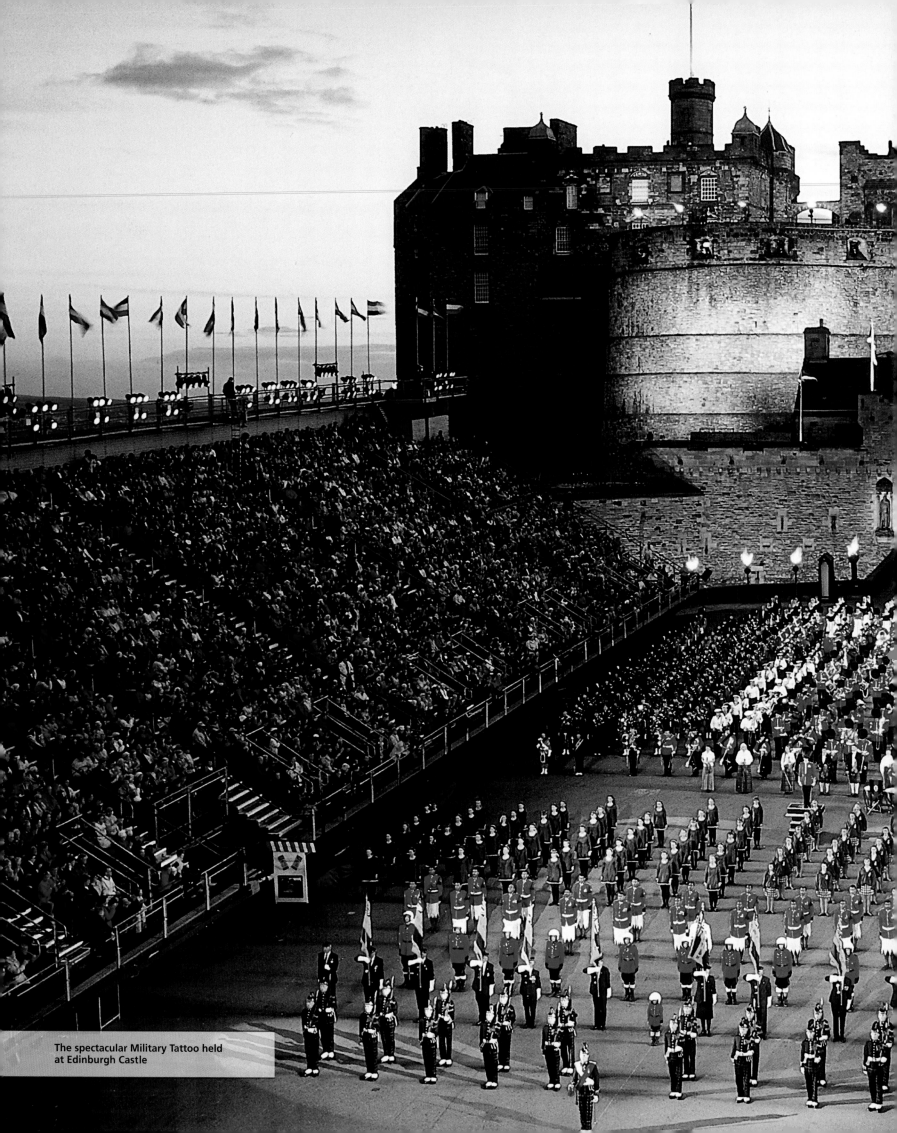

The spectacular Military Tattoo held
at Edinburgh Castle

STAINED GLASS

York Minster has an exceptional collection of medieval stained glass. The glass was generally colored during production, using metal oxides to produce the desired color, then worked on by craftsmen on site. When a design had been produced, the glass was first cut, then trimmed to shape. Details were painted on using iron oxide-based paints that were fused to the glass by firing in a kiln. Individual pieces were then leaded together to form the finished window. Part of the fascination of the minster glass is its variety of subject matter. Some windows, including the **Great East Window**, were paid for by lay donors who specified a particular subject; others reflect ecclesiastical patronage.

THE DECORATED GOTHIC STYLE

An example of this second phase of Gothic architecture in England (c. 1275–1380) is the **Chapter House**, which radiates elegantly against the backdrop of York Minster. Delicate carvings, fine stained-glass windows, elaborate tracery, and experimental vaulting typify the Decorated Gothic style. Carvings of foliage, animals, and human figures can be viewed above the stalls. Inside the **nave**, complex tracery can be seen throughout.

YORK MYSTERY PLAYS

These 48 medieval dramas, which relate the history of the world from the mystery of God's creation to the Last Judgment, were originally performed between the 14th and the 16th centuries for the feast of Corpus Christi. The York Mystery Plays, or cycles, are one of only four complete English mystery play cycles to have survived. They are divided into short episodes and performed by actors standing on a wagon. The entertainers then ride through the city streets, pausing at a number of venues to perform. It was customary for different guilds to adopt the productions that often bore a connection to their trade. For example, shipbuilders were responsible for the portrayal of Noah's Ark, bakers played the Last Supper, and butchers staged the death of Christ. This cycle tradition was revived for the Festival of Britain in 1951 and has been performed every three to four years since.

York Minster

The largest Gothic cathedral in northern Europe *(Gothic Style, see p.54)*, York Minster is 519 ft (158 m) long and 249 ft (76 m) wide across its transepts, and houses the biggest collection of medieval stained glass in Britain. The word "minster" usually refers to a cathedral served by monks, but priests always served at York. The first minster began as a wooden chapel used to baptize King Edwin of Northumbria in 627. There have been several cathedrals on or near the site, including an 11th-century Norman structure. The present minster was begun in 1220 and completed 250 years later. In July 1984, the south transept roof was destroyed by fire. Restoration cost $4 million.

Central sunflower in the rose window

▼ **Great East Window**
The size of a tennis court, this is the largest surviving expanse of medieval stained glass in the world. From 1405 to 1408, the Bishop of Durham paid glazier John Thornton four shillings a week to complete a celebration of the Creation.

East transept

Choir
This has a vaulted entrance with a 15th-century boss of the Assumption of the Virgin.

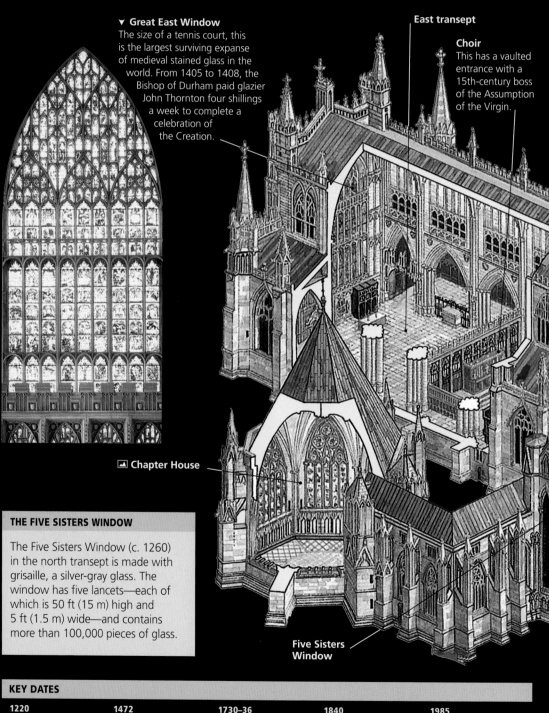

🔲 **Chapter House**

THE FIVE SISTERS WINDOW

The Five Sisters Window (c. 1260) in the north transept is made with grisaille, a silver-gray glass. The window has five lancets—each of which is 50 ft (15 m) high and 5 ft (1.5 m) wide—and contains more than 100,000 pieces of glass.

Five Sisters Window

KEY DATES

1220	1472	1730–36	1840	1985
Construction of York Minster begins on the site of several earlier churches.	The cathedral is completed and consecrated.	York Minster is restored and its floor entirely relaid in patterned marble.	Fire damages the nave; repairs are completed four years later.	The roof in the south transept is rebuilt following a fire in 1984.

▲ Chapter House
A Latin inscription near the entrance of the octagonal, rib-vaulted meeting room for the Dean and Chapter (1260–85) reads, "As the rose is the flower of flowers, so this is the house of houses."

▲ Central Tower
Reconstructed in 1420–65 (after partial collapse in 1407) from a design by the master stonemason William Colchester, the tower is 230 ft (70 m) high and its geometrical roof has a central lantern.

▲ Nave

West Towers ➤
The 15th-century decorative paneling and elaborate pinnacles on the west towers contrast with the simpler design of the north transept.

South transept

16th-century rose window

Choir Screen ▲

Great West Window
Added between 1338 and 1339 by master stonemason Ivo de Raghton, this is often called the "Heart of Yorkshire" because of its heart-shaped tracery symbolizing the Sacred Heart of Christ.

◪ Choir Screen
Sited between the choir and the nave, this beautiful 15th-century stone screen depicts the kings of England from William I to Henry VI, and has a canopy of angels.

◪ Nave
Work began on the nave in 1291 and was completed in the 1350s. It was severely damaged by fire in the 19th century. Rebuilding costs were heavy, but it was reopened with a peal of bells in 1844.

Great West Door
This leads into the main body of the cathedral.

Westminster Abbey, London

Since the 13th century, Westminster Abbey has been the burial place of Britain's monarchs and the setting for many coronations and royal weddings. It is one of the most beautiful buildings in London, with an exceptionally diverse array of architectural styles, ranging from the austere French Gothic of the nave to the astonishing complexity of the Lady Chapel. Half national church, half national museum, the abbey's aisles and transepts are crammed with an extraordinary collection of tombs and monuments honoring some of Britain's greatest public figures, from politicians to poets.

FAMOUS TOMBS AND MONUMENTS

Many sovereigns and their consorts are buried in Westminster Abbey. Some tombs are deliberately plain, while others are lavishly decorated. The shrine of the Saxon king Edward the Confessor and various tombs of medieval monarchs are located at the heart of the abbey (**St. Edward's Chapel**). The Grave of the Unknown Warrior in the **nave** commemorates those killed in World War I who had no formal resting place. One unnamed soldier is buried here. Monuments to a number of Britain's greatest public figures crowd the aisles. Memorials to literary giants such as Chaucer, Shakespeare, and Dickens can be found in the South Transept (**Poets' Corner**).

THE LADY CHAPEL

Work on the chapel began in 1503, on the orders of King Henry VII. It was intended to enshrine Henry VI, but it was Henry VII himself who was finally laid to rest here in an elaborate tomb. The highlight of this chapel, completed in 1519, is the vaulted roof, a glorious example of Perpendicular architecture. The undersides of the choir stalls (1512) are beautifully carved with exotic and fantastic creatures. The chapel contains the fine tomb of Elizabeth I, who reigned 1558–1603, and that of her half-sister, Mary I, who ruled 1553–8.

THE CORONATION CEREMONY

Every monarch since William the Conqueror, except Edward V and Edward VIII, has been crowned in Westminster Abbey. Many elements in this solemn and mystical ceremony date from the reign of Edward the Confessor (1042–66). The king or queen proceeds to the abbey, accompanied by some of the crowns, scepters, orbs, and swords that form the royal regalia. The jewelled State Sword, one of the most valuable swords in the world, represents the monarch's own sword. He or she is anointed with holy oil, to signify divine approval, and invested with ornaments and royal robes. The climax of the ceremony is when St. Edward's Crown is placed on the sovereign's head; there is a cry of "God Save the King" (or Queen), the trumpets sound, and guns at the Tower of London are fired.

▼ *Lady Nightingale's Memorial* by Roubiliac (1761), north transept

Shakespeare monument at Poets' Corner

◄ **Chapter House**

▼ **Nave**
At a height of 102 ft (31 m), the nave is the highest in England. The ratio of height to width is 3:1.

◄ **The Lady Chapel**
The chapel, built in 1503–12, has superb late-Perpendicular vaultings, and choir stalls dating from 1512.

◄ **Flying Buttresses**
The abbey's enormous flying buttresses help to redistribute the great weight of nave's soaring roof.

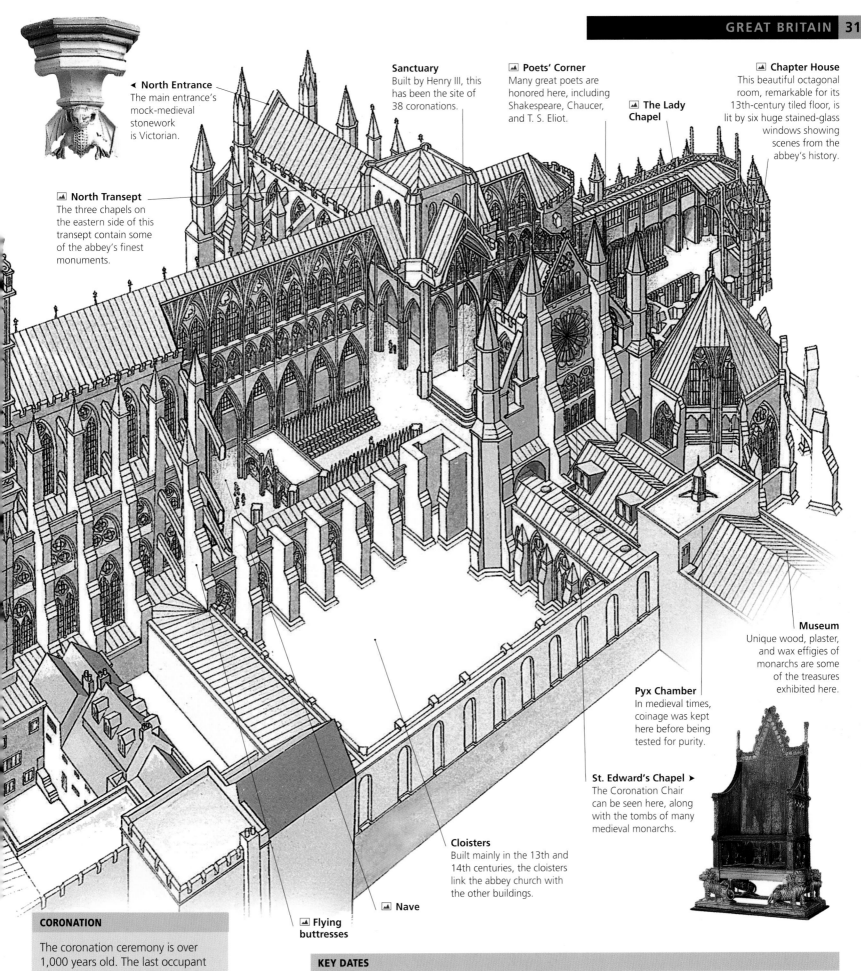

◄ North Entrance
The main entrance's mock-medieval stonework is Victorian.

▣ North Transept
The three chapels on the eastern side of this transept contain some of the abbey's finest monuments.

Sanctuary
Built by Henry III, this has been the site of 38 coronations.

▣ Poets' Corner
Many great poets are honored here, including Shakespeare, Chaucer, and T. S. Eliot.

▣ The Lady Chapel

▣ Chapter House
This beautiful octagonal room, remarkable for its 13th-century tiled floor, is lit by six huge stained-glass windows showing scenes from the abbey's history.

Museum
Unique wood, plaster, and wax effigies of monarchs are some of the treasures exhibited here.

Pyx Chamber
In medieval times, coinage was kept here before being tested for purity.

St. Edward's Chapel ►
The Coronation Chair can be seen here, along with the tombs of many medieval monarchs.

Cloisters
Built mainly in the 13th and 14th centuries, the cloisters link the abbey church with the other buildings.

▣ Nave

▣ Flying buttresses

CORONATION

The coronation ceremony is over 1,000 years old. The last occupant of the Coronation Chair was the present queen, Elizabeth II. She was crowned on June 2, 1953, by the Archbishop of Canterbury in the first televised coronation.

KEY DATES

1065	1245	1503	1745	1953
Edward the Confessor founds the original abbey, which becomes the coronation church.	Henry III demolishes the old abbey and begins work on Westminster Abbey as seen today.	Work commences on the construction of the stunning Lady Chapel.	The west towers, encased in Portland stone, are completed.	Queen Elizabeth I's coronation is the most watched in the abbey's history.

St. Paul's Cathedral, London

The Great Fire of London in 1666 left the medieval cathedral of St. Paul's in ruins. The architect Christopher Wren was commissioned to rebuild it, but his design for a church on a Greek Cross plan (where all four arms are equal) met with considerable resistance. The authorities insisted on a conventional Latin cross, with a long nave and short transepts, to focus the congregation's attention on the altar. Despite the compromises, Wren created a magnificent, world-renowned Baroque cathedral. Built between 1675 and 1710, it has been the setting for many state ceremonies.

▲ West Front and Towers
Added by Wren in 1707, the towers' design was inspired by the Italian Baroque architect Boromini.

PORTLAND STONE

Wren constructed St. Paul's of durable Portland Stone from Dorset quarries, thought to be the optimum material to withstand London's climate. More than 300 years of continuous use, and air pollution, have taken their toll, but advanced technology has made it possible to clean the exposed stonework, restoring it to its original cream color.

◄ Nave
An imposing succession of massive arches and saucer domes open out into the vast space below the cathedral's main dome.

West Portico
Two stories of coupled Corinthian columns are topped by a pediment carved with reliefs showing the conversion of St. Paul.

KEY DATES

1675–1710	1723	1810	1940
Wren's St. Paul's Cathedral is built. It is the fourth church to occupy the site.	Wren is the first person to be interred in the cathedral's crypt.	Many precious artifacts are lost in a major robbery.	Slight bomb damage occurs during the London Blitz in World War II.

◄ Whispering Gallery

◄ Dome

▣ Dome
At 370 ft (113 m), the elaborate dome is one of the highest in the world.

Stone Gallery

Balustrade
This was added in 1718, against Wren's wishes.

▣ West front

West porch

Main entrance, approached from Ludgate Hill

◄ Choir Stalls

Lantern
This weighs a massive 850 tons.

Golden Gallery
There are splendid views over London from here.

Oculus
The cathedral floor can be seen through this opening.

CHRISTOPHER WREN

Sir Christopher Wren (1632–1723) began his impressive architectural career at the age of 31. He became a leading figure in the reconstruction of London after the devastating Great Fire of 1666, building a total of 52 new churches. Although Wren never visited Italy, his work was influenced by Roman, Renaissance, and Baroque architecture.

Whispering Gallery
The dome's unusual acoustics mean that words whispered against the wall in this gallery can be heard clearly on the opposite side.

Choir
Jean Tijou, a Huguenot refugee, created much of the fine wrought-ironwork here in Wren's time, including the choir screens.

Choir Stalls
The 17th-century choir stalls and organ case were made by Grinling Gibbons (1648–1721), a woodcarver from Rotterdam. He and his team of craftsmen worked on these intricate carvings for two years.

High Altar
The present altar was made in 1958 and features a canopy based on Wren's designs.

Entrance to Golden, Whispering, and Stone galleries

Entrance to crypt

South Portico
This was inspired by the porch of Santa Maria della Pace in Rome. Wren absorbed the detail by studying a collection of architectural engravings.

Nave

ATLANTIC OCEAN

• Edinburgh

NORTH SEA

IRELAND

GREAT BRITAIN

Birmingham •

THE NETHERLANDS

ST. PAUL'S CATHEDRAL, LONDON ○

BELGIUM

FRANCE

FAMOUS TOMBS

St. Paul's Cathedral is the final resting place of Sir Christopher Wren, whose tomb is marked by a slab. The inscription states, "Reader, if you seek a monument look around you." Around 200 tombs of famous figures and popular heroes can be found in the crypt, such as Nelson, naval hero of the Battle of Trafalgar (1805), and the Duke of Wellington, hero of the Battle of Waterloo (1815). Other tombs and memorials include those of the composer Sir Arthur Sullivan, the sculptor Sir Henry Moore, and artists Sir John Everett Millais and Joshua Reynolds. Florence Nightingale, famous for her pioneering work in nursing standards and the first woman to receive the Order of Merit, is also buried here, as is Alexander Fleming, who discovered penicillin.

THE INTERIOR

The cathedral's cool, beautifully ordered, ornate and spacious interior is instantly striking. The **nave**, **transepts**, and **choir** are arranged in the shape of a cross, as in a medieval cathedral, but Wren's Classical vision shines through this conservative floor plan, forced on him by the Church authorities. The interior is dominated by the vast cupola (**dome**), which is decorated with monochrome frescoes by Sir James Thornhill. Master woodcarver Grinling Gibbons produced intricate carvings of cherubs, fruits, and garlands (**choir stalls**), while the French Huguenot wrought-ironwork genius Jean Tijou created the sanctuary gates.

SPECIAL EVENTS

Aided by some of the finest craftsmen of his day, Christopher Wren created an interior of grand majesty and Baroque splendor (*Baroque Style, see p.80*), a worthy setting for the many great ceremonial events that have taken place here. These include the funerals of Admiral Lord Nelson (1806), the Duke of Wellington (1852), and Sir Winston Churchill (1965). Celebrated royal occasions have included the wedding of Prince Charles and Lady Diana Spencer (1981) and Queen Elizabeth II's Golden Jubilee (2002). The cathedral also provided the venue for a special service to mark the September 11, 2001, attacks in the United States.

The Tower of London

Soon after he became king in 1066, William the Conqueror built a castle to guard the entrance to London from the Thames Estuary. In 1097, the White Tower, standing today at the center of the complex, was completed in sturdy stone; other fine buildings were added over the centuries to create one of the most powerful and formidable fortresses in Europe. The tower has served as a royal residence, an armory, a treasury, and, most famously, as a prison for enemies of the crown. Many prisoners were tortured, and among those who met their death here were the "Princes in the Tower," the sons and heirs of Edward IV. Today, the tower is a popular attraction, housing the Crown Jewels and other priceless exhibits—powerful reminders of royal might and wealth.

THE CROWN JEWELS

One of the world's best-known collections of precious objects includes the regalia of crowns, scepters, orbs, and swords used at coronations and other state occasions. Most date from 1661, when Charles II commissioned replacements for regalia destroyed by Parliament after the execution of Charles I. Only a few older pieces survived, hidden until the restoration of the monarchy in 1660—notably, Edward the Confessor's (r. 1327–77) sapphire ring, now incorporated into the Imperial State Crown. The crown was remade for Queen Victoria and has been worn at every coronation since.

The Sovereign's Orb (1661), a hollow gold sphere encrusted with jewels

The Sovereign's Ring (1831)

Jewel House ▲
Among the magnificent Crown Jewels is the Scepter with the Cross of 1660 (above), which contains the world's biggest diamond.

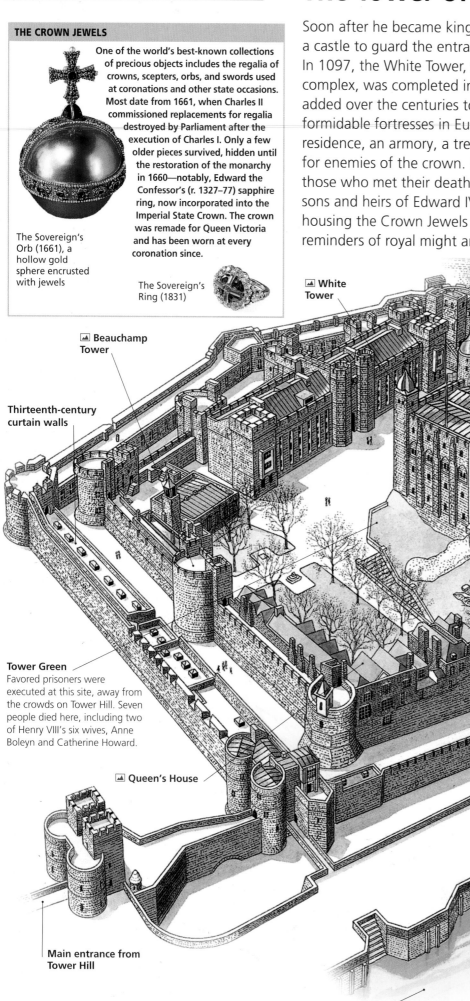

🖼 **White Tower**

🖼 **Beauchamp Tower**

🖼 **Chapel of St John**

Thirteenth-century curtain walls

Tower Green
Favored prisoners were executed at this site, away from the crowds on Tower Hill. Seven people died here, including two of Henry VIII's six wives, Anne Boleyn and Catherine Howard.

🖼 **Queen's House**

🖼 **Traitors' Gate**
This infamous entrance was used for prisoners brought from trial in Westminster Hall.

Main entrance from Tower Hill

River Thames

Bloody Tower ▶
Edward IV's two sons were put in the tower by their uncle, Richard of Gloucester (subsequently Richard III), after their father died in 1483. The princes, depicted here by John Millais (1829–96), mysteriously disappeared and Richard was crowned later that year. In 1674, the skeletons of two children were found nearby.

White Tower ➤
When the tower was completed in 1097, it was the tallest building in London, at 90 ft (27 m) high.

Nineteenth-century Tower Bridge, which overlooks the Tower of London ➤

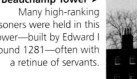

Beauchamp Tower ➤
Many high-ranking prisoners were held in this tower—built by Edward I around 1281—often with a retinue of servants.

Salt Tower
Prisoners' inscriptions are carved into the walls of this tower's two residential rooms, which were used as prison cells during Tudor times.

Queen's House ➤
This Tudor building is the sovereign's official residence at the tower.

Traitors' Gate ➤

"Beefeaters" ➤
Thirty-seven Yeoman Warders guard the tower and live here. Their uniforms harken back to Tudor times.

▲ **Chapel of St. John**
This austerely beautiful Romanesque chapel is a particularly fine example of Norman architecture.

THE LEGEND OF THE RAVENS

The tower's most celebrated residents are a colony of seven ravens. It is not known when they first settled here, but these scavenger birds would have arrived soon after the castle was constructed to feed off the abundant refuse. Their presence has been protected by a legend that says that should the birds desert the tower, the kingdom will fall. In fact, they have their wings clipped on one side, making flight impossible. The Ravenmaster, one of the "**Beefeaters**," looks after the birds.

FAMOUS PRISONERS

The tower has been prison to kings, queens, and notorious characters throughout its history. One of the first monarchs to be held here was Henry VI, who was murdered while at prayer in 1471. The Duke of Clarence, brother of Edward IV, was convicted of treason and killed by drowning in a cask of wine in 1478. Two of Henry VIII's wives, and his former chancellor, Sir Thomas More, were beheaded here. Even Elizabeth I was held in the tower for two months, and on her death in 1603, Sir Walter Raleigh, her favorite explorer, was imprisoned and later executed. The last prisoner, held in the **Queen's House** in 1941, was Rudolf Hess, deputy leader of the Nazi party.

THE WHITE TOWER

Work on the **White Tower**, the oldest surviving building in the tower, was begun in 1078. It was designed as a palace-fortress to accommodate the king and the Constable of the Tower, the garrison commander. Each had their own rooms, including a hall for public occasions, a partitioned chamber, and a chapel. When the fortress was enlarged a century later, both king and constable moved to new residences. On the upper two stories, the monarch's elegant royal suite was used to hold distinguished prisoners. The ceremonial chambers were twice their present height. Rising through two floors is the **Chapel of St. John**, an exquisite early-Norman church. This was once decorated with rich furnishings, painted stonework, and stained-glass windows, but these were removed in 1550 during the English Reformation. In the 1600s, the tower served as a storehouse and armory.

TORTURE AND DEATH

Early prisoners in the Tower of London, who were sentenced to execution, could look forward to a drawn-out death. In the 14th and 15th centuries, many would have been hanged, drawn, and quartered, or burned at the stake, although some may have been stretched on a rack first. Others were disemboweled or hacked to pieces.

KEY DATES

1078	1533	1601	1841
Work begins on building the White Tower.	Henry VIII marries Anne Boleyn at the tower.	The last victim of the ax is beheaded on Tower Green.	Fire destroys part of the White Tower.

Hampton Court Palace, London

Ceiling decoration in the Queen's Drawing Room

Cardinal Wolsey, influential Archbishop of York to Henry VIII, began building Hampton Court in the early 16th century. Originally it was not a royal palace, but was intended as Wolsey's riverside country house. Later, in 1528, Hampton Court was seized by the king when Wolsey fell from royal favor. The buildings and gardens were then twice rebuilt and extended into a grand palace, first by Henry himself and then, in the 1690s, by William III and Mary II, who employed Christopher Wren as architect. There is a striking contrast between Wren's Classical royal apartments and the Tudor turrets, gables, and chimneys elsewhere. The inspiration for the gardens as they are today comes largely from the time of William and Mary, for whom Wren created a vast, formal Baroque landscape, with radiating avenues of majestic limes and many collections of exotic plants.

ROYAL TENNIS COURT AND THE MAZE

Henry VIII had the **Royal Tennis Court** built in the 16th century, as he was very fond of the game. Legend says that he was playing tennis at Hampton Court while his second wife, Anne Boleyn, was being executed. When William III moved into the palace in 1689, he had the gardens and the buildings remodeled. Wren's design for the gardens included the **Fountain Garden** and the **Maze**. The Maze was planted with hornbeams until the 18th century, when they were replaced with yews and hollies.

THE CHAPEL ROYAL AND THE GREAT HALL

Cardinal Wolsey had the **Chapel Royal** built during his time at Hampton Court. As soon as King Henry VIII moved in, he refurbished the chapel and installed its impressive vaulted ceiling in 1535–6. The chapel subsequently became the location for many decisive moments in Henry's life—it was here that he learned of his fifth wife Katherine Howard's infidelity and married his last wife, Catherine Parr. The **Great Hall**, with its delightful hammerbeam roof and Gothic fireplaces, was also part of Henry's rebuilding of Hampton Court. Stained-glass windows were added to the beautiful hall, showing the king flanked by the coats of arms of his six wives.

CARDINAL WOLSEY AND HENRY VIII

The English statesman and cardinal Thomas Wolsey (c. 1475–1530) was considered the most powerful person in England after the king. During Henry VIII's reign, from 1509, Wolsey was given the role of managing England's foreign affairs, as well as being the king's adviser. This important position earned Wolsey a lot of wealth, but he also had enemies. His downfall came when Henry wanted a church annulment from his first wife, Catherine of Aragon, so he could marry Anne Boleyn. Wolsey, aware that his life would be in danger if he did not achieve Henry's demand, proceeded slowly with a request to the pope. This angered the king, and also Anne, who used her influence to remove Wolsey from court. A few years later, Wolsey died suddenly on his way to face trial for treason.

◄ Long Water
A man-made lake runs almost parallel with the Thames, from the Fountain Garden across the Home Park.

◄ Maze

▼ Fountain Garden

▲ Clock Court
The so-called Anne Boleyn's Gateway is at the entrance to Clock Court. Henry VIII's Astronomical Clock, created in 1540, is also located here.

▼ Mantegna Gallery
Andrea Mantegna's nine canvases depicting *The Triumphs of Caesar* (1480s) are housed here.

▲ East Front

▲ Pond Garden
This sunken water garden was part of Henry VIII's elaborate designs.

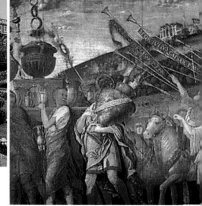

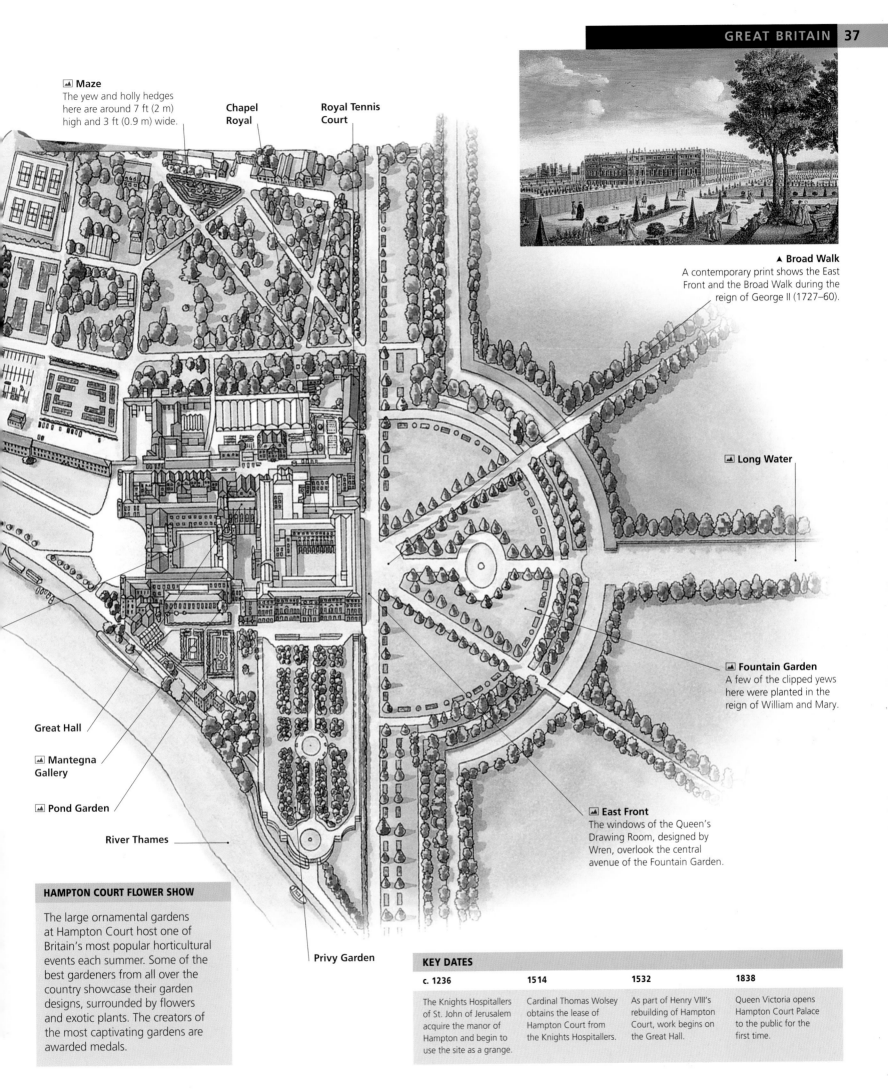

⊿ Maze
The yew and holly hedges here are around 7 ft (2 m) high and 3 ft (0.9 m) wide.

Chapel Royal

Royal Tennis Court

▲ Broad Walk
A contemporary print shows the East Front and the Broad Walk during the reign of George II (1727–60).

⊿ Long Water

⊿ Fountain Garden
A few of the clipped yews here were planted in the reign of William and Mary.

Great Hall

⊿ Mantegna Gallery

⊿ Pond Garden

River Thames

⊿ East Front
The windows of the Queen's Drawing Room, designed by Wren, overlook the central avenue of the Fountain Garden.

Privy Garden

HAMPTON COURT FLOWER SHOW

The large ornamental gardens at Hampton Court host one of Britain's most popular horticultural events each summer. Some of the best gardeners from all over the country showcase their garden designs, surrounded by flowers and exotic plants. The creators of the most captivating gardens are awarded medals.

KEY DATES

c. 1236	1514	1532	1838
The Knights Hospitallers of St. John of Jerusalem acquire the manor of Hampton and begin to use the site as a grange.	Cardinal Thomas Wolsey obtains the lease of Hampton Court from the Knights Hospitallers.	As part of Henry VIII's rebuilding of Hampton Court, work begins on the Great Hall.	Queen Victoria opens Hampton Court Palace to the public for the first time.

Stonehenge

Built in several stages from about 3000 BC, Stonehenge is Europe's most famous prehistoric monument. We can only guess at the rituals that took place here, but the alignment of the stones leaves little doubt that the circle is connected with the sun and the passing of the seasons, and that its builders possessed a sophisticated understanding of both arithmetic and astronomy. Contrary to popular belief, the circle was not built by the Druids; this Iron Age priestly cult flourished in Britain from around 250 BC, more than 1,000 years after Stonehenge was completed.

An impression of the completed prehistoric monument

THE BELL-BEAKER CULTURE

It is believed that the Beaker people emerged in Britain around 2200 BC. Their name derives from the distinctive bell-shaped pottery cups found in their burial mounds. They are credited with building the **Bluestone Circle** at Stonehenge because concentric circles were typical of their culture and much of their pottery was unearthed in the vicinity. Their advanced construction techniques suggest that the Beaker people were sun worshipers, as well as highly organized and skilled craftsmen. They created the **Avenue**, which runs directly toward the midsummer sun, and widened the entrance to the henge, aligning it more precisely with the sunrise of the summer solstice.

THE SITE

Despite centuries of archeological, religious, and mystical interest in Stonehenge, the site's original purpose remains unknown. The building of this inscrutable prehistoric megalith has been attributed to Greeks, Phoenicians, Druids, and Atlanteans. Theories on the reason it was built range from sacrificial ceremonies to astronomical calendars. Unearthed evidence of burials suggests that human sacrifices took place here, and most experts agree that Stonehenge has religious foundations. The arrangement of the stones fuels beliefs in an astronomical purpose. The significance of this site must have been great, as the stones used were not quarried locally but brought from as far away as Wales.

THE DRUIDS

Archeologists once claimed that Stonehenge was built by the Druids, the priestly class of the ancient Celts, who performed ritualistic ceremonies and sacrifices here. Although the site is still associated with the Druids, radiocarbon dating has proved that it was raised more than 1,000 years before they were established in the region, and they may have used the existing site as a temple. Today, Stonehenge is famous for modern Druid ceremonies and festivals. English Heritage, who control the site, permit Druid gatherings in the inner circle each year for the solstices and equinoxes. However, the site itself is cordoned off to protect against damage caused by an increasing number of tourists.

RECONSTRUCTION OF STONEHENGE

This illustration shows what Stonehenge probably looked like about 4,000 years ago. The stones remaining today create a strong impression of how incredible the original site would have been to see.

Heel Stone
A large sarsen stone quarried in the Marlborough Downs stands at the entrance to the site. It casts a long shadow straight to the heart of the inner circle on midsummer's day.

Slaughter Stone
Named by 17th-century antiquarians who believed Stonehenge to be a place of human sacrifice, this was in fact one of a pair of stones that formed a doorway.

Outer Bank
Dug around 3000 BC, this is the oldest part of the site.

Avenue
Built by the Beaker people, this dirt path forms a ceremonial approach to the site.

Station Stones
Four pillar stones stood inside the bank. Two, diagonally opposite each other, had mounds and ditches.

PREHISTORIC WILTSHIRE

Ringing the horizon around Stonehenge are scores of circular barrows, or burial mounds, where ruling class members were honored with burial close to the temple site. Ceremonial bronze weapons, jewelry, and other finds excavated around Stonehenge can be seen in the museums at Salisbury and Devizes.

KEY DATES

3000–1000 BC	1648	1900	1978	1984
Stonehenge is constructed in three phases.	The site is recognized as a prehistoric religious base.	On New Year's eve, two of the Sarcen Circle stones fall down.	The British government prohibits visitors from walking within the stone circle.	Stonehenge is added to UNESCO's World Heritage Site list.

BUILDING OF STONEHENGE

Stonehenge's scale is astonishing given that the only tools available were made of stone, wood, and bone. The labor involved in quarrying, transporting, and erecting the huge stones was such that its builders must have been able to command vast numbers of people. One method is explained here.

A sarsen stone was moved on rollers and levered down into a waiting pit.

With levers supported by timber packing, the stone was gradually raised by 200 men.

The pit around the base was packed tightly with stones and chalk.

Alternate ends of the top stone, or lintel, were levered up.

The lintel was supported by a timber platform.

The lintel was then levered sideways onto the upright stones.

Bluestone Circle
Erected around 2000 BC out of some 80 slabs quarried in Wales, it was never completed.

Horseshoe of Sarsen Trilithons
There were originally five trilithons (three stones) within the Sarcen and Bluestone circles, each comprising two upright sarcen (hard sandstone) stones topped by a horizontal lintel.

Sarsen Circle
The central part of the monument is made up of four concentric stone arrangements: two circles and two horseshoes. These 30 stones form the outermost circle.

Horseshoe of Bluestones
These stones are thought to have been transported from Wales on a combination of sledges and rafts.

▲ Finds
From a burial mound near Stonehenge, these prehistoric finds are now part of Devizes museum's exceptional collection.

Winter Solstice ▼
There are many lunar and solar alignments. The inner horseshoe faces the winter solstice sunrise.

Restoration of Stonehenge ►
Formal excavation and restoration work on the site only began during the 20th century.

▼ The Prehistoric Site
This was possibly a ceremonial area for fertility, birth, and death rituals. Evidence of burials and cremations exists nearby and inside the circle.

▲ Stonehenge as it is today
The ruins of Stonehenge reflect the grand structure that existed 4,000 years ago. Only half of the original stones remain, due to natural weathering and human destruction.

Midsummer sunrise over Stonehenge

Canterbury Cathedral

This glorious high-vaulted cathedral was designed in the French Gothic style *(Gothic Style, see p.54)* by William of Sens in 1070 and was the first Gothic church in England. It was built to reflect Canterbury's growing ecclesiastical rank as a major center of Christianity by the first Norman archbishop, Lanfranc, on the ruins of an Anglo-Saxon cathedral. Enlarged and rebuilt many times, it remains an exceptional example of the different styles of medieval architecture. The most significant moment in its history came in 1170, when Archbishop Thomas Becket was murdered here. In 1220, Becket's body was moved to a new shrine in Trinity Chapel, which, until Henry VIII destroyed it, was one of Christendom's chief pilgrimage sites.

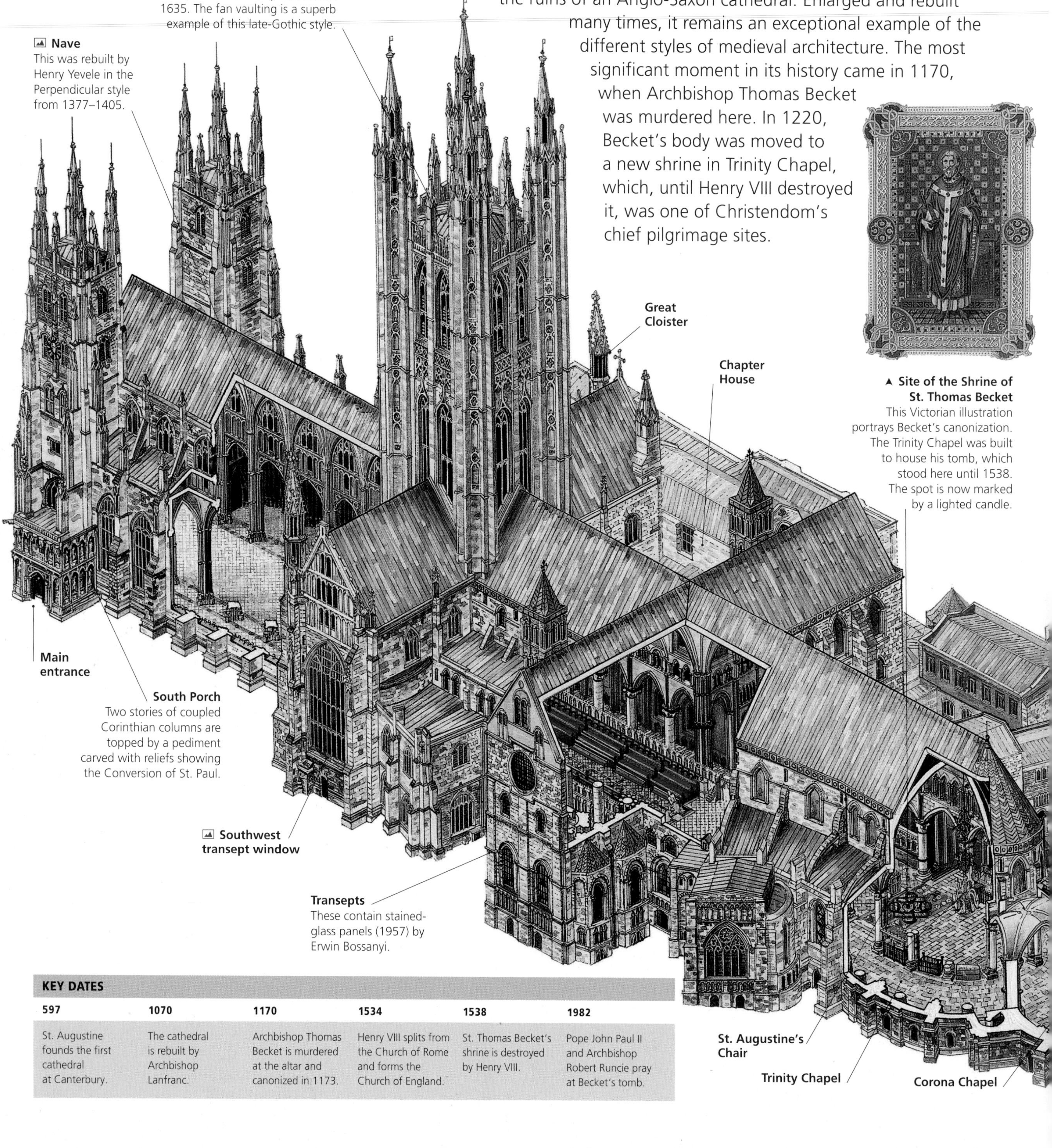

⊿ Bell Harry Tower
The central tower was built in 1496 to house a bell donated by Prior Henry (Harry) of Eastry. The present Bell Harry was cast in 1635. The fan vaulting is a superb example of this late-Gothic style.

⊿ Nave
This was rebuilt by Henry Yevele in the Perpendicular style from 1377–1405.

Great Cloister

Chapter House

▲ Site of the Shrine of St. Thomas Becket
This Victorian illustration portrays Becket's canonization. The Trinity Chapel was built to house his tomb, which stood here until 1538. The spot is now marked by a lighted candle.

Main entrance

South Porch
Two stories of coupled Corinthian columns are topped by a pediment carved with reliefs showing the Conversion of St. Paul.

⊿ Southwest transept window

Transepts
These contain stained-glass panels (1957) by Erwin Bossanyi.

St. Augustine's Chair

Trinity Chapel

Corona Chapel

KEY DATES					
597	**1070**	**1170**	**1534**	**1538**	**1982**
St. Augustine founds the first cathedral at Canterbury.	The cathedral is rebuilt by Archbishop Lanfranc.	Archbishop Thomas Becket is murdered at the altar and canonized in 1173.	Henry VIII splits from the Church of Rome and forms the Church of England.	St. Thomas Becket's shrine is destroyed by Henry VIII.	Pope John Paul II and Archbishop Robert Runcie pray at Becket's tomb.

THE CANTERBURY TALES

Considered to be the first great English poet, Geoffrey Chaucer (c. 1345–1400) is chiefly remembered for *The Canterbury Tales*, a boisterous and witty saga about a group of pilgrims who travel from London to Becket's shrine. The pilgrims represent a cross-section of 14th-century English society and the tales are one of the most entertaining works of early English literature.

Wife of Bath,
The Canterbury Tales

ST. AUGUSTINE

In 597, Pope Gregory the Great sent Augustine on a mission to convert the English to Christianity. Augustine founded a church on the present-day site of Canterbury Cathedral and became its first archbishop.

Bronze of Jesus on the main entrance to the cathedral precinct ➤

Southwest Transept Window ➤
The cathedral's unique collection of stained glass gives a precious glimpse into medieval beliefs and practices. This depiction of the 1,000-year-old Methuselah is a detail from the southwest transept window.

Nave ▼
At 328 ft (100 m), the nave makes Canterbury Cathedral Europe's longest medieval church. In 1984, parts of an Anglo-Saxon cathedral were found beneath the nave.

Black Prince's Tomb ▲
This copper effigy is on the tomb of Edward, Prince of Wales, who died in 1376.

▼ **Bell Harry Tower**

ST. THOMAS BECKET

When Archbishop Theobold died in 1161, King Henry II saw the opportunity to increase his power over the Church by consecrating his faithful adviser, Thomas Becket, as the Archbishop of Canterbury—the most prominent ecclesiastical role in the kingdom. The king mistakenly believed that this would allow him to exert pressure on the Church. Becket's loyalty shifted and the struggle between Church and monarch for ultimate control of the realm culminated in the murder of Becket on December 29, 1170, by four knights attempting to gain the king's favor. People flocked to mourn him and, three days later, a series of miracles took place that were attributed to Becket. After Becket's canonization in 1173, Canterbury Cathedral became a major center of pilgrimage.

THE ENGLISH REFORMATION

In 1534, Henry VIII broke with the Church of Rome when the pope refused to divorce him from Catherine of Aragon. The Archbishop of Canterbury, Thomas Cranmer, was made to do so instead. The Church of England was created, with Henry as its supreme head and the Archbishop of Canterbury its ecclesiastical guide. The *Book of Common Prayer*, compiled by Cranmer, became the cornerstone of the Church of England.

THE BLACK PRINCE

Edward, Prince of Wales (1330–76), known as "The Black Prince," gained popularity as leader of the victorious English army at the Battle of Crécy in 1346. He again emerged triumphant in 1356, at the Battle of Poitiers, when the French king, John the Good, was captured and brought to Canterbury Cathedral to worship at St. Thomas's tomb. As heir to the throne, Edward wanted to be buried in the crypt, but it was thought appropriate that this hero be laid to rest alongside the tomb of St. Thomas in the **Trinity Chapel**. The copper effigy on the **Black Prince's Tomb** is one of the most impressive in the cathedral. The Black Prince was outlived by his father, Edward III, but his son was crowned Richard II in 1377 at the age of ten.

THE NETHERLANDS

RUBENS' HOUSE, ANTWERP

Brussels

GERMANY

BELGIUM •Liège

FRANCE

LUXEMBOURG

PETER PAUL RUBENS (1577–1640)

Rubens had apprenticeships with prominent Antwerp artists from an early age and was inspired to visit Italy in 1600 to study and copy the work of the Italian Renaissance masters. On returning to Antwerp in 1608, Rubens' reputation earned him an appointment as court painter to the governors of the Low Countries, the Archduke Albert and his wife, the Infanta Isabella. He became the most renowned Baroque painter in Europe, combining Flemish realism with the Classical imagery of Italian Renaissance art. After 1626, he was assigned diplomatic missions and nominated to the courts of Charles I in England, Marie de' Medici in France and Felipe IV in Spain. In 1630, having helped to conclude a treaty between England and Spain, he was knighted by Charles I for his peacemaking efforts. In his later years, Rubens focused once more on his painting.

RUBENS IN ANTWERP

On his return to Antwerp in 1608, Rubens was swamped by commissions from the nobility, Church, and state. He painted pictures for church altarpieces, etched, engraved, designed tapestries, and planned entire pageants. His well-run **studio**, modeled on those in Italy, was able to meet the demand and under his guidance, a school of superior artists flourished.

RUBENS' HOUSE DESIGN

Rubens' sojourn in Italy (1600–08) influenced his views on architecture as well as painting. Rubens' House was embellished to reflect his love of Italian Renaissance forms, incorporating Classical arches and sculpture *(Renaissance Style, see p.131)*. His style boldly contrasted with the architectural traditions of the day and bears witness to his voracious creativity. It was here that he received prominent guests throughout his career. The house is entered as Rubens intended: through the main gate, which leads to an inner courtyard that creates an imposing impression of the surrounding features. The opulent **Baroque Portico** *(Baroque Style, see p.80)* between the courtyard and the **Formal Gardens** was designed by the artist himself. The renovations completed in 1946 were based on the artist's original sketches.

Rubens' House, Antwerp

Peter Paul Rubens' home and studio for the last 30 years of his life, from 1610 to 1640, is found on Wapper Square in Antwerp. The city bought the premises just before World War II, but the house had fallen into disrepair, and what can be seen today is the result of careful restoration. Rubens' House *(Rubenshuis)* is divided into two sections and offers a fascinating insight into how the artist lived and worked. To the left of the entrance are the narrow rooms of the artist's living quarters, equipped with period furniture. Behind this part of the house is the *kunstkamer*, or art gallery, where Rubens exhibited both his own and other artists' work, and entertained his friends and wealthy patrons such as the Archduke Albert and the Infanta Isabella. To the right of the entrance lies the main studio, a spacious salon where Rubens worked on—and showed—his paintings.

Statue of Neptune in the courtyard

◄ Kunstkamer
This art gallery contains a series of painted sketches by Rubens. At the far end is a semicircular dome, modeled on Rome's Pantheon, displaying a number of marble busts.

◄ Bedroom

RELIGIOUS WORKS

Rubens was a fervent Roman Catholic, prompting magnificent religious and allegorical masterpieces. Several of these can be seen in Antwerp, including the beautiful ceiling of the Jesuit church of St. Ignatius and a triptych in the Cathedral of Our Lady.

◄ Rubens' Studio
It is estimated that Rubens produced some 2,500 paintings in this large, high-ceilinged room. In order to meet this huge number of commissions, Rubens often sketched a work before passing it on to be completed by other artists employed in the studio.

▼ Dining Room

Baroque Portico ▼

Familia Kamer
The family sitting room is cosy, with a pretty, tiled floor. It overlooks Wapper Square.

⊿ Bedroom
The Rubens family lived in the Flemish section of the house, with its small rooms and narrow passages.

⊿ Dining Room
Intricately fashioned leather panels line the walls of this room, which also displays a noted work by Frans Snyders.

⊿ Kunstkamer

Chequered mosaic tiled floor

⊿ Rubens' studio

▼ Formal Gardens
The small garden is laid out formally and its charming pavilion dates from Rubens' time.

⊿ Baroque Portico
One of the few remaining original features, this was designed by Rubens, and links the older house with the Baroque section. It features a frieze with scenes from Greek mythology.

► Facade of Rubens' House
The older, Flemish part of the house sits next to the later house, whose elegant early-Baroque façade was designed by Rubens.

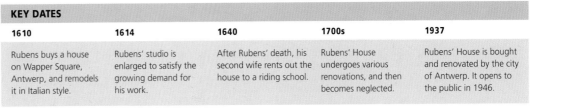

KEY DATES				
1610	**1614**	**1640**	**1700s**	**1937**
Rubens buys a house on Wapper Square, Antwerp, and remodels it in Italian style.	Rubens' studio is enlarged to satisfy the growing demand for his work.	After Rubens' death, his second wife rents out the house to a riding school.	Rubens' House undergoes various renovations, and then becomes neglected.	Rubens' House is bought and renovated by the city of Antwerp. It opens to the public in 1946.

Het Loo Palace, Apeldoorn

Stadtholder William III, the future king of England, built the magnificent Het Loo Palace, regarded as the "Versailles of the Netherlands," as a royal hunting lodge in the 17th century. Generations of the House of Orange used the lodge as a summer palace. The main architect was Jacob Roman (1640–1716); the interior decoration and garden design were the responsibility of Daniel Marot. The building's Classical façade *(Classical Style, see p.137)* belies the opulence of its lavish interior; extensive restoration work was completed on both in 1984.

Engraving of William III of Orange (1650–1702)

THE HOUSE OF ORANGE-NASSAU

The marriage of Hendrik III of Nassau-Breda and Claudia of Chalon-Orange established the House of Orange-Nassau in 1515. Since that time, the family has played a central role in the political life of the Netherlands. The House of Orange is also important in British history. In 1677, William III of Orange married his first cousin, the English princess Mary Stuart. William and Mary became king and queen of England in 1689 when Mary's father, James II, went into exile in France, and the couple ruled as joint monarchs.

HET LOO PALACE INTERIOR

The Orange-Nassau family continued to use Het Loo Palace as a royal summer house until 1975. The palace is now a museum, and painstaking restoration has re-created its 17th-century appearance. The interior, which is sumptuously decorated with rich materials, is laid out symmetrically, with the royal apartments located to the east and west of the Great Hall. The wings of the palace contain exhibitions of court costumes, along with documents, paintings, silver, and china belonging to the House of Orange-Nassau over three centuries.

THE GARDENS AND FOUNTAINS

In 1686, the **Formal Gardens** surrounding the palace were laid out and soon became celebrated. The designer was Daniel Marot (1661–1752), who added a host of small details such as wrought-iron railings and garden urns. The gardens, which include the **Queen's Garden** and **King's Garden**, were designed to be strictly geometrical. They were decorated with formal flower beds and embellished with fountains, borders, topiary and cascades. Statues were placed throughout. Today, the King's Garden features clipped box trees and pyramid-shaped juniper trees. At the center stands an octagonal white marble basin with a spouting triton and gilt sea dragons. The slightly raised **Upper Garden** is home to the impressive King's Fountain, which is fed by a natural spring and operates 24 hours a day. It is a classic, eye-catching feature in a royal garden.

QUEEN WILHELMINA

After the death of the Dutch King William III (r. 1848–90), his daughter Wilhelmina was the first female to rule the country as queen (r. 1890–1948). During her reign, Wilhelmina used the Het Loo Palace as her summer retreat.

Royal Bedroom
The wall coverings and draperies in this luxuriously furnished bedroom (1713) are of rich orange damask and purple silk.

Stadtholder William III's Closet
The walls of William's private study (1690) are covered in embossed scarlet damask. His favorite paintings and Delftware pieces are exhibited here.

Queen Mary II's Bedroom

King's Garden

King William III's Bedroom

Main entrance

THE FORMAL GARDENS

Old prints, records, and plans were used as the guidelines for re-creating Het Loo's formal gardens, which lie in the vast acres behind the palace. Grass was planted over the original walled and knot gardens in the 18th century, and this was cleared in 1975. By 1983, the intricate floral patterns had been reestablished, replanting had begun, the Classical fountains had been renovated and the water supply fully restored. The garden reflects the late 17th century belief that art and nature should operate in harmony.

Upper Garden
Queen's Garden
Het Loo Palace
King's Garden
Lower Garden

Formal section of the gardens

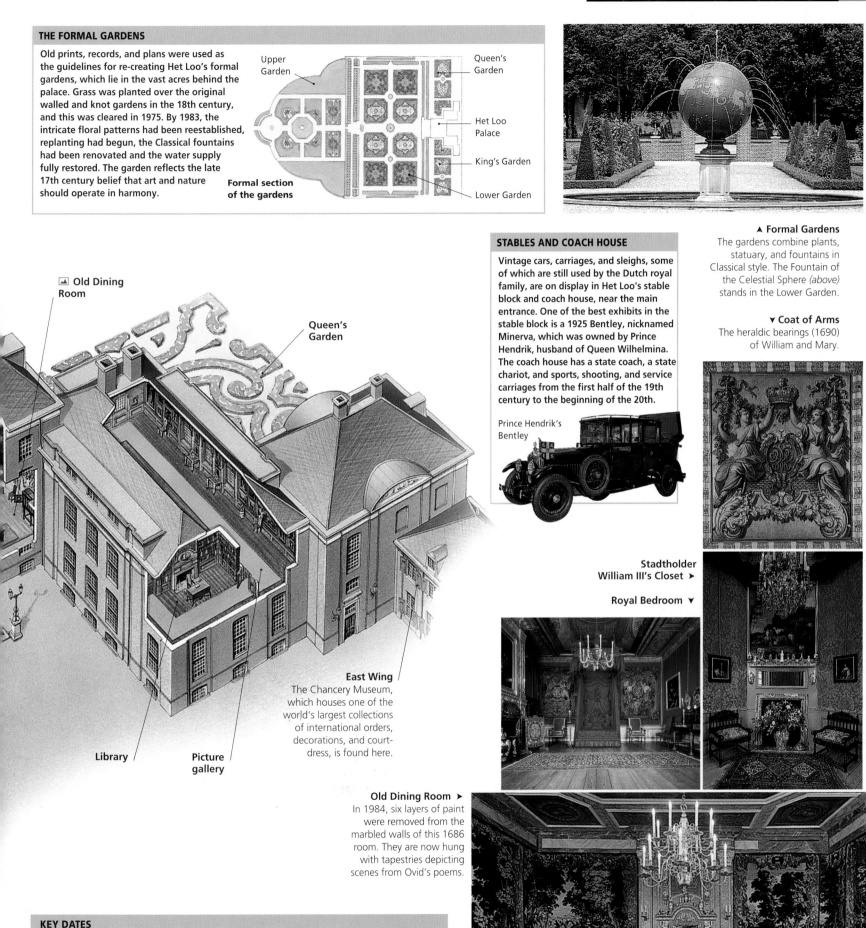

Old Dining Room

Queen's Garden

STABLES AND COACH HOUSE

Vintage cars, carriages, and sleighs, some of which are still used by the Dutch royal family, are on display in Het Loo's stable block and coach house, near the main entrance. One of the best exhibits in the stable block is a 1925 Bentley, nicknamed Minerva, which was owned by Prince Hendrik, husband of Queen Wilhelmina. The coach house has a state coach, a state chariot, and sports, shooting, and service carriages from the first half of the 19th century to the beginning of the 20th.

Prince Hendrik's Bentley

▲ **Formal Gardens**
The gardens combine plants, statuary, and fountains in Classical style. The Fountain of the Celestial Sphere (above) stands in the Lower Garden.

▼ **Coat of Arms**
The heraldic bearings (1690) of William and Mary.

Stadtholder William III's Closet ➤

Royal Bedroom ▼

East Wing
The Chancery Museum, which houses one of the world's largest collections of international orders, decorations, and court-dress, is found here.

Library
Picture gallery

Old Dining Room ➤
In 1984, six layers of paint were removed from the marbled walls of this 1686 room. They are now hung with tapestries depicting scenes from Ovid's poems.

KEY DATES

1684–6	1691–4	1814	1984
Building of the Het Loo Palace for Prince William III and Princess Mary.	King William III commissions new building works on the palace.	Het Loo Palace becomes the property of the Dutch state.	Restoration of the house and garden is completed.

Amiens Cathedral

A masterpiece of engineering and Gothic architecture (*Gothic Style, see p.54*) carried to a bold extreme, Amiens' Notre-Dame Cathedral is also the largest cathedral in France. Building work started around 1220 and took just 50 years, financed by profits from the cultivation of woad, a plant valued for its blue dye. Built to house the head of St. John the Baptist brought back from the Crusades, which is still on display, the cathedral became a magnet for pilgrims. After restoration by the architect Viollet-le-Duc in the mid-19th century, and miraculously surviving two world wars, the cathedral is famous for its wealth of statues and reliefs.

▲ **Weeping Angel**
Sculpted by Nicolas Blasset in 1628, this sentimental statue in the ambulatory became a popular image during World War I.

GOTHIC ORNAMENTATION

Like all Gothic churches, Amiens Cathedral is richly decorated. Sculpture served to detract attention from structural features, making a virtue out of a necessity, as with grotesque gargoyles that disguise waterspouts, or natural forms decorating columns. Even where the carvings would not be seen at close hand, they were still produced with tremendous skill and care. Amiens' **choir stalls** alone are decorated with more than 4,000 wooden carvings of figures, many representing local trades of the day, residents of Amiens and biblical figures.

VIOLLET-LE-DUC

The renowned architect and theorist Eugène Emmanuel Viollet-le-Duc (1814–79) worked on the restoration of the cathedral in the 1850s. Trained in both architecture and medieval archeology, he was a leading figure in France's Commission for Historical Monuments, which undertook early restoration work on many architectural landmarks, including Notre-Dame in Paris. Today, he is best known for his encyclopedic writings on French architecture and design, especially the *Analytical Dictionary of French Architecture from the 11th–16th Centuries* (1854–68).

BUILDING AMIENS CATHEDRAL

The cathedral was designed by the French architect Robert de Luzarches, and inspired by the Gothic cathedral at Reims, France. Work began in 1220 and by 1236, the façade, **Rose Window**, and portals were complete. By this stage, the architect Thomas de Cormont had taken over from de Luzarches, who had died prematurely in about 1222. De Cormont directed the building of the choir and apse. The cathedral was finished by 1270 and this speed of execution perhaps explains the building's coherence and purity of style. Research has shown that the figures on the beautiful west portal would originally have been brightly painted. Modern laser technology has enabled experts to assess the original coloring of the sculptures, and a light show is put on periodically to illuminate the portal, re-creating how it would have looked over 700 years ago.

KEY DATES			
1220	**1279**	**1849**	**1981**
Bishop Evrard de Fouilly begins work on the foundations of the cathedral.	The relics of St. Firmin and St. Ulphe are presented, attended by the kings of France and England.	Restoration of the cathedral takes place under the direction of the architect Viollet-le-Duc.	Amiens Cathedral joins the list of UNESCO World Heritage Sites.

◄ **Rose Window**

◄ **Choir Screens**
Vivid scenes from the lives of St. Firmin and St. John, carved in the 15th–16th centuries, adorn the walkway.

▲ **Towers**
Two towers of unequal height frame the cathedral's west front. The south tower was completed in 1366, the north in 1402. The spire was replaced twice, in 1627 and 1887.

◄ **Choir Stalls**

▲ **West Front**
The King's Gallery, a row of 22 colossal statues representing the kings of France, spans the west front. They are also thought to symbolize the kings of Judah.

◄ **Nave**

North tower

ST. FIRMIN

The patron saint of Amiens, St. Firmin was born in Pamplona, Spain, in around 272. After ordination, he was sent to northern France, where he pursued his mission boldly, unafraid of persecution, and soon settled in Amiens. His persuasive preaching led to his beheading by the Romans in around 303.

Rose Window
This immense, 16th-century window has a diameter of 43 ft (13 m) and features flamboyant tracery.

▲ Central Portal
Above the doors are scenes from the Last Judgment and there is a statue of Christ between the doors.

West front

Flying Buttresses
A double row of 22 elegant flying buttresses support the cathedral.

St. Firmin Portal
This portal is decorated with figures and scenes from the life of St. Firmin, the martyr who brought Christianity to Picardy and became the first bishop of Amiens.

Nave
Soaring 138 ft (42 m) high, with support from 126 slender pillars, the airy, brightly lit nave is a hymn to the vertical.

Choir Stalls
The 110 oak choir stalls (1508–19) are delicately carved with more than 3,500 biblical, mythical, and real-life figures.

Central portal

Choir screens

Calendar
Sculptures in the north portal depict the signs of the zodiac and their corresponding monthly labors—from seed-sowing to grape-treading—offering an insight into everyday life in the 13th century.

Flooring
Originally laid down in 1288, this was re-assembled in the late 19th century. The faithful followed its labyrinthine path on their knees.

Mont-St-Michel

Shrouded by mist and encircled by sea, the enchanting silhouette of Mont-St-Michel soars proudly above glistening sands. Now linked to the mainland by a causeway, the island of Mont-Tombe (Tomb on the Hill) stands at the mouth of the Couesnon River, crowned by an abbey that almost doubles its height. This superb example of a fortified abbey ranks as one of the most significant sites of pilgrimage in Christendom. Lying strategically on the frontier between Brittany and Normandy, Mont-St-Michel grew from a humble 8th-century oratory to become a Benedictine monastery of great influence. Pilgrims known as *miquelots* journeyed from afar to honor the cult of St. Michael, and the monastery was a renowned center of medieval learning. After the French Revolution, the abbey became a prison. It is now a national monument that draws one million visitors a year.

OVER THE CENTURIES

The 10th-century abbey
Richard I, Duke of Normandy, founded this great Benedictine abbey in 966.

The 11th-century abbey
The Romanesque church was built between 1017 and 1144 (*Romanesque Style, see p.122*).

The 18th-century abbey
The number of monks slowly dwindled, and in 1790 the abbey was disbanded and turned into a political prison.

THE FORTIFICATIONS

Mont-St-Michel became a symbol of French national identity when its defensive 15th-century walls protected it against fierce cannon attacks in the Hundred Years' War. The whole of Normandy was conquered by the English, except this well-fortified island.

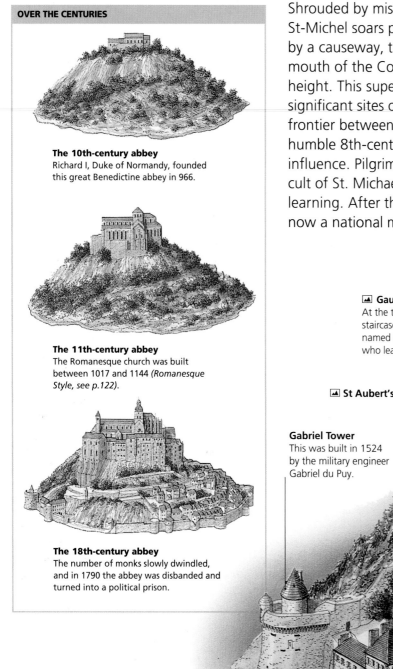

Gautier's Leap
At the top of the inner staircase, this terrace is named after a prisoner who leaped to his death.

St Aubert's Chapel

Gabriel Tower
This was built in 1524 by the military engineer Gabriel du Puy.

Abbey
Protected by high walls, the abbey and its church occupy an impregnable position on the island.

Ramparts
Fortified walls with imposing towers were built to withstand attacks by the English during the Hundred Years' War (1337–1453).

Entrance

KEY DATES

708	966	1446–1521	1863–74	1877–9	1895–7	1922	1979
St. Aubert builds an oratory dedicated to St. Michael on Mont-Tombe.	Duke Richard I founds the Benedictine abbey.	A flamboyant Gothic choir replaces the Romanesque one in the abbey church.	The prison closes and the abbey is declared a national monument.	A causeway is built, linking Mont-St-Michel and mainland France.	The belfry, spire, and statue of St. Michael are added.	Religious services resume in the abbey church.	Mont-St-Michel is added to UNESCO's World Heritage Site list.

▲ Tides of Mont-St-Michel
Extremely strong tides in the Baie du Mont-St-Michel act as a natural defense. They rise and fall with the lunar calendar and can reach speeds of 6 mph (10 km/h) in spring.

▲ St. Aubert's Chapel
This small 15th-century chapel, built on an outcrop of rock, is dedicated to St. Aubert, the founder of Mont-St-Michel.

Église St-Pierre
A dramatic statue of St. Michael slaying a dragon can be seen in the elaborately carved side chapel of this medieval church.

▲ Gautier's Leap

Ramparts ▶

King's Tower

Arcade Tower
This provided lodgings for the abbot's soldiers.

Liberty Tower

Grande Rue ▶
Now crowded with restaurants, the pilgrims' route, followed since the 12th century, climbs up past Église St-Pierre to the gates of the abbey.

Abbey Cloister ▶
Inside the abbey is a 13th-century Anglo-Norman covered gallery. It surrounds an open-air garden where the monks would meditate.

BISHOP AUBERT

For centuries, the Mont was recognized as a sacred site of devotion, where both Druids and Romans worshiped. In 708, Aubert, Bishop of the nearby town of Avranches, had a vision in which the Archangel Michael commanded t hat a chapel be built in his honor on Mont-St-Michel. In response, Bishop Aubert had an oratory erected on the summit, his belief inspiring one of Christianity's most spectacular holy sites. The faithful came to appeal for the archangel's protection and Mont-St-Michel soon became an important place of pilgrimage. Although nothing remains of Bishop Aubert's original oratory, it is thought to have been situated on the west side of the rock, on the ground where **St. Aubert's Chapel** now stands.

THE ABBEY

The three levels of the abbey reflect the monastic hierarchy. The monks lived at the highest level, in the enclosed world of the church, the refectory and the elegant columns of the cloister. In 1776, three bays in the church's nave were pulled down to create the West Terrace, which has fine views of the coastline. Monks ate in the long, narrow refectory, which is flooded with light through its tall windows. On the middle level, the abbot entertained his noble guests. Soldiers and pilgrims further down the social scale were received at the lowest level of the abbey, in the almonry. The three-story complex of *La Merveille* (The Miracle), added to the north side in the early 13th century, is a Gothic masterpiece (*Gothic Style, see p.54*).

THE MONT PRISON

The monastery first served as a prison in the 15th century under the reign of Louis XI, whose political opponents were kept here in famously severe conditions. During the French Revolution, the monks were dismissed and the abbey once again functioned as a penitentiary, with aristocrats, priests, and political adversaries imprisoned within its walls. Prominent figures, including writers such as Chateaubriand and Victor Hugo, protested against this practice, but Mont-St-Michel remained a state prison for 73 years until October 20, 1863, when a decree was passed returning the abbey to divine worship.

The soaring pinnacles of Notre-Dame, Paris—a superb example of French Gothic architecture

Notre-Dame, Paris

South Rose Window

No other building is so strongly associated with the history of Paris as the cathedral of Notre-Dame. It stands majestically on the Ile de la Cité, in the heart of the city. When the first stone was laid in 1163, it marked the start of 170 years of toil by armies of medieval architects and craftsmen. Since then, a succession of coronations and royal marriages has taken place within its walls. Built on the site of a Roman temple, the cathedral is a masterpiece of Gothic architecture. When it was completed, in about 1330, it was 430 ft (130 m) long and featured flying buttresses, a large transept, a deep choir, and 228-ft (69-m) high towers.

THE HUNCHBACK OF NOTRE-DAME

The novel *Notre-Dame de Paris* (1831), published in English as *The Hunchback of Notre-Dame*, was written by the Romantic French novelist Victor Hugo (1802–85). The hunchback of the title is the bell-ringer Quasimodo, ward of the cathedral, and the novel tells the story of his doomed love for a dancer, Esmeralda. Notre-Dame features strongly in the work and Hugo used his book to rail against its neglect, declaring that medieval cathedrals were "books in stone" and should be treasured. The novel aroused widespread interest in the restoration of the cathedral.

THE INTERIOR

Notre-Dame's interior grandeur is strikingly apparent in its high-vaulted central nave. This is bisected by a huge **transept**, at either end of which is a medieval rose window, 43 ft (13 m) in diameter. Works by famous sculptors adorn the cathedral. Among them are Jean Ravy's choir screen carvings, Nicolas Coustou's *Pietà*, which stands on a gilded base sculpted by François Girardon, and Antoine Coysevox's statue of Louis XIV. The 13th-century stained-glass **North Rose Window** depicts the Virgin encircled by figures from the Old Testament. A 14th-century statue of the Virgin and Child stands against the transept's southeast pillar.

GOTHIC STYLE

The Gothic style emerged in France around the end of the 12th century with the Basilica of St-Denis (1137–1281), north of Paris, where most of the French monarchs are buried. The pointed arch, the ribbed vault, tracery, and the rose window were all used to great effect there and were important features of the Gothic style. The desire to build taller, ever more magnificent, light-filled ecclesiastical buildings grew. Another key feature emerged with the use of flying buttresses, which provided support for high walls and helped redistribute their weight. With its soaring interior and stained-glass filtered light from the large rose windows, Notre-Dame Cathedral is one of the best-known and most impressive examples of the Gothic style. Across Europe in many countries, architects took to the style with enthusiasm.

◄ West Façade and Portals
Two huge towers, three main doors, superb statuary, a central rose window and an openwork gallery are impressive features of the cathedral's west façade.

◄ South Rose Window
This window depicts the Virgin in a medallion of rich reds and blues.

◄ Galerie des Chimères
The cathedral's famous 19th-century gargoyles *(chimères)* hide behind a large upper gallery between the towers.

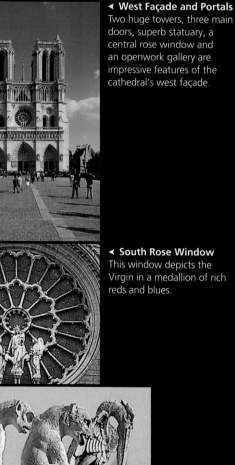

⊡ West façade and portals

⊡ Galerie des Chimères

⊡ West Rose Window

Portal of the Virgin
The Virgin surrounded by saints and kings is a fine composition of 13th-century statues.

King's Gallery
This is a line of statues of the 28 kings of Judah and Israel.

◄ Flying Buttresses
Jean Ravy's spectacular flying buttresses at the east end of the cathedral have a span of 50 ft (15 m).

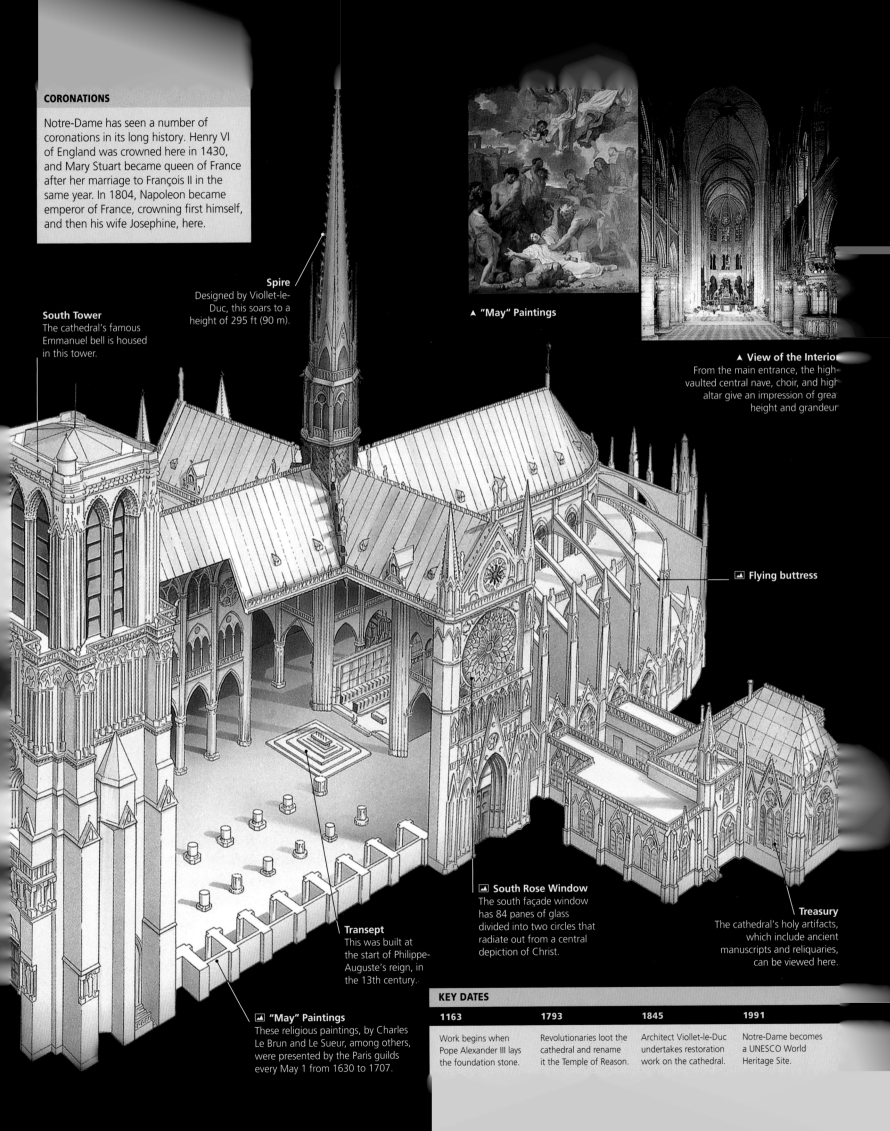

CORONATIONS

Notre-Dame has seen a number of coronations in its long history. Henry VI of England was crowned here in 1430, and Mary Stuart became queen of France after her marriage to François II in the same year. In 1804, Napoleon became emperor of France, crowning first himself, and then his wife Josephine, here.

Spire
Designed by Viollet-le-Duc, this soars to a height of 295 ft (90 m).

South Tower
The cathedral's famous Emmanuel bell is housed in this tower.

▲ **"May" Paintings**

▲ **View of the Interior**
From the main entrance, the high-vaulted central nave, choir, and high altar give an impression of great height and grandeur

▣ **Flying buttress**

▣ **South Rose Window**
The south façade window has 84 panes of glass divided into two circles that radiate out from a central depiction of Christ.

Transept
This was built at the start of Philippe-Auguste's reign, in the 13th century.

Treasury
The cathedral's holy artifacts, which include ancient manuscripts and reliquaries, can be viewed here.

▣ **"May" Paintings**
These religious paintings, by Charles Le Brun and Le Sueur, among others, were presented by the Paris guilds every May 1 from 1630 to 1707.

KEY DATES

1163	1793	1845	1991
Work begins when Pope Alexander III lays the foundation stone.	Revolutionaries loot the cathedral and rename it the Temple of Reason.	Architect Viollet-le-Duc undertakes restoration work on the cathedral.	Notre-Dame becomes a UNESCO World Heritage Site.

Arc de Triomphe, Paris

After his greatest victory, at the Battle of Austerlitz in 1805, Napoleon promised his men, "You shall go home beneath triumphal arches." The first stone of what was to become the world's most famous and largest triumphal arch was laid the following year. However, disruptions to architect Jean Chalgrin's plans, and the demise of Napoleonic power, delayed the completion of this monumental building until 1836. Standing 164 ft (50 m) high, the arch is now the customary starting point for victory celebrations and parades.

Triumph of Napoleon

◄ East façade of the Arc de Triomphe

◄ Departure of the Volunteers in 1792
François Rude's work shows French citizens leaving to defend the nation. This patriotic relief is commonly known as "La Marseillaise."

THE BATTLE OF VERDUN

On the day this World War I battle started in 1916, the sword carried by the figure representing France broke off from *Departure of the Volunteers in 1792*. The relief was covered up so that the public would not interpret it as a sign of misfortune.

▼ General Marceau's Funeral
Marceau defeated the Austrians in 1795, only to be killed when fighting them the following year.

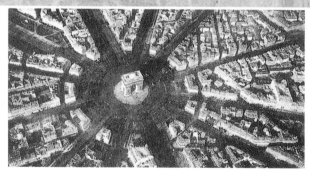

Frieze
Running around the arch is a frieze executed by Rude, Brun, Jacquet, Laitié, Caillouette, and Seurre the Elder. The east façade shows the departure of the French armies for new campaigns. The west side shows their victorious return.

Battle of Aboukir
A bas-relief by Seurre the Elder depicts a scene of Napoleon's victory over the Turkish army in 1799.

◄ Place Charles de Gaulle
Twelve avenues radiate from the triumphal arch at the center of this busy road junction. Some bear the names of important French military leaders. Baron Haussman, in charge of urban planning under Napoleon III, created the star-shaped configuration.

◪ Triumph of Napoleon
J. P. Cortot's high-relief celebrates the Treaty of Vienna peace agreement of 1810. Victory, History, and Fame surround Napoleon.

Tomb of the Unknown Soldier ▼
A symbolic "eternal flame" burns over the grave of this French victim of World War I.

KEY DATES

1806	1815	1836	1885	1920
Napoleon commissions Jean Chalgrin to build the triumphal arch.	With Napoleon's downfall, the construction of the arch ceases.	The arch is finally completed: 15 years after Napoleon's death.	The body of French poet and novelist Victor Hugo is laid in state beneath the arch.	An unknown World War I soldier is buried at the center of the arch.

NAPOLEON'S NUPTIAL PARADE

Napoleon divorced Josephine in 1809 because she was unable to bear him children. A diplomatic marriage was arranged in 1810 with Marie-Louise, daughter of the Austrian emperor. Napoleon wanted to pass through the Arc on the way to the wedding at the Louvre, but work had barely begun. So Chalgrin built a full-scale model on the site for the couple to pass beneath.

Napoleon with his new wife

Thirty Shields
Just below the top of the arch is a row of 30 shields, each of which carries the name of a victorious Napoleonic battle.

East façade

Viewing Platform
The top of the arch, reached via an elevator or by climbing the 284 steps, affords one of the best views in Paris.

Battle of Austerlitz
Another battle victory is depicted on a frieze on the north side of the arch. Napoleon's army is seen breaking up the ice on Lake Satschan—a tactic that led to the drowning of thousands of enemy troops.

◪ General Marceau's Funeral

Officers' names
The names of 558 French generals of the Imperial Army are engraved on the inner face of the arch.

Entrance to the museum

◪ Departure of the Volunteers in 1792

CARVED RELIEFS

The west façade of the arch is adorned with colossal reliefs. *The Resistance of the French in 1814* is depicted on the right. Here, a soldier defends his family and is encouraged by the embodiment of the future. *The Peace of 1815*, on the left, shows a man, protected by Minerva, Goddess of Wisdom, returning his sword to its scabbard. These reliefs are by the sculptor Antoine Étex. Above them are two bas-reliefs. The left frame depicts the *Capture of Alexandria* (1798), as General Kléber urges his troops forward. The right frame shows the *Passage of the Bridge of Arcola* (1796), with Napoleon advancing against the Austrians. The south façade details the *Battle of Jemmapes* (1792).

THE BATTLE OF AUSTERLITZ

Napoleon commissioned the arch in 1806 to honor his soldiers, who had achieved a masterful victory at the Battle of Austerlitz in 1805. Heavily outnumbered, Napoleon led the Allies to believe that his army was weak and successfully lured them into a vulnerable position. Fierce battle ensued, forcing the Allies to retreat across frozen Lake Satschan in Austria. It is believed that Napoleon's army fired on the ice in an attempt to drown the fleeing enemy. The armies of Russia and Austria, members of the Third Coalition alliance against France in the Napoleonic Wars, were destroyed.

NEO-CLASSICAL STYLE

The power, might and learning of Western Europe was represented in the 18th and the first half of the 19th centuries by architecture inspired by that of ancient Greece and Rome. The traditional principles of the Classical style were extended and adapted as the culture of the ancient world was increasingly revealed, documented and disseminated. This new Classicism was seen as an ideal match for the ambitions of the powerful European states, whether autocratic or witnessing the birth pangs of democracy, and also of the young United States of America. The Neo-Classical style is defined by elaborate details and a refined sense of proportion: hallmarks of ancient Classical architecture that could be adapted for every conceivable purpose.

Château de Versailles

A magnificent palace with sumptuous interiors and splendid gardens, Versailles represents the glory of Louis XIV's reign. Starting in 1668 with his father's modest hunting lodge, the king commissioned the largest palace in Europe, with 700 rooms, 67 staircases, and 1,800 acres (730 ha) of landscaped parkland. Architect Louis Le Vau built a series of wings that expanded into an enlarged courtyard. They were decorated with marble busts, antique trophies, and gilded roofs. Jules Hardouin-Mansart took over in 1678 and added the two immense north and south wings. He also designed the chapel, which was finished in 1710. Charles le Brun planned the interiors and André Le Nôtre redesigned the gardens.

Gold crest from the Petit Trianon

RESIDENTS OF VERSAILLES

In 1682, Louis XIV declared Versailles the official seat of the French government and court. During his reign, life in this sumptuous Baroque palace (Baroque Style, see p.80) was ordered by rigid etiquette. Under Louis XV (1715–74), it became increasingly opulent with the help of Madame de Pompadour, the king's mistress, who set a taste for elegance that soon spread across Europe. In 1789, Louis XVI was forced to leave Versailles when it was invaded by a Revolutionary Parisian mob. The palace was subsequently looted and left until the reign of Louis-Philippe (1830–48), who converted part of it into a museum of French history.

THE GARDENS

André Le Nôtre (1613–1700), France's greatest landscape gardener, created magnificent château gardens. His superb architectural orchestration, Classical vision and sense of symmetry are seen in the sweeping vistas of Versailles, his greatest triumph. The gardens are styled into regular patterns of flowerbeds and box hedges, paths and groves, ornate pools of water, and fountains. Geometric paths and shrubberies are features of the formal gardens. The **Petit Trianon**, a small château built as a retreat for Louis XV, is found in the gardens.

INSIDE THE CHÂTEAU

The lavish main apartments are on the first floor of the vast château complex. Around the **Marble Courtyard** are the private apartments of the king and queen. On the garden side are the state apartments, where official court life took place. These were richly decorated by Charles Le Brun with colored marble, stones, and wood carvings, murals, velvet, silver and gilded furniture. Starting with the **Salon d'Hercule**, each state room is dedicated to an Olympian deity. The **Salon d'Apollon**, dedicated to the god Apollo, was Louis XIV's throne room. The climax is the **Hall of Mirrors**, stretching 230 ft (70 m) along the west façade. Great state occasions were held in this room, where 17 mirrors face tall, arched windows. Another highlight is the **Chapelle Royale**, with the first floor reserved for the royal family and the ground floor for the court.

◄ South Wing
The wing's original apartments for great nobles were replaced in 1837 by Louis-Philippe's museum of French history.

Louis XIV statue
Erected by Louis-Philippe in 1837, this bronze equestrian statue of the Sun King stands where a gilded gateway once marked the beginning of the Royal Courtyard.

Clock ▼
Hercules and Mars flank the clock overlooking the Marble Courtyard.

▲ Marble Courtyard

Chapelle Royale ►

▼ North Wing

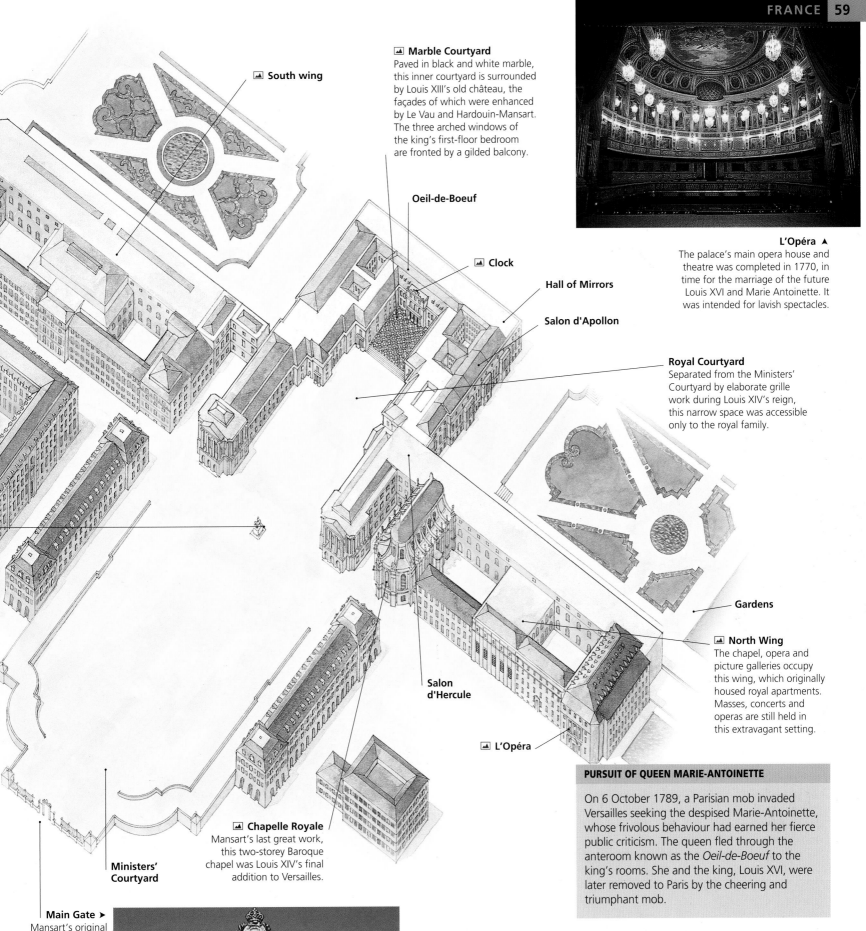

South wing

Marble Courtyard
Paved in black and white marble, this inner courtyard is surrounded by Louis XIII's old château, the façades of which were enhanced by Le Vau and Hardouin-Mansart. The three arched windows of the king's first-floor bedroom are fronted by a gilded balcony.

Oeil-de-Boeuf

Clock

Hall of Mirrors

Salon d'Apollon

L'Opéra ▲
The palace's main opera house and theatre was completed in 1770, in time for the marriage of the future Louis XVI and Marie Antoinette. It was intended for lavish spectacles.

Royal Courtyard
Separated from the Ministers' Courtyard by elaborate grille work during Louis XIV's reign, this narrow space was accessible only to the royal family.

Gardens

North Wing
The chapel, opera and picture galleries occupy this wing, which originally housed royal apartments. Masses, concerts and operas are still held in this extravagant setting.

Salon d'Hercule

L'Opéra

Chapelle Royale
Mansart's last great work, this two-storey Baroque chapel was Louis XIV's final addition to Versailles.

Ministers' Courtyard

Main Gate ▶
Mansart's original gateway grille, surmounted by the royal arms, is the entrance to the Ministers' Courtyard.

PURSUIT OF QUEEN MARIE-ANTOINETTE

On 6 October 1789, a Parisian mob invaded Versailles seeking the despised Marie-Antoinette, whose frivolous behaviour had earned her fierce public criticism. The queen fled through the anteroom known as the *Oeil-de-Boeuf* to the king's rooms. She and the king, Louis XVI, were later removed to Paris by the cheering and triumphant mob.

KEY DATES

1668	1671	1833	1919
Le Vau starts the construction of the château.	Decorator Charles Le Brun begins work on the château's interiors.	Louis-Philippe turns the château into the Museum of the History of France.	The Treaty of Versailles is signed in the Hall of Mirrors, ending World War I.

THE ROYAL PORTAL

Following the devastating fire of 1194, a decision was taken to retain the magnificent, still-standing west entrance (**Royal Portal**), which was a survivor of the earlier Romanesque church *(Romanesque Style, see p.122)*. Although this created a variation in architectural styles, it was an astute decision that resulted in the survival of some of the finest sculpture of the early Middle Ages. The Royal Portal, carved between 1145 and 1155, is the most ornamental of the cathedral's three entrances. The features of the statues in the portal are lengthened in Romanesque style and depict figures from the Old Testament. The portal represents the glory of Christ.

THE STAINED GLASS OF CHARTRES

Donated by aristocracy, the merchant brotherhoods and royalty between 1210 and 1240, the cathedral's glorious array of **stained-glass windows** is world-renowned. More than 150 windows illustrate biblical stories and daily life in the 13th century. Each window is divided into panels, which are usually read from left to right and bottom to top (Earth to heaven). The bottom panel of the Blue Virgin Window depicts Christ's conversion of water into wine. During both world wars, the windows were dismantled piece by piece and removed for safety. There is an ongoing program, begun in the 1970s, to restore the windows.

GOTHIC STATUARY

There are around 4,000 statues at Chartres Cathedral. Fortunately, having remained virtually untouched since being sculpted in the 13th century, they are in a remarkable state of preservation. Incredible examples, tracing the evolution of Gothic sculpture, are clustered around the north and south portals. The north porch is devoted to representations of such Old Testament figures as Joseph, Solomon, the Queen of Sheba, Isaiah, and Jeremiah. Scenes from Christ's childhood and the Creation of the World are also illustrated. The **South Porch** portrays the Last Judgment, and episodes in the lives of the saints. The hundreds of figures decorating both portals were originally painted in bright colors.

Chartres Cathedral

Part of the Vendôme Chapel window

One of the greatest examples of French Gothic architecture *(Gothic Style, see p.54)*, Chartres Cathedral was built around the remains of an earlier Romanesque church which had been partly destroyed by fire. The result is a blend of styles, with the original north and south towers, south steeple, west portal, and crypt enhanced by lofty Gothic additions. Peasant and lord alike helped to rebuild the church in just 25 years. Few alterations were made after 1250, and fortunately Chartres was unscathed by the Wars of Religion and the French Revolution.

◄ Royal Portal
The central tympanum of the Royal Portal (1145–55) shows Christ in Majesty.

◄ Stained-Glass Windows

Steeple
The north tower's steeple dates from the start of the 16th century. Flamboyant Gothic in style, it contrasts sharply with the solemnity of its Romanesque counterpart on the south tower.

▼ Vaulted Ceiling

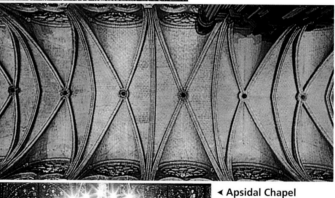

◄ Apsidal Chapel

🖼 Royal Portal

◄ Nave

◄ Crypt

VEIL OF THE VIRGIN

The miraculous survival of this relic after the fire of 1194 made Chartres a pilgrimage site and attracted generous donations. The veil is said to have been worn by the Virgin Mary when she gave birth to Jesus.

THE LABYRINTH

Set into the stone floor of the nave is a labyrinth (13th century), a feature often seen in Gothic churches. As a penance, pilgrims would follow the tortuous route on their knees, echoing the Way of the Cross. The jouney of 859 ft (262 m), around 11 bands of broken concentric circles, took at least one hour to complete.

Vaulted Ceiing
A network of ribs supports the vaulted ceiling.

Nave
As wide as the Romanesque crypt below it, the Gothic nave reaches a soaring height of 121 ft (37 m).

Apsidal Chapel
This chapel houses the cathedral's oldest treasure, the *Veil of the Virgin* relic. More artifacts can be seen in the St. Piat Chapel, whose lower level was once the chapter house.

Stained-Glass Windows
Chartres' windows cover a surface area of more than 28,000 sq ft (2,600 sq m).

South Porch
The sculpture on the South Porch (1197–1209) reflects New Testament teaching.

Labyrinth

West Front
The lower half of the west façade is a surviving part of the original Romanesque church.

Crypt
This is the largest crypt in France, most of it dating from the early 11th century. It comprises two parallel galleries, a series of chapels and the 9th-century St. Lubin's vault.

KEY DATES

1020	1194	1220s	1260	1507	1836	1974
Works starts on a Romanesque basilica with a huge crypt.	A fire partly destroys the Romanesque cathedral.	The cathedral is rebuilt, with new parts in the early Gothic style.	The cathedral is formally consecrated.	A Flamboyant Gothic steeple is added to the north tower.	The cathedral's wooden roof is damaged by fire.	The cathedral is added to UNESCO's World Heritage Site list.

Château de Chenonceau

Stretching romantically across the Cher River, this French Renaissance château *(Renaissance Style, see p.131)* was the residence of queens and royal mistresses, including Catherine de' Medici and Diane de Poitiers. Transformed over the centuries from a modest manor and water mill into a castle designed solely for pleasure, it is surrounded by elegant formal gardens and wooded grounds. The interior rooms have been restored to their original style, and a small waxwork museum illustrates the building's history. The site also includes a stable with a miniature train ride down the lovely tree-lined drive, and several restaurants.

THE FIRST FIREWORKS

After the death of her husband, King Henri II, in 1559, Catherine de' Medici moved into Chenonceau and staged lavish balls in her goal to surpass his mistress, Diane de Poitiers. At a feast for her son François II and his wife Mary Stuart in 1560, the celebrations moved into the formal gardens, where guests were treated to the first fireworks display in France.

▲ **The Three Graces**
Painted by Charles-André Van Loo (1705–65), *The Three Graces* depicts the pretty Mailly-Nesle sisters, all royal mistresses.

▲ **Formal Gardens**

🖼 **Cabinet Vert**

🖼 **Chapelle**
The chapel has a vaulted ceiling and pilasters sculpted with acanthus leaves and cockle shells. The stained glass, ruined by a bomb in 1944, was replaced in 1953.

🖼 **To formal gardens**

Louise de Lorraine's Room
After the assassination of her husband, King Henri III, in 1589, Queen Louise had this room painted black and decorated with monograms, tears, and knots in white.

Tour des Marques
This tower is the only surviving part of the 15th-century castle of the Marques family.

KEY DATES

1521	1526	1547	1559	1789	1913
The medieval Chenonceau is acquired by Thomas Bohier. His wife, Catherine Briçonnet, supervises the rebuilding of the château.	The château is seized from the Bohier family by King François I for unpaid debts to the Crown.	Diane de Poitiers, King Henri II's lifelong mistress, moves into the château and lays out the gardens.	On the death of King Henri II, Catherine de' Medici takes the building from Diane de Poitiers.	The castle is spared in the French Revolution thanks to its liberal owner, Madame Dupin.	The Menier family buys Chenonceau and still owns it today.

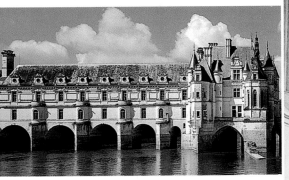

Grand Galerie ➤
Chenonceau's Florentine-style Grande Galerie stretches across the Cher River for 200 ft (60 m).

Chapelle ➤

Grande Galerie Interior ▼

CHÂTEAU DE CHENONCEAU

GERMANY

• Paris

SWITZERLAND

FRANCE

BAY OF BISCAY

• Bordeaux

ITALY

Marseille •

SPAIN

MEDITERRANEAN SEA

THE FORMAL GARDENS

As the mistress of Henri II, Diane de Poitiers wanted a surrounding fit for a king and set about creating her grand, **formal gardens** along the banks of the Cher River. Divided into four triangles and protected from flooding by elevated stone terraces, they were planted with an extensive selection of flowers, vegetables, and fruit trees. When Catherine de' Medici arrived at Chenonceau, she created her own garden from a program devised by Bernard Palissy in his *Drawings of a Delectable Garden* (1563). Today, more than 4,000 flowers are planted in the gardens each year.

THE CREATION OF CHENONCEAU

Catherine Briçonnet, wife of the royal chamberlain, was the first of many women who added her feminine touches to Chenonceau. During his reign (1547–59), King Henri gave the castle to his mistress, Diane de Poitiers, who went on to dramatically transform it. She redecorated its interiors, built a bridge over the Cher River and constructed a formal garden. When the king died, his wife, Catherine de' Medici, reclaimed the château from Diane and set about erasing her presence. She redesigned the castle and built the **Grande Galerie** on the bridge above the Cher. Over the centuries, other women have shaped Chenonceau's destiny and design, including Louise de Lorraine, who was bequeathed the castle in 1589, the enlightened Louise Dupin, friend of the writers Voltaire and Rousseau, in the 18th century, and Madame Pelouze in the 19th century.

THE INTERIOR

The elegant Grande Galerie, designed by Catherine de' Medici to hold her festivities, dominates Chenonceau. Lit by 18 windows stretching from an exposed-joists ceiling, its enamelled tiled floor leads into royal bedrooms, including Diane de Poitiers', covered in Flemish **tapestries**. The small tiles in the first floor hall are stamped with fleur de lys crossed by a dagger. Marble medallions brought from Italy by Catherine de' Medici hang above the doors, including those of her bedroom, which is full of 16th-century furnishings and tapestries depicting biblical scenes.

Cabinet Vert ➤
The walls of Catherine de' Medici's study were originally covered with green velvet.

Grande Galerie
Catherine de' Medici added this elegant gallery to the bridge designed by Philibert de l'Orme in 1556–9 for Diane de Poitiers.

CHÂTEAU CHENONCEAU GUIDE

The main living area was in the turreted pavilion in the middle of the Cher River. Four principal rooms open off the Vestibule on the ground floor: the Salle des Gardes and the Chambre de Diane de Poitiers, both hung with 16th-century tapestries; the Chambre de François I, with a Van Loo painting; and the Salon Louis XIV. Lavish rooms on the first floor include the Chambre de Catherine de' Medici and the Chambre de Vendôme.

Ground floor

KEY

1. Vestibule
2. Salle des Gardes
3. Chapelle
4. Terrasse
5. Librairie de Catherine de' Medici
6. Cabinet Vert
7. Chambre de Diane de Poitiers
8. Grande Galerie
9. Chambre de François I
10. Salon Louis XIV
11. Chambre des Cinq Reines
12. Cabinet des Estampes
13. Chambre de Catherine de' Medici
14. Chambre de Vendôme
15. Chambre de Gabrielle d'Estrées

First floor

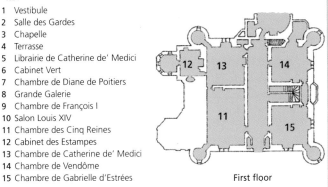

Tapestries ▲
As was the practice in the 16th century, Chenonceau is hung with Flemish tapestries that both warm and decorate its well-furnished rooms.

Catherine de' Medici's graceful Grande
Galerie, Château de Chenonceau

Rocamadour

Pilgrims have flocked to Rocamadour since the discovery in 1166 of an ancient grave and sepulcher containing an undecayed body, said to be that of the early Christian hermit St. Amadour. King Louis IX, St. Bernard, and St. Dominic were among many who visited the site as a spate of miracles were heralded, it is claimed, by the bell above the Black Virgin and Child in the Chapel of Notre-Dame. Although the town suffered with the decline of pilgrimages in the 17th and 18th centuries, it was heavily restored in the 19th century. Still a holy shrine, as well as a popular tourist destination, the site above the Alzou valley is phenomenal. The best views of the town can be had from the hamlet of L'Hospitalet.

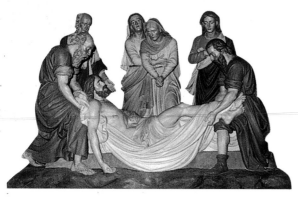

▲ Stations of the Cross
Pilgrims encounter the Cross of Jerusalem and 14 stations marking Jesus' journey to the cross on their way up the hillside to the château.

▲ Rocamadour Town
Now a pedestrian precinct, the town's main street is lined with souvenir shops to tempt the throngs of pilgrims and visitors.

◄ Grand Stairway

THE SPORTELL

Crafted in either lead, bronze, tin, silver or gold, the Sportell was a medallion bearing an image of the Virgin Mary and Child that was carried by pilgrims who had visited Rocamadour. During the Middle Ages, it was often worn as an amulet, sewn onto a hat or coat, and served as a pass to cross certain war-torn regions.

◄ General View
Rocamadour is at its most breathtaking in the sunlight of early morning: the cluster of medieval houses, towers, and battlements seems to sprout from the base of the cliff.

▲ Chapel of Notre-Dame

Chapel of St. Michael
Well-preserved 12th-century frescoes can be seen on the exterior of this chapel, which is sheltered by an overhanging rock.

Tomb of St. Amadour
The body of the hermit from whom the town took its name (Rock of Amadour) was once held in this small sanctuary beneath the basilica.

Museum of Sacred Art

◿ Grand Stairway
Pilgrims would climb this broad flight of steps on their knees as they said their rosaries. The stairway leads to the church square on the next level, around which seven main pilgrim chapels are grouped.

KEY DATES

1166	1172	1193–1317	1479	1562	1858–72
The preserved body of Zaccheus, later renamed St. Amadour, is discovered.	*The Book of Miracles* is drafted, with the testimonies of miracles granted to pilgrims.	More than 30,000 pilgrims flock to the religious site.	The Chapel of Notre-Dame (Miracles Chapel) is constructed.	Rocamadour's chapels are plundered by Protestants.	Rocamadour's restoration is supervised by abbot Jean-Baptiste Chevalt.

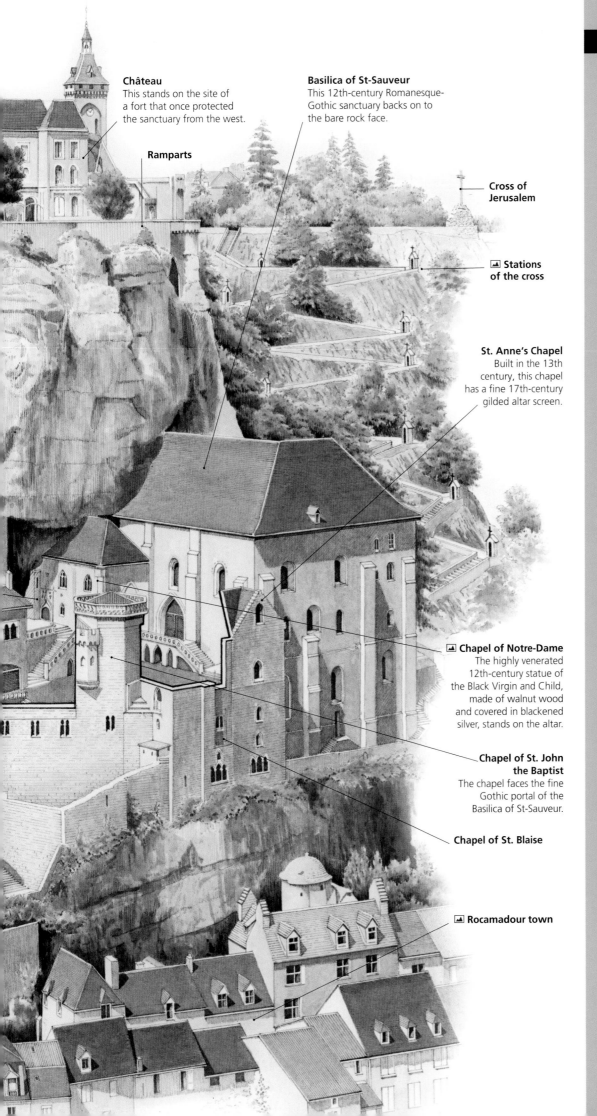

Château
This stands on the site of a fort that once protected the sanctuary from the west.

Ramparts

Basilica of St-Sauveur
This 12th-century Romanesque-Gothic sanctuary backs on to the bare rock face.

Cross of Jerusalem

🖼 **Stations of the cross**

St. Anne's Chapel
Built in the 13th century, this chapel has a fine 17th-century gilded altar screen.

🖼 **Chapel of Notre-Dame**
The highly venerated 12th-century statue of the Black Virgin and Child, made of walnut wood and covered in blackened silver, stands on the altar.

Chapel of St. John the Baptist
The chapel faces the fine Gothic portal of the Basilica of St-Sauveur.

Chapel of St. Blaise

🖼 **Rocamadour town**

ST. AMADOUR

There are various stories about the life of St. Amadour. One legend claims that he was Zaccheus of Jericho, who knew and conversed with Jesus during his time on Earth. His wife, St. Veronica, gave Jesus a cloth to wipe his face during his journey to Calvary. After Jesus' crucifixion, Zaccheus and his wife fled from Palestine to escape religious persecution. On their travels, the couple met St. Martial, Bishop of Limoges, in Aquitaine, France, who was preaching the Gospel. They continued to Rome, and while there they witnessed the martyrdoms of St. Peter and St. Paul. The death of his wife led Zaccheus back to France and the place later named after him, where he stayed until he died in AD 70.

CHAPEL OF NOTRE-DAME

This Romanesque chapel (*Romanesque Style, see p.122*) was built in the 15th century close to the site where St. Amadour's body was found. Considered the holiest of Rocamadour's chapels, it houses the famous statue of the **Black Virgin and Child**. Pilgrims who heard about the statue flocked to the shrine, often climbing the **Grand Stairway** on their knees as they prayed for the forgiveness of their sins. A 9th-century bell hangs in the chapel's vault and is thought to ring when a miracle occurs. Saints and kings also made the journey to the chapel, including England's King Henry II. Legend says that he was cured of an illness when he prayed before the Black Virgin and Child.

ROCAMADOUR'S MUSEUM

The **Museum of Sacred Art** is housed in the Bishop's Palace, which was constructed by the abbots of Tulle in the 13th century. The museum was restored in 1996 and is dedicated to the French composer Francis Poulenc (1899–1963), who was inspired to compose *Litanies to the Black Virgin* after visiting Rocamadour. The museum's collection of statues, paintings, and religious artifacts has been assembled from different sites around Rocamadour. Particularly interesting is the 17th-century statue of the prophet Jonah, carved in wood, and the fine lanterns, vases, and chalices that are still used in various religious ceremonies at Rocamadour.

Bremen Town Hall

A brick façade in the style of the Weser Renaissance makes Bremen Town Hall one of the northernmost Renaissance masterpieces to be found in mainland Europe *(Renaissance Style, see p.131)*. Behind the façade lies a magnificent late-Gothic manifestation of civic pride *(Gothic Style, see p.54)*. The rectangular building is decorated with medieval statuary, including life-size sandstone sculptures of Emperor Charlemagne and the seven electors, four prophets, and four wise men. The frieze above the building's arcade is an allegory of human history.

Wine cask, Ratskeller

THE STATUE OF ROLAND

This 33-ft (10-m) high statue of Roland has been a fixture of Bremen's Market Square for some 600 years. A Christian knight and nephew of Charlemagne, the Holy Roman Emperor (r. 800–814), Roland symbolizes the town's independence. His gaze is directed toward the cathedral, the residence of the bishop, who often sought to restrict Bremen's autonomy. Roland's sword of justice symbolizes the judiciary's independence, and its engraved motto confirms the emperor's edict, conferring town rights on Bremen. The statue was carved in 1404 by a member of the Parléř family, a well-known clan of architects and sculptors. It was the prototype for 35 similar statues in other German towns.

WESER RENAISSANCE

Bremen's Gothic Town Hall owes much of its splendor to its magnificent **façade**. Having been completely reworked by the architect Lüder von Bentheim in 1595–1612, this façade is considered an outstanding example of Weser Renaissance architecture, the predominant style throughout the Weser region of northern Germany between 1520 and 1630. Nobles who had toured Italy returned home inspired by the Renaissance architecture they had seen and attempted to replicate it in their own designs. The **ornamental gables** and frieze along the arcade are both typical of this style, as are the richly sculptured projecting oriels.

THE RATSKELLER

To the west side of the Town Hall is the entrance to the **Ratskeller**. One of the oldest wine cellars in Germany, it has been serving wine since 1405. Today, more than 650 wines can be sampled here, all of which are from German wine-growing regions and some of which are stored in decoratively carved wine casks. The Ratskeller's atmosphere has inspired many artists and writers. For example, its setting provided the basis for Wilhelm Hauff's book, *Fantasies in the Bremer Ratskeller* (1827), which later inspired the German Impressionist painter Max Slevogt to paint the humorous frescoes in the Hauff Room.

⊿ Upper Hall
New laws were passed in the splendid Upper Hall, which occupies the entire first floor.

Model sailing ships
Suspended from the ceiling, these are reminiscent of Bremen's role as a major port.

Main entrance

⊿ Ratskeller
This Gothic wine cellar stores hundreds of different wines. Murals by Max Slevogt (1927) decorate the walls.

KEY DATES

1251	1405–10	1595–1612	1620	1905	1909–13	1927
Inauguration of Bremen's first civic building, the *domus consulum*.	The dilapidated town hall is replaced by a new Gothic structure.	The structure is renovated and a new façade built overlooking the Market Square.	The Bacchus and what is now the Hauff Room for the storage of wine are built.	Completion of the Golden Chamber in German Art Nouveau style.	Addition of the New Town Hall on the east side of the building.	Completion of the murals in the Hauff Room.

⊡ Fireplace Room

⊡ Gobelin Room

▲ Statue of Roland on the Market Square in Bremen

▲ Ornamental Gable

⊡ **The Judgment of Solomon**

▲ **Façade**
The original Gothic building was clad with a magnificent Weser Renaissance façade designed by Lüder von Bentheim in 1595–1612.

The Judgment of Solomon ▶
The 16th-century mural of Solomon's court in the Upper Hall is a reference to the room's dual function as a council chamber and a courtroom.

Golden Chamber ▶

THE MUSICIANS OF BREMEN

On the northern side of the Town Hall is a bronze statue of the four animals—a donkey, dog, cat, and rooster—immortalized in the Grimm Brothers' fairy tale of *The Musicians of Bremen*. It was cast by Gerhard Marcks in 1951.

Upper Hall ▶

⊡ **Golden Chamber**
The lower room of the two-story Güldenkammer offers exquisite examples of Jugendstil (German Art Nouveau), created during a makeover by the artist Heinrich Vogeler (1872–1942) in 1905. The gilded leather wallpaper dates from the 17th century.

Fireplace Room ▼
Adjoining the Gobelin Room, the elegant Fireplace Room owes its name to a high, French marble fireplace.

⊡ **Ornamental Gable**
The architect Lüder von Bentheim gave the Town Hall façade a local touch by adding a decorative Flemish-style stepped gable that is five stories high.

Gobelin Room ▶
This room derives its charm from a large, exquisitely wrought tapestry produced by the 17th-century Gobelin workshop in Paris.

Cologne Cathedral

The history of Germany's greatest Gothic cathedral (*Gothic Style, see p.54*) is unusually long and complicated. The foundation stone of the present cathedral was laid on August 15, 1248, and the presbytery consecrated in 1322. The cathedral was built gradually until around 1520, but remained unfinished until the 19th century. The building was finally completed in 1842–80, according to the rediscovered, original Gothic designs. Once the world's tallest building, Cologne Cathedral still boasts the world's largest church façade.

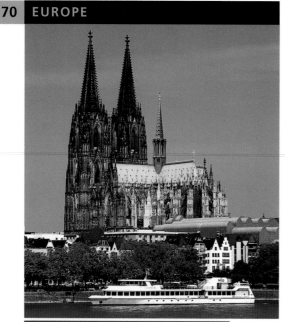

◄ **View of the cathedral from the Rhine River**

EARLIER CHURCHES

Several churches had come and gone on the site by the time the first cathedral was completed in 870. Today's larger Gothic cathedral became necessary because of the number of pilgrims wanting to see the Shrine of the Three Kings.

◄ **Pinnacles**

◄ **Gothic Stalls**
The massive oak stalls, built in 1308–11, were the largest that had ever been made in Germany.

▲ **Shrine of the Three Kings**
This huge Romanesque reliquary was made by Nikolaus von Verdun in 1181–1220 to hold the relics of the Three Kings. The relics, acquired by the cathedral in the 12th century, put Cologne on the pilgrimage map.

◄ **Mailänder Madonna**
This fine early-Gothic carving of the Milan Madonna and Child dates from around 1290. It is currently displayed in the Marienkapelle.

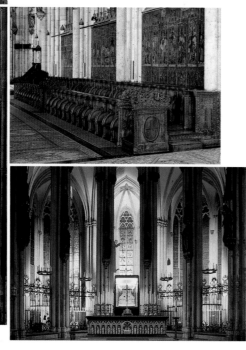

◄ **High Altar**
The Gothic altar slab, which dates back to the consecration of the presbytery, depicts the Coronation of the Virgin Mary, flanked by the 12 Apostles.

▲ **Cathedral Interior**

Main entrance

KEY DATES

1248	1265	c.1530	1794	1801	1842–80	1996
Work begins on a new cathedral to house the relics of the Three Kings.	The outer walls of the choir and adjacent chapels are completed.	Work on the cathedral halts with the south tower 190 ft (58 m) in height.	French troops use the cathedral as a warehouse and stables during the French Revolutionary Wars.	The cathedral is reconsecrated and the city's citizens demand that it is completed.	Building work recommences and the cathedral is finished according to the medieval plans.	Cologne Cathedral becomes a UNESCO World Heritage Site.

◄ Altar of
the Magi

▲ Treasury
Housed in the cathedral's 13th-century
stone cellar vaults, the treasury contains a
large collection of golden objects, including
the Engelbert Reliquary (c. 1630) above.

◫ Pinnacles
Elaborately decorated,
spirelike structures top
the supporting pillars.

Semicircular Arches
These arches were used to
transfer the thrust of the
vaults onto the buttresses.

◫ Gothic stalls

◫ High altar

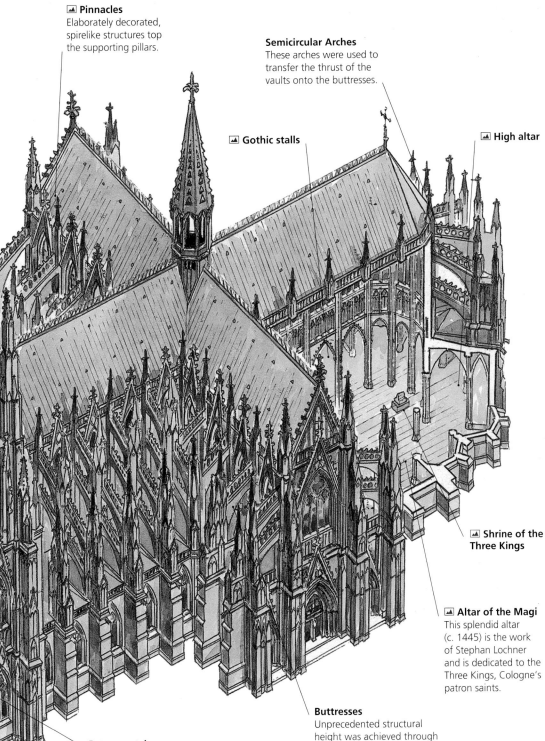

**◫ Shrine of the
Three Kings**

◫ Altar of the Magi
This splendid altar
(c. 1445) is the work
of Stephan Lochner
and is dedicated to the
Three Kings, Cologne's
patron saints.

Buttresses
Unprecedented structural
height was achieved through
the use of flying buttresses,
which support the entire bulk
of the cathedral.

Petrusportal
The portal of St. Peter, the only
one built in the second half of
the 14th century, has five
Gothic figures.

THE CATHEDRAL BELLS
The 3.4-ton bell cast in 1418 in honor of the
Three Kings was tuned to the note B. It hung
in a belfry adjacent to the cathedral, but in
1437 it was moved to the south tower. Eleven
years later, it was joined by Europe's largest
bell, the 10-ton *Pretiosa* (Precious One), tuned
to G. When rung together, the bells produced
a G-major chord. In 1449, the 4.3-ton
Speciosa (Beautiful One) was added. It was
tuned to A, so that Cologne Cathedral would
be the first church to have its bells tuned to a
melody rather than a chord. The first bell has
since been replaced.

THE CHOIR
Around 30 years after the cathedral's
foundation stone was laid, the pillars of the
choir were decorated with early-Gothic statues
of Christ, the Virgin Mary and the 12 Apostles.
These larger-than-life figures are clad in
splendid robes. Above them there is a choir
of angels playing musical instruments,
symbolizing the heavenly music played to
celebrate the celestial coronation of the Virgin
Mary. The coronation itself is depicted in
the figures of Christ and Mary. A similar
interpretation, dating from 1248, can be
seen in the church of Sainte-Chapelle in Paris.
There, too, 12 of the pillars supporting the
building symbolize the 12 Apostles as the most
important pillars of the Christian church.

SHRINE OF THE THREE KINGS
The **Shrine of the Three Kings**, the largest
reliquary in the Western world, is located
near the **high altar**. Studded with precious
and semiprecious stones, this lidded sarcophagus is a masterpiece of medieval
goldsmithery. Its sides are decorated with
images of the prophets and Apostles, the
adoration of the kings and the baptism of
Christ. The rear features a portrait of Rainald
von Dassel, archbishop of Cologne (1159–67).
As chancellor to Emperor Barbarossa (r. 1152–
90), the archbishop is said to have brought the
mortal remains of the Three Kings from Milan
to Cologne in 1164. On January 6 every year,
the front of the shrine is opened to reveal the
golden-crowned skulls of the kings.

Würzburg Residence

A masterpiece of German Rococo, the Residence was commissioned by two prince-bishops, the brothers Johann Philipp Franz and Friedrich Karl von Schönborn, as an Episcopal palace. Its construction between 1720 and 1744 was supervised by several architects, including Johann Lukas von Hildebrandt and Maximilian von Welsch. However, the Residence is mainly associated with the name of Balthasar Neumann, the then young and unknown creator of its remarkable Baroque staircase *(Baroque Style, see p.80).*

Sculpture in the Residence garden

TIEPOLO

Born in Venice, the Italian painter Giovanni Battista Tiepolo (1696–1770) is considered the last great master of Venetian art. He created numerous altarpieces and frescoes for churches, castles, palaces, and villas in Italy and Germany. Almost all the interior decoration of the Würzburg Residence was created by Tiepollo, including magnificent ceiling frescoes in the **Imperial Hall** and above the staircase, or **Treppenhaus**, completed from 1751 to 1753.

ROCOCO STYLE

The Residence is such a fine example of German Rococo that it had a style named after it: Würzburg Rococo. Typical of this style are the vast *trompe-l'oeil* painted ceilings and large, domed rooms. The term Rococo is derived from the French word *rocaille*, meaning "rock-work," a decorative trend for both interiors and façades featuring abstract, shell-like forms and curves. Trees, flowers, and Chinese scenes were among the most popular motifs. Stucco craftsmen and woodcarvers became as revered as architects and painters for the quality and splendor of their work.

THE PATRONS

Many of those involved in the building of the Würzburg Residence were members of the Schönborn family, a powerful 18th-century dynasty of princes and electors on the rivers Rhine, Maine, and Moselle. Among them was Johann Philipp von Schönborn, who became prince-bishop of Würzburg in 1719. He was succeeded by his brother, Friedrich Karl, one of the chief instigators of the Würzburg Residence project. The brothers engaged renowned architects and painters from all over Europe for what was to become a *Gesamtkunstwerk*—a unique synthesis of various branches of the arts into a total experience. The Residence was devastated by a fire during World War II and underwent a painstaking 27 million-dollar reconstruction program between 1950 and 1987. Today, 40 rooms are open to the public, with a splendid array of 18th-century furniture, frescoes, tapestries, and other treasures.

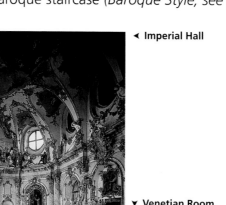

◄ **Imperial Hall**

FRESCO DETAILS

Tiepolo was not without a sense of humor: on the Treppenhaus fresco he included a portrait of the architect Balthasar Neumann dressed as an artillery officer and with his dog by his side.

▼ **Venetian Room**
This room is named after a tapestry depicting the Venetian Carnival. Further ornaments include decorative panels with paintings by Johann Thalhofer, a pupil of Rudolph Byss.

▼ **Treppenhaus**
The work of the Venetian artist Giovanni Battista Tiepolo, the largest fresco in the world adorns the vault of the staircase. It is an allegorical depiction of the four continents.

▲ **Garden Hall**
This low, vaulted hall, supported by slender marble columns, has Rococo stuccowork by Antonio Bossi dating from 1749. There is also a painting on the ceiling by Johan Zick, dating from 1750, depicting *The Feast of the Gods and Diana Resting*.

Hofkirche ►

KEY DATES

1720–44	1732–92	1751–53	1765	1945	1981	2003
Building of the Würzburg Residence.	The Residence garden is laid out and landscaped.	Decoration of the Residence with ceiling frescoes by Tiepolo.	Ludovico Bossi oversees the decorative stuccowork in the stairwell.	The palace is damaged in a bombing raid during World War II.	The Residence becomes a UNESCO World Heritage Site.	The restoration of Tiepolo's Treppenhaus frescoes begins.

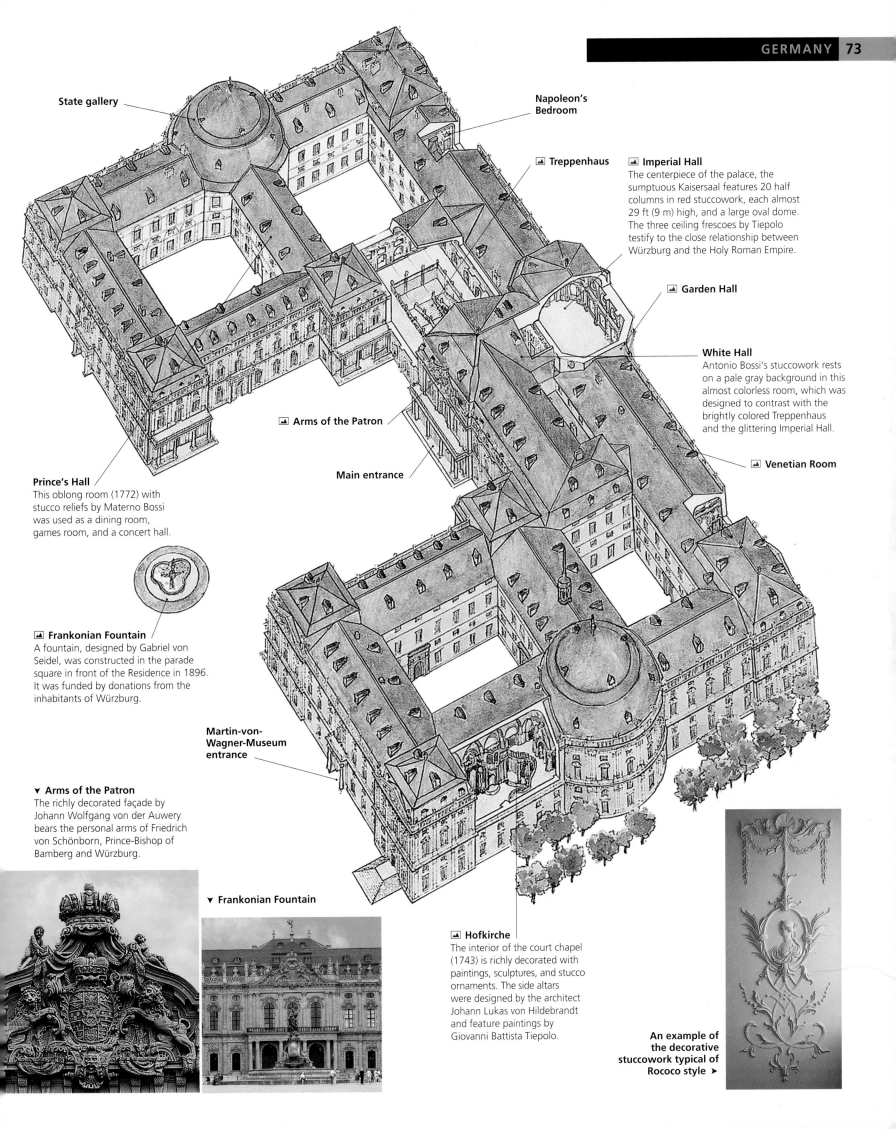

State gallery

Napoleon's Bedroom

⬛ **Treppenhaus**

⬛ **Imperial Hall**
The centerpiece of the palace, the sumptuous Kaisersaal features 20 half columns in red stuccowork, each almost 29 ft (9 m) high, and a large oval dome. The three ceiling frescoes by Tiepolo testify to the close relationship between Würzburg and the Holy Roman Empire.

⬛ **Garden Hall**

White Hall
Antonio Bossi's stuccowork rests on a pale gray background in this almost colorless room, which was designed to contrast with the brightly colored Treppenhaus and the glittering Imperial Hall.

⬛ **Arms of the Patron**

⬛ **Venetian Room**

Main entrance

Prince's Hall
This oblong room (1772) with stucco reliefs by Materno Bossi was used as a dining room, games room, and a concert hall.

⬛ **Frankonian Fountain**
A fountain, designed by Gabriel von Seidel, was constructed in the parade square in front of the Residence in 1896. It was funded by donations from the inhabitants of Würzburg.

Martin-von-Wagner-Museum entrance

▼ **Arms of the Patron**
The richly decorated façade by Johann Wolfgang von der Auwery bears the personal arms of Friedrich von Schönborn, Prince-Bishop of Bamberg and Würzburg.

▼ **Frankonian Fountain**

⬛ **Hofkirche**
The interior of the court chapel (1743) is richly decorated with paintings, sculptures, and stucco ornaments. The side altars were designed by the architect Johann Lukas von Hildebrandt and feature paintings by Giovanni Battista Tiepolo.

An example of the decorative stuccowork typical of Rococo style ▶

Heidelberg Castle

Towering over the city, this majestic red sandstone structure is a vast residential complex that was built between the 12th and 17th centuries. Originally a supremely well-fortified Gothic castle (*Gothic Style, see p.54*), but now mostly in ruins, this was the seat of the House of Wittelsbach palatines. After remodeling in the 16th century, the castle became one of Germany's most beautiful Renaissance residences (*Renaissance Style, see p.131*). However, its splendor was extinguished during the Thirty Years' War (1618–48) and the 1689 war with France, when most of the structure was destroyed.

Ruprecht III's coat of arms

HEIDELBERG ROMANTICISM

Heidelberg is widely held to be Germany's most romantic city and Heidelberg Castle was a favorite target of early 19th-century revisionism, with poets such as Achim von Arnim, Clemens Brentano, Ludwig Görres, and Joseph von Eichendorff recasting it as the cradle of German Romanticism. The ruins came to symbolize the artistic, intellectual, and political return to Germany's national roots that the poets so much wanted to see. It was during this period that Count Charles de Graimberg acted to prevent further looting of stone from the site in an attempt to preserve the ruins. Even today, the sprawling castle complex provides an extraordinarily majestic scene. Since being destroyed by the French in the 17th century, this once-important residence is regarded as Germany's most palatial ruin.

RUPRECHT III

One of the most important figures in the history of Heidelberg Castle was Elector Ruprecht III, a member of the Wittelsbach dynasty. Born in Amberg in 1352, Ruprecht became Elector of the Palatinate in 1398 and spearheaded a successful campaign to depose Wenceslas, the Holy Roman Emperor, in 1400. Ruprecht was elected emperor in his place, although his election was not universally recognized. He died in Oppenheim in 1410, having failed to restore the crown to its former glory.

STYLISTIC ACCRETIONS

Inside the Gothic-style **Ruprecht's Palace**, there are two models of the castle showing the various additions through the ages. In 1524, Ludwig V added a residential building known as Ludwig's Palace. The Glazed Palace (1549), which is named after its mirrored hall, symbolizes the architectural transition from Gothic to Renaissance style. **Ottheinrich's Palace** is a splendid example of German early-Renaissance architecture, while **Friedrich's Palace** has a typical late-Renaissance façade. This was followed by the **English Palace**. The jewel in the crown was undoubtedly the castle garden of Friedrich V (r. 1613–19), once described as the eighth wonder of the world.

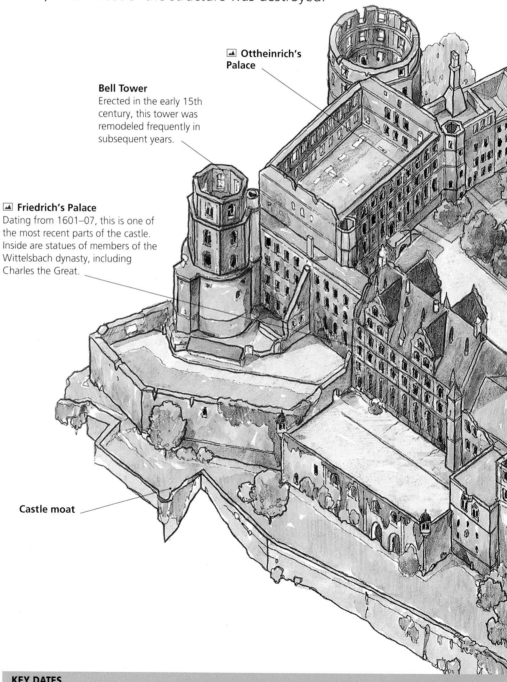

Ottheinrich's Palace

Bell Tower
Erected in the early 15th century, this tower was remodeled frequently in subsequent years.

Friedrich's Palace
Dating from 1601–07, this is one of the most recent parts of the castle. Inside are statues of members of the Wittelsbach dynasty, including Charles the Great.

Castle moat

KEY DATES

Mid-1100s	1400	1556–9	1614–19	1689–93	1742–64	1810
Construction of a castle begins under Count Palatine Conrad.	Ruprecht III's palace is built—the first use of the castle as a royal residence.	Ottheinrich builds his Renaissance-style palace.	A garden is commissioned by Prince-Elector Friedrich V for his wife.	The castle is destroyed in the War of the Palatine Succession.	Reconstruction takes place but fire destroys several buildings.	Attempts are made to preserve the castle ruins.

△ Gunpowder Tower
Built during the reign of the Elector Ruprecht, this 14th-century tower once formed part of the castle defenses. It was damaged by lightning in 1764, after which the townspeople took its stone for building.

▲ Friedrich's Palace

Fountain Hall
This Gothic loggia features early Romanesque columns taken from the palace of Charlemagne in Ingelheim.

▲ Ottheinrich's Palace
The German Pharmacy Museum is housed within the shell of this Renaissance building. It features Baroque and Rococo workshops and a traveling pharmacy.

◄ Gunpowder Tower

▼ Ruprecht's Palace

Gate Tower

Main entrance

△ Ruprecht's Palace
Built in around 1400 by a master-builder from Frankfurt, this is the oldest surviving part of the castle.

▲ Panoramic View
Heidelberg Castle has survived as a picturesque ruin, and its imposing structure occupies a commanding position. From its terrace there is a beautiful view of the medieval Old Town of Heidelberg.

English Palace ►

△ English Palace
These imposing ruins in the castle complex are the remains of a 17th-century building that Friedrich V built for his wife, Elizabeth Stuart.

THE GIANT WINE CASK

To the left of Friedrich's Palace, a staircase leads to the cellars where a giant wine cask is stored. This symbol of the electors' love of good wine was built in 1750 and holds 48,620 gallons (221,000 liters). The wine was piped directly from the cask to the King's Hall.

Church of the Holy Ghost ►
Palatine electors' tombs can be seen in this early 15th-century church in Heidelberg's Old Town.

Neuschwanstein Castle

Set amid magnificent mountain scenery on the shores of the Schwansee (Swan Lake), the fairy-tale Neuschwanstein Castle was built in 1869–91 for the eccentric Bavarian King Ludwig II, to a plan by the theater designer Christian Jank. On deciding to build this imposing residence, the king had undoubtedly been inspired by Wartburg Castle in Thuringia, which he visited in 1867. But Neuschwanstein is no ordinary castle—behind the pale gray granite exterior, which combines a variety of styles, the interior is equipped with several late 19th-century technological innovations.

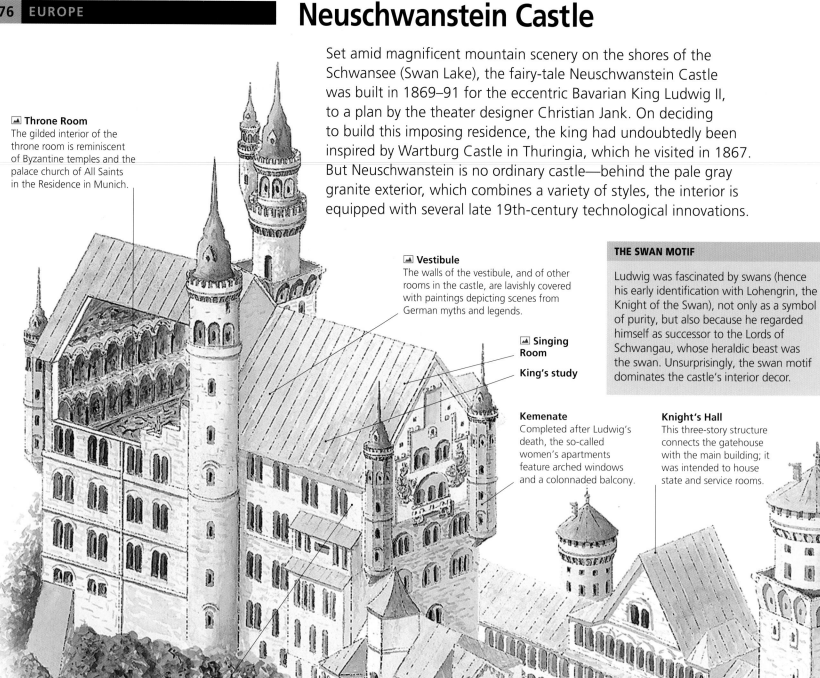

▲ Throne Room
The gilded interior of the throne room is reminiscent of Byzantine temples and the palace church of All Saints in the Residence in Munich.

▲ Vestibule
The walls of the vestibule, and of other rooms in the castle, are lavishly covered with paintings depicting scenes from German myths and legends.

▲ Singing Room

King's study

Kemenate
Completed after Ludwig's death, the so-called women's apartments feature arched windows and a colonnaded balcony.

Knight's Hall
This three-story structure connects the gatehouse with the main building; it was intended to house state and service rooms.

THE SWAN MOTIF

Ludwig was fascinated by swans (hence his early identification with Lohengrin, the Knight of the Swan), not only as a symbol of purity, but also because he regarded himself as successor to the Lords of Schwangau, whose heraldic beast was the swan. Unsurprisingly, the swan motif dominates the castle's interior decor.

▲ Dining Room

Arcades
Two-story arcades surround the castle.

▲ Courtyard

Gatehouse
Completed in 1872, this served as temporary accommodation for the king. He had an apartment on the second floor.

LUDWIG'S CHILDHOOD HOME

In 1832, Ludwig's father bought the remains of a 12th-century fortress in the Bavarian village of Schwangau. He rebuilt it in Neo-Gothic style (*Gothic Style, see p.54*) as Hohenschwangau Castle. As a child, Ludwig was captivated by its frescoes, which depict various legends.

Hohenschwangau Castle

Castle Building ➤
Neuschwanstein is the archetypal fairy-tale castle. It has provided the inspiration for countless toy models, book illustrations, and movie sets.

Throne Room ➤

▼ Vestibule

▲ Courtyard
The heart of the castle was supposed to have been a mighty 295-ft (90-m) high tower with a Gothic castle church. It was never built, but in 1988 its planned position was marked in white stone.

Dining Room ➤
Like many other rooms in the palace, the dining room includes fabulous pictures, intricately carved panels and beautifully decorated furniture, all bearing witness to the skill and artistry of 19th-century craftsmen.

▲ Singing Room
The Sängersaal was modeled on the singing room at Wartburg Castle in Eisenach.

Main entrance

◄ Tapestry Room in another of Ludwig's palaces, Linderhof.

LUDWIG'S BUILDINGS

Today, King Ludwig II of Bavaria (1845–86) is known above all for his extravagant building projects, which include the royal villa of Linderhof, near Neuschwanstein, and the palace at Herrenchiemsee in eastern Bavaria. While Neuschwanstein was an attempt to re-create the building styles of the Middle Ages (**castle building**), Herrenchiemsee was inspired by the Château de Versailles in France. Linderhof was originally a hunting lodge which, from 1869 onward, was repeatedly rebuilt, its interior shaped largely by Ludwig's fantasy world. The main inspiration here, as at Herrenchiemsee, was the French Rococo style of Louis XIV (*Rococo Style, see p.72*), as is evident from the Gobelin tapestries that adorn the **Tapestry Room**.

A MODERN CASTLE

The medieval character of Neuschwanstein is illusory, for hidden behind the façade is what was, for the period, state-of-the-art technology. The royal chambers, for example, all have central heating and there is running water on every floor with both hot and cold water in the kitchens. There is a dumb waiter linking the kitchens with the **dining room**. The third and fourth floors of the castle even have telephone jacks and an electric bell system, which Ludwig could use to summon his servants and adjutants (assistants).

PICTURE CYCLE

Ludwig's choice of interior decor was inspired by the operas of German composer Richard Wagner (1813–83). Yet, although Ludwig commissioned set painter Christian Jank to create the interior design, most of the murals depict scenes taken not from operas, but from the same medieval sagas that Wagner himself used as a source. They feature Tannhäuser, a poet, Lohengrin, the Knight of the Swan, and Parsifal, King of the Holy Grail. Murals in the **Singing Room** show one of the legendary singing contests held at Wartburg Castle in the 13th century. Scenes from Wagner's opera *Lohengrin* (1846–48) decorate the King's Chambers. Josef Aigner and Ferdinand Piloty were among the artists employed.

KEY DATES

1868	1869	1873	1880	1884	1886	1891
Ludwig makes known his plans to build a new castle.	The foundation stone is laid. The king hopes the work will take just three years.	The gatehouse is constructed; the king lives there for a number of years.	A ceremony marks the completion of all five floors.	Ludwig occupies the castle but dies soon after in mysterious circumstances.	Seven weeks after Ludwig II's death, the castle is opened to visitors.	The castle is completed, but many of the rooms are left bare.

The magnificent setting of the fairy-tale
Neuschwanstein Castle

St. Gallen Monastery

The Benedictine abbey in St. Gallen, established in 720, was one of the most important monasteries in Europe, as well as being a leading center for the arts, letters, and sciences. A priceless library was gathered and monks came from far and wide to copy manuscripts, many of which still exist. Only the crypt remains of the Romanesque church and monastery built in the 9th century. The present Baroque cathedral and abbey, by architects Peter Thumb and Johann Michael Beer, were completed in 1766 and feature exquisite Rococo decorations *(Rococo Style, see p.72)*.

Baroque confessional

THE CRYPT

Several calamitous fires destroyed much of the Romanesque Episcopal church erected in 830–37 on the site where the Cathedral of St. Gall now stands. The only part of the building to have survived the ravages of time is the 9th–10th century **crypt**, which became an integral part of the Baroque cathedral. The bishops of St. Gall have long found their final resting place here—a tradition that has continued to the present day. Among those buried in the cathedral are Abbot Otmar, founder of the abbey, who, ten years after his death in 769, was interred in St. Otmar's Crypt beneath what is now the west gallery, and Bishop Otmar Mäder, who died in 2003.

THE ABBEY LIBRARY

Built in the second half of the 18th century, the abbey library is richly decorated with ceiling frescoes, intricate stuccowork, wood-carving, and intarsia. The two-story reading room, containing walnut and cherry bookcases reaching to the ceiling, is especially impressive. Around 130,000 leather-bound volumes and 2,000 manuscripts are housed here. These include such bibliophilic treasures as a copy of the *Song of the Nibelungen* and *Codex Abrogans* (790), a dictionary of synonyms believed to be one of the oldest existing written documents in German. The best-known item in the collection is the *St. Gallener Klosterplan*, showing the layout of an ideal Benedictine monastery. Copied from an earlier manuscript by monks in the early 9th century, this document is thought to have been the blueprint for the St. Gallen Monastery.

BAROQUE STYLE

Baroque was the predominant style for much of the 17th and early 18th centuries. Whereas in Italy, the golden age of Baroque was the high Baroque of 1630–80, Germany saw a flourishing of late Baroque well beyond 1700. The hallmarks of Baroque architecture are its preference for dynamic, curvaceous forms and broken gables; its *Gesamtkunstwerk*, or fusion of the arts to create an exuberant whole; and its liberal use of ornamentation and sculpture.

ST. GALL

According to the Gallus-Vita (835) by Walahfrid Strabo, the Abbey of St. Otmar was founded on the site where a monk named Gallus (c. 560–650)—later canonized as St. Gall—built a hermit's shelter for himself in 612.

◢ **High Altar**
The painting of the *Assumption of the Virgin* on the high altar is by Francesco Romanelli. Dating from 1645, it was later heavily retouched.

◢ **Thrones**
Two thrones by Franz Joseph Anton Feuchtmayer, decorated with paintings by Franz Joseph Stälzer, stand in the choir stalls.

Choir Stalls ▶
The Baroque choir stalls
(1763– 70), made of walnut
and decorated with paintings
and gilding, are by Franz
Joseph Anton Feuchtmayer
and Franz Joseph Stälzer.

▲ Crypt
Beneath the cathedral is the
crypt of the earlier church. Its
walls retain fragments of 10th-
century frescoes above the altar.

⊡ **Confessionals**
The 11 Baroque confessionals
in the nave are crowned with
medallions featuring reliefs
by Franz Joseph Anton
Feuchtmayer and Anton
Dirr dating from 1761–3.

High Altar ▶

Ceiling Frescoes ▶
The ceiling is decorated
with frescoes by Joseph
Wannenmacher.

⊡ **Pulpit**

**Main
entrance**

⊡ **Ceiling frescoes**

⊡ **Choir stalls**

Pulpit ▶
The fine Rococo pulpit,
decorated with figures of
the Evangelists and of
angels, was made by
Anton Dirr in 1786.

▲ Throne

KEY DATES

c. 720	816–37	1529	1755–67	1758–67	1805	1824	1983
An abbey is founded by a priest named Otmar to preserve St. Gall's relics.	A Benedictine abbey with a basilica is constructed.	The people of St. Gallen expel the monks. They return in 1532.	The Baroque Episcopal church is built with an opulent nave and stuccowork.	The abbey library is built to house the priceless collection of illuminated manuscripts.	Under Napoleon's influence, the monastery is dissolved.	The Episcopal church is elevated to the status of a cathedral.	St. Gallen Monastery becomes a UNESCO World Heritage Site.

St. Stephen's Cathedral, Vienna

Situated in the medieval center of Vienna, St. Stephen's Cathedral is the soul of the city itself; it is no coincidence that urns containing the entrails of some of the powerful Habsburg family lie in a vault beneath its main altar. A church has stood on the site for more than 800 years, but all that remains of the original 13th-century Romanesque structure is the Giant's Doorway and the Heathen Towers. The Gothic nave, choir, and side chapels are the result of a major rebuilding program in the 14th and 15th centuries *(Gothic Style, see p.54)*. The lofty vaulted interior contains an impressive collection of works of art spanning several centuries.

Carving of Rudolf IV

RUDOLF THE FOUNDER

In 1359, Duke Rudolf IV of Austria, later known as Rudolf the Founder, laid the foundation stone for the Gothic enlargement of what was then a Romanesque church *(Romanesque Style, see p.122)*. Born in 1339, Rudolf became a duke in 1358 and campaigned tirelessly to have St. Stephen's Church granted its independence from the bishop of Passau and elevated to the status of a cathedral. But it was not until 1469 that Vienna, under Frederick III, became a diocese in its own right. On Rudolf's death in 1365, a monument to him was placed in front of the **high altar**. In 1945, it was moved to the Ladies' Choir. Rudolf is buried in the ducal vault, next to his wife, Katharina.

CATACOMBS

The extensive **catacombs** beneath the cathedral were excavated in around 1470 to relieve pressure on Vienna's main cemetery. For the next 300 years, the people of Vienna were interred in the catacombs and by the time Emperor Joseph II put a stop to the practice in 1783, around 10,000 of them had been laid to rest here. At the heart of the complex is the Habsburg Vault, built by Rudolf IV in 1363. This houses 15 sarcophagi belonging to the early Habsburgs and 56 urns, which contain the entrails of the later Habsburgs who, from 1633 onward, were buried in the imperial vault of the Capuchin Monastery Church. Vienna's archbishops are interred beneath the Apostles' Choir in the Episcopal vault of 1953.

ANTON PILGRAM

One of the cathedral's leading craftsmen was Anton Pilgram (c. 1460–1515), a master-builder from Brünn. His sandstone **pulpit** (1514–15) inside the nave contains portraits of the Four Fathers of the Church (theologians representing four physiognomic temperaments) and is considered a masterpiece of late-Gothic stone sculpture. Pilgram even included a portrait of himself as a "watcher at the window" beneath the pulpit steps. There is another **portrait of Pilgram** in the cathedral. Here, the builder and sculptor is shown peeping through a window into the church. Pilgram signed this work with the monogram "MAP 1513."

ST. JOHANNES CAPISTRANO

On the exterior wall of the choir is a pulpit built after the Christian victory over the Turks at Belgrade in 1456. It was from here that the Italian Franciscan Johannes Capistrano (1386–1456) is said to have preached against the Turkish invasion while on a visit to Austria in 1451. Capistrano had been appointed governor of Perugia, but was imprisoned while on a peace mission. After having a vision of St. Francis, he joined the Franciscans and became a priest in 1425. In 1454 he assembled troops for the Crusade against the Turks. This event is depicted in the statue above the pulpit showing Capistrano trampling on a Turkish invader. He was canonized in 1690.

16th-century statue of St. Johannes Capistrano

Heathen Towers
These towers, together with the massive Giant's Doorway, are part of the Romanesque church and stand on the site of an earlier heathen shrine.

Pilgram's pulpit

Main entrance

Symbolic Number "05"
The sign of the Austrian Resistance Movement was carved here in 1945.

TOOTHACHE FIGURE

According to a legend, the "Zahnwehherrgott," a sculpture of a man in agony, punished those who ridiculed him by inflicting them with a toothache. Only when they atoned for their sins did the pain subside. The figure is located beneath the north tower.

North Tower
According to legend, the "Eagle" tower was never completed because its master-builder, Hans Puchsbaum, broke a pact he had made with the devil by pronouncing a holy name. The devil then caused him to fall to his death.

⊡ **Portrait of Pilgram**

⊡ **Spire**

⊡ **Entrance to catacombs**

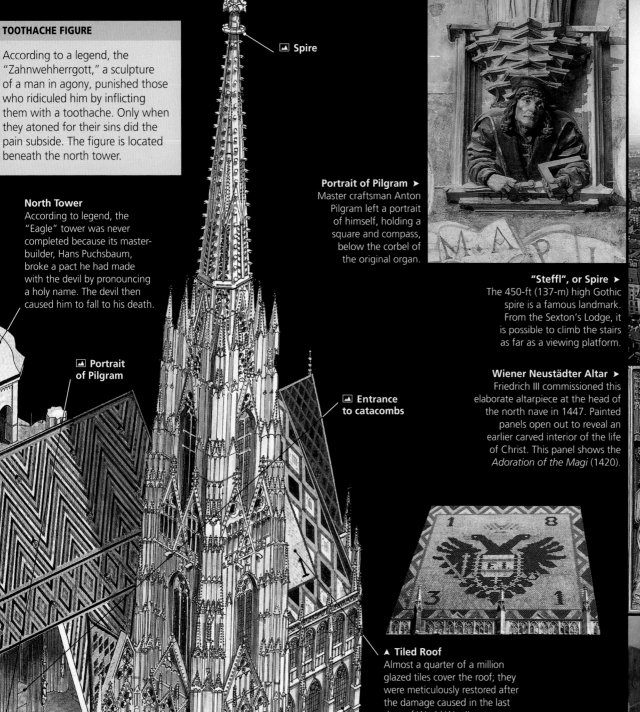

Portrait of Pilgram ➤
Master craftsman Anton Pilgram left a portrait of himself, holding a square and compass, below the corbel of the original organ.

"Steffl", or Spire ➤
The 450-ft (137-m) high Gothic spire is a famous landmark. From the Sexton's Lodge, it is possible to climb the stairs as far as a viewing platform.

Wiener Neustädter Altar ➤
Friedrich III commissioned this elaborate altarpiece at the head of the north nave in 1447. Painted panels open out to reveal an earlier carved interior of the life of Christ. This panel shows the *Adoration of the Magi* (1420).

▲ **Tiled Roof**
Almost a quarter of a million glazed tiles cover the roof; they were meticulously restored after the damage caused in the last days of World War II.

Catacombs ▲

High Altar
Constructed from black marble between 1640 and 1660, this is adorned with an altarpiece by Tobias Pock depicting the martyrdom of St. Stephen.

Singer Gate ➤

Lower vestry

⊡ **Singer Gate**
This was once the entrance for male visitors. A sculpted relief above the door details scenes from the life of St. Paul.

KEY DATES

1137–47	1300s	1433	1556–78	1722	1945–60	2001
The first Romanesque church is built.	Work begins on Gothic additions, including a choir.	The "Steffl," or spire, on the south tower, is completed.	The dome is added to the north tower.	The church is elevated to cathedral status.	The cathedral is damaged during World War II and reconstructed.	The cathedral becomes a UNESCO World Heritage Site.

Schönbrunn Palace, Vienna

The former summer residence of the imperial Habsburg family takes its name from a beautiful spring found on the site. Leopold I asked the Baroque architect Johann Bernhard Fischer von Erlach to design a residence here in 1695, but it was not until Empress Maria Theresa employed the Rococo architect Nikolaus Pacassi in the mid-18th century that it was completed (*Rococo Style, see p.72*). Fine gardens complement the palace.

Empress Maria Theresa

▲ **Large Rosa Room**

SCHÖNBRUNN PALACE GUIDE

The suite of rooms to the right of the Blue Staircase was occupied by Franz Joseph I and Elisabeth. The rooms in the east wing include Maria Theresa's bedroom and rooms used by Grand Duke Karl.

KEY
- ☐ Empress Elisabeth's apartments
- ☐ Franz Joseph I's apartments
- ☐ Ceremonial and reception rooms
- ☐ Maria Theresa's rooms
- ☐ Grand Duke Karl's rooms
- ☐ Closed to visitors

◄ **Round Chinese Cabinet**

◄ **Vieux-Lacque Room**

▾ **Great Gallery**
Used for imperial banquets, the gallery has a lovely ceiling fresco by Gregorio Guglielmi.

🔲 **Round Chinese Cabinet**
Maria Theresa used this white and gold room for private discussions with her state chancellor, Prince Kaunitz. The walls are adorned with lacquered panels.

🔲 **Great Gallery**

Hidden Staircase
This leads to the apartment of the state chancellor, above which he had secret conferences with Empress Maria Theresa.

🔲 **Blue Chinese Salon**

Chapel

🔲 **Vieux-Lacque Room**
During her widowhood, Maria Theresa lived in this room, which is decorated with exquisite Oriental lacquered panels.

Napoleon Room

Millions' Room
Maria Theresa's conference room features superb Rococo decor.

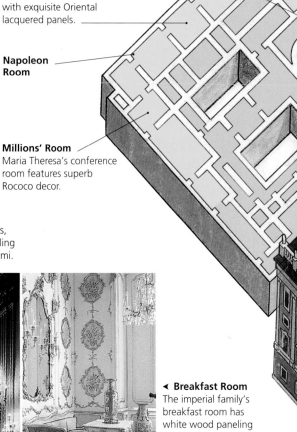

◄ **Breakfast Room**
The imperial family's breakfast room has white wood paneling inlaid with appliqué floral designs worked by Maria Theresa and her daughters.

Main entrance

⌲ **Breakfast Room**

⌲ **Large Rosa Room**
This is one of three rooms decorated with monumental Swiss and Italian landscape paintings by Josef Rosa, after whom the room is named.

Blue Chinese Salon ▲
This Rococo room, with its Chinese scenes, was where the last Habsburg emperor, Karl I, signed his abdication in 1918.

Billiard Room
This is the first of a suite of rooms that provide a glimpse of Emperor Franz Joseph's life at the palace.

Blue Staircase
Pacassi converted what was once a dining hall into a ceremonial stairway in 1745.

THE CARRIAGE MUSEUM

One wing of the palace, formerly housing the Winter Riding School, now contains a marvelous collection of coaches used by the imperial family and Viennese court. It includes more than 60 carriages dating back to the 17th century, as well as riding uniforms, horse tack, saddles, coachmen's liveries, and paintings and drawings of horses and carriages. The main exhibit is the richly decorated and carved coronation coach of Emperor Charles VI.

Coronation coach of Charles VI

A MILITARY MAN

When visiting Schönbrunn, Emperor Franz Joseph I would sleep in a simple, iron-framed bed, as befit a man who felt more at home in the field. He died at the palace in 1916, after nearly 68 years on the throne.

MARIA THERESA

The daughter of Emperor Charles VI, Maria Theresa (1717–80) became archduchess of Austria and queen of Hungary and Bohemia on her father's death in 1740. Five years later, her husband, Duke Francis Stephen of Lorraine, was recognized as Holy Roman Emperor. Maria Theresa instigated numerous reforms in the spirit of the Enlightenment. She initiated state-supported elementary schools, introduced a new penal code, and reduced taxation. She also worked toward unifying Habsburg lands by centralizing control over the empire. One of her 16 children was Marie-Antoinette, who married Louis XVI of France.

PREVIOUS PALACES

Schönbrunn Palace stands on the site of the Katterburg, a 14th-century castle that belonged to the Neuburg Convent. By the time Emperor Maximilian II bought the property in 1569, it included a mansion, a mill and stables. Maximilian intended to turn it into a pleasure palace and a zoo, and indeed a palace was finally built in the mid-17th century by the widow of Emperor Ferdinand II. She named it "Schönbrunn" after the "Schönen Brunnen" (beautiful spring), discovered by Emperor Matthew II while hunting on the estate in 1612. This first palace was destroyed by the Turks during the Siege of Vienna in 1683. Emperor Leopold I acquired the estate in 1686 and commissioned today's palace.

CEREMONIAL STATE ROOMS

As architect to the court of Empress Maria Theresa, Nikolaus Pacassi oversaw the enlargement and redesign of Schönbrunn Palace. Together with Rococo artists and craftsmen, including Albert Bolla, Gregorio Guglielmi, Isidor Canevale, and Thaddaeus Adam Karner, Pacassi was responsible for creating the interiors of both the state rooms and the private quarters. The **Large Rosa Room** and the **Millions' Room**, for example, feature frescoes and stuccowork in the Rococo style commissioned by Maria Theresa herself. The Schönbrunn Palace is renowned for its intricate gilded stuccowork, elegant mirrored galleries, and exotic chinoiserie.

KEY DATES

1696	1728	1743–63	1775–80	1918	1996
Fischer von Erlach begins work on Emperor Leopold I's new residence.	Emperor Charles VI purchases Schönbrunn and later makes a gift of it to his daughter, Maria Theresa.	Nikolaus Pacassi enlarges Schönbrunn into a palatial imperial and family residence in the Rococo style.	Court architect Johann Ferdinand Hetzendorf von Hohenberg redesigns the gardens.	As the Habsburg Empire ends, the palace passes to the Austrian state.	Schönbrunn Palace is added to UNESCO's World Heritage list.

Royal Castle, Warsaw

A grand example of Baroque architecture, the original Royal Castle (Zamek Królewski) was planned on the site of a Mazovian fortress when Zygmunt III Vasa decided to move Poland's capital from Cracow to Warsaw in 1596. It was designed in the early-Baroque manner *(Baroque Style, see p.80)* by the Italian architects Giovanni Trevano, Giacomo Rodondo, and Matteo Castelli between 1598 and 1619. Successive rulers remodeled the castle many times. Following its destruction in World War II, the castle was rebuilt between 1971 and 1984, and many of the original furnishings were returned. This massive undertaking was funded largely by donations from the Polish people.

Tabletop from 1777

▲ Canaletto Room
The walls of this room are decorated with 23 scenes of Warsaw by Bernardo Bellotto (1720–80), a Venetian painter who was known in Poland by the name of his famous uncle.

◄ Crown Princes' Rooms

◄ Deputies' Chamber
The Constitution of May 3 was formally adopted here in 1791. The coats of arms of all the administrative regions and territories of the Republic are depicted on the walls and a royal throne is also on show.

◄ Apartment of Prince Stanisław Poniatowski

◄ Zygmunt Tower
This tower, 200 ft (60 m) high, was built in 1619. It is crowned by a cupola with a spire. It is also known as the Clock Tower (Zegarowa), since a clock was installed in 1622.

⊿ Great Assembly Hall
Decorated with 17 pairs of golden columns, the hall is one of the castle's most elaborate rooms. It was used for state occasions, banquets, and balls.

⊿ Crown Princes' Rooms
Historical paintings by Jan Matejko are displayed in a gallery in these former royal apartments.

⊿ Deputies' Chamber

⊿ Zygmunt Tower

Main entrance

Great Assembly Hall ▼

◄ Marble Room
Decorated in 16th-century style with colored marble and *trompe l'œil* painting, this room also features 22 magnificent portraits of Polish kings by Marcello Bacciarelli.

KEY DATES

Early 1300s	1598	1939–44	1980	1984
The dukes of Mazovia build a fortress on the site of the Royal Castle.	Construction begins on the Baroque addition.	The Royal Castle is destroyed in World War II.	The Old Town and castle become a UNESCO World Heritage Site.	The restored Royal Castle opens to the public.

Knights' Hall
The finest piece in this beautiful room is the Neo-Classical sculpture of Chronos by Jakub Monaldi (right).

⬛ **Marble Room**

CONSTITUTION

The Constitution of May 3 was an experiment in democratic reform—the first of its kind in Europe. Members of Poland's parliament had to swear an oath of allegiance to it in St. John's Cathedral.

Lanckoroński Gallery
This second-floor gallery contains two paintings by Rembrandt—*Portrait of a Young Woman* and *Scholar at his Desk*.

Royal Apartments
King Stanisław's bedroom, dressing room and study were located here.

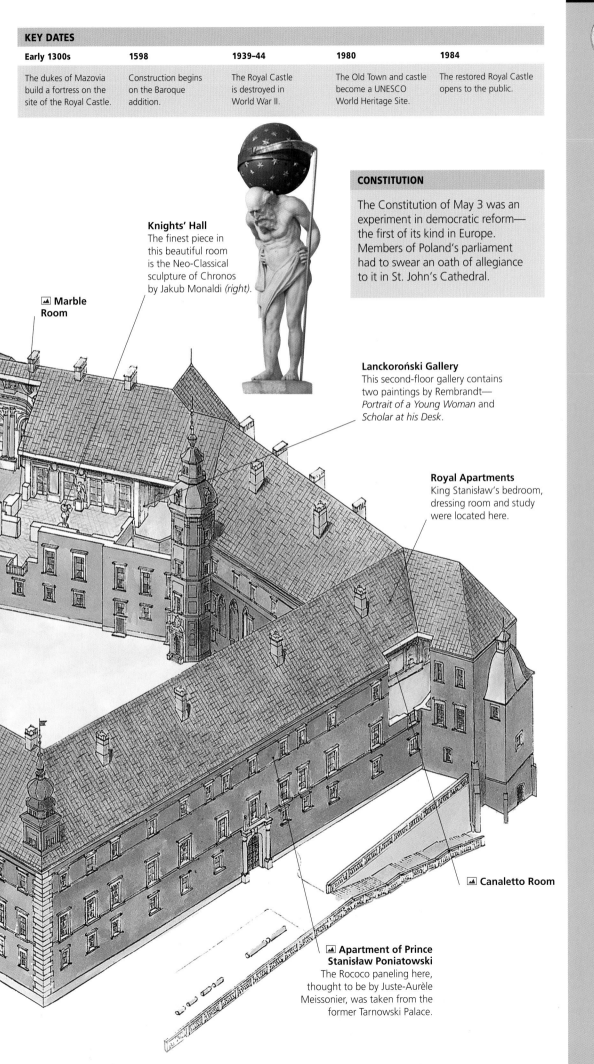

⬛ **Canaletto Room**

⬛ **Apartment of Prince Stanisław Poniatowski**
The Rococo paneling here, thought to be by Juste-Aurèle Meissonier, was taken from the former Tarnowski Palace.

INSIDE THE CASTLE

The Royal Castle's fascinating interior is the result of its dual role as a royal residence and as the seat of the *Sejm* (parliament). A tour of the castle visits lavish royal apartments as well as the **Deputies' Chamber** and the Senate. Rooms have been meticulously reconstructed in the style of the 18th century, and many of the furnishings and *objets d'art* are original to the castle. These include statues, paintings, and even fragments of woodwork and stucco that were rescued from the building and hidden during World War II. The **Canaletto Room** displays the 18th-century paintings of Warsaw by an Italian artist that were used as source material for the rebuilding of the castle.

THE GALLERIES

Among the many permanent exhibitions in the castle, two galleries are of particular interest. The Gallery of Decorative Arts is a showcase for 17th–18th century ceramics, glass, furniture, textiles, bronzes, silverware, and jewelry. Around 200 pieces are on display, including an Etruscan vase saved from the original castle. In the **Lanckoroński Gallery** there are paintings from the former royal gallery of King Stanisław August Poniatowski, donated by the Lanckoroński family in 1994. The collection includes works by Rembrandt, Teniers the Younger, and Anton von Maron.

POLAND'S LAST KING

Born in 1732, King Stanisław August Poniatowski (r. 1764–95) was the son of the palatine of Mazovia. He spent his early life in St. Petersburg, where he was introduced to the future empress, Catherine the Great, who took him as her lover. Russia was eager to add Poland to its empire and, perhaps to this end, Catherine promised the Polish crown to Poniatowski. When he fell out of favor and was sent back to Warsaw, she engineered his election as king of Poland in 1764. He introduced economic reforms, promoted the arts and sciences, and presided over the adoption of the Constitution of May 3, 1791. But Poniatowski was unable to repel his mighty neighbors: by 1795 Poland had lost its statehood and the king was forced to abdicate.

Old-New Synagogue, Prague

Built in around 1270, this is the oldest surviving synagogue in Europe and one of the earliest Gothic buildings in Prague *(Gothic Style, see p.54)*. The synagogue has survived fires, slum clearances in the 19th century, and several Jewish pogroms. Residents of the city's Jewish Quarter (Josefov) have often had to seek refuge within its walls and today it is the religious center for Prague's Jewish community. It was called the New Synagogue until another synagogue was built nearby—this was later destroyed.

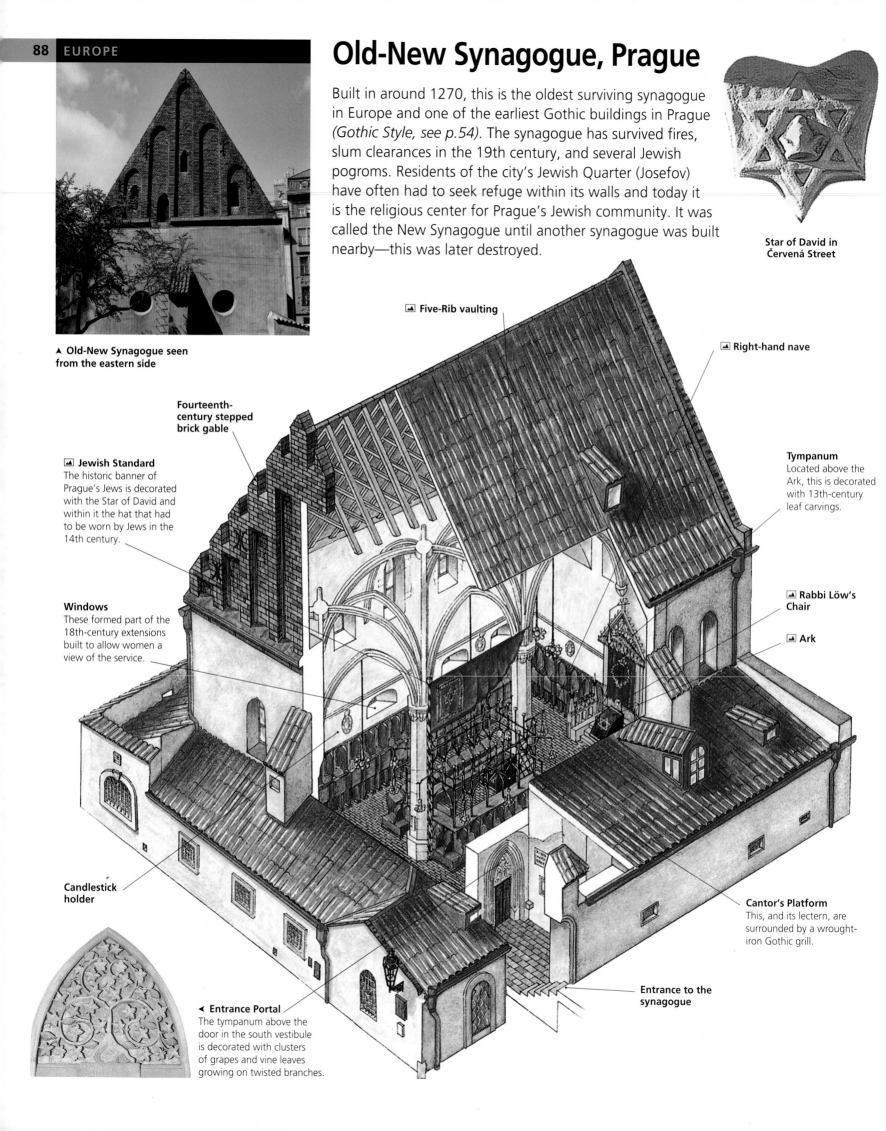

Star of David in Červená Street

▲ **Old-New Synagogue seen from the eastern side**

🔺 **Five-Rib vaulting**

🔺 **Right-hand nave**

Fourteenth-century stepped brick gable

Tympanum
Located above the Ark, this is decorated with 13th-century leaf carvings.

🔺 **Jewish Standard**
The historic banner of Prague's Jews is decorated with the Star of David and within it the hat that had to be worn by Jews in the 14th century.

🔺 **Rabbi Löw's Chair**

🔺 **Ark**

Windows
These formed part of the 18th-century extensions built to allow women a view of the service.

Candlestick holder

Cantor's Platform
This, and its lectern, are surrounded by a wrought-iron Gothic grill.

Entrance to the synagogue

◄ **Entrance Portal**
The tympanum above the door in the south vestibule is decorated with clusters of grapes and vine leaves growing on twisted branches.

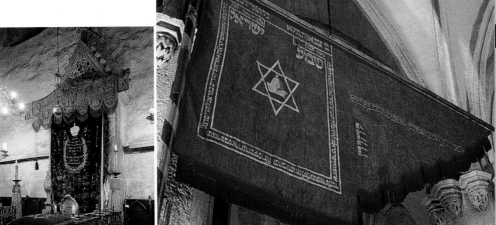

▲ Ark
This shrine is the holiest place in the synagogue and holds the sacred scrolls of the Torah.

Jewish Standard ▲

RABBI LÖW AND THE GOLEM

The great scholar Rabbi Löw was director of the Talmudic school (which studied the Torah) in the late 16th century. According to legend, he made a being, the Golem, from clay and brought it to life by placing a magic stone tablet in its mouth. The Golem went berserk, so the rabbi removed the tablet and hid the creature in the Old-New Synagogue's rafters.

Etching of Rabbi Löw

Right-Hand Nave ▶
The glow from the bronze chandeliers provides light for worshipers using the seats lining the walls.

Rabbi Löw's Chair ▶
A Star of David marks the chair of Chief Rabbi Löw, placed where the distinguished 16th-century scholar used to sit.

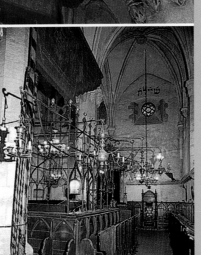

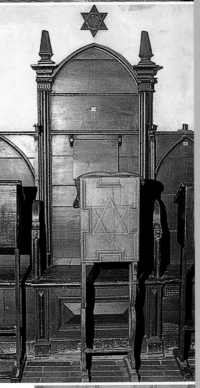

OLD JEWISH CEMETERY

Near the Old-New Synagogue is the Old Jewish Cemetery. For more than 300 years, this was the only burial ground permitted for Jews. More than 100,000 people are estimated to be buried here. The oldest gravestone dates from 1439, and the last burial was in 1787.

Five-Rib Vaulting ▶
Two massive octagonal pillars inside the hall support the five-rib vaults.

KEY DATES

1200s	1700s	1883	1992
Work starts on building the New Synagogue.	Construction of the women's gallery on the western and northern sides of the synagogue.	The architect Joseph Mocker begins renovation work on the building.	The Historic Center of Prague becomes a UNESCO World Heritage Site.

THE INTERIOR

This Gothic hall, with its distinctive crenellated gable, has been a house of prayer for over 700 years. Its twin-nave has a ribbed, vaulted ceiling. To avoid the sign of the cross, a fifth rib was added (**five-rib vaulting**) and decorated with vine leaves, symbolizing the fertility of the land, and ivy. In a two-story building the women's gallery would be upstairs, but here it is located in the vestibule. The number 12 is a recurring feature throughout the synagogue, probably in reference to the 12 tribes of Israel.

THE JEWISH GHETTO

The Old-New Synagogue stands in Josefov, once Prague's Jewish Ghetto. The area is named after Emperor Josef II, who partially relaxed the discrimination against Jews during his reign in the 18th century. For centuries, Prague's Jews had suffered from oppressive laws—in the 16th century, they had to wear a yellow circle as a mark of shame. In the 1890s, the ghetto slums were razed, but a handful of buildings survived, including the Jewish Town Hall and a number of synagogues. During World War II, the Nazis occupied Prague and almost two-thirds of the city's Jewish population perished in the Holocaust, mainly in Terezín concentration camp, situated northwest of Prague.

THE SYNAGOGUE

The Old-New Synagogue is one of three synagogues in Prague where services are held today. Admonishing worshipers on their way into the synagogue are the following words inscribed on the **entrance portal**: "Revere God and observe his commandments! For this applies to all mankind." Inside, men and women are segregated for religious rituals. Services are held in the main prayer hall and are reserved for men only; those attending must keep their heads covered. Women may follow the rituals from the adjacent women's gallery, where they can stand and watch through small slot **windows**. In the center of the hall is the *bima*, similar to a wrought-iron cage, with a lectern from which the Torah is read daily (**cantor's platform**). Above this is a red **Jewish Standard**, a copy of the 1716 original.

Silhouetted statues on Charles Bridge,
Prague, at dawn

CHARLES BRIDGE, PRAGUE

Plzeň

CZECH REPUBLIC

Brno

GERMANY

POLAND

AUSTRIA

SLOVAKIA

Charles Bridge, Prague

Prague's most familiar monument, connecting the city's Old Town with the Little Quarter, was the city's only crossing over the Vltava River until 1741. It is 1,706 ft (520 m) long and built of sandstone blocks. Now pedestrianized, at one time it could take four carriages abreast. Today, due to wear and tear, many of its statues are copies. The Gothic Old Town Bridge Tower *(Gothic Style, see p.54)* is one of the finest buildings of its kind.

THE BRIDGE'S SCULPTORS

The sculptor Matthias Braun (1684–1738), who was born near Innsbruck and learned his craft in Austria and Italy, came to Prague in 1710. His first work, the statue of **St. Luitgard**, was produced when he was only 26. Other sculptors were Johann Brokoff (1652–1718), of German origin, and his sons Michael and Ferdinand. The latter produced some of Charles Bridge's most dynamic figures, such as **St. Adalbert** and **St. Francis Xavier**, which shows the Jesuit missionary supported by three Moorish and two Asian converts.

EMULATING ROME

Charles Bridge was named after Charles IV, crowned Holy Roman Emperor in 1355, who wanted the bridge to echo the ancient Rome of the Caesars. However, it was not until the late 17th century that statues inspired by Roman sculpture were placed on the bridge. The statues mainly depict saints, including **St. Vitus**, the bridge's patron saint. Cherubs, dice, and a centurion's gauntlet form part of the statue of **The Madonna and St. Bernard**. Nearby, the Dominicans are shown with the Madonna and their emblem, a dog (**The Madonna, St. Dominic, and St. Thomas**).

THE LIFE OF ST. JOHN NEPOMUK

The cult of St. John Nepomuk, who was canonized in 1729, was promoted by the Jesuits to rival the revered Czech martyr Jan Hus, whose reformist preaching earned him a huge following in the early 15th century. Jan Nepomucký, vicar-general of the Archdiocese of Prague, was arrested in 1393 by Wenceslas IV, along with others who had displeased the king over the election of an abbot. John died under torture and his body was bound and thrown off Charles Bridge. He is commemorated by a statue (**St. John Nepomuk**) and a bronze relief depicting him being thrown off the bridge. St. John Nepomuk is a popular figure and statues modeled on this one can be seen in countries throughout Central Europe, especially on bridges.

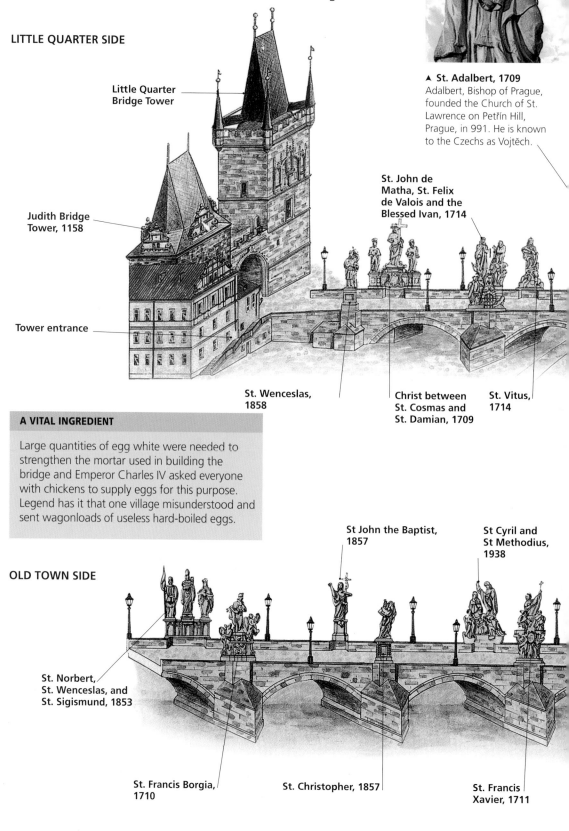

LITTLE QUARTER SIDE

Little Quarter Bridge Tower

Judith Bridge Tower, 1158

Tower entrance

▲ **St. Adalbert, 1709**
Adalbert, Bishop of Prague, founded the Church of St. Lawrence on Petřín Hill, Prague, in 991. He is known to the Czechs as Vojtěch.

St. John de Matha, St. Felix de Valois and the Blessed Ivan, 1714

St. Wenceslas, 1858

Christ between St. Cosmas and St. Damian, 1709

St. Vitus, 1714

A VITAL INGREDIENT

Large quantities of egg white were needed to strengthen the mortar used in building the bridge and Emperor Charles IV asked everyone with chickens to supply eggs for this purpose. Legend has it that one village misunderstood and sent wagonloads of useless hard-boiled eggs.

St John the Baptist, 1857

St Cyril and St Methodius, 1938

OLD TOWN SIDE

St. Norbert, St. Wenceslas, and St. Sigismund, 1853

St. Francis Borgia, 1710

St. Christopher, 1857

St. Francis Xavier, 1711

▲ **View from Little Quarter Bridge Tower**
The tall pinnacled wedge tower gives a superb view of the city of 100 spires.

▲ **St. Luitgard, 1710**
This statue, sculpted by Matthias Braun, is based on a blind Cistercian nun's celebrated vision in which Christ appeared and permitted her to kiss his wounds.

▲ **St. John Nepomuk**

▲ **Bridge Tower Sculptures**
Peter Parléř's sculptures include St. Vitus, the bridge's patron saint, Charles IV, and Wenceslas IV.

▲ **Thirty Years' War**
In the last hours of this war, the Old Town was saved from the invading Swedish army. The truce was signed in the middle of the bridge in 1648.

▲ **Crucifix (17th century)**

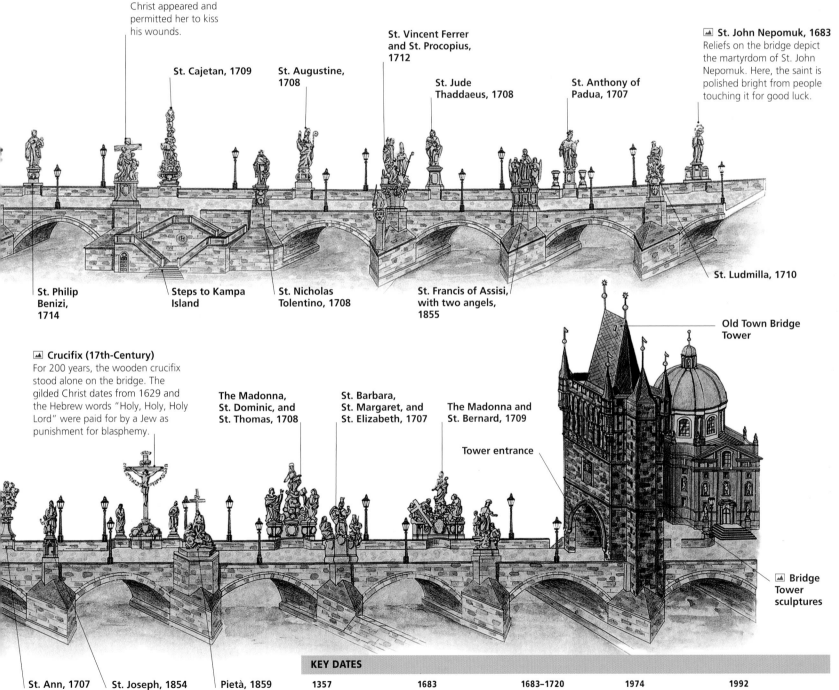

St. Vincent Ferrer and St. Procopius, 1712

St. Cajetan, 1709

St. Augustine, 1708

St. Jude Thaddaeus, 1708

St. Anthony of Padua, 1707

⬚ **St. John Nepomuk, 1683**
Reliefs on the bridge depict the martyrdom of St. John Nepomuk. Here, the saint is polished bright from people touching it for good luck.

St. Philip Benizi, 1714

Steps to Kampa Island

St. Nicholas Tolentino, 1708

St. Francis of Assisi, with two angels, 1855

St. Ludmilla, 1710

⬚ **Crucifix (17th-Century)**
For 200 years, the wooden crucifix stood alone on the bridge. The gilded Christ dates from 1629 and the Hebrew words "Holy, Holy, Holy Lord" were paid for by a Jew as punishment for blasphemy.

The Madonna, St. Dominic, and St. Thomas, 1708

St. Barbara, St. Margaret, and St. Elizabeth, 1707

The Madonna and St. Bernard, 1709

Old Town Bridge Tower

Tower entrance

⬚ **Bridge Tower sculptures**

St. Ann, 1707   St. Joseph, 1854   Pietà, 1859

KEY DATES

1357	1683	1683–1720	1974	1992
Charles IV commissions Peter Parléř to construct a new bridge, replacing the Judith Bridge.	The first statue, of St. John Nepomuk, is placed at the center of the bridge.	Statues by the Brokoffs and Braun are erected along the bridge.	The bridge becomes a pedestrian area and a focal point of the city.	The Historic Center of Prague joins the UNESCO list of World Heritage Sites.

Parliament, Budapest

Imre Steindl's rich Neo-Gothic Parliament *(Gothic Style, see p.54)* is Hungary's largest building and a symbol of Budapest. Hungarian materials, techniques, and master craftsmen were used in its construction on the bank of the Danube River. The building is 880 ft (268 m) long and 315 ft (96 m) high. The north wing houses the offices of Hungary's prime minister, while the south wing contains those of the president of the Republic.

One of the pair of lions at the main entrance

IMRE STEINDL

Professor of architecture at Hungary's Technical University, Imre Steindl (1839–1902) won the competition to design Hungary's Parliament. The building was intended to symbolize the country's thriving democracy. Steindl drew inspiration from Charles Barry and A. W. Pugin's Neo-Gothic Houses of Parliament in London. However, for the internal spaces, including the superb **Dome Hall**, he also used references from the Baroque *(Baroque Style, see p.80)* and Renaissance *(Renaissance Style, see p.131)* styles as well.

SACRED CROWN OF ST. STEPHEN I

The first Hungarian king, St. Stephen I (c. 975–1038), received the royal crown from Pope Sylvester II in the year 1000. The crown became a symbol of Christianity and all Hungarian kings who followed after Stephen I were crowned with the sacred diadem. Many today believe that the crown bears little resemblance to the original crown, because over the centuries it has been lost and stolen. Battles and wars have also been fought for possession of the crown. At the end of World War II, it was taken to the US for safekeeping and returned to Hungary with much fanfare in 1978. The crown now resides in Hungary's Parliament.

PARLIAMENT'S STATUES

Surrounding the external façade of the Parliament building are 90 statues, which include some of the country's past monarchs, prime ministers, writers, and revolutionaries. A statue of the Transylvanian prince Ferenc Rákóczi II (1676–1735), who fought the Habsburgs for Hungary's freedom, is at the southern end. Nearby is a seated statue of the Hungarian writer József Attila (1905–37). His first collection of poems was published when he was 17. Adorning the **north wing** is the statue of Lajos Kossuth (1802–94), who fought for Hungary's independence for six months in 1849 before being driven into exile. Next to it is a statue of the democratic prime minister and revolutionary Mihály Károlyi (1875–1955). He ruled Hungary for five months in 1919 until he was forced into exile after the government was overthrown by the Communists.

PARLIAMENT VASE

In 1954, the Herend Porcelain Manufactory made the first Parliament Vase. It stood in the Dome Hall for ten years and was then moved to the Herend Museum. A new vase was created in 2000 to mark Hungary's 1,000 years of statehood.

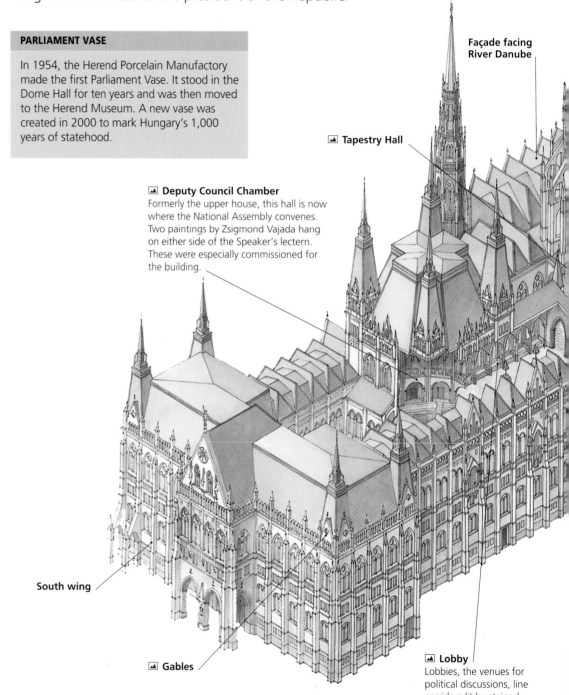

Façade facing River Danube

🔲 **Tapestry Hall**

🔲 **Deputy Council Chamber**
Formerly the upper house, this hall is now where the National Assembly convenes. Two paintings by Zsigmond Vajada hang on either side of the Speaker's lectern. These were especially commissioned for the building.

South wing

🔲 **Gables**

🔲 **Lobby**
Lobbies, the venues for political discussions, line corridors lit by stained-glass windows.

KEY DATES

1882	1885	1902	1987
Imre Steindl wins the competition for the design of the Parliament building.	The foundation stone is laid along the Danube embankment.	Work on the Parliament building is completed.	The historic area of Budapest, including the Parliament building, is inscribed as a UNESCO World Heritage Site.

Dome Hall
Adorning the massive pillars that support Parliament's central dome are figures of some of the rulers of Hungary.

Dome

Old Upper House Hall

North wing

Main Staircase
The best contemporary artists were invited to decorate the interior. The sumptuous main staircase features ceiling frescoes by Károly Lotz and sculptures by György Kiss.

Royal Insignia
The Crown Jewels of Hungary, except the Coronation Mantle, are kept in the Dome Hall.

Main entrance

▼ Deputy Council Chamber

General View ➤
The magnificent dome marks the central point of the Parliament building. Although the façade is elaborately Neo-Gothic, the ground plan follows Baroque conventions.

▼ Carved Stones
Over 500,000 stones were carved for the exterior decoration.

▲ Gables
Almost every corner of the Parliament building features gables with lacelike pinnacles based on Gothic sculptures.

Tapestry Hall ➤
This hall is decorated with a Gobelin tapestry illustrating Prince Árpád, with seven Magyar leaders under his command, signing a peace treaty and blood oath.

Old Upper House Hall ➤
This vast hall is virtually a mirror image of the National Assembly Hall. Both halls have public galleries running around a horseshoe-shaped interior.

Dome ▼
The ceiling of the 315-ft (96-m) high dome is covered in an intricate design of Neo-Gothic gilding combined with heraldic decoration.

▼ Main Staircase

▼ Lobby

▼ Dome Hall

RUSSIA

THE WINTER PALACE, ST. PETERSBURG

THE SMALL AND LARGE HERMITAGE

Catherine the Great hired architect Yuriy Velten to erect the Small Hermitage so she could privately entertain her chosen friends at court. The building was designed in Baroque style with Classical features to blend in with Rastrelli's Baroque Winter Palace. After the Small Hermitage was completed, Catherine decided to house her newly acquired collection of more than 255 paintings in the building. The Large Hermitage was built a few years later to accommodate the tsarina's vast library and works of art. Over the centuries, Catherine's original collection has been added to. There are now more than 3 million pieces of art displayed in the Small and Large Hermitage, as well as in an ensemble of buildings that includes the Winter Palace. There are exhibits from the Stone Age up to the 20th century, including works by Matisse, Rembrandt, and Cézanne.

BARTOLOMEO RASTRELLI

The Italian architect Rastrelli (1700–71) studied under his father and assisted him during his appointment as architect for Czar Peter I. In 1722, Rastrelli took on his own commissions in Moscow and St. Petersburg, which established him as a brilliant Baroque architect. During Elizabeth's reign, he was appointed Chief Court Architect and went on to design several buildings, including the grandiose Winter Palace. When Catherine the Great ascended the throne, Rastrelli retired from court as the empress preferred a stricter, Classical style.

CATHERINE II

Czarina Elizabeth chose the German-born princess Catherine (1729–96), the future Catherine the Great, as a wife for her successor, Peter III. When he ascended the throne in 1762, Catherine had resided in Russia for 18 years and had fully immersed herself in Russian culture. Six months into Peter's reign, Catherine and her allies at the imperial guard had the czar killed. She was then crowned ruler of Russia in 1763. During her reign she implemented many reforms and expanded Russian territory. Art and trade flourished and new academies were built, including the Russian Academy of Sciences and the Academy of Fine Art.

The Winter Palace, St. Petersburg

This superb example of Baroque architecture *(Baroque Style, see p.80)* was the home of the Russian czars and czarinas, including Catherine the Great, from the late 18th century. Built for Czarina Elizabeth (r. 1741–62), the opulent Winter Palace was the finest achievement of Italian architect Bartolomeo Rastrelli. Though the exterior has changed little, the interiors were subsequently altered by a number of architects and then largely restored after a fire gutted the palace in 1837. After the assassination of Alexander II in 1881, the imperial family rarely lived here. In July 1917, the Provisional Government took the palace as its headquarters, which led to its storming by the Bolsheviks.

Bartolomeo Rastrelli, court architect until 1763

Armorial Hall
With its huge gilded columns, this vast chamber covers more than 8,600 sq ft (800 sq m). It houses the European silver collection and a restored imperial carriage.

1812 Gallery
Built in 1826, this has portraits of Russian military heroes of the Napoleonic Wars, most by English artist George Dawe.

Hall of St. George
Monolithic columns and wall facings of Italian Carrara marble are features of this room.

Small Throne Room

To Large Hermitage

Field Marshals' Hall
The devastating fire of 1837 broke out in this reception room.

Jordan Staircase
This vast, sweeping staircase (1762) was Rastrelli's masterpiece. It was from here that the imperial family watched the Epiphany ceremony of baptism in the Neva, which celebrated Christ's baptism in the Jordan River.

Nicholas Hall
The largest room in the palace, this was always used for the first ball of the season.

North façade overlooking the River Neva

KEY DATES

1754–62	1764–75	1771–87	1917	1990
The Winter Palace is constructed by Bartolomeo Rastrelli.	The Small Hermitage by Yuriy Velten is built for Catherine II's art collection.	Catherine's art collection grows and a second extension, the Large Hermitage, also by Yuriy Velten, is added.	Anatoly Lunacharsky of the Soviet Government declares the Winter Palace and the Hermitage state museums.	The city of St. Petersburg, including the Winter Palace and Hermitage, is declared a UNESCO World Heritage Site.

▲ **Jordan Staircase**

▲ **Small Throne Room**
Dedicated in 1833 to the memory of
Peter the Great, this room houses a
silver-gilt English throne made in 1731.

▲ **Alexander Hall**

🖼 **Alexander Hall**
Architect Aleksandr Bryullov
employed a mixture of Gothic
vaulting and Neo-Classical stucco
bas-reliefs of military themes in
this reception room of 1837.

French Rooms
Designed by Bryullov
in 1839, these house a
collection of 18th-century
French art.

**South façade on
Palace Square**

White Hall
This room was decorated
for the wedding of the
future Alexander II in 1841.

Malachite Room ▲
More than 2 tons of
ornamental stone were
used in this sumptuous
room (1839), which is
decorated with malachite
columns and vases,
gilded doors, and rich
parquet flooring.

**Golden
Drawing
Room** ▶

▲ **Dark Corridor**
The French and Flemish
tapestries here include *The
Marriage of Emperor
Constantine*, made in Paris
in the 17th century to
designs by Rubens.

🖼 **Golden Drawing Room**
Created in the 1850s, this room
was extravagantly decorated in the
1870s with all-over gilding of walls
and ceiling. It houses a display of
Western European carved gems.

🖼 **Dark Corridor**

West wing

Gothic Library
The wood-paneled library
was created by Meltzer in
1894. This, and other
rooms in the northwest
part of the palace, were
adapted to suit Nicholas
II's bourgeois lifestyle.

Rotunda
Built in 1830, this connected
the private apartments in the
west with the state apartments
on the palace's north side.

🖼 **Malachite Room**

STORMING THE PALACE

On the evening of October 25,
1917, the Bolsheviks fired some
blank shots at the Winter Palace,
storming it soon after to arrest
the Provisional Government that
resided there. The Communists
took over power and the Russian
Revolution was a fact.

▲ **Detail, Chapel of the Entry of Christ into Jerusalem**

◄ **Chapel of St. Cyprian**
This is one of eight main chapels commemorating the campaigns of Ivan the Terrible against the town of Kazan, to the east of Moscow. It is dedicated to St. Cyprian, whose feast is on October 2, the day after the last attack.

St. Basil's Cathedral, Moscow

Regarded as one of the most beautiful monuments to the Russian Orthodox Church, St. Basil's has come to represent Moscow and Russia to the outside world. Commissioned by Ivan the Terrible to celebrate the capture of the Mongol stronghold of Kazan in 1552, the cathedral was completed in 1561. It is reputed to have been designed by the architect Postnik Yakovlev. According to legend, Ivan was so amazed at the beauty of Yakovlev's work that he had him blinded so that he could never design anything as exquisite again. The church was officially called the Cathedral of the Intercession, because the final siege of Kazan began on the Feast of the Intercession of the Virgin. However, it is more usually known as St. Basil's after the "holy fool," Basil the Blessed, whose remains are interred in the cathedral's ninth chapel.

RED SQUARE

St. Basil's Cathedral is located in Red Square in the heart of Moscow. The name of the square is derived from the Russian word *krasnyy*, which originally meant "beautiful" but later came to denote "red."

◄ **Chapel of the Entry of Christ into Jerusalem**

◄ **Main iconostasis**

▼ **Colorful, onion-shaped dome, part of the façade of St. Basil's**

Bell tower

Chapel of the Trinity

◢ **Domes**
Following a fire in 1583, the original helmet-shaped cupolas were replaced by ribbed or faceted onion domes. It is only since 1670 that the domes have been painted in many colors; at one time St. Basil's was white, with golden domes.

◢ **Chapel of St. Cyprian**

Chapel of the Three Patriarchs

Chapel of St. Basil
The ninth chapel to be added to the cathedral was built in 1588 to house the remains of the "holy fool," Basil the Blessed.

Entrance
An exhibition on the cathedral's history, and armor and weapons dating from the time of Ivan the Terrible, can be seen here.

▲ **Central Chapel of the Intercession**
Light floods in through the windows of the tent-roofed central church, which soars to a height of 200 ft (61 m).

KEY DATES

1555	1583	1812	1918	1929	1990s
Building work commences, and St. Basil's is completed six years later.	Onion-shaped domes are built to replace the original cupolas destroyed by fire.	Napoleon's cavalry stable their horses in St. Basil's during his invasion of Russia.	The Communist authorities close the cathedral and melt down its bells.	St. Basil's is turned into a museum dedicated to the Russian conquest of Kazan.	St. Basil's is declared a UNESCO World Heritage Site in 1990, and returned to the Orthodox Church in 1991.

Tent roof on the
Central Chapel

🔺 Central
Chapel of the
Intercession

Chapel of
St. Nicholas

Chapel of
St. Varlaam of
Khutynskiy

Tiered gables

Chapel of Bishop
Gregory

MININ AND POZHARSKIY STATUE

A bronze by Ivan Martos depicts two heroes from
the Time of Troubles (1598–1613): the butcher Kuzma
Minin and Prince Dmitriy Pozharskiy. The men raised
a volunteer force to
fight the invading
Poles and, in 1612, led
their army to victory
when they drove them
out of the Kremlin. The
statue was erected
in 1818 in the center
of Red Square. It was
moved to its present
position, in front of
St. Basil's, during
the Soviet era.

Monument
to Minin and
Prince Pozharskiy

🔺 **Chapel of the Entry of
Christ into Jerusalem**
This chapel was used as a
ceremonial entrance during
the annual Palm Sunday
procession. On this day,
the patriarch rode from the
Kremlin to St. Basil's on a horse
disguised to look like a donkey.

🔺 **Main Iconostasis**
The Baroque-style iconostasis in the
Central Chapel of the Intercession
dates from the 19th century. However,
some of the icons contained in it were
painted much earlier.

Gallery
Running around the outside of
the Central Chapel, the gallery
connects it to the other eight
chapels. It was roofed over at
the end of the 17th century
and the walls and ceilings were
decorated with floral tiles in the
late 18th century.

BASIL, THE "HOLY FOOL"

Born in 1464 into a peasant family in the village
of Yelokhovoe, Basil worked as an apprentice
to a shoemaker. His skill at divining the future
soon became apparent and at the age of 16
he left for Moscow. There he undertook the
ascetic challenge of walking the city's streets
barefoot, educating Muscovites in piety.
Although he was often derided and beaten for
his sermonizing, his fortune changed in 1547,
when he foresaw the fire of Moscow and was
credited with preventing it from destroying the
entire city. On Basil's death, at the age of 88,
Czar Ivan the Terrible carried his body to the
cathedral for burial. He was canonized in 1579.

CATHEDRAL DESIGN

St. Basil's Cathedral consists of nine churches
dedicated to different saints. Each of these,
with the exception of the **Central Chapel of
the Intercession**, symbolizes the eight assaults
on Kazan and is topped by a multicolored
dome. All of the churches are uniquely
decorated and different in size from each other,
giving the structure an all-around balance. The
building is designed to be viewed from every
angle, hence the absence of a single main
façade. In plan, the eight churches form an
eight-pointed star. The four larger domes form
the endpoints of an imaginary cross with the
Central Chapel in the middle, and the smaller
churches between the larger ones.

ICON PAINTING IN RUSSIA

The Russian Orthodox Church uses icons for
both worship and teaching and there are strict
rules for creating each image. Iconography is a
symbolic art, expressing in line and color the
theological teaching of the Church. Icons are
thought to be imbued with power from the
saint they depict and are often invoked for
protection during wartime. The first icons were
brought to Russia from Byzantium. Kiev, today
the capital of Ukraine, was Russia's main icon-
painting center until the Mongols conquered
it in 1240. The Moscow school was founded
in the late 15th century when Ivan the Terrible
decreed that artists must live in the Kremlin. The
great icon painters Dionysius and Andrey Rublev
were members of this renowned school.

Onion-shaped domes of
St. Basil's Cathedral, Moscow

PORTUGAL
Porto
ATLANTIC OCEAN
PALACE OF PENA, SINTRA
Lisbon
SPAIN
Faro

BARON VON ESCHWEGE

In 1839, Ferdinand of Saxe-Coburg-Gotha acquired the well-positioned land of a former monastery and appointed the German architect Baron von Eschwege (1777–1855) to construct a fabulous summer palace. Von Eschwege turned the king's extravagant dreams into reality and, over the following decade, he erected a fantasy palace around the restored ruins of the monastery. On a nearby crag is the statue of a warrior-knight that supposedly guards the palace. It is an enormous stone sculpture whose base bears an engraving of the baron's coat of arms.

THE PALACE'S DESIGN

Ferdinand's passion for the arts, and for scientific progress, resulted in an eclectic mix of architectural styles that included Gothic (*Gothic Style, see p.54*), Renaissance (*Renaissance Style, see p.131*) and elements of the rich, indigenous Portugeuse style, Manueline. Painted in shades of pink, blue, and yellow, the exterior of the building is lavishly carved or covered with *azulejo* tile arrangements, with golden domes, crenellated turrets, and gargoyles. Inside the palace, highlights include the Renaissance retable by sculptor Nicolau Chanterène (**chapel altarpiece**) and the exotic furniture, which contribute to the prevailing air of decadence.

ROMANTICISM

Sintra has long been regarded as an enchanting place of outstanding beauty, internationally revered by kings, noblemen, and artists. In 1809, the English poet Lord Byron described its verdant beauty as "glorious Eden," and further praise was given in *Os Lusíadas*, Portugal's celebrated 16th-century epic poem by Luís Vaz de Camões. The Palace of Pena's garish union of styles, including exotic Gothic traces, made it a forerunner of European Romanticism.Largely inspired by Bavarian palaces, Arab, Portuguese, German, Classical, and Romantic influences were combined to create a unique, and at times bizarre, effect. The surrounding grounds of the **Parque da Pena** are also of striking romantic beauty, filled with exotic trees and shrubs and containing the chalet Ferdinand had built for his mistress.

Palace of Pena, Sintra

On the highest peaks of the Serra de Sintra stands the spectacular Palace of Pena. This eclectic medley of architectural styles was built in the 19th century for the husband of the young Queen Maria II (r. 1834–53), Ferdinand of Saxe-Coburg-Gotha—King Dom Fernando II of Portugal. It stands over the ruins of a Hieronymite monastery founded here in the 15th century on the site of the chapel of Nossa Senhora da Pena. The outlandish rooms of the enchanting summer palace are filled with oddities from all over the world. The monarchy was overthrown in 1910 and with the declaration of the Republic, the palace became a museum, preserved as it was when the royal family lived here.

FERDINAND: KING CONSORT

Ferdinand was known in Portugal as "the artist king." Like his cousin Albert, who married Britain's Queen Victoria, he loved nature, art, and the new inventions of the time. Ferdinand enthusiastically adopted his new country and devoted his life to the arts. In 1869, 16 years after the death of Maria II, Ferdinand married his mistress, the opera singer Countess Edla. His lifelong dream of building the palace at Pena was realized in 1885, the year he died.

Ferdinand

ENTERTAINMENT

The palace hosts a number of live events throughout the year. These include concerts of classical music, exhibitions, ballets, and historical plays performed by internationally acclaimed artistes.

⊿ Manuel II's Bedroom
This oval-shaped room is decorated with green walls and a stuccoed ceiling. A portrait of Manuel II, the last king of Portugal, hangs above the fireplace.

Kitchen
Copper pots and utensils still hang around the iron stove here. A dinner service bears the coat of arms of Ferdinand II.

▲ Triton Arch

⊿ Entrance arch

KEY DATES

1400s	1839	1840s	1910	1995
The Hieronymite monastery of Nossa Senhora da Pena is founded here.	Ferdinand of Saxe-Coburg-Gotha buys the ruins of the monastery with the intention of turning it into a palace.	Baron von Eschwege puts the king's ideas into effect, preserving the original monastery cloister and chapel.	The palace is classified as a national monument and opens to the public as a museum.	The palace, along with the city of Sintra, are added to UNESCO's World Heritage list.

Chapel Altarpiece
The impressive 16th-century alabaster and marble retable was sculpted by Nicolau Chanterène. Each niche portrays a scene of the life of Christ, from the manger to the Ascension.

Cloister
Decorated with colorful patterned tiles, this is part of the original monastery buildings.

⤬ Arab Room
Marvelous *trompe-l'oeil* frescoes cover the walls and ceiling of the Arab Room, one of the loveliest in the palace. The Orient was a great inspiration to Romanticism.

⤬ Ballroom
This spacious room is sumptuously furnished with German stained-glass windows, precious Oriental porcelain, and four life-size turbaned torchbearers holding giant candelabras.

Arab Room ▾

⤬ Triton Arch
This is encrusted with Neo-Manueline decoration and is guarded by a fierce sea monster.

Parque da Pena, overlooked by the Palace of Pena ▶

▾ Entrance Arch
A studded archway with crenellated turrets greets visitors at the entrance to the palace. The palace buildings are painted in the original daffodil yellow and strawberry pink.

▾ Manuel II's Bedroom

▾ Ballroom

Santiago de Compostela Cathedral

As befits one of the great shrines of Christendom, this monument to St. James is a majestic sight, dominated by its soaring twin Baroque towers *(Baroque Style, see p.80)*. The rest of the cathedral dates from the 11th–13th centuries, although it stands on the site of Alfonso II's 9th-century basilica. Through the famous Pórtico da Gloria is the same interior that greeted pilgrims in medieval times. The choir, designed by Maestro Mateo, has been completely restored.

ST. JAMES THE GREAT

According to tradition, James returned to Jerusalem after preaching in Spain and was the first Apostle to be martyred. His body is thought to have been translated, some claim miraculously, to a burial site in Galicia. A bishop is said to have discovered the relics some 750 years later in 819, guided by a divine vision. A church was erected in St. James' honor on the sacred spot. The Moors destroyed Santiago in 997, yet the saint's tomb was spared (**crypt**). This, and subsequent Christian victories, led to St. James becoming Spain's patron saint, and forged the cathedral's reputation as one of Christendom's major pilgrimage sites.

THE ROAD TO SANTIAGO

In the Middle Ages, 500,000 pilgrims a year flocked to the cathedral from all over Europe. Several pilgrimage roads converge on Santiago de Compostela. The various routes, marked by the cathedrals, churches, and inns built along them, are still used by travelers today; the main road from the Pyrenees is known as the French Route. To qualify for a certificate, pilgrims must produce a stamped and dated pilgrim passport and have covered the final 62 miles (100 km) on foot or horseback, or have cycled the last 125 miles (200 km).

PÓRTICO DA GLORIA

The Romanesque pillars, pointed arches, and ribbed vaulting *(Romanesque Style, see p.122)* of this doorway were carved in part by Maestro Mateo (the lintel of the central arch bears his signature and the date 1188). Its three arches are carved with almost 200 expressive biblical figures. Christ sits at the center, baring his wounds, flanked by his Apostles and the 24 Elders of the Apocalypse, who are carrying musical instruments. St. James is seated below Christ, perched before the richly sculpted central column. Several indentations are visible on this column, which also depicts the Tree of Jesse. These have been created by the millions of pilgrims who have touched this spot with their hands as a gesture of thanks for their safe journey. On the other side, pilgrims bend to rest their heads on the statue of the **Santos dos Croques** hoping to gain wisdom.

The gigantic *botafumeiro*

Twin Towers
These are the cathedral's highest structures, soaring to 243 ft (74 m).

Statue of St. James

⊡ West Façade
The richly sculpted Baroque Obradoiro façade was added in the 18th century.

⊡ Pórtico da Gloria
Statues of the Apostles and prophets decorate the 12th-century Doorway of Glory, the original entrance to the cathedral.

Santos dos Croques
The Saint of Bumps has greeted pilgrims since the 12th century. Touching this statue with the forehead is said to impart luck and wisdom.

THE SCALLOP SHELL

As the symbol of St. James, scallop shells were worn by pilgrims in the Middle Ages to show that they had journeyed to his shrine. Houses willing to accept passing pilgrims en route hung shells over their doors.

⊡ Tapestry Museum
Tapestries dating from the early 16th century are displayed in the museum above the chapter house and library. Some of the later tapestries are based on works by Goya.

KEY DATES

1075	1750	1879	1985
Work on the cathedral begins on the site of the church destroyed by the Moors.	The Baroque west façade of the building is completed.	St. James' remains, hidden in 1700, are rediscovered during building work.	The Old Town of Santiago is added to UNESCO's World Heritage Site list.

Botafumeiro
This giant censer is swung high above the altar by eight men during important services.

High altar

Mondragon Chapel
Fine wrought-iron grills and vaulting can be seen in this chapel of 1521.

Clock tower

Crypt

Porta das Praterias

Cloisters

Chapter house

▲ **High Altar**
Visitors can pass behind the ornate high altar to embrace the silver mantle of the 13th-century statue of St. James.

West Façade ▶

Porta das Praterias ▶
The 12th-century Goldsmiths' Doorway is rich in bas-relief sculptures of biblical scenes.

▲ **Tapestry Museum**

Crypt ▶
The relics of St. James and two disciples are said to lie in a tomb in the crypt, under the altar, in the original 9th-century foundations.

◀ **Pilgrim Passport**
This provides proof of a pilgrim's journey.

Guggenheim Museum, Bilbao

The jewel in Bilbao's revitalization program, the Museo Guggenheim unites art and architecture. The building itself is a star attraction: a mind-boggling array of silvery curves by the architect Frank O. Gehry, which are alleged to resemble a ship or flower. The Guggenheim's collection represents an intriguingly broad spectrum of modern and contemporary art, and includes works by Abstract Impressionists such as Willem de Kooning and Mark Rothko. Most of the art shown here is displayed as part of an ongoing series of temporary exhibitions and major retrospectives. Some of these are also staged at the Guggenheim museums in New York, Venice, and Berlin.

Architect Frank O. Gehry

FRANK O. GEHRY

Canadian-born architect Frank O. Gehry studied architecture at the University of Southern California and then urban planning at Harvard before setting up his own firm in 1962. His early work is notable for its use of unusual materials, including chain-link and corrugated metal. Later works have possessed an almost sculptural quality, made possible by computer design, creating distinctive, unique modern landmarks. During his career, Gehry has been awarded large-scale public and private commissions in the US, Japan, and Europe.

THE BUILDING

The Guggenheim is a breathtaking combination of curling fragmented shapes, limestone blocks, and glass walls and panels that beam light into the building. The central space (**Atrium**), one of the pioneering design features, is crowned by a metal dome and skylight. Framing this vast area is a futuristic vision of suspended curved walkways, glass lifts, and soaring staircases that lead to the 19 galleries. Ten of the galleries have a conventional rectangular form, and can be recognized from the outside by their stone finish. The other rooms are erratically shaped, and identified by their exterior titanium paneling (**titanium façade**). Volumes and perspectives have been manipulated throughout to blend the overall sculpted design with the surrounding landscape, referencing Bilbao's industrial past.

THE COLLECTION

The collection is arranged over three levels around the Atrium, with Mark Rothko's *Untitled* (1952) marking the chronological start. It comprises works by significant artists of the late 20th century, ranging from the earliest avant-garde movements to present-day genres. The artists include Eduardo Chillida, Yves Klein, Willem de Kooning, Robert Motherwell, Clyfford Still, Antoni Tàpies, and Andy Warhol. There are also artworks by emerging Basque and Spanish artists. The museum's own permanent collection is supplemented by important pieces from the Solomon R. Guggenheim Museum in New York and the Peggy Guggenheim Collection in Venice.

Tower
Positioned on the far side of the bridge, this was designed to resemble a sail. It is not an exhibition space.

⬛ Roofscape
The Guggenheim's prowlike points and metallic material make it comparable to a ship.

Puente de la Salve
This bridge was incorporated into the design of the building, which extends underneath it.

Snake
This mammoth sculpture by Richard Serra was created from hot-rolled steel. It is more than 100 ft (30 m) long.

⬛ Arcelor Mittal Gallery

SYMBOLISM

Built to rescue the city from economic decline, the museum uses materials and shapes to convey Bilbao's industrial past of steel and shipbuilding while simultaneously symbolizing its commitment to its future.

KEY DATES

1991	1993	1994	1997
Plans to build the museum are approved.	Frank O. Gehry presents his museum design model.	Work begins on the museum building.	The Guggenheim Museum is opened to the public.

Arcelor Mittal Gallery ▸
Formerly known as the Fish Gallery because of its flowing, fishlike shape, this is the largest gallery in the museum. It is dominated by a series of steel sculptures by Richard Serra called *Snake* and *The Matter of Time* (right).

▣ Atrium
The space in which visitors to the museum first find themselves is the extraordinary 200-ft (60-m) high Atrium. It serves as an orientation point and its height makes it a dramatic setting for exhibiting large pieces.

▲ Atrium

Second floor balcony

Puppy
American artist Jeff Koons created this sculpture of a dog with a coat of flowers irrigated by an internal system. Originally a temporary feature, its popularity earned it a permanent spot.

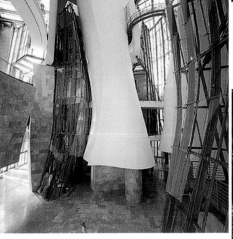

▾ View from the City
Approaching from the Calle de Iparraguirre, the museum stands out amid more traditional buildings.

Main entrance

Roofscape ▸

Restaurant
Designed and owned by star chef Martín Berasategui, this serves local specialties.

Titanium Façade ▸
Rarely seen in buildings, titanium is more commonly used for aircraft parts. In total, 60 tons were used, but the layer is only 0.1 inch (3 mm) thick.

▣ Water garden beside the Nervión River

Water Garden ▸
On the west side of the museum, a sweeping concrete promenade connects the Nervión River with a water garden.

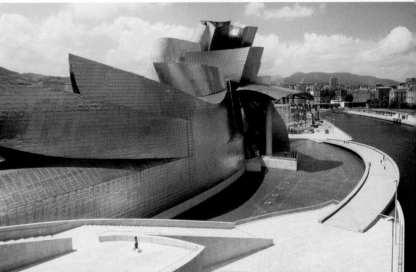

Titanium curves at the Guggenheim
Museum, Bilbao

Sagrada Família, Barcelona

Europe's most unconventional church, the Temple Expiatori de la Sagrada Família is an emblem of a city that likes to think of itself as individualistic. Crammed with symbolism inspired by nature, and striving for originality, it is Antoni Gaudí's greatest work. In 1883, a year after building had begun on a Neo-Gothic church on the site *(Gothic Style, see p.54)*, the task of completing it was given to Gaudí, who changed everything, extemporizing as he went along. It became his life's work; he lived like a recluse on the site for 16 years and was buried in the crypt. On his death, only one tower on the Nativity Façade had been completed, but work continued after the Spanish Civil War and several more have since been finished to his plans. Work continues today, financed by public subscription.

Stained-glass window

MODERNISME

Toward the end of the 19th century, a new style of art and architecture, a variant of Art Nouveau, was born in Barcelona. Modernisme became a means of expression for Catalan nationalism and attempted to reestablish a local identity that had waned under the rule of Castilian Madrid. The style is characterized by curved lines and a profuse use of colored tiles and tiled mosaics. It counted Josep Puig i Cadafalch, Lluís Domènech i Montaner and, above all, Antoni Gaudí among its major exponents; the style's radical appearance is one of the principal attractions of Barcelona today.

ANTONI GAUDÍ

Born into a family of artisans, Antoni Gaudí (1852–1926) studied at Barcelona's School of Architecture. Inspired by a nationalistic search for a romantic medieval past, his work was supremely original. His most celebrated building is the Sagrada Família, to which he devoted his life from 1883. He gave all his money to the project and often went from house to house begging for more, until his death a few days after being run over by a tram. Gaudí designed, or collaborated on designs, for almost every known medium. He combined bare, un-decorated materials—wood, rough-hewn stone, rubble, and brickwork—with meticulous craftwork in wrought iron and stained glass.

SYMBOLISM

Gaudí united nature and religion in his symbolic vision of the Sagrada Família. The church has three monumental façades. The east front (**Nativity Façade**) is directed toward the rising Sun and dedicated to the birth of Christ. Flora and fauna, spring and summer symbols, fruits, birds, and flowers adorn this façade. The west front (**Passion Façade**) represents Christ's Passion and death, with columns eerily reminiscent of bones combined with a lack of decoration to reflect the loss that death brings. The Glory Façade to the south has not yet been constructed, but is projected to be the largest of all. Gaudí intended the interior of the church to evoke the idea of a forest (**nave**). Columns are "planted" symbolically like tree trunks, and dappled light filters in through skylights.

THE FINISHED CHURCH

Gaudí's initial ambitions have been scaled down over the years, but the design for the completion of the building remains impressive. Still to come is the central tower, which will be encircled by four large towers representing the Evangelists. Four towers on the Glory (south) Façade will match the existing four on the Passion (west) and Nativity (east) façades. An ambulatory—like an inside-out cloister—will run around the outside of the building.

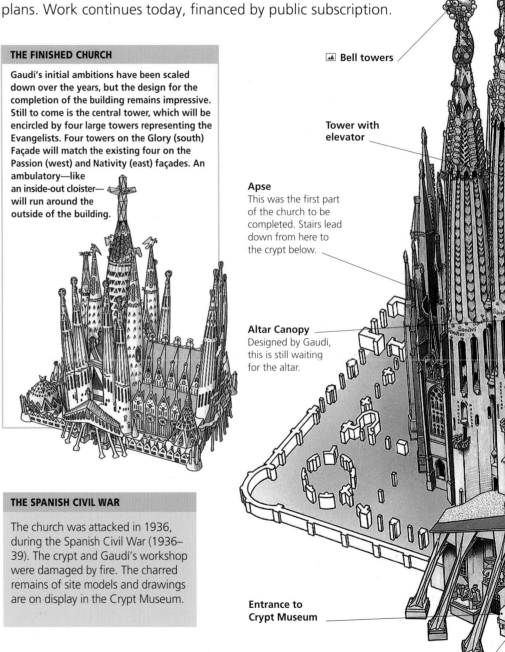

⛰ Bell towers

Tower with elevator

Apse
This was the first part of the church to be completed. Stairs lead down from here to the crypt below.

Altar Canopy
Designed by Gaudí, this is still waiting for the altar.

Entrance to Crypt Museum

THE SPANISH CIVIL WAR

The church was attacked in 1936, during the Spanish Civil War (1936–39). The crypt and Gaudí's workshop were damaged by fire. The charred remains of site models and drawings are on display in the Crypt Museum.

KEY DATES

1882	1884	1893	1954
Work begins on a church in a traditional Neo-Gothic style.	Gaudí takes over as the lead architect and immediately changes the project.	Gaudí begins the Nativity Façade, which reflects his love of nature.	Work resumes following the Civil War and continues to this day.

⛰ Passion Façade
This bleak façade was completed in the late 1980s by artist Josep Maria Subirachs. A controversial work, its sculpted figures, which represent Jesus' pain and sacrifice, are often angular and sinister.

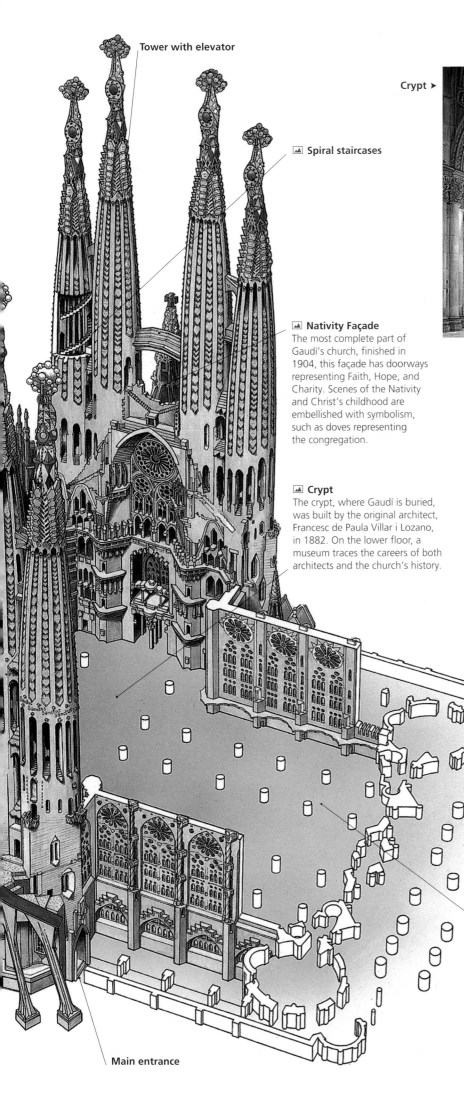

Tower with elevator

Spiral staircases

Nativity Façade

The most complete part of Gaudí's church, finished in 1904, this façade has doorways representing Faith, Hope, and Charity. Scenes of the Nativity and Christ's childhood are embellished with symbolism, such as doves representing the congregation.

Crypt

The crypt, where Gaudí is buried, was built by the original architect, Francesc de Paula Villar i Lozano, in 1882. On the lower floor, a museum traces the careers of both architects and the church's history.

Main entrance

Crypt ►

Spiral Staircases ►
Viewed from the top, these spiral stone stairways resemble snail shells. The steps allow access to the bell towers and upper galleries.

Nave ►

▲ Nativity Façade

Passion Façade ►

Nave
In the nave, which is still under construction, fluted pillars will support four galleries above the aisles, while skylights let in natural light.

Bell Towers ►
Eight of the 12 spires, one for each Apostle, have been built. They are topped by Venetian mosaics.

El Escorial, Madrid

Felipe II's imposing gray palace of San Lorenzo de El Escorial stands out against the foothills of the Sierra de Guadarrama to the northwest of Madrid. It was built between 1563 and 1584 in honor of St. Lawrence, and its unornamented severity set a new architectural style that became one of the most influential in Spain. The interior was conceived as a mausoleum and contemplative retreat rather than a splendid residence. The palace's artistic wealth, which includes some of the most important works of art in the royal Habsburg collections, is concentrated in the museums, chapter houses, church, royal pantheon, and library. In contrast, the royal apartments are remarkably modest.

Fresco by Luca Giordano

◄ Museum of Art
Flemish, Italian, and Spanish paintings are displayed in the museum, located on the first floor. One of the highlights is *The Calvary*, by 15th-century Flemish artist Rogier van der Weyden.

◄ Basilica

ST. LAWRENCE

On August 10, 1557—St. Lawrence's Day—King Felipe II defeated the French in battle and immediately vowed to build a monastery in the saint's honor. El Escorial's shape, based on that of a gridiron, is said to recall the instrument of St. Lawrence's martyrdom.

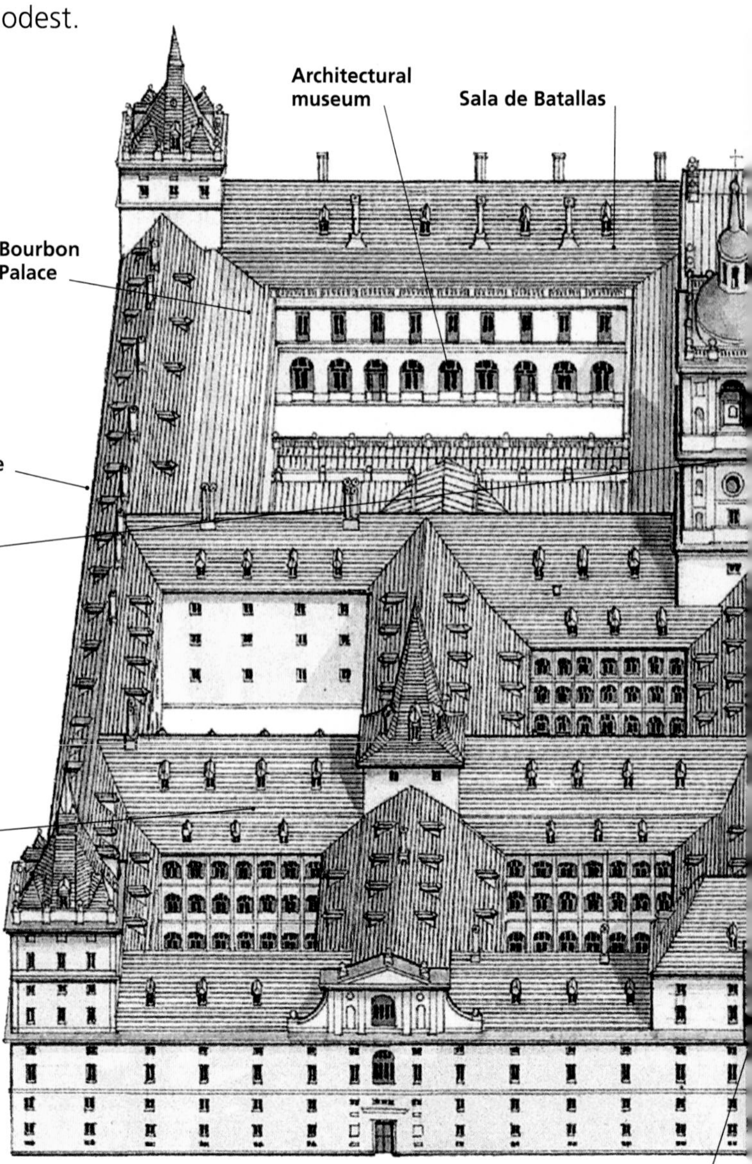

◄ Library

▼ Chapter Houses

◄ Royal Pantheon
The funerary urns of Spanish monarchs line this octagonal marble mausoleum.

Architectural museum

Sala de Batallas

Bourbon Palace

Main entrance

▲ Basilica
The highlight of this huge decorated church is the lavish altarpiece. The chapel houses a superb marble sculpture of the Crucifixion by Cellini.

Alfonso XII College
This was founded by monks in 1875 as a boarding school.

▲ Library
The library's impressive array of 40,000 books incorporates King Felipe II's personal collection. On display are precious manuscripts, including a poem by Alfonso X the Learned. The 16th-century ceiling frescoes are by Pellegrino Tibaldi (1527–96).

◄ The Glory of the Spanish Monarchy, by Luca Giordano

The building of El Escorial ▶
When chief architect Juan Bautista de Toledo died in 1567 he was replaced by Juan de Herrera, royal inspector of monuments. The plain architectural style of El Escorial is called *desornamentado*, which literally means "unadorned."

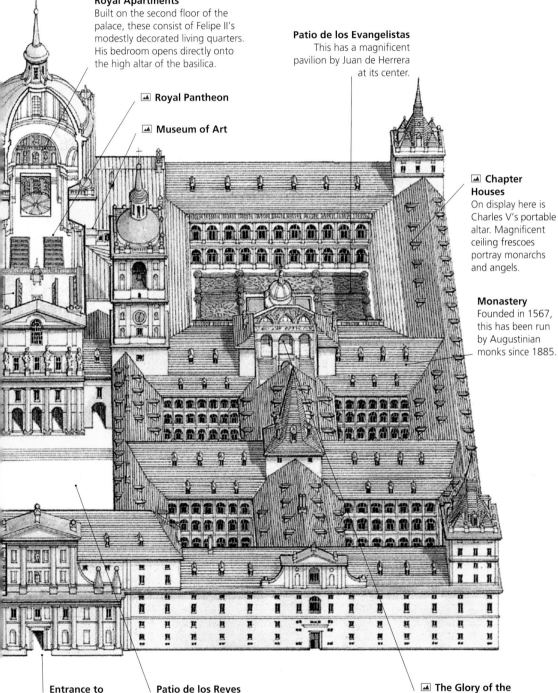

Royal Apartments
Built on the second floor of the palace, these consist of Felipe II's modestly decorated living quarters. His bedroom opens directly onto the high altar of the basilica.

Patio de los Evangelistas
This has a magnificent pavilion by Juan de Herrera at its center.

▣ **Royal Pantheon**

▣ **Museum of Art**

▣ **Chapter Houses**
On display here is Charles V's portable altar. Magnificent ceiling frescoes portray monarchs and angels.

Monastery
Founded in 1567, this has been run by Augustinian monks since 1885.

Entrance to basilica only

Patio de los Reyes

▣ **The Glory of the Spanish Monarchy, by Luca Giordano**
This beautiful fresco, above the main staircase, depicts Charles V and Felipe II, and scenes of the building of the monastery.

KEY DATES

1563	1581	1654	1984
The foundation stone of the monastery is laid.	Work on the basilica is finished.	The Royal Pantheon is completed.	El Escorial is added to UNESCO's World Heritage Site list.

THE LIBRARY
Established by Felipe II (r. 1556–98), this was Spain's first public library. In 1619, a decree was issued demanding that a copy of each new publication in the empire be sent here. At its zenith, it contained some 40,000 books and manuscripts. The long Print Room has a marble floor and a glorious vaulted ceiling. The ceiling frescoes depict Philosophy, Grammar, Rhetoric, Dialectics, Music, Geometry, Astrology, and Theology. The wooden shelving was designed by Juan de Herrera (1530–97). On the four main pillars are portraits of the royal house of Habsburg—Carlos I (Emperor Charles V), Felipe II, Felipe III, and Carlos II.

THE PANTHEONS
Directly beneath the high altar of the basilica is the **Royal Pantheon**, where almost all Spanish monarchs since Carlos I have been laid to rest. Adorned with black marble, red jasper, and Italian gilt bronze decorations, it was finished in 1654. Kings lie on the left of the altar and queens on the right. The most recent addition to the pantheon was the mother of Juan Carlos I in 2000. Of the eight other pantheons, one of the most notable is that of Juan de Austria, Felipe II's half-brother, who became a hero after defeating the Turks at the Battle of Lepanto in 1571. Also worth seeing is La Tarta, a white marble polygonal tomb resembling a cake, where royal children are buried.

THE BASILICA
Historically, only the aristocracy were permitted to enter the **basilica**, and the townspeople were confined to the vestibule at the entrance. The basilica contains 45 altars. Among its highlights is the exquisite statue of C*hrist Crucified* (1562) in Carrara marble by the Italian sculptor Benvenuto Cellini. It is found in the chapel to the left of the entrance, with steps leading up to it. On either side of the high altar, above the doors leading to the **Royal Apartments**, are fine gilded bronze cenotaphs of Charles V and Felipe II worshiping with their families. The enormous altarpiece was designed by Juan de Herrera with colored marble, jasper, gilt-bronze sculptures, and paintings. The central tabernacle took seven years to craft.

THE NASRID DYNASTY

The Reconquista—a series of campaigns by Christian kingdoms to recapture territory lost to the Moors since 711—started in northern Spain, arriving in Andalusia with a Christian victory in 1212. As the Christians infiltrated the Moorish empire, Granada became the principal Muslim stronghold in Spain. The Nasrids came to power in the kingdom of Granada in 1236, ushering in a prolonged period of peace and prosperity. Muhammad I, founder of the Nasrid dynasty, undertook the construction of the Alhambra and the Generalife in 1238, building a fortified complex of singular beauty that became the official residence of the Nasrid sultans. Granada finally fell in 1492 to Ferdinand and Isabella, the Catholic Monarchs.

THE GENERALIFE

Located west of the Alhambra, the Generalife was the country estate of the Nasrid kings. Here, they could escape the intrigues of the palace and enjoy the tranquillity high above the city. The name Generalife, or Yannat al Arif, has various interpretations, perhaps the most pleasing being "the garden of lofty paradise." The gardens, begun in the 13th century, have been modified over the years. They originally contained orchards and pastures for animals.

MOORISH ARCHITECTURE

The palaces of the Moors were designed with gracious living, culture, and learning in mind. Space, light, water, and ornamentation were combined to harmonious effect. The Alhambra has all the key features of Moorish architecture: arches, stuccowork, and ornamental use of calligraphy. The elaborate stuccowork (**Sala de los Abencerrajes**) typifies the Nasrid style. Reflections in water, combined with an overall play of light, are another central feature. Water often had to be pumped from a source far beneath the palaces (**Patio de los Leones**). The Moors introduced techniques for making fantastic mosaics of tiles in sophisticated geometric patterns to decorate their palace walls. The word azulejo derives from the Arabic for "little stone." Exquisite azulejos, made of unicolored stones, can be seen throughout the Alhambra complex.

The Alhambra, Granada

A magical use of space, light, water, and decoration characterizes this most sensual piece of Moorish architecture. The Islamic Moors first arrived in Spain in 710. By the late 13th century, only the Nasrid kingdom of Granada remained under their control, and the Alhambra is the most remarkable structure to have survived from this period. Seeking to belie an image of waning power, the Moors created their idea of paradise on Earth in this palace-fortress. Modest materials were used, but they were superbly worked. Restored in the late 1800s after centuries of neglect and pillage, the Alhambra's delicate craftsmanship dazzles the eye.

Sala de los Reyes

THE ALHAMBRA AT NIGHT

Night visits provide a magical view of the Alhambra complex, when subtle, indirect lighting contrasts with the bright city lights. Nocturnal visits only give access to the outdoor areas of the Nasrid palaces.

Sala de la Barca

🔲 **Salón de Embajadores**
The ceiling of this sumptuous throne room, built from 1334–54, represents the seven heavens of the Muslim cosmos.

🔲 **Patio de Arrayanes**

Patio de Machuca

🔲 **Patio del Mexuar**

Entrance

KEY DATES

1236	1238	1492	1984
The Nasrid dynasty comes to power in the sole remaining Islamic state in Spain, the Kingdom of Granada.	Construction of the Alhambra palace complex begins under the first Nasrid ruler.	The Nasrid dynasty surrenders to the Catholic Monarchs during the Reconquista.	The Alhambra and the Generalife are added to UNESCO's World Heritage list.

▲ Palacio del Partal
A pavilion with an arched portico and a tower is all that remains of this palace, the oldest building in the Alhambra.

▲ Patio de los Leones
Built by Muhammad V (1354–91), this patio is lined with arcades supported by 124 slender marble columns. At its center, a fountain rests on 12 marble lions.

▲ Patio de la Acequia, Generalife

▼ Patio de Arrayanes
This pool, set amid myrtle hedges and graceful arcades, reflects light into the surrounding halls.

Washington Irving's Apartments
The celebrated American author wrote his *Tales of the Alhambra* (1832) here.

Baños Reales

◪ Palacio del Partal

Jardín de Lindaraja

◪ Sala de los Reyes
This great banqueting hall was used to hold extravagant parties and feasts. Beautiful ceiling paintings on leather, from the 14th century, depict tales of hunting and chivalry.

Puerta de la Rawda

Sala de las Dos Hermanas
With its honeycomb dome, the Hall of the Two Sisters is regarded as the ultimate example of Spanish-Islamic architecture.

◪ Sala de los Abencerrajes

◪ Patio de los Leones

Sala de los Abencerrajes ▶
This hall takes its name from a noble family that was the rival of the Nasrid sultan Boabdil. According to legend, he had them massacred while they attended a banquet here. The geometrical ceiling pattern was inspired by Pythagoras' theorem.

Salón de Embajadores ▶

Palace of Charles V
Built in 1526, this houses a collection of Spanish-Islamic art, the highlight of which is the Alhambra vase.

PLAN OF THE ALHAMBRA

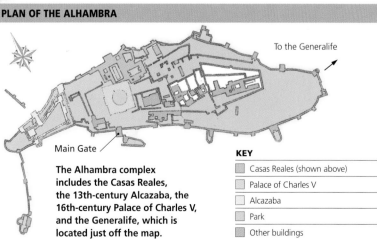

To the Generalife

Main Gate

The Alhambra complex includes the Casas Reales, the 13th-century Alcazaba, the 16th-century Palace of Charles V, and the Generalife, which is located just off the map.

KEY
- Casas Reales (shown above)
- Palace of Charles V
- Alcazaba
- Park
- Other buildings

Patio del Mexuar ▶
This council chamber, completed in 1365, was where the reigning Nasrid sultan heard the petitions of his subjects and held meetings with his ministers.

St. Mark's Basilica, Venice

This stunning basilica, built on a Greek-cross plan and crowned with five huge domes, clearly shows the influence of Byzantine architecture *(Byzantine Style, see p.148)*, which had been brought to Venice via the city's extensive links with the East. The present basilica is the third church to stand on this site. The first, built to enshrine the body of St. Mark, was destroyed by a fire. The second was pulled down in the 11th century to make way for a more spectacular edifice, built to reflect the escalating power of the Venetian Republic. In 1807, St. Mark's succeeded San Pietro in the administrative district of Castello as the cathedral of Venice; it had until then served as the doge's chapel for state ceremonies.

▲ St. Mark and Angels
The statues crowning the central arch are additions from the early 15th century.

◄ Horses of St. Mark

▼ Baptistry Mosaics
Herod's Banquet (1343–54) is one of the mosaics in a cycle of scenes from the life of St. John the Baptist.

Pentecost Dome
This was probably the first dome to be decorated with mosaics. It shows the Descent of the Holy Ghost as a dove.

▣ St. Mark and Angels

Museo Marciano

▣ Horses of St. Mark
These four horses are replicas of the gilded bronze originals, now protected inside the Museo Marciano.

▼ One of the ornate, jeweled panels from the Pala d'Oro

▲ Central Doorway Carvings
The central arch features 13th-century carvings of the *Labors of the Month*.

◄ Ciborium

◄ Façade Mosaics
This 17th-century mosaic shows the smuggling out of Alexandria of St. Mark's remains, reputedly under slices of pork to get them past the Muslim guards.

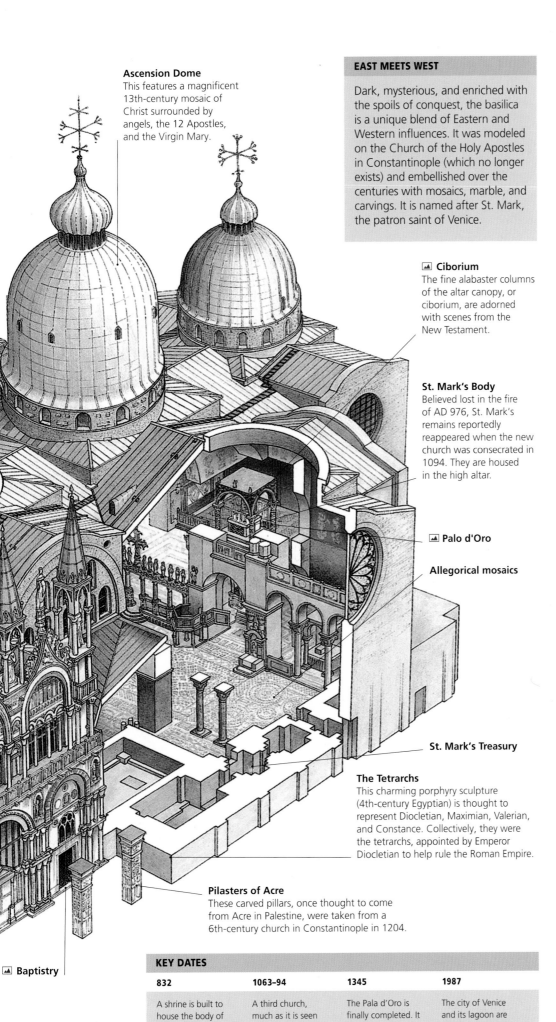

Ascension Dome
This features a magnificent 13th-century mosaic of Christ surrounded by angels, the 12 Apostles, and the Virgin Mary.

EAST MEETS WEST

Dark, mysterious, and enriched with the spoils of conquest, the basilica is a unique blend of Eastern and Western influences. It was modeled on the Church of the Holy Apostles in Constantinople (which no longer exists) and embellished over the centuries with mosaics, marble, and carvings. It is named after St. Mark, the patron saint of Venice.

Ciborium
The fine alabaster columns of the altar canopy, or ciborium, are adorned with scenes from the New Testament.

St. Mark's Body
Believed lost in the fire of AD 976, St. Mark's remains reportedly reappeared when the new church was consecrated in 1094. They are housed in the high altar.

Palo d'Oro

Allegorical mosaics

St. Mark's Treasury

The Tetrarchs
This charming porphyry sculpture (4th-century Egyptian) is thought to represent Diocletian, Maximian, Valerian, and Constance. Collectively, they were the tetrarchs, appointed by Emperor Diocletian to help rule the Roman Empire.

Pilasters of Acre
These carved pillars, once thought to come from Acre in Palestine, were taken from a 6th-century church in Constantinople in 1204.

Baptistry

KEY DATES

832	1063–94	1345	1987
A shrine is built to house the body of St. Mark the Evangelist, brought from its tomb in Alexandria in Egypt.	A third church, much as it is seen today, is built on the site.	The Pala d'Oro is finally completed. It was commissioned in 976.	The city of Venice and its lagoon are added to UNESCO's World Heritage list.

PALA D'ORO

The most valuable treasure held in St. Mark's Basilica is the **Pala d'Oro** (Golden Altar Screen). This jewel-spangled altarpiece is situated behind the high altar, beyond the chapel of St. Clement. The Pala consists of 250 enamel paintings on gold foil, enclosed within a silver-gilt Gothic frame. The subjects include scenes from the life of Christ and the life of St. Mark. Begun in Byzantium in 976, the altarpiece was enlarged and embellished over the centuries. Following the fall of the Venetian Republic in 1797, Napoleon removed some of the precious stones, but the screen still gleams with jewels such as pearls, rubies, sapphires, and amethysts.

ST. MARK'S TREASURY

Although **St. Mark's Treasury** was plundered after the Napoleonic invasion in the late 18th century, and much depleted by a fundraising sale of jewels in the early 19th century, it nevertheless possesses a precious collection of Byzantine silver, gold, and glasswork. Today, the treasures, 283 pieces in all, are mainly housed in a room with remarkably thick walls believed to have been a 9th-century tower of the original Doge's Palace. A dazzling array of exhibits by Byzantine and Venetian craftsmen includes chalices, goblets, reliquaries, two intricate icons of the Archangel Michael, and an 11th-century silver-gilt reliquary made in the form of a five-domed basilica.

ST. MARK'S MUSEUM

A stairway from the basilica's atrium leads up to the **Museo Marciano**, or church museum. The original **Horses of St. Mark**—which stood on the basilica's façade for centuries before being replaced by the replicas seen today—are housed here. Stolen from the Hippodrome (and ancient racecourse) in Constantinople (now Istanbul) in 1204, their origin, either Roman or Hellenistic, remains a mystery. Also on display are Paolo Veneziano's 14th-century *Pala Feriale*, painted with stories from the life of St. Mark, medieval illuminated manuscripts, fragments of ancient mosaics, and antique tapestries. There are splendid views of the basilica's interior from the museum's gallery and the Piazza San Marco can be seen from the external loggia.

Ornate exterior of St. Mark's Basilica, Venice

Doge's Palace, Venice

At the heart of the powerful Venetian Republic, the magnificent Doge's Palace was the official residence of the doge (ruler). Originally built in the 9th century, the present palace dates from the 14th and early 15th centuries and is adorned with glorious paintings and sculptures. To create their airy Gothic masterpiece *(Gothic Style, see p.54)*, the Venetians perched the bulk of the palace (built in pink Veronese marble) on top of an apparent fretwork of loggias and arcades (built from white Istrian stone).

Mars, by Sansovino

SALA DEL CONSIGLIO DEI DIECI

This was the meeting room of the immensely powerful Council of Ten, founded in 1310 to investigate and prosecute people for crimes concerning the security of the state. Napoleon pilfered some of the paintings by Paolo Veronese from the ceiling, but two of the finest found their way back in 1920: *Age and Youth* and *Juno Offering the Ducal Crown to Venice* (both 1553–54). Offenders awaited sentence in the nearby room, the **Sala della Bussola**. In the same room is a *bocca di leone* (lion's mouth), used to post secret denunciations, one of several in the palace. Convicts were sent across the **Bridge of Sighs** for incarceration.

THE BRIDGE OF SIGHS

According to legend, the Bridge of Sighs, built in 1600 to link the Doge's Palace with the new prisons, takes its name from the lamentations of the prisoners as they made their way over to the offices of the feared State Inquisitors. Just below the leaded roof of the Doge's Palace are the *piombi* cells. Prisoners held here were more comfortable than those in the *pozzi* cells in the dungeons at ground level. One of the more famous inmates was the Venetian libertine Casanova, who was incarcerated here in 1755. He made a daring escape from his cell in the *piombi* through a hole in the roof.

CHOOSING A DOGE

The Doge's Palace was the Venetian Republic's seat of power, and home to its rulers. New doges were nominated in the Sala dello Scrutinio, and were chosen from the members of the Maggior Consiglio, Venice's Great Council. A lengthy and convoluted system was used to count votes during dogal elections: a method designed to prevent candidates from bribing their way to power. Once elected, a doge occupied the post for the rest of his lifetime, but numerous restrictions were placed on him in an attempt to prevent him from exploiting his position. Despite the precautions, many doges met their deaths in office, or were sent into exile for activities such as conspiring against the state. Others survived in office for many years: the diplomat doge Leonardo Loredan ruled for 20 years.

▼ The Bridge of Sighs, with the Ponte della Paglia beyond.

▼ Loggia

Scala dei Giganti
The 15th-century Giant's Staircase is crowned by Jacopo Sansovino's huge statues of Mars and Neptune, symbols of Venice's power.

Arco Foscari
This triumphal arch features copies of Antonio Rizzo's 15th-century marble statues of Adam and Eve.

◄ Scala dei Giganti

Porta della Carta
This 15th-century Gothic gate is the principal entrance to the palace. From it, a vaulted passageway leads to the Arco Foscari and the internal courtyard.

Main entrance

▲ Torture Chamber

▼ Sala del Maggior Consiglio
This vast hall was used as a meeting place for members of Venice's Great Council. Tintoretto's huge *Paradise* (1590) fills the end wall.

Porta della Carta ►

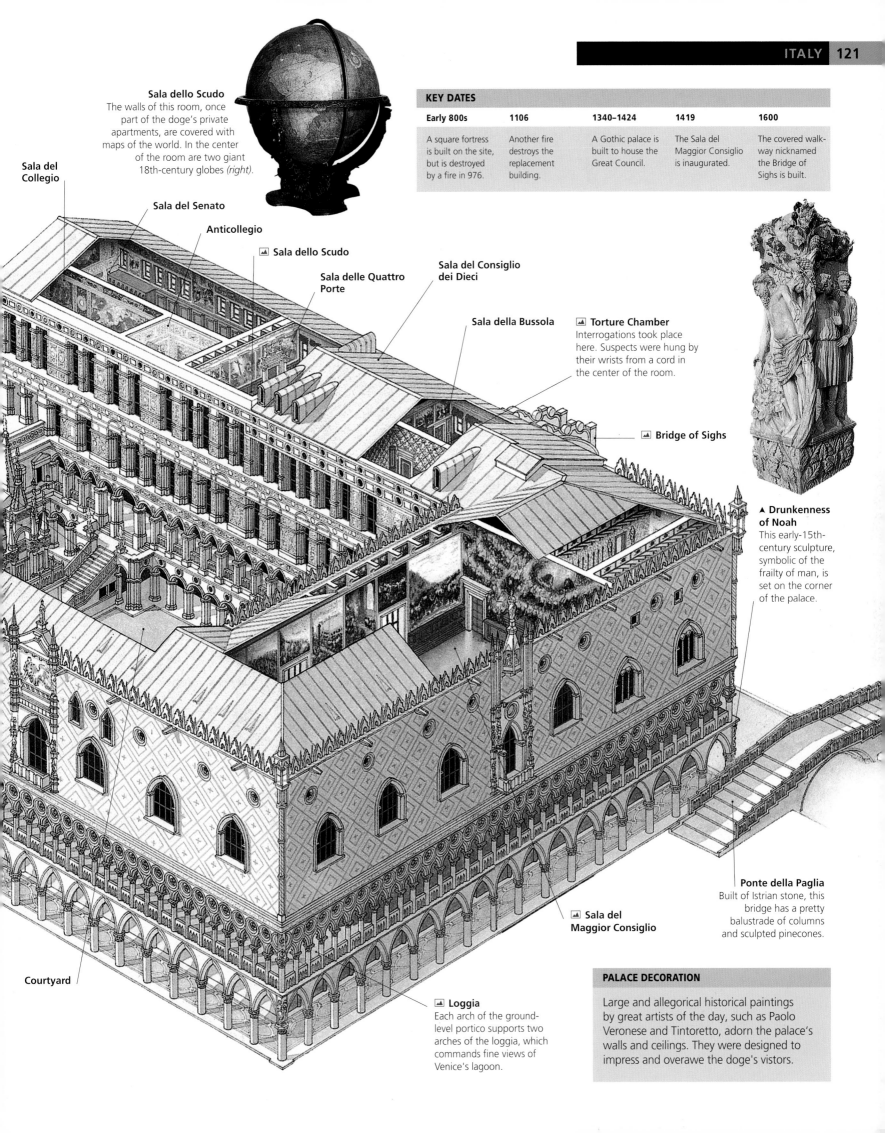

Sala dello Scudo
The walls of this room, once part of the doge's private apartments, are covered with maps of the world. In the center of the room are two giant 18th-century globes (right).

Sala del Collegio

Sala del Senato

Anticollegio

🔼 Sala dello Scudo

Sala delle Quattro Porte

Sala del Consiglio dei Dieci

Sala della Bussola

KEY DATES

Early 800s	1106	1340–1424	1419	1600
A square fortress is built on the site, but is destroyed by a fire in 976.	Another fire destroys the replacement building.	A Gothic palace is built to house the Great Council.	The Sala del Maggior Consiglio is inaugurated.	The covered walkway nicknamed the Bridge of Sighs is built.

🔼 **Torture Chamber**
Interrogations took place here. Suspects were hung by their wrists from a cord in the center of the room.

🔼 **Bridge of Sighs**

▲ **Drunkenness of Noah**
This early-15th-century sculpture, symbolic of the frailty of man, is set on the corner of the palace.

Ponte della Paglia
Built of Istrian stone, this bridge has a pretty balustrade of columns and sculpted pinecones.

🔼 **Sala del Maggior Consiglio**

Courtyard

🔼 **Loggia**
Each arch of the ground-level portico supports two arches of the loggia, which commands fine views of Venice's lagoon.

PALACE DECORATION

Large and allegorical historical paintings by great artists of the day, such as Paolo Veronese and Tintoretto, adorn the palace's walls and ceilings. They were designed to impress and overawe the doge's vistors.

Campo dei Miracoli, Pisa

Pisa's world-famous Leaning Tower is just one of the splendid buildings rising from the lawns of the "Field of Miracles." It is joined by the Duomo, a triumph of marble decoration; Italy's largest baptistry, with an acoustically perfect interior; and the Campo Santo cemetery, containing Roman sarcophagi and sculptures. The buildings combine Moorish elements, such as inlaid marble in geometric patterns (arabesques), with delicate Romanesque colonnading and spiked Gothic niches and pinnacles.

Carved support, Duomo pulpit

ROMANESQUE STYLE

When Charlemagne was crowned emperor of the Holy Roman Empire in 800, he encouraged an ambitious wave of church-building throughout Western Europe. Massive vaults and arches, characteristic of ancient Roman architecture, were combined with elements from Byzantium and the Middle East, and from the Germans, Celts, and other northern tribes in Western Europe. This fusion created a number of local styles known as Romanesque, meaning "in the manner of the Roman." Romanesque buildings are characterized by their vast size, sturdy piers, and semicircular arches. Decoration is carved into the structural fabric, rather than painted on. An important innovation was the replacement of timber construction with stone vaulting, which increased resistance to fire.

CARRARA MARBLE

The fine, snow-white marble quarried in Massa-Carrara province in Tuscany was the stone of choice for many Italian sculptors and architects during the Renaissance. Carrara marble was a great favorite of Michelangelo and many of his most famous works are sculpted from it. The 300 or so quarries, located near the city of Carrara, date back to Roman times, making this the world's oldest industrial site in continuous use. In Carrara itself today there are showrooms and workshops where the marble is worked into sheets or made into ornaments. The house in which Michelangelo stayed when buying marble is marked by a plaque.

THE LEANING TOWER OF PISA

The tower is not the only leaning building on this site: the shallow foundations and sandy silt subsoil create problems for all of the structures. However, none tilts so famously as the **Leaning Tower**. The tower began to tip sideways even before the third story was finished. Despite this, construction continued until the tower's completion in 1350, when the addition of the bell chamber brought its total height to 179 ft (54.5 m). Recent engineering interventions have corrected the tilt by 15 inches (38 cm). Measures adopted included the use of counterweights and the introduction of ten anchors. The tower was reopened in 2001.

PISAN ARCHITECTURE

The Romanesque architectural style of Pisa, with its tiers of open colonnades on a background of marble and arcaded themes, was to spread widely, and examples can be found throughout Italy and as far afield as Zadar in Croatia.

Campo Santo
This former cemetery was built in 1278 around soil brought back from the Holy Land. Once decorated with extensive frescoes, it was the burial place of Pisa's wealthy for centuries.

The Triumph of Death
These late 14th-century frescoes depict various allegorical scenes, including a knight and a lady overwhelmed by the stench of an open grave.

Capella del Pozzo
This domed chapel was added in 1594.

Baptistry

Upper gallery

◄ Baptistry Pulpit by Nicola Pisano
This great marble pulpit, completed in 1260, is carved with lively scenes from the life of Christ.

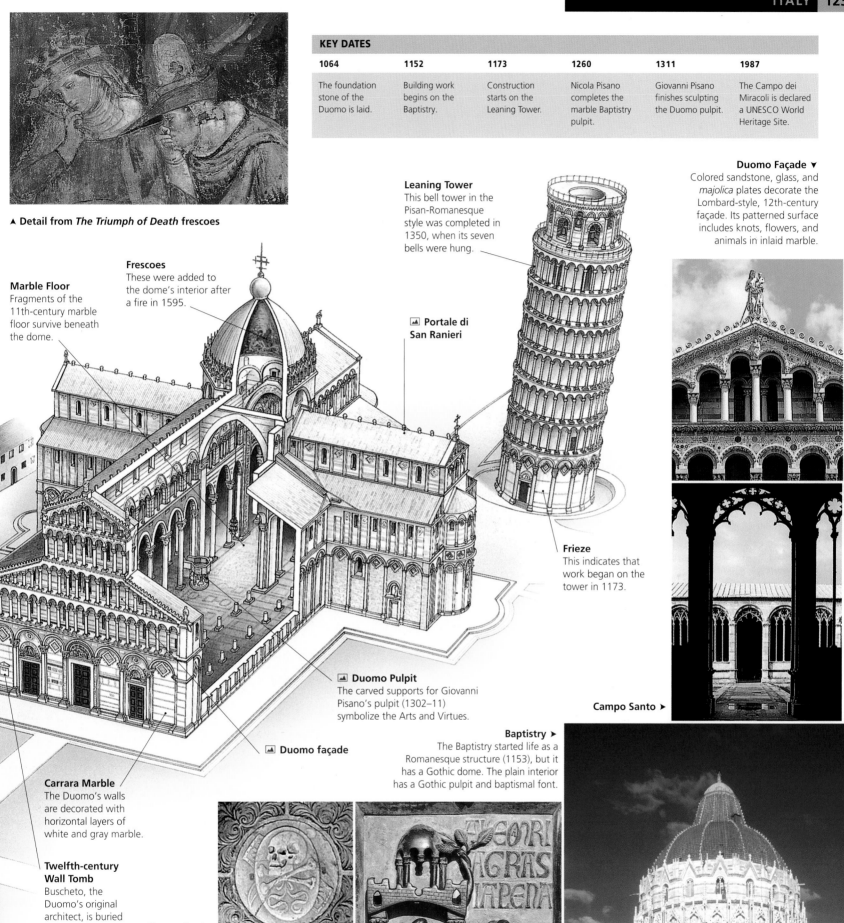

▲ Detail from *The Triumph of Death* frescoes

KEY DATES

1064	1152	1173	1260	1311	1987
The foundation stone of the Duomo is laid.	Building work begins on the Baptistry.	Construction starts on the Leaning Tower.	Nicola Pisano completes the marble Baptistry pulpit.	Giovanni Pisano finishes sculpting the Duomo pulpit.	The Campo dei Miracoli is declared a UNESCO World Heritage Site.

Duomo Façade ▼
Colored sandstone, glass, and *majolica* plates decorate the Lombard-style, 12th-century façade. Its patterned surface includes knots, flowers, and animals in inlaid marble.

Leaning Tower
This bell tower in the Pisan-Romanesque style was completed in 1350, when its seven bells were hung.

Marble Floor
Fragments of the 11th-century marble floor survive beneath the dome.

Frescoes
These were added to the dome's interior after a fire in 1595.

🖾 **Portale di San Ranieri**

Frieze
This indicates that work began on the tower in 1173.

🖾 **Duomo Pulpit**
The carved supports for Giovanni Pisano's pulpit (1302–11) symbolize the Arts and Virtues.

Campo Santo ▶

🖾 **Duomo façade**

Carrara Marble
The Duomo's walls are decorated with horizontal layers of white and gray marble.

Twelfth-century Wall Tomb
Buscheto, the Duomo's original architect, is buried in the last blind arch on the left side of the façade.

Baptistry ▶
The Baptistry started life as a Romanesque structure (1153), but it has a Gothic dome. The plain interior has a Gothic pulpit and baptismal font.

Campo Santo Memorial ▶

Portale di San Ranieri ▶
Bonanno Pisano's bronze panels for the Duomo's south transept doors depict the life of Christ. Palm trees and Moorish buildings show Arabic influence.

Cathedral and Baptistry, Florence

Rising above the heart of the city, this richly decorated cathedral (Santa Maria del Fiore) and its massive dome have become Florence's most famous symbols. Typical of the Florentine determination to lead in all things, the cathedral is still the Tuscan city's tallest building, and Europe's fourth-largest church. The Baptistry, with its celebrated bronze doors and host of mosaic panels inside, is one of Florence's oldest buildings. The Campanile, designed by Giotto in 1334, was finally completed in 1359, 22 years after his death.

Sir John Hawkwood, by Paolo Uccello, in the cathedral

THE CATHEDRAL WORKS MUSEUM

This informative museum consists of a series of rooms dedicated to the history of the cathedral. The main ground floor room contains statues from Arnolfo di Cambio's workshop, which once occupied the cathedral's niches. Nearby is Donatello's *St. John,* and Michelangelo's *Pietà* can be seen on the staircase. The upper floor contains two choir lofts from the 1430s by Luca della Robbia and Donatello. The haunting statue *La Maddalena* is also by Donatello.

EAST DOORS OF THE BAPTISTRY

Lorenzo Ghiberti's famous bronze **Baptistry** doors were commissioned in 1401 to mark the city's deliverance from the plague. Ghiberti was chosen for the project after a competition involving seven leading artists of the day, including Donatello, Jacopo della Quercia, and Brunelleschi. The trial panels by Ghiberti and Brunelleschi are so different from the Florentine Gothic art of the time, notably in the use of perspective and individuality of figures, that they are often regarded as the first works of the Renaissance. Michelangelo enthusiastically dubbed the **East Doors** the "Gate of Paradise." Ghiberti worked on them from 1424 to 1452, after spending 21 years on the **North Doors.** The original relief panels are now on display in the Museo dell'Opera del Duomo.

BRUNELLESCHI'S DOME

A stunning feat of technical as well as artistic skill, the cathedral's **dome** is the epitome of Florentine Renaissance architecture (*Renaissance Style, see p.131*). Construction took more than 14 years, and only began after a lengthy period of planning and model-building, during which the dome's architect, Filippo Brunelleschi (1377–1446), worked hard to convince the sceptics that the project was feasible. At one point, he even built a large-scale model by the river to demonstrate that the dome was technically achievable. The dome spans 140 ft (43 m) and is not buttressed; instead, a double wall of spirally laid bricks was strengthened by the use of stone chains. Despite his brilliance as an engineer and architect, Brunelleschi was not made chief architect until 1445, a year before his death.

▲ **Campanile**
At 278 ft (85 m), the Campanile is 20 ft (6 m) shorter than the dome. It is clad in white, green, and pink Tuscan marble.

◄ **Chapels at the East End**
The three apses have five chapels each and are crowned by smaller copies of the dome. The 15th-century stained glass is by Ghiberti.

North Doors

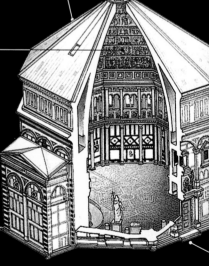

◄ **Baptistry**
Colorful 13th-century mosaics depicting the *Last Judgment* decorate the ceiling above the octagonal font, where many famous Florentines, including Dante, were baptized. The doors are by Andrea Pisano (south) and Lorenzo Ghiberti (north and east).

KEY DATES

c. 1059–1150	1294–1302	1334–59	1875–87	1982
Probable construction of the current Baptistry in the Florentine Romanesque style.	Building work begins on the cathedral, to a design by Arnolfo di Cambio.	The Campanile is built, supervised by Giotto, Andrea Pisano and Francesco Talenti.	The Neo-Gothic façade is added, designed by Emilio de Fabris and Augustino Conti.	The cathedral and Baptistry are declared a UNESCO World Heritage Site.

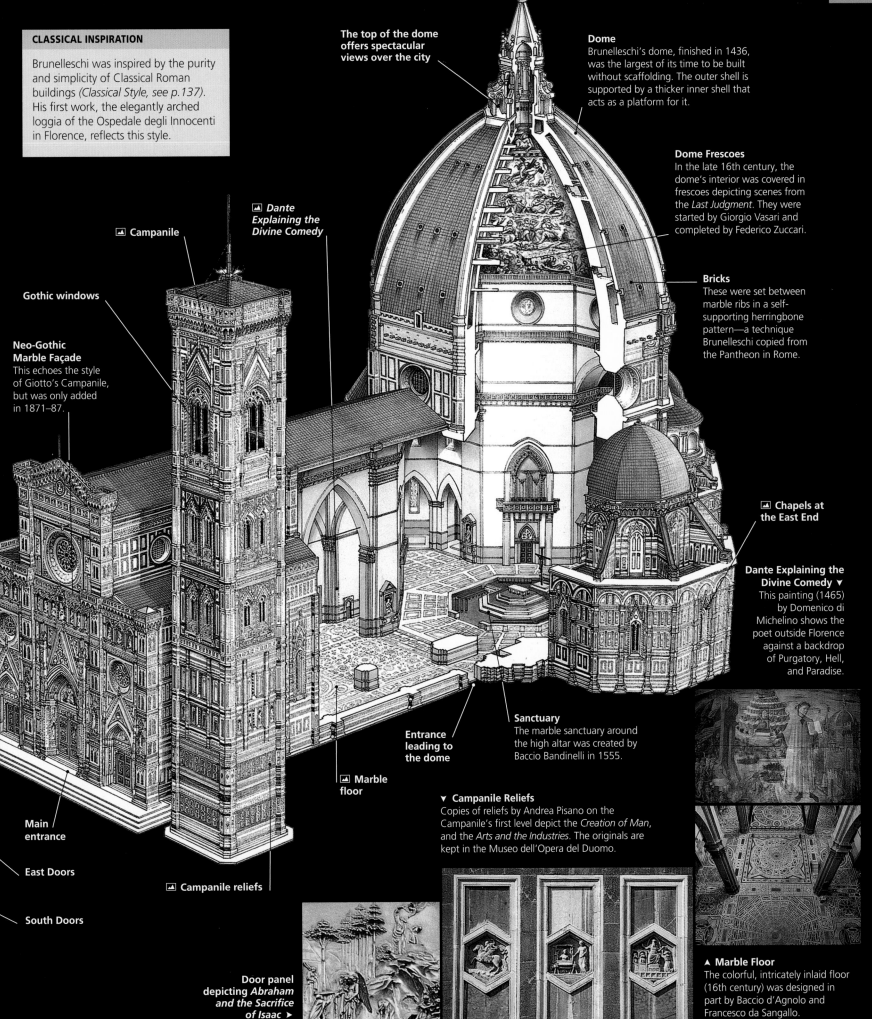

CLASSICAL INSPIRATION

Brunelleschi was inspired by the purity and simplicity of Classical Roman buildings *(Classical Style, see p.137)*. His first work, the elegantly arched loggia of the Ospedale degli Innocenti in Florence, reflects this style.

The top of the dome offers spectacular views over the city

Dome
Brunelleschi's dome, finished in 1436, was the largest of its time to be built without scaffolding. The outer shell is supported by a thicker inner shell that acts as a platform for it.

Dome Frescoes
In the late 16th century, the dome's interior was covered in frescoes depicting scenes from the *Last Judgment*. They were started by Giorgio Vasari and completed by Federico Zuccari.

Bricks
These were set between marble ribs in a self-supporting herringbone pattern—a technique Brunelleschi copied from the Pantheon in Rome.

🖾 **Campanile**

🖾 *Dante Explaining the Divine Comedy*

Gothic windows

Neo-Gothic Marble Façade
This echoes the style of Giotto's Campanile, but was only added in 1871–87.

🖾 **Chapels at the East End**

Dante Explaining the Divine Comedy ▼
This painting (1465) by Domenico di Michelino shows the poet outside Florence against a backdrop of Purgatory, Hell, and Paradise.

Main entrance

East Doors

South Doors

🖾 **Campanile reliefs**

Entrance leading to the dome

Sanctuary
The marble sanctuary around the high altar was created by Baccio Bandinelli in 1555.

🖾 **Marble floor**

▼ **Campanile Reliefs**
Copies of reliefs by Andrea Pisano on the Campanile's first level depict the *Creation of Man*, and the *Arts and the Industries*. The originals are kept in the Museo dell'Opera del Duomo.

Door panel depicting *Abraham and the Sacrifice of Isaac* ►

▲ **Marble Floor**
The colorful, intricately inlaid floor (16th century) was designed in part by Baccio d'Agnolo and Francesco da Sangallo.

Basilica of St. Francis, Assisi

One of the greatest Christian shrines in the world, the Basilica of St. Francis is visited by a vast number of pilgrims throughout the year. It is the burial place of St. Francis, and building work began two years after the saint's death in 1226. Over the following century, its Upper and Lower churches were decorated by the foremost artists of the day, among them Cimabue, Simone Martini, Pietro Lorenzetti, and Giotto, whose frescoes on the *Life of St. Francis* are among the most renowned in Italy.

▲ View of the Basilica and Friary
For centuries, Assisi has been dominated by the humble figure of St. Francis, whose followers have filled the beautiful medieval hilltown with churches, monasteries, and shrines.

◀ Façade
The façade and its rose window are early examples of Italian Gothic architecture.

◀ Lower Church
Side chapels were created here in the 13th century to accommodate the growing number of pilgrims.

◀ Cappella di San Martino
The frescoes in this chapel on the *Life of St. Martin* (1315) are by the Sienese painter Simone Martini. This panel shows the *Death of the Saint*. Martini was also responsible for the fine stained glass in the chapel.

◀ Upper Church

⊞ Upper Church
The soaring Gothic lines *(Gothic Style, see p.54)* of the 13th-century Upper Church symbolize the heavenly glory of St. Francis. This style also influenced later Franciscan churches.

Choir
Built in 1501, this features a 13th-century stone papal throne.

Campanile
This was built in 1239.

⊞ Frescoes by Lorenzetti

Steps to the Treasury

⊞ Lower Church

◀ Frescoes by Lorenzetti
The bold composition of Pietro Lorenzetti's *The Deposition* (1323) is based around the truncated Cross and focuses the viewer's attention on the twisted figure of Christ.

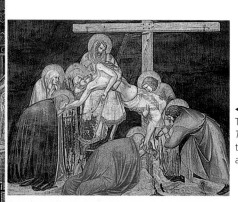

Crypt
This contains the tomb of St. Francis, who was buried here in 1230.

⊞ St. Francis
Cimabue's simple painting (c. 1280) captures the humility of the revered saint.

THE POETRY OF ST. FRANCIS

In order to reach a wide audience, St. Francis preached and wrote in his native tongue, instead of using the Latin texts of the Church of Rome. He wrote simple, lyrical hymns that everyone could understand. In the *Laudes Creaturarum* (Praise of the Creatures), a milestone in Italian vernacular poetry, he praised all of God's creation.

▲ **Frescoes by Giotto**
The Ecstasy of St. Francis is one of 28 panels that make up Giotto's cycle on the *Life of St. Francis* (c. 1290–95).

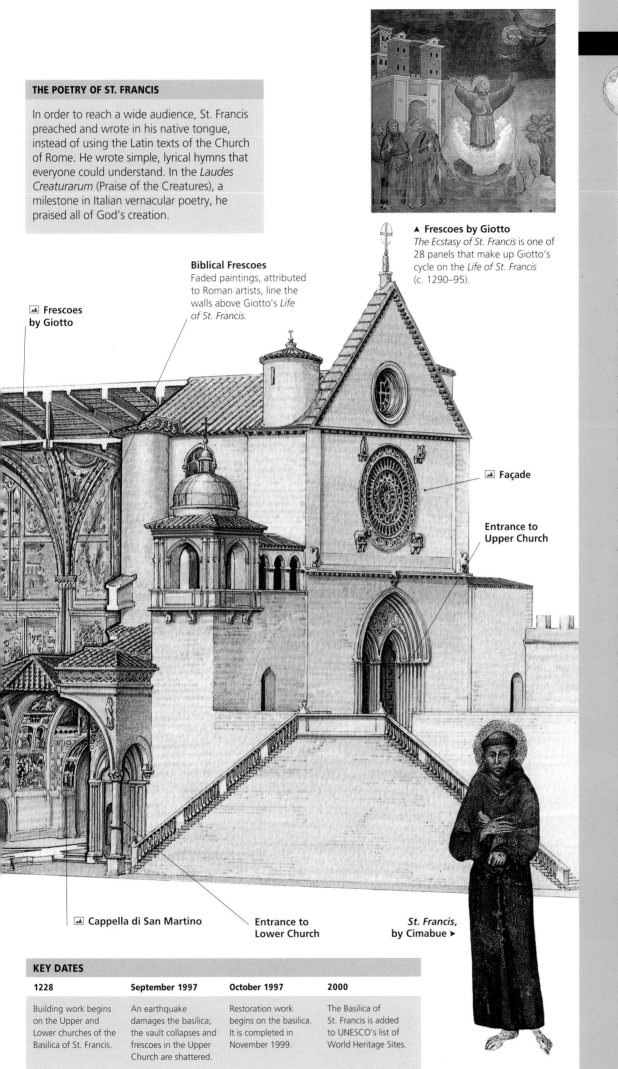

Biblical Frescoes
Faded paintings, attributed to Roman artists, line the walls above Giotto's *Life of St. Francis*.

☑ **Frescoes by Giotto**

☑ **Façade**

Entrance to Upper Church

☑ **Cappella di San Martino**

Entrance to Lower Church

St. Francis, by Cimabue ▶

ST. FRANCIS

The highly revered St. Francis was born in Assisi in 1182 to a rich family. During his mid-20s, he decided to reject his family's wealth and live a life of poverty, chastity, meditation, and prayer. He looked after the sick and extended his care to birds and animals. His humble spirituality soon attracted numerous followers and he established a religious order, the Friars Minor, in 1209. The order was orally recognized by Pope Innocent III the same year, and in 1223, it was officially confirmed by Pope Honorius III. A Franciscan order of nuns, the Poor Clares, was founded in 1215. St. Francis died in Assisi in 1226 and was canonized two years later. He was made the patron saint of Italy in 1939.

THE EARTHQUAKES OF 1997

In 1997, two strong earthquakes hit Umbria, leaving 11 people dead and tens of thousands homeless. A large number of centuries-old buildings were also badly damaged. The eastern part of the province was the most affected, with the basilica in Assisi suffering the worst structural upheaval. In the **Upper Church**, the vaults in the two bays collapsed, shattering ancient frescoes by Cimabue, and others attributed to Giotto. However, the great St. Francis cycle (**frescoes by Giotto**) survived, as did the stained-glass windows. Painstaking restoration followed, and the church reopened to the public in November 1999.

GIOTTO'S FRESCOES

The work of the great Tuscan architect and artist Giotto di Bondone (1267–1337) is often seen as the inspirational starting point for Western painting. He broke away from the ornate, but highly formalized, Byzantine style to visualize naturalness and human emotions, placing three-dimensional figures in convincing settings. The St. Francis cycle was painted "al fresco" by spreading paint onto a thin layer of damp, freshly laid plaster. Pigments were drawn into the plaster by surface tension and the color became fixed as the plaster dried. The pigments reacted with the lime in the plaster to produce strong, rich colors. The technique is not suited to damp climates, but had been used for centuries in hot, dry Italy.

KEY DATES

1228	September 1997	October 1997	2000
Building work begins on the Upper and Lower churches of the Basilica of St. Francis.	An earthquake damages the basilica; the vault collapses and frescoes in the Upper Church are shattered.	Restoration work begins on the basilica. It is completed in November 1999.	The Basilica of St. Francis is added to UNESCO's list of World Heritage Sites.

▲ Outer Wall of the Colosseum

Colosseum, Rome

Rome's great amphitheater was commissioned by the Emperor Vespasian in AD 72 on the marshy site of a lake in the grounds of Nero's palace, the Domus Aurea. Deadly gladiatorial combats and wild animal fights were staged free of charge by the emperor and wealthy citizens for public viewing. The Colosseum was built to a practical design, with its 80 arched entrances allowing easy access for 55,000 spectators, but it is also a building of great Classical beauty *(Classical Style, see p.137)*. The drawing here shows how it looked at the time of its inauguration in AD 80. It was one of several similar amphitheaters built in the Roman Empire, and some survive—at El Djem in North Africa, Nîmes, and Arles in France and Verona in northern Italy. Despite being damaged over the years by neglect and theft, it remains a majestic sight.

Vespasian, founder of the Colosseum

◄ Internal Corridors

Vomitorium
Vomitoria were wide corridors situated below or behind a tier of seats, through which thousands of spectators could file in and out quickly.

⊡ Outer Wall
Stone plundered from the façade during the Renaissance was used to build several palaces and bridges, and part of St. Peter's.

◄ **Beneath the Arena**
In the late 19th century, excavations exposed the network of underground rooms where the animals were kept.

Bollards
These anchored the velarium.

▲ **Looking across the ancient Forum to the Colosseum in Rome**

◄ **Colossus of Nero**
The Colosseum may have acquired its name from this huge gilt-bronze statue, which stood near the amphitheater.

Velarium
This huge awning shaded spectators from the sun. Supported on poles fixed to the upper story of the building, it was hoisted into position with ropes anchored to bollards outside the stadium.

ITALY 129

KEY DATES

AD 72	81–96	248	1980
The Colosseum is commissioned by Emperor Vespasian.	The amphitheater is completed during the reign of Emperor Domitian.	Games are held to mark the 1,000th anniversary of Rome's founding.	Rome's historic center is added to UNESCO's World Heritage list.

A GLADIATOR'S LIFE

Gladiator fights were not mere brawls, but professional affairs between trained men. Gladiators lived and trained in barracks and a range of different fighting styles was practiced, each with its own expert coach. Larger barracks had a training arena where men could get used to fighting in front of noisy spectators.

▲ **Gladiator Graffiti**
Gladiators fought one-to-one, as shown in this graffiti from the Colosseum. A *secutor* gladiator carrying a short sword is pitched against a *retiarius* gladiator armed with a trident and a net.

GLADIATORIAL FIGHTS IN THE ARENA
The emperors of Rome held impressive shows, which often began with animals performing circus tricks. Then, on came the gladiators, who fought each other to the death. Gladiators were usually slaves, prisoners of war, or condemned criminals. When one was killed, attendants dressed as Charon, the mythical ferryman of the dead, carried his body off on a stretcher and sand was raked over the blood in preparation for the next bout. A badly wounded gladiator would surrender his fate to the crowd. The "thumbs-up" sign from the emperor meant he could live, while "thumbs-down" meant that he would die. The victor in a gladiator fight became an instant hero and was sometimes rewarded with freedom.

EMPEROR VESPASIAN
Titus Flavius Vespasianus (**Founder of the Colosseum**) was Roman emperor for a decade from AD 69. At that time, Rome was in complete disarray, the legacy of Emperor Nero's reign. Vespasian's rule is noted for the stability and relative peace he brought to the empire. He instigated a number of building projects, including a temple dedicated to Claudius on the Celian Hill; a Temple of Peace near the Forum; and, most famously, the Colosseum. At the time of his death in 79, the amphitheater was still incomplete, and it was left to his sons and successors, Titus and Domitian, to finish the work.

INSIDE THE COLOSSEUM
The stadium was built in the form of an ellipse, with tiers of seats around a vast central arena. The different social classes were segregated, and the consul and emperor had their own separate entrances and boxes. A complex of rooms, passages and elevators lay in the subterranean area (**beneath the arena**), and this was where men, animals, and scenery were moved around. Cages for the animals were found at the lowest level, beneath the wooden arena floor. When the animals were needed, the cages were moved upward to the arena by means of winches and the animals were released. A system of ramps and trap doors enabled them to reach the arena.

◪ **Internal Corridors**
These were designed to allow the large and often unruly crowd to move freely and to be seated within 10 minutes of arriving at the Colosseum.

Inner Walls
These were formed of brick.

Entry Routes
Used to take the spectators to their seats, these were reached by means of staircases to the various levels of the amphitheater.

Podium
This large terrace was where the emperor and the wealthy upper classes had their seats.

Corinthian columns

Ionic columns

Doric columns

Arched Entrances
All 80 entrances were numbered. Each spectator had a *tessera* (small square tile) with an entrance number stamped on it.

FLORA OF THE COLOSSEUM

By the 19th century, the Colosseum was heavily overgrown. Different microclimates in various parts of the ruins had created an impressive variety of herbs, grasses, and wild flowers. Several botanists were inspired to study and catalog them and two books were published, one listing 420 different species.

Borage, a herb

St. Peter's Basilica, Rome

Catholicism's most sacred shrine, the sumptuous, marble-clad St. Peter's Basilica draws pilgrims and tourists from all over the world. It holds hundreds of precious works of art, some salvaged from the original 4th-century basilica built by Emperor Constantine, others commissioned from Renaissance and Baroque artists. The dominant tone is set by Bernini, who created the baldacchino twisting up below Michelangelo's huge dome. He also created the cathedra in the apse, with four saints supporting a throne that contains fragments once thought to be relics of the chair from which St. Peter delivered his first sermon.

13th-century mosaic by Giotto, Grottoes

▲ **Piazza San Pietro**
On Sundays, and on special occasions such as religious festivals and canonizations, the pope blesses the crowds from a balcony overlooking Bernini's colonnaded square in front of St. Peter's Basilica.

◄ **Monument to Pope Alexander VII**
Bernini's last work in St. Peter's was finished in 1678 and shows the Chigi pope among the allegorical figures of Truth, Justice, Charity, and Prudence.

◄ **Michelangelo's Pietà**
Protected by glass since an attack in 1972, this beautiful marble sculpture of Mary holding the dead Christ was created in 1499.

▼ **Tomb of Pius XI in the Grottoes**

▣ Dome of St. Peter's
The 448-ft (136.5-m) high Renaissance dome was designed by Michelangelo, although it was not completed in his lifetime.

Two minor cupolas by Vignola (1507–73)

Staircase
537 narrow steps lead to the summit of the dome.

▣ Baldacchino
Commissioned by Pope Urban VIII in 1624, Bernini's extravagant Baroque canopy stands above St. Peter's tomb.

▣ Monument to Pope Alexander VII

▣ Papal Altar

Entrance to Historical Artistic Museum and Sacristy

St. Peter's Basilica is 610 ft (186 m) long

Nave
Markings on the floor of the nave show how other churches compare in length.

▼ **Dome of St. Peter's**

▼ **Baldacchino**

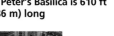

◄ **Papal Altar**
This stands over the crypt where St. Peter is reputedly buried.

ST. PETER

One of the most important and revered saints, Peter was one of the first two disciples of Christ. Peter's apostolate brought him to Rome in AD 44, where he established the Church of Rome. The saint is traditionally associated with two keys, one for Earth and one for heaven.

KEY DATES

AD 64	324	1506	1546	1980
St. Peter is crucified and buried in Rome.	Roman Emperor Constantine builds a basilica over the tomb of St. Peter.	Pope Julius II lays the first stone of a new basilica.	Michelangelo is appointed chief architect.	The properties of the Holy See join the list of UNESCO World Heritage Sites.

Grottoes
A fragment of a 13th-century mosaic by Giotto, salvaged from the old basilica, can be found in the Grottoes, where many popes are buried.

Statue of St. Peter
The extended foot of this 13th-century bronze statue has worn thin and shiny from the touch of pilgrims over the centuries.

Façade Statues
The façade is topped by 13 travertine stone statues depicting Christ, John the Baptist, and 11 of the Apostles.

HISTORICAL PLAN OF ST PETER'S BASILICA

St. Peter was buried in AD 64 in a necropolis near his crucifixion site in the Circus of Nero. Constantine built a basilica on the burial site in 324. In the 15th century, the old church was found to be unsafe and had to be demolished. It was rebuilt in the 16th and 17th centuries. By 1614, the façade was ready, and in 1626 the new church was consecrated.

KEY
- Circus of Nero
- Constantinian
- Renaissance
- Baroque

Michelangelo's *Pietà*

Façade by Carlo Maderno (1614)

▲ **Filarete Doors**
These bronze doors from the old basilica were decorated with biblical reliefs by Filarete between 1439 and 1445.

Holy Door
This entrance is only used in Holy Years.

Main entrance

Atrium by Carlo Maderno

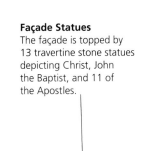

MICHELANGELO
The great Florentine artist, sculptor, architect, poet, and engineer Michelangelo Buonarroti (1475–1564) was one of the towering figures of the Renaissance. One of his very early works, the **Pietà**, a technically accomplished masterpiece produced when he was only 25, is in St. Peter's Basilica. Michelangelo felt that he was primarily a sculptor, but in 1508 he accepted Pope Julius II's commission to paint the ceiling of the Sistine Chapel in the Vatican. When it was completed, in 1512, it was immediately hailed as a masterpiece of the age. In 1546, Michelangelo was appointed chief architect of St. Peter's Basilica and devoted the last decades of his life to the building.

GIANLORENZO BERNINI
This Italian sculptor, architect, set designer, and painter was the outstanding figure of the Baroque era in Italy. Born in Naples in 1598, the son of a sculptor, the young Bernini was quickly acknowledged as having a precocious talent for marble. He became the favorite architect, sculptor, and town planner to three successive popes, and transformed the look of Rome with his churches, palaces, piazzas, statues, and fountains. He worked on various parts of St. Peter's Basilica for more than 57 years.

RENAISSANCE STYLE
Brunelleschi's design for the Ospedale degli Innocenti (1419–24) in Florence, with its Classically inspired slender columns and semicircular arches, ushered in a new era of architecture in Italy. In the following decades, the Renaissance style spread to other urban centers in Italy. The vanguard of the movement relocated to Rome in the late 15th and early 16th centuries. By this point, Renaissance styles had reached most of Europe and even as far as Moscow, via Venice. The Renaissance (or "rebirth") in building design was intended to be rational and humane. Taking inspiration from the principal elements of architecture—square, cube, circle, and sphere—architects began to plan buildings according to mathematical proportions. Streets were widened and planning led to a focus on monuments and fountains.

Pompeii

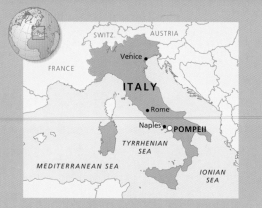

When Mount Vesuvius erupted in AD 79, the town of Pompeii, near modern-day Naples, was complely buried in 20 ft (6 m) of pumice and ash. It was rediscovered in the 16th century, but serious excavation only began in 1748. This amazing find revealed an entire town petrified in time. Houses, temples, works of art, and everyday objects have been unearthed, all in a remarkably good state of preservation, providing a unique insight into everyday life at the height of the Roman Empire.

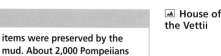

Pompeiian vase in Naples' archeological museum

VILLA OF THE MYSTERIES

This large villa outside Pompeii's city walls, on Via dei Sepolcri, was built in the early 2nd century BC. Initially designed as an urban dwelling, it was later extended into an elegant country house. The villa is famous for its interior decoration and contains a series of well-preserved fresco cycles. The most famous is in the salon and features 29 brightly colored, life-size figures against a red background. They are believed to represent a bride's initiation into the Dionysian mysteries, or a postulant's initiation into the Orphic mysteries. Some scholars say this subject was depicted because the owner was a priestess of the Dionysian cult, which was widespread in southern Italy at the time.

VIA DELL'ABBONDANZA AND VIA STABIANA

Once the liveliest, busiest street in Pompeii, **Via dell'Abbondanza** was lined with private homes and shops selling a wide range of goods. Felt and tanned hide were sold at the shop of Verecundus, and farther along, there is also a well-preserved laundry. Among the inns (thermoplia), the most famous belonged to Asellina, whose obliging foreign waitresses are depicted in graffiti on the wall. The inn still has a record of the proceeds of that fateful day in AD 79: 683 sesterces. The Via Stabiana was a major road, used by carriages traveling between Pompeii and the port and coastal districts. On the west side stood the Stabian Baths.

LIFE IN POMPEII

In the 1st century AD, Pompeii was a prosperous place. Once Etruscan, and later Greek, it was by AD 79 a thriving Roman commercial center, with baths, amphitheaters, temples, and luxurious villas for the wealthy. The **House of Julia Felix** occupies an entire block, divided into the owner's quarters and rented dwellings and shops. The house also had baths, which were open to the public. On the highest spot in Pompeii was the rectangular, paved **Forum**, once the market place. This was the center of public life and the focus for the most important civic functions, both secular and religious. The **Amphitheater** (80 BC) was used for gladiatorial combat and is the oldest of its kind in the world.

VESUVIUS AND THE CAMPANIAN TOWNS

Almost 2,000 years after the eruption of Mount Vesuvius, the Roman towns in its shadow are still being released from the petrification that engulfed them. Pompeii and Stabiae (Castellammare di Stabia), to the southeast of Naples and the volcano, were smothered by hot ash and pumice stone. The roofs of the buildings collapsed under the weight of the volcanic debris. To the west, Herculaneum (Ercolano) vanished under a sea of mud. A large number of its buildings have survived, their roofs intact, and many domestic items were preserved by the mud. About 2,000 Pompeiians perished, but few, if any, of the residents of Herculaneum died.

Much of our knowledge of the daily lives of the ancient Romans derives from the excavations of Pompeii and Herculaneum. Most of the objects from them are now held in Naples' Museo Archeologico Nazionale, creating an outstanding archeological collection. Although Mount Vesuvius has not erupted since 1944, it rumbles occasionally, causing minor earthquakes.

Casts of a mother and child in the archeological museum in Naples

◄ **Scene from the famous fresco cycle in the Villa of the Mysteries**

◄ **Macellum**
Pompeii's marketplace was fronted by a portico with two moneychangers' kiosks.

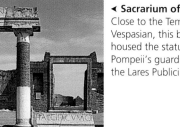

☒ House of the Vettii

House of the Faun

Forum baths

House of the Faun
The famous villa of the wealthy patrician Casii is named after this bronze statuette (right). The mosaic Battle of Alexander, now in the Museo Archeologico Nazionale in Naples, also originated here.

◄ **Sacrarium of the Lares**
Close to the Temple of Vespasian, this building housed the statues of Pompeii's guardian deities, the Lares Publici.

◄ **Amphitheatre and Sports Ground**

▼ **Via dell'Abbondanza**

Villa of the Mysteries

WESTERN POMPEII

This illustration shows part of the western area of Pompeii, where the most impressive and intact Roman ruins are located (*Classical Style, see p.137*). There are several large patrician villas in the eastern area, where some wealthy residents built their homes, but much of eastern Pompeii still awaits excavation.

PLAN OF POMPEII

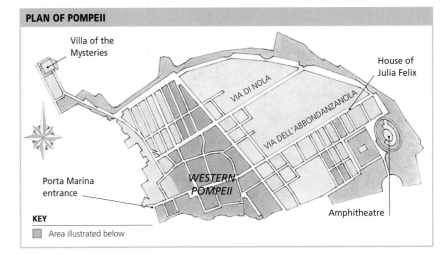

Villa of the Mysteries

VIA DI NOLA

House of Julia Felix

VIA DELL'ABBONDANZANOLA

Porta Marina entrance

WESTERN POMPEII

Amphitheatre

KEY

☐ Area illustrated below

Bakery of Modesto

Thirty-three bakeries have so far been found in Pompeii. The carbonized remains of loaves of bread were found in this one, revealing that the oven was in use at the time of the eruption.

▲ Via dell'Abbondanza

This was one of the original and most important roads through Pompeii. Many houses, shops, and inns lined the route.

▲ Amphitheater and Sports Ground

Situated in the southeastern corner of the town, Pompeii's amphitheater dates to 70 BC. It survived the eruption of Vesuvius almost intact, making it the world's oldest surviving Roman amphitheater.

Teatro Grande

VICOLO DEI VETTI

VIA DELLA FORTUNA

VIA DEGLI AUGUSTALI

VICOLO DEL LUPANARE

VIA DEL FORO

VIA DELL'ABBONDANZA

▲ Cave canem

This "Beware of the Dog" mosaic is from the threshold of a house in Pompeii.

▲ Macellum

▲ Sacrarium of the Lares

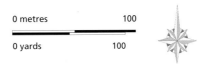

0 metres 100

0 yards 100

Forum

THE ART OF POMPEII

Villas and public areas such as theaters were richly decorated with lively wall frescoes, mosaics, and statues, some of which miraculously survived the eruption. Designs and themes were strongly influenced by late-Classical and Hellenistic art, and clients often commissioned close copies of Greek originals.

◄ House of the Vettii

This partly reconstructed patrician villa of the wealthy merchants Aulus Vettius Conviva and Aulus Vettius Restitutus contains wonderful frescoes.

KEY DATES

c. 8th century BC	August AD 79	1594	1860	1997
Building of Pompeii on an important crossroad by a people from central Italy.	Vesuvius erupts and Pompeii and Stabiae are showered with debris and completely buried for centuries.	Workers digging a trench in the area known as Civita discover traces of the ancient town.	Giuseppe Fiorelli becomes director of excavations; the town is gradually uncovered by archeologists.	The Archeological Area of Pompeii is added to UNESCO's World Heritage list.

Basilica of Euphrasius, Poreč

This 6th-century church, a Byzantine masterpiece *(Byzantine Style, see p.148)*, is decorated with splendid mosaics on a gold background. The Basilica of Euphrasius was constructed for Bishop Euphrasius between 539 and 553 by enlarging the 4th-century Oratory of St. Maurus, one of the earliest Christian religious sites in the world. Over the centuries, the building has undergone several alterations. Some of the original floor mosaics have survived—they were discovered during restoration work in the 19th century.

Mosaic in the apse

ST. MAURUS AND BISHOP EUPHRASIUS

Little is known about the lives of St. Maurus, the first bishop of Poreč, and Bishop Euphrasius. In the 4th century, St. Maurus built an oratory used by early Christians for secret worship. Legend says that he endured a martyr's death during the Roman Emperor Diocletian's persecution of Christians. In the 6th century, his body was transferred from a cemetery near the basilica to the **Votive Chapel**. The influential Bishop Euphrasius sought the best craftsmen for the construction of his basilica and created one of the greatest architectural complexes of the period.

BYZANTINE MOSAIC TECHNIQUE

The art of mosaic, especially in churches, peaked during the Byzantine period. Small, colored glass pieces were inlaid onto the walls, while hard-wearing natural stones and marbles were encrusted into the floors. In the 6th century, mosaicists began to use gold and silver glass tesserae in their designs to reflect the maximum amount of light. Most mosaics depicted biblical scenes or saints, but a few also included images of the builders. Bishop Euphrasius commissioned marvelous Byzantine designs for his basilica. The most impressive is that of the Virgin and Child in the apse, flanked by images of St. Maurus and Euphrasius (**apse mosaics**).

THE INTERIOR

The Basilica of Euphrasius is entered through the **atrium**, which contains traces of the Byzantine mosaics that were restored in the 19th century. Nearby is the **baptistry**, built with a wooden roof in the 5th century and remodeled during the construction of Euphrasius's basilica. Christian converts were baptized in the central font until the 15th century. Inside the basilica, beautiful mosaics, made partly from semi-precious stones and mother-of-pearl, are still visible, especially in the apse and the **ciborium**. Several fires and earthquakes over the centuries have altered the shape of the building; the southern wall of the central nave was destroyed in the 15th century and later rebuilt with Gothic windows *(Gothic Style, see p.54)*. On the western side of the basilica is the Holy Cross Chapel, adorned with a 15th-century polyptych by the Venetian artist Antonio Vivarini.

⊿ Apse Mosaics
Mosaics from the 6th century cover the apse. On the triumphal arch are Christ and the Apostles; on the vault, the Virgin enthroned with Child and two Angels; to the left are St. Maurus, Bishop Euphrasius with a model of the basilica, and Deacon Claud with his son.

⊿ Ciborium
Dominating the presbytery is a beautiful 13th-century ciborium, or canopy, supported by four marble columns. It is decorated with mosaics.

⊿ Sacristy and Votive Chapel
Past the sacristy's left wall is a triple-apsed chapel with a mosaic floor from the 6th century. The remains of saints Maurus and Eleuterius lie here.

Floor Mosaic
The remains of a mosaic floor from the 4th-century oratory can be seen in the church's garden.

▼ Apse Mosaics

▼ Virgin and Child mosaic in the apse

KEY DATES

539–53	1277	1800s	1997
The Basilica of Euphrasius is built on the site of the Oratory of St. Maurus.	A great marble ciborium is built, ordered by Otto, Bishop of Poreč.	Restoration work on the basilica repairs centuries of damage.	The Basilica of Euphrasius is inscribed on UNESCO's World Heritage List.

THE POREČ MUSEUM

Near the Basilica of Euphrasius is the regional museum, which was opened in 1884. It contains more than 2,000 exhibits, including mosaics from as early as the 3rd century, as well as crosses, altarpieces, and choir stalls.

Interior

Atrium
This has a roughly square portico with two columns on each side. Tombstones and a variety of archeological finds dating from the medieval period are displayed in this area.

Baptistry

▼ Interior of the Basilica
The entrance leads to a large church with a central nave and two side aisles. The 18 marble columns are topped by Byzantine and Romanesque capitals carved with depictions of animals. All bear the monogram of Euphrasius.

Sacristy and Votive Chapel ▶

▼ Baptistry
This octagonal building dates from the 6th century. In the center is a baptismal font and there are also fragments of mosaic. To the rear rises a 16th-century bell tower.

Atrium ▶

Ciborium ▼

Bishop's Palace
A triple-aisled building dating from the 6th century, this now houses several paintings by Antonio da Bassano, a polyptych by Antonio Vivarini, and a painting by Palma il Giovane.

Acropolis, Athens

In the mid-5th century BC, the Athenian statesman Perikles persuaded the Athenians to begin a program of building work that has come to represent the political and cultural achievements of ancient Greece. Three new contrasting temples were built on the Acropolis, together with a monumental gateway. The Theater of Dionysos on the south slope was developed further in the 4th century BC, and the Theater of Herodes Atticus was added in the 2nd century AD.

▲ The Acropolis today
The Acropolis provides a stunning backdrop to the modern city of Athens and is Greece's most visited site. Having survived earthquakes, fires, and wars for over 2,500 years, today its monuments are under threat from the atmospheric pollution that is slowly softening their marble.

Moschophoros,
Acropolis Museum

◄ Porch of the Caryatids

▼ Propylaia

◄ Temple of Athena Nike
This temple to Athena of Victory is on the west side of the Propylaia. It was built in 426–421 BC.

◄ Theater of Dionysos, figure of the comic satyr Silenus

▼ Sculpture on the east pediment of the Parthenon

🖼 Porch of the Caryatids
These statues of women were used in place of columns on the south porch of the Erechtheion. The originals, four of which are now in the Acropolis Museum, have been replaced by casts.

Olive Tree
In Greek mythology, Athena and Poseidon competed to be patron deity of Athens. Athena won by giving the gift of an olive tree. Today, a olive tree grows on the spot where she planted hers.

🖼 Propylaia
This was built in 437–432 BC to form a new entrance to the Acropolis.

🖼 Temple of Athena Nike

Beulé Gate
This was the first entrance to the Acropolis.

◄ Theatre of Herodes Atticus
Also known as the Odeion of Herodes Atticus, this superb theater was originally built in AD 161. It was restored in 1955 and is used today for outdoor concerts.

LOCATOR MAP

KEY

▓ Area illustrated below

Acropolis Museum
Built in 1878, the museum is located on the southeastern corner of the site. It exhibits stone sculptures from the Acropolis monuments and artifacts from on-site excavations.

⛰ Parthenon
Although few sculptures are left on this famous temple to Athena, some can still be admired, including those on the east pediment.

Two Corinthian Columns
These are the remains of monuments erected by sponsors of successful dramatic performances.

Panagía Spiliótissa
This chapel is set in a cave in the Acropolis rock.

▼ Theatre of Dionysos
The theater seen today was built by Lykourgos in 342–326 BC. A figure of the comic satyr Silenus can be seen here.

Shrine of Asklepios

Stoa of Eumenes

Acropolis Rock
As the highest part of the city, the rock is an easily defended site. It has been inhabited for almost 5,000 years.

KEY DATES

3000 BC	510 BC	451–429 BC	AD 267	1987
The first of the settlements is built on the Acropolis.	The Delphic Oracle declares the Acropolis a holy place of the gods.	A lavish building program is begun by Perikles.	Much of the Acropolis is destroyed by the Germanic Heruli tribe.	UNESCO inscribes the Acropolis as a World Heritage Site.

ACROPOLIS MUSEUM

The museum is devoted to finds from the Acropolis. Divided chronologically, the collection begins with 6th-century BC works that include fragments of painted pedimental statues, such as *Moschophoros*, or Calf-Bearer, a young man carrying a calf on his shoulders (c. 570 BC). Two rooms house a unique group of *korai* (votive statues of maidens offered to Athena) from c. 500 BC. The *korai* illustrate the development of ancient Greek art—moving from the formal bearing of the *Peplos Kore* to the more natural body movement of the *Almond-Eyed Kore*. The museum's collection ends with the original four caryatids from the south porch of Erechtheion (**Porch of the Caryatids**).

THE PARTHENON

Built as an expression of the glory of Athens, this temple (**Parthenon**) was designed to house a 40-ft (12-m) high statue of Athena Parthenos (Maiden) sculpted by Pheidias. Taking nine years to complete, the building was finally dedicated to the goddess in 438 BC. The temple was 230 ft (70 m) long and 100 ft (30 m) wide, with a striking red, blue, and gold entablature. The sculptors used visual tricks to counteract the laws of perspective, making the building completely symmetrical. Over the centuries, it has served as a church, a mosque, and an arsenal.

CLASSICAL STYLE

At the heart of Greek architecture were the Classical "orders"—the types and styles of columns and the forms of structures and decoration that followed on from them. Of these, Doric is the earliest; the column has no base, a fluted shaft, and a plain capital. The Ionic column is a lighter development from the Doric; the fluted shaft has a base and a volute capital. The Corinthian, with its plinth and fluted shaft, is a variant of the Ionic and distinctive in its ornate capital. The capitals of the columns were representations of natural forms, as in the rams' horns of the Ionic or the stylized acanthus leaves of the Corinthian. Other architectural features included pediments (triangular structures crowning the front of the temples), caryatids (sculptures used as columns), and friezes of relief sculptures, used to adorn exteriors.

Statues adorning the south porch of the
Erectheion on the Acropolis, Athens

Monastery of St. John, Pátmos

The Monastery of St. John is one of the most important places of worship for Orthodox and Western Christians alike. It was founded in 1088 by a monk, the Blessed Christodoulos, in honor of St. John the Divine, author of the Bible's *Book of Revelation*. One of the richest and most influential monasteries in Greece, its towers and buttresses make it look like a fairy-tale castle, but were built to protect its religious treasures, which are now the star attraction for the thousands of pilgrims and tourists who visit every year.

▲ The Hospitality of Abraham
This is one of the most important of the 12th-century frescoes that were found in the chapel of the Panagía.

ST. JOHN AND THE HOLY CAVE

Inside the church of Agía Anna, near the Monastery of St. John, is the **Holy Cave of the Apocalypse**. It was here that St. John had the vision of fire and brimstone that inspired the New Testament's *Book of Revelation*. The cave contains the rock where John dictated his vision to his disciple, Próchoros, and the indentation where the saint is said to have rested his head each night. Also visible is the cleft in the rock from where the voice of God is said to have spoken to John. The cave also has 12th-century wall paintings and icons from 1596 of St. John and the Blessed Christodoulos by the Cretan painter Thomás Vathás.

◄ Holy Cave of the Apocalypse, where St. John lived and worked

THE BLESSED CHRISTODOULOS

The Christian monk Christodoulos (slave of Christ) was born around 1020 in Asia Minor. He spent much of his life building monasteries on several Greek islands. He was given permission by the Byzantine Emperor Alexios I Comnenos (r. 1081–1118) to build a temple on Pátmos, in honor of the Apostles. Christodoulos laid the foundation stone for the Monastery of St. John, but died in 1093 before it was completed. His remembrance celebrations are held each year in Pátmos on March 16 and October 21.

Kitchens

Monks' Refectory
This room contains two marble tables taken from the Temple of Artemis, which originally occupied the site.

▲ Chrysobull

▼ Main Courtyard

THE TREASURY

Also known as the library, the **treasury** contains a vast and important collection of theological and Byzantine works. There is a central room, decorated with plastered arches supported by stone columns, off which lie other rooms displaying religious artifacts. Priceless icons and sacred art, including vestments, chalices, and Benediction crosses, can be viewed. Floor-to-ceiling bookcases, built into the walls, store religious manuscripts and biographical materials, many written on parchment. Manuscripts of note include the *Book of Job*, sermons by St. George the Theologue, the Purple Code, and a 14th-century volume containing images of the Evangelists entitled *Gospel of Four*. The treasury also possesses 15th- to 18th-century embroidered stools and mosaics, as well as beautiful 17th-century furnishings. There are also garments worn by past bishops, some woven in gold thread.

▲ Icon of St. John
This 12th-century icon is the most revered in the monastery and is housed in the *katholikon*, the monastery's main church.

▼ Monastery of St. John above the village of Chóra

▼ Chapel of the Holy Cross

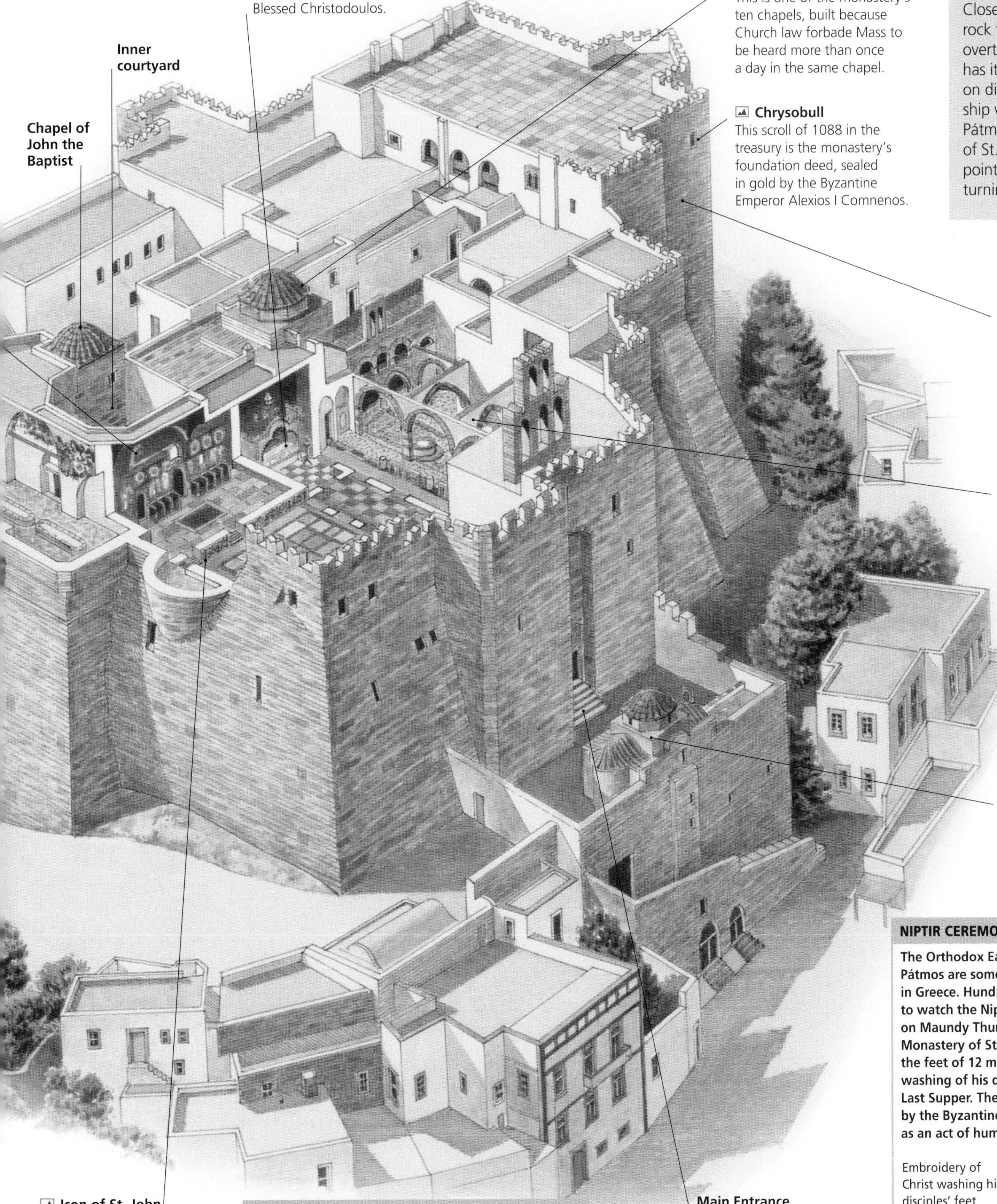

Chapel of Christodoulos
This contains the tomb and silver reliquary of the Blessed Christodoulos.

Inner courtyard

Chapel of John the Baptist

🖼 **Chapel of the Holy Cross**
This is one of the monastery's ten chapels, built because Church law forbade Mass to be heard more than once a day in the same chapel.

🖼 **Chrysobull**
This scroll of 1088 in the treasury is the monastery's foundation deed, sealed in gold by the Byzantine Emperor Alexios I Comnenos.

SHIP OF STONE

Close to Pátmos is a rock that resembles an overturned ship. Legend has it that Christodoulos, on discovering that a pirate ship was on its way to Pátmos, seized an icon of St. John the Divine and pointed it at the ship, turning it to stone.

Treasury
This houses more than 200 icons, 300 pieces of silverware, and a dazzling collection of jewels.

🖼 **Main Courtyard**
Frescoes of St. John from the 18th century adorn the outer narthex of the *katholikon*, whose arcades form an integral part of the courtyard.

Chapel of the Holy Apostles
This chapel lies just outside the monastery's gate.

NIPTIR CEREMONY

The Orthodox Easter celebrations on Pátmos are some of the most important in Greece. Hundreds of people visit Chóra to watch the Niptír (washing) ceremony on Maundy Thursday. The abbot of the Monastery of St. John publicly washes the feet of 12 monks, reenacting Christ's washing of his disciples' feet before the Last Supper. The rite was once performed by the Byzantine emperors as an act of humility.

Embroidery of Christ washing his disciples' feet

🖼 **Icon of St. John**

KEY DATES

1088	1999
The Monastery of St. John is constructed, with a heavily fortified exterior.	The Monastery of St. John and the Holy Cave of the Apocalypse are inscribed as a UNESCO World Heritage Site.

Main Entrance
This 17th-century gateway leads up to the cobbled main courtyard. Its walls have slits for pouring boiling oil over marauders.

Palace of the Grand Masters, Rhodes

Built in the 14th century by the Knights of Rhodes, who occupied Rhodes from 1309 to 1522, this fortress within a fortress was the seat of 19 Grand Masters, the nerve center of the Collachium, or Knights' Quarter, and the final refuge for Rhodes' citizens in times of danger. It was destroyed by an accidental explosion in 1856 and restored by the Italians in the early 20th century as a residence for Mussolini and King Victor Emmanuel III. The palace contains some priceless mosaics from sites in Kos, after which some of the rooms are named. It also houses two exhibitions—Ancient Rhodes and Medieval Rhodes.

Gilded angel candle-holder in the palace

▲ **Medusa Chamber**
The mythical Gorgon Medusa, with her hair of writhing serpents, forms the centerpiece of this important late-Hellenistic mosaic. The chamber also features Chinese and Islamic vases.

Central Courtyard

🖼 **Chamber with Colonnades**
An Early Christian mosaic from the 5th century AD decorates the floor of this room. Two elegant colonnades support the roof.

Thyrsus Chamber

🖼 **Battlements**
The palace's heavy fortifications were designed to be the last line of defense in the event of the city walls being breached.

Entrance to Ancient Rhodes exhibition

Second Cross-Vaulted Chamber
Once used as the governor's office, this room is paved with an intricately decorated mosaic from Kos that dates from the 5th century AD.

First Cross-Vaulted Chamber

🖼 **Medusa Chamber**

🖼 **Main Gate**

Entrance

🖼 **Laocoön Chamber**
A copy of the "Laocoön" group, a famous sculpture depicting the deaths of the Trojan priest Laocoön and his two sons, dominates this hall. The original, created by Rhodian artists Athenodoros, Agesandra and Polydoros in the 1st century AD, is in Rome's Vatican Museum.

Second Chamber
This contains a late-Hellenistic mosaic and carved choir stalls.

Grand Staircase

First Chamber
This room has a late-Hellenistic mosaic and 16th-century choir stalls.

Entrance to Medieval Rhodes exhibition

Chamber of the Nine Muses
Busts of the Nine Muses of Greek mythology can be seen in the mosaic on this room's floor.

THE KNIGHTS OF THE ORDER

Men were drawn from noble Roman Catholic families all over Europe to join the Order of the Knights of St. John; however, there were never more than 600 knights at any one time. Those who entered the order swore vows of chastity, obedience, and poverty.

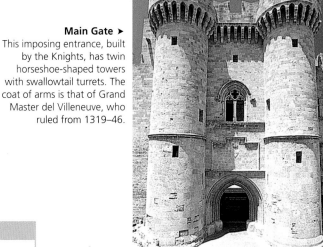

Main Gate ➤
This imposing entrance, built by the Knights, has twin horseshoe-shaped towers with swallowtail turrets. The coat of arms is that of Grand Master del Villeneuve, who ruled from 1319–46.

▼ Battlements

THE FIRST GRAND MASTER

Foulkes de Villaret (1305–19), a French knight, was the first Grand Master. He negotiated to buy Rhodes from the Lord of the Dodecanese, Admiral Vignolo de Vignoli, in 1306. This left the Knights with the task of conquering the island's in-habitants. The Knights of Rhodes, as they became known, remained here until their expulsion in 1522. The Villaret name lives on in Villaré, one of the island's white wines.

Foulkes de Villaret

Central Courtyard ➤
Hellenistic statues taken from the Odeion in Kos line the Central Courtyard. Its north side is paved with geometric marble tiles.

The Knights Street (Odhos Ippoton) ➤
This cobbled medieval street leads to the palace. Along its length are the most important public and private buildings erected by the Knights.

▲ Chamber with Colonnades

KEY DATES

1300s	1856	1937–40	1988
The Palace of the Grand Masters is constructed by the Knights of Rhodes.	The palace is accidentally demolished by a gunpowder explosion.	The building is restored by Italian architect Vittorio Mesturino.	The Medieval City of Rhodes, including the Palace of the Grand Masters, is inscribed as a UNESCO World Heritage Site.

▲ Laocoön Chamber

MOSAIC FLOORS AND STATUES FROM KOS

During the restoration of the palace, beautiful Hellenistic, Roman, and Early Christian mosaics were taken from buildings on the nearby island of Kos and used to rebuild the palace's floors, including those of the **Chamber with Colonnades** and the **Medusa Chamber**. The magnificent statues displayed in the **Central Courtyard** were also brought in from Kos; they date from the Hellenistic and Roman periods.

THE KNIGHTS OF RHODES

Founded in the 11th century by merchants from Amalfi, the Order of Knights Hospitallers of St. John guarded the Holy Sepulcher and defended Christian pilgrims in Jerusalem. They became a military order after the First Crusade (1096–9), but took refuge in Cyprus in 1291 when Jerusalem fell to the Muslim Mamelukes. They then bought Rhodes from the Genoese and conquered the Rhodians in 1309. A Grand Master was elected for life to govern the order, which was divided into seven Tongues, or nationalities: France, Italy, England, Germany, Spain, Provence, and Auvergne. Each Tongue protected an area of the city wall known as a Curtain. The Knights built some fine examples of medieval military architecture, including 30 castles in Greece's Dodecanese islands.

EXHIBITIONS

The Ancient Rhodes exhibition is situated off the **Central Courtyard** in the north wing of the palace. Its marvelous collection is a result of 45 years of archeological investigation on the island, and includes vases and figurines—dating from the prehistoric period up to the founding of the city in 408/7 BC—excavated from the Minoan site at Trianda. Also on display are jewelry, pottery, and grave stelae from the tombs of Kamiros, Lindos, and Ialysos, which date from the 8th and 9th centuries BC. In the south and west wings is the splendid **Medieval Rhodes exhibition**. Covering the 4th century AD to the city's conquest by the Ottoman Turks in 1522, the displays here provide an insight into trade and everyday life in Rhodes in Byzantine and medieval times, with Byzantine icons, Italian and Spanish ceramics, armor, and military memorabilia on view.

Topkapı Palace, Istanbul

The official residence of the Ottoman sultans for more than 400 years, the magnificent Topkapı Palace was built by Mehmet II between 1459 and 1465, shortly after his conquest of Constantinople (now Istanbul). It was not conceived as a single building, but rather as a series of pavilions contained by four enormous courtyards, a stone version of the tented encampments from which the nomadic Ottomans had emerged. Initially, Topkapı served as the seat of government and contained a school in which civil servants and soldiers were trained. However, the government was moved to the Sublime Porte in Istanbul in the 16th century. Sultan Abdül Mecid I left Topkapı in 1853 in favor of Dolmabahçe Palace. In 1924, two years after the sultanate was abolished, the palace was opened to the public as a museum.

Seventh-century jewel-encrusted jug, Treasury

LIFE IN THE HAREM

The word "harem" derives from the Arabic for "forbidden." It was the residence of the sultan's wives, concubines, children, and mother (the most powerful woman), who were guarded by black slave eunuchs. The sultan and his sons were the only other men allowed into the harem. The concubines were slaves, gathered from the farthest corners of the Ottoman empire and beyond. Their goal was to become a favorite of the sultan and bear him a son. Competition was stiff, for at its height a harem had more than 1,000 women. Topkapı's **harem** was laid out by Murat III in the 16th century. The last women left in 1909.

MEHMET II

Capturing the strategically important city of Constantinople from the Byzantines in 1453 was one of Mehmet II's greatest achievements and a turning point in the development of the Ottoman empire. Mehmet (1432–81) was the son of Murat II and a slave girl. He became known as "the conqueror," not only for taking Constantinople, but also for his successful campaigns in the Balkans, Hungary, the Crimea, and elsewhere. In 30 years as sultan, he rebuilt his new capital, reorganized the government, codified the law and set up colleges that excelled in mathematics and astronomy.

PALACE COLLECTIONS

On display throughout the palace are the glittering treasures amassed by the Ottoman sultans during their 470-year reign. In addition to diplomatic gifts and items commissioned from palace craftsmen, many objects were booty brought back from military campaigns. The **kitchens** contain cauldrons and utensils used to prepare food for the 12,000 residents, and Chinese porcelain carried along the Silk Route. The **Treasury** holds thousands of precious and semiprecious stones: highlights include the bejeweled Topkapı dagger (1741), and the 86-carat Spoonmaker's diamond. Mehmet II's sumptuous silk kaftan is among the imperial costumes in the **Hall of the Campaign Pages**. In the **Pavilion of the Holy Mantle** are some of the holiest relics of Islam, such as the mantle once worn by the Prophet Mohammed.

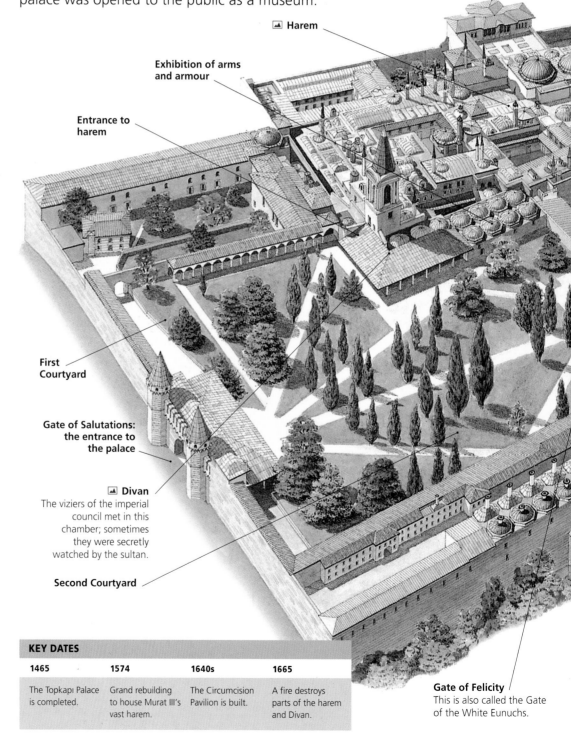

◢ **Harem**

Exhibition of arms and armour

Entrance to harem

First Courtyard

Gate of Salutations: the entrance to the palace

◢ **Divan**
The viziers of the imperial council met in this chamber; sometimes they were secretly watched by the sultan.

Second Courtyard

Gate of Felicity
This is also called the Gate of the White Eunuchs.

KEY DATES			
1465	**1574**	**1640s**	**1665**
The Topkapı Palace is completed.	Grand rebuilding to house Murat III's vast harem.	The Circumcision Pavilion is built.	A fire destroys parts of the harem and Divan.

▲ Iftariye Pavilion
Under the golden roof of this pavilion, Sultan Ahmed III awarded gold coins to those who had entertained him during a festival to honor the circumcision of his sons in 1720.

◄ Harem
This was a labyrinth of exquisite rooms where the sultan's wives and concubines lived.

▼ Divan

THE CAGE

A new sultan would order the execution of his brothers to avoid succession contests. From the 17th century, brothers were spared, but were incarcerated in the notorious "Cage," a set of rooms in the harem.

Circumcision Pavilion

Exhibition of clocks

Pavilion of the Holy Mantle

Throne room

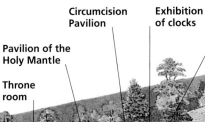

⛰ Baghdad Pavilion

Exhibition of miniatures and manuscripts

The Fourth Courtyard is a series of gardens dotted with pavilions

Third Courtyard

⛰ Treasury

Baghdad Pavilion ►
In 1639, Murat IV built this pavilion to celebrate his capture of Baghdad. Its walls have exquisite blue-and-white tile work.

Hall of the Campaign Pages

Kitchens
These now contain an exhibition of ceramics, glass, and silverware.

Library of Ahmet III ►
Erected in 1719, the library is an elegant marble building. This ornamental fountain is set into the wall below its main entrance.

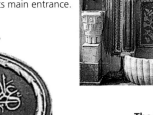

Süleyman I's tuğra (monogram) ►

The harem's Imperial Hall, used for staging entertainments ►

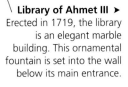

The magnificent interior of Haghia
Sophia, Istanbul

Haghia Sophia, Istanbul

Print of Haghia Sophia from the mid-19th century

The "Church of the Holy Wisdom," Haghia Sophia is among the world's greatest architectural achievements. More than 1,400 years old, it stands as a testament to the sophistication of 6th-century Constantinople, and had a huge influence on architecture in the centuries that followed. The vast edifice was built over two earlier churches and inaugurated by the Byzantine emperor Justinian I in 537. In the 15th century, the Ottomans converted it into a mosque: the minarets, tombs, and fountains date from this period. To help support the structure's great weight, the exterior has been buttressed on numerous occasions, which has partly obscured its original shape.

THE GROUND FLOOR

The interior of Haghia Sophia succeeds in imparting a truly celestial feel. Highlights include the fine Byzantine **mosaics**, mostly dating from the 9th century or later. The most conspicuous features at ground level are those added by the Ottoman sultans after the conquest of Istanbul in 1453, when the church was converted into a mosque. These comprise the *mihrab*, a niche indicating the direction of Mecca; the *minbar*, a platform used by the *imam* to deliver sermons; the **Sultan's loge**, a safe place in which the sultan could pray; and the **Kürsü**, a throne used by the *imam* while reading from the Koran.

UPPER WALLS AND DOME MOSAICS

The apse is dominated by a large and striking mosaic showing the Virgin with the infant Jesus on her lap. Two other mosaics, unveiled in 867, depict the archangels Gabriel and Michael, although only fragments of the latter remain. Portraits of the saints Ignatius the Younger, John Chrysostom, and Ignatius Theophorus adorn niches in the north tympanum. In a concave area at the base of the dome is a mosaic of the six-winged **seraphim**. The dome is decorated with Koranic inscriptions (**calligraphic roundels**). It was once covered in gold mosaic tiles.

BYZANTINE STYLE

When Emperor Constantine I (r. 306–337) chose Byzantium for his capital and renamed it Constantinople, he amassed artists, architects, and craftsmen to build his new imperial city. They came mainly from Rome, bringing with them an Early Christian style. Eastern influences were added to this and a distinct Byzantine style evolved. Churches, once based on a longitudinal design, became centralized—as at Haghia Sophia—with an eastern apse and three aisles. Mosaics depicting angels, archangels and saints, in hierarchical order, covered the interiors and the Virgin Mary would be pictured in one of the domes. Figures were front-on, with large, penetrating eyes, and set against a gold background. Sculpture took the form of small relief carvings, rather than figures. The Byzantines were also sophisticated metalworkers, producing bronze church doors inlaid with silver.

WEEPING PILLAR

Crowds often gather around the pillar of St. Gregory the Miracle-Worker in the northwest corner of the ground floor. Moisture seeping from this brass-clad column is believed to have healing powers.

 Byzantine Frieze
Among the ruins of the monumental entrance to the second church on the site (dedicated in AD 415) is a frieze of sheep.

Nave

Kürsü

Imperial Gate

Buttress

Entrance

Outer narthex

Inner narthex

Galleries
These were originally used by women during services.

KEY DATES

360	532	1453	1934
Inauguration of the first Haghia Sophia on the site. A bigger church is built in 415; it burns down in 532.	Anthemius of Tralles and Isidore of Miletus are commisioned to build a new church.	After conquering Constantinople, the Ottomans convert Haghia Sophia into a mosque.	Haghia Sophia is secularized and turned into a museum.

Mosaics ▶
The church's splendid Byzantine mosaics include this one at the end of the south gallery. It depicts Christ flanked by Emperor Constantine IX and his wife, the Empress Zoe.

▲ **Mausoleum of Selim II**

▲ **Nave**
Visitors cannot fail to be staggered by this vast space, which is covered by a huge dome reaching a height of 184 ft (56 m).

Seraphim
A mosaic of a six-winged angel has recently been uncovered on one of the triangular sections that support the dome.

Caligraphic Roundels ▶
The eight calligraphic roundels—painted wooden plaques—were added in the 19th century.

📷 **Calligraphic roundel**

Sultan's loge

Muezzin mahfili (preacher's pew)

📷 **Mosaics**

Brick minaret

Coronation Square
This square of patterned marble flooring marks the supposed location of the Byzantine emperor's throne.

Library of Sultan Mahmut I

Ablutions Fountain ▶
Built around 1740, this fountain is an exquisite example of Turkish Rococo style. Its projecting roof is painted with floral reliefs.

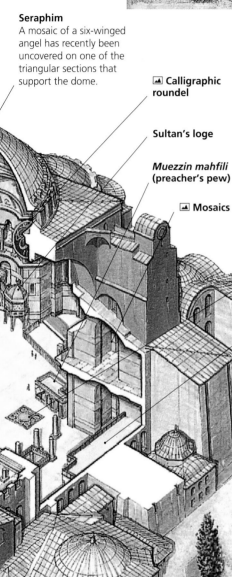

Mausoleum of Mehmet III

📷 **Mausoleum of Selim II**
The oldest of the three mausoleums was completed in 1577 to the plans of Sinan, Süleyman I's imperial architect. Its exquisite interior is entirely covered with Iznik tiles.

Byzantine Frieze ▲

Mausoleum of Murat III
The sultan was buried here in 1599. By the time of his death, he had fathered 103 children.

Exit

Baptistry
Part of the 6th-century church, this now serves as the tomb of two Ottoman sultans.

📷 **Ablutions fountain**

HISTORICAL PLAN OF HAGHIA SOPHIA

Nothing remains of the first 4th-century church on this spot, but there are traces of the second one from the 5th century, which burned down in 532. Earthquakes have taken their toll on the third Haghia Sophia, which has been strengthened and added to many times.

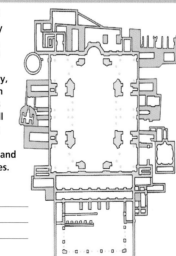

KEY
- 5th-century church
- 6th-century church
- Ottoman additions

Ephesus

One of the best-preserved ancient cities in the world, Ephesus is a fine example of Classical architecture *(Classical Style, see p.137)*. A Greek city was first established here in around 1000 BC and it soon rose to prominence as a center for the worship of Cybele, the Anatolian mother goddess. The city we see today was built by Alexander the Great's successor, Lysimachus, in the 4th century BC. But it was under the Romans that Ephesus became the chief port in the Aegean. Most of the surviving structures date from this period. The city declined when the harbor silted up, but it played an important role in the spread of Christianity. It is said that the Virgin Mary spent her last days nearby, cared for by St. John the Evangelist, and two ecumenical councils of the early Church were held here in AD 431 and 449.

Statue of Artemis in Ephesus Museum

CHURCH OF ST. MARY

Occupying a place of particular significance in the development of Christianity, the Church of St. Mary, located near the entrance to the site, is believed to be the first church in the world dedicated to the Virgin Mary. It was here, in AD 431, that the Council of the Church accepted that Jesus, son of the Virgin Mary, was also the son of God. Used as a warehouse in the Roman era, the long, narrow building has been altered over time and was at one point used for training priests. In the 4th century, it was converted into a basilica with a central nave and two aisles. Later, an apse was created on the eastern wall and, to the western side of the church, a circular baptistry with a central pool was built. Additions dating from the 6th century include a domed chapel situated between the apse and the entrance of the original church.

EPHESUS MUSEUM

The archeological museum at Selçuk, 2 miles (3 km) from the excavations, is one of the most important in Turkey. It contains many of the remarkable artifacts uncovered at Ephesus since World War II. An entire hall is devoted to Artemis, the Greek goddess of chastity, hunting, and the moon. Other exhibits feature marble and bronze statues, ancient frescoes, and wall paintings, jewels, Mycenean vases, gold and silver coins, Corinthian column heads, tombs, bronze and ivory friezes, and the altar from the **Temple of Domitian**.

GENERAL LYSIMACHUS

On the death of Alexander the Great in 323 BC, the Macedonian empire—including Ephesus—was divided among his generals. Lysimachus (360–281 BC) was entrusted with Thrace. He soon added Asia Minor, and in 286 BC he took Ephesus, heralding a new era for the city. It was already a strategic trading port, but the receding coastline and silt-filled harbor threatened its livelihood. Lysimachus first dredged the harbor. Then he moved the city to its present site, fortified it with huge walls and renamed it (for a brief time) Arsinoe, after his third wife. The city soon became densely populated and began to prosper.

▼ **Colonnaded Street**

◄ **Temple of Hadrian**

Private Houses ▲
Murals in the houses opposite the Temple of Hadrian indicate that these were the homes of wealthy Ephesians.

Gate of Hercules ▼
The gate at the entrance to Curetes Street takes its name from two reliefs showing Hercules draped in a lion skin. Originally a two-story structure, and believed to date from the 4th century AD, it had a large central arch with winged victories on the upper corners of the archway. Curetes Street was lined with statues of civic notables.

▼ **Library of Celsus**

← Church of St. Mary

Commercial Agora
This was the city's main market place. Three of its four sides were surrounded by a portico that contained shops.

Skene
The stage building featured elaborate ornamentation.

⊡ Theater
Carved into the flank of Mount Pion during the Hellenistic period, this was designed for theatrical performances. Later alterations by the Romans also allowed gladiatorial contests to be held here.

⊡ Library of Celsus
Built in AD 114–117 by Consul Gaius Julius Aquila for his father, the library was damaged first by the Goths and then by an earthquake in AD 1000. The statues occupying the niches in front are Sophia (Wisdom), Arete (Virtue), Ennoia (Intellect), and Episteme (Knowledge).

Marble Street
This short street, once flanked by columns, is paved with large, uneven marble blocks.

HOUSE OF THE BLESSED VIRGIN

According to the Bible, Jesus asked St. John the Evangelist to care for his mother after his death. John brought Mary with him to Ephesus in AD 37, and she spent the last years of her life here in a modest stone house. The House of the Blessed Virgin is located at Meryemana, 5 miles (8 km) from the center of Ephesus. The shrine, known as the Meryemana Kultur Parkı, is revered by both Christians and Muslims and is a place of pilgrimage, especially around August 15 (Assumption).

Brothel
This was adorned with a statue of Priapus, the Greek god of fertility.

Temple of Hadrian
Built to honor a visit by Emperor Hadrian in AD 123, the relief marble work on the façade portrays mythical gods and goddesses.

A FISH AND A BOAR

According to legend, Androklos asked the oracle at Delphi where he should build his city. He was told, "A fish and a boar will show you the place." When he crossed the Aegean and went ashore to cook a fish, a bush caught fire and a boar ran out. Ephesus was founded on that spot.

⊡ Gate of Hercules

The House of the Blessed Virgin

⊡ Private houses

Odeon
This small roofed theater was built in AD 150. It was used for meetings, and as a concert venue.

⊡ Colonnaded Street
Lined with Ionic and Corinthian columns, this street runs from the Baths of Varius to the Temple of Domitian.

Temple of Domitian
This 1st-century temple was the first at Ephesus to be built in honor of an emperor.

◄ Theater

Baths of Varius

Huge statues of Queen Nefertari and Ramses II on Nefertari's temple at Abu Simbel, Egypt

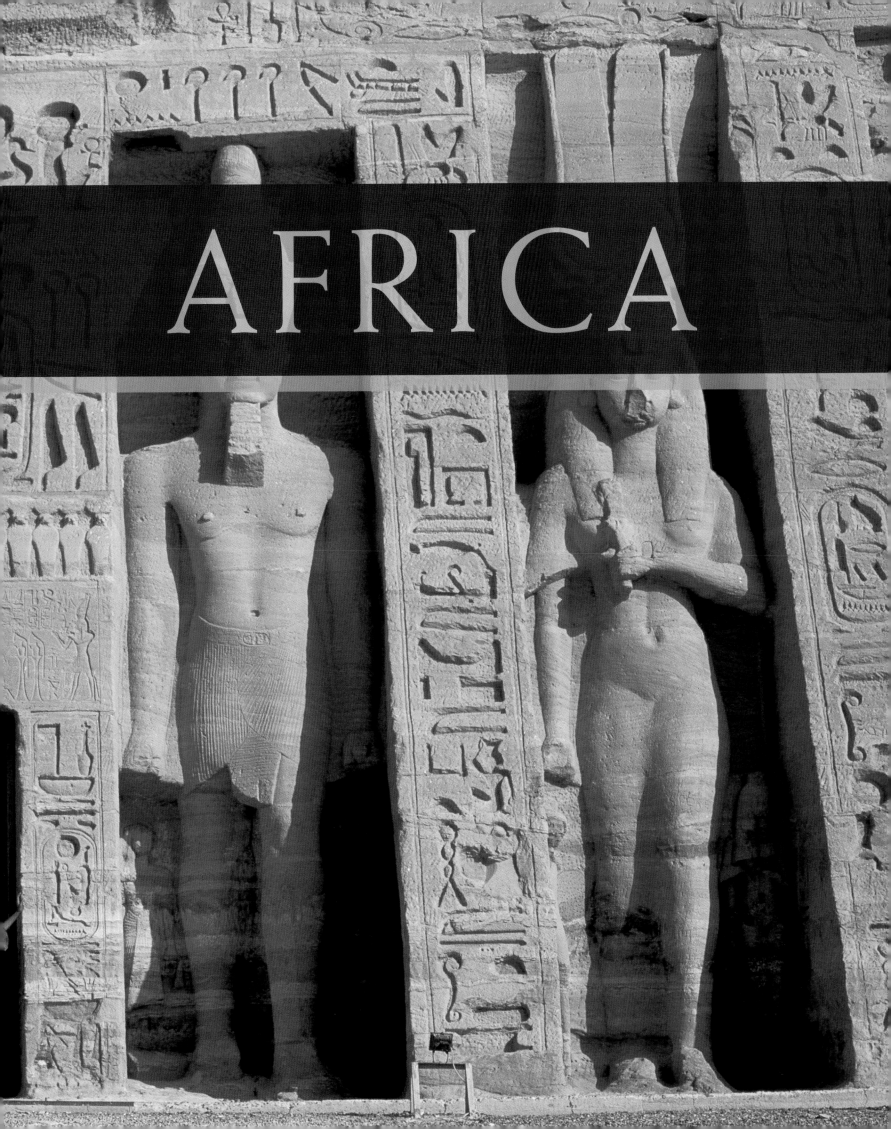

AFRICA

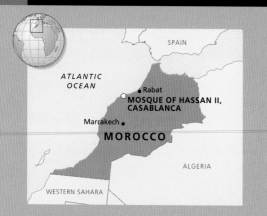

Mosque of Hassan II, Casablanca

With a prayer hall that can accommodate 25,000 people, the Mosque of Hassan II is the second-largest religious building in the world after the mosque in Mecca. The complex covers 96,840 sq ft (9,000 sq m), with two-thirds of it built over the sea. The minaret, the lighthouse of Islam, is 656 ft (200 m) high, and two laser beams reaching over a distance of 18.5 miles (30 km) shine in the direction of Mecca. The building was designed by Michel Pinseau and it took 35,000 craftsmen to build it. With carved stucco, *zellij* tile work, a painted cedarwood ceiling and marble, onyx, and travertine cladding, the mosque is a monument to Moroccan architectural virtuosity.

HASSAN II

Moulay Hassan succeeded to the throne of Morocco on the death of his father in 1961. A skillful politician, he alternated liberalizing policies with repression. He introduced the country's first constitution in 1962 and parliamentary elections in 1963, but the road to reform was rocky. When Spain withdrew from the mineral-rich Western Sahara in 1975, Hassan initiated the Green March, in which 350,000 civilians crossed the border to assert Morocco's claim to the region. Spain agreed to the transfer of power, but Algerian-backed Polisario Front guerrillas began a violent campaign for independence. A ceasefire was agreed to in 1991. Hassan II died in 1999.

INSIDE THE MOSQUE

The waterfront Mosque of Hassan II is the crowning glory of the king's reign. Built for his 60th birthday, the mosque was mainly financed by donations from the Moroccan people. Inside, the massive marble-floored **prayer hall** sparkles in the glow of Venetian chandeliers. Cedarwood from Morocco's Middle Atlas range has been shaped and carved to form **doors** and screens and the paneling of 70 cupolas. Even the sliding roof is painted and gilded. The **hammam** (traditional bathhouse) is below the prayer hall.

MUSLIM BELIEFS AND PRACTICES

Muslims believe in one God (Allah), and their holy book, the Koran, shares many stories and prophets with the Bible. However, Muslims hold that Jesus was just one in a line of prophets, the last being Mohammed, who brought the final revelation of God's truth to mankind. Muslims believe that Allah communicated the texts of the Koran to Mohammed through the Archangel Gabriel. Muslims pray five times a day, wherever they may be, and the calls to prayer are broadcast from the mosque. Those who visit a mosque to pray remove their shoes and wash their feet, head, and hands outside before entering. Inside, women and men pray in separate areas. When praying, Muslims face Mecca in Saudi Arabia. In a prayer hall, the direction is indicated by the *mihrab* (a niche in the wall). Kneeling and lowering the head to the ground are gestures of humility and respect for Allah.

Mosque door, interior view

⊿ Minaret

⊿ Fountains

⊿ Marble
Used throughout the building—on the columns of the prayer hall, doorways, fountains, and stairs—marble is everywhere. It is also sometimes combined with granite and onyx.

⊿ Minbar
The *minbar*, or pulpit, located at the western end of the prayer hall, is particularly ornate. It is decorated with verses from the Koran.

⊿ Prayer Hall
The vast prayer hall measures 656 ft (200 m) by 328 ft (100 m). The central part of the roof can be opened to the sky.

Hammam

KEY DATES

1980	1986	1993
King Hassan II declares his intention to build a landmark mosque.	Construction begins on the Mosque of Hassan II.	The mosque is finished, four years after the king's 60th birthday.

VISITING A MOSQUE

Unusually in Morocco, the Mosque of Hassan II is open to non-Muslims on guided tours. It is important for both sexes to dress modestly when visiting the mosque. Shoes should be removed, and shoulders and knees covered. Men must take off their hats and women are asked to cover their hair with a headscarf.

Women's Gallery
Above two mezzanines, and hidden from view, this gallery extends over 57,000 sq ft (5,300 sq m) and can hold up to 5,000 women.

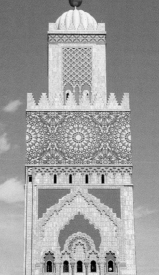

▲ **Doors**
Seen from the exterior, these are double doors in the shape of pointed arches framed by columns. Many are clad in incised bronze.

🖼 **Dome**

🖼 **Royal Door**

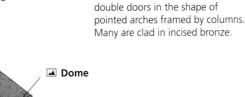

Columns

🖼 **Doors**

Windows
Wooden latticework *mashrabiya* screenwork at the windows protects those within from prying eyes.

▲ **Fountains**
These are decorated with *zellij* tile work and framed with marble arches and columns.

◄ **Minaret**
Its vast size—it is the tallest minaret in the world—and exquisite decoration make this an exceptional building.

▼ **Mosque viewed from the sea**

Marble ➤

Royal Door ➤
This is decorated with traditional motifs engraved on brass and titanium.

▼ **Dome**
The cedarwood-paneled interior of the dome, over the prayer hall, glistens with carved and painted decoration.

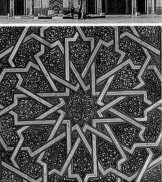

🖼 **Stairway to the Women's Gallery**
The stairway features decorative woodcarving, multiple arches, and marble, granite, and onyx columns, arranged in a harmonious ensemble.

▼ **Stairway to the women's gallery**

▼ **Minbar**

▼ **Prayer Hall**

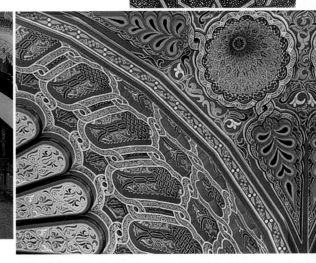

Great Mosque, Kairouan

The Sidi Oqba Mosque, or Great Mosque, is the oldest and most impressive Muslim place of worship in North Africa and is Islam's fourth holiest site after Mecca, Medina, and Jerusalem. The founder of Kairouan, Uqba ibn Nafi, built a small mosque on the site in AD 670. As the city thrived, the mosque was rebuilt and enlarged several times: in 703, again in 774, in 836, and 863. It reached its current dimensions by the end of the 9th century, but its design and ornamentation continued to evolve up to the 19th century.

Ornately decorated column in the prayer hall

▲ Entrance to the Mosque
There are two entrances to the prayer hall from the road. Non-Muslims are not permitted to enter, but they may look in through the open doors.

◄ Entrance to the Courtyard

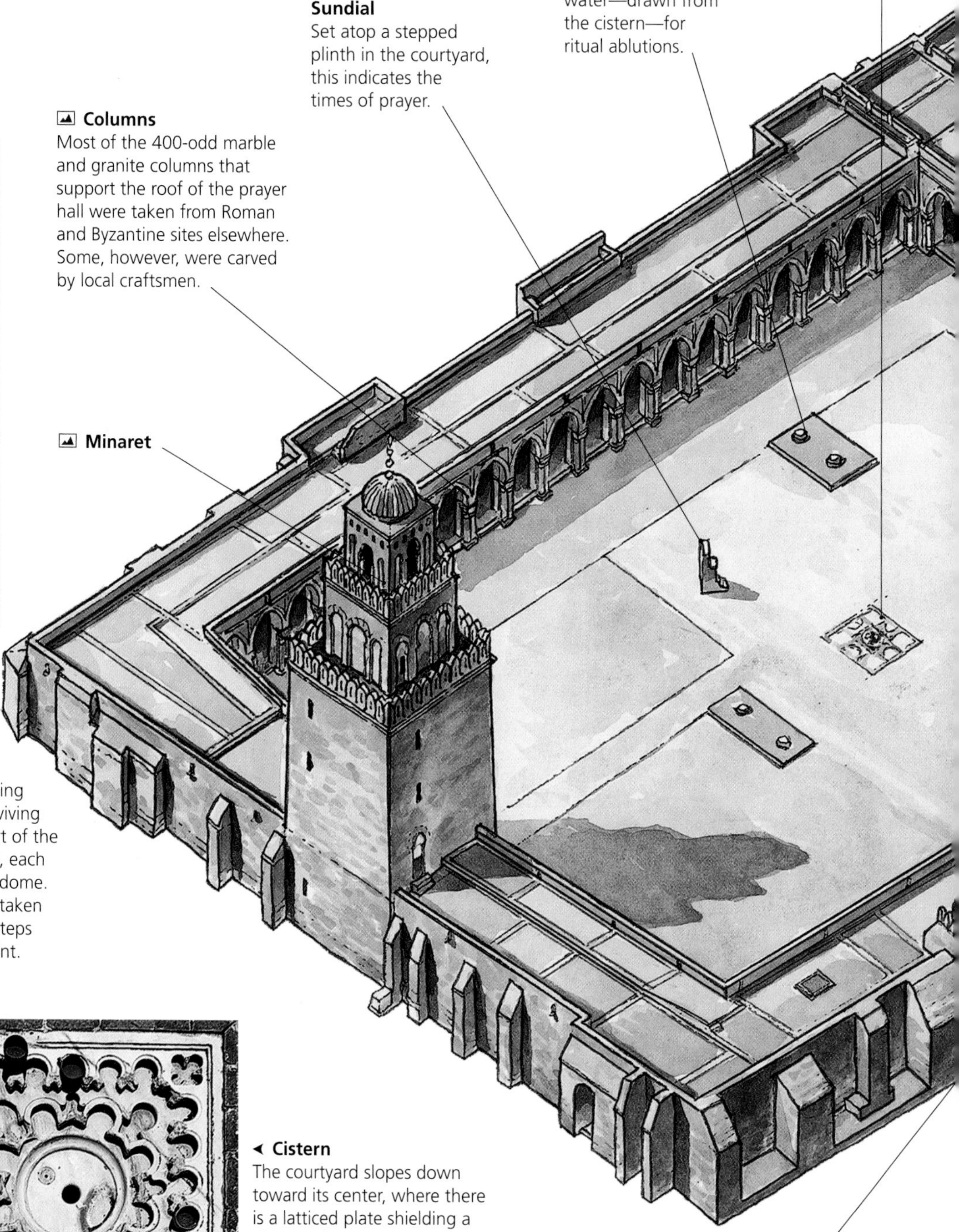

▦ Columns
Most of the 400-odd marble and granite columns that support the roof of the prayer hall were taken from Roman and Byzantine sites elsewhere. Some, however, were carved by local craftsmen.

▦ Minaret

Sundial
Set atop a stepped plinth in the courtyard, this indicates the times of prayer.

Wells
These provide the water—drawn from the cistern—for ritual ablutions.

▦ Cistern

▲ Cloisters
Surrounding the courtyard on three sides are cloisters giving shade and protection from the elements.

◄ Minaret
Built between 724 and 728, this imposing square minaret is one of the oldest surviving towers of its kind, and is the oldest part of the Great Mosque. It rises in three sections, each diminishing in size, and is topped by a dome. The lower stories are built from blocks taken from Roman buildings. There are 129 steps leading up to the minaret's highest point.

▼ Dome

◄ Cistern
The courtyard slopes down toward its center, where there is a latticed plate shielding a cistern. The plate has a decorative function but also prevents the water, which drains into the cistern, from becoming polluted.

▦ Entrance to the Courtyard
Six gates are set into the wall surrounding the courtyard. The main entrance is through a gate surmounted by a dome.

Decoration ▶
The richly decorated mosque contains some rare examples of ceramic decorative features. Plant motifs and geometric forms are popular.

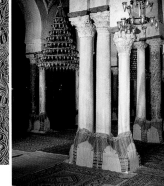

Prayer Hall ▲

☑ Cloisters

☑ Dome
The exterior of the mosque's dome shows the position of the 9th-century tiled *mihrab* (a niche that indicates the direction of Mecca).

Minbar
The *minbar*, or pulpit, is made out of teak. It was commissioned by the Aghlabid emir, Abu Ibrahim, and built in around 863.

☑ Entrance to the mosque

☑ Prayer Hall
This hall is divided into 17 long naves divided by arcades. The two wider naves form a "T" shape.

KAIROUAN CARPETS

Kairouan is a carpet-making center, a tradition going back hundreds of years, and it is renowned for the quality of its rugs. However, the large rug in the Great Mosque's prayer hall was a gift from Saudi Arabia.

GREAT MOSQUE, KAIROUAN

Tunis
MEDITERRANEAN SEA
TUNISIA
ALGERIA
LIBYA

UQBA IBN NAFI AND KAIROUAN

At the time of the Prophet Mohammed's death in 632, Muslims only ruled Arabia. However, by 750, the Arab Muslims had achieved one of the most spectacular conquests in history, ruling over the Middle East, Central Asia, and North Africa. In 670, the Muslim leader Uqba ibn Nafi crossed the desert from Egypt as part of the conquest of North Africa. Establishing military posts along the way, he stopped to camp at the location of modern-day Kairouan. Legend tells of a golden cup being discovered in the sand, which was recognized as one that had disappeared from Mecca several years previously. When the cup was picked up, a spring emerged from the ground which, it was declared, was supplied by the same source as that of the holy Zem-Zem well in Mecca. Uqba founded his capital and swept on to conquer Morocco.

ISLAM'S FOURTH HOLIEST CITY

Kairouan grew in importance to become the capital of the Aghlabid dynasty in the 9th century. When the Fatimids took power in 909, they moved their capital elsewhere. By the 11th century, Kairouan's political and economic power had been surpassed by other cities, but it never lost its holy status. As a religious center it continued to grow in prominence, with the mosque proving a powerful magnet for pilgrims from Muslim territories throughout northern and Saharan Africa. Today, Kairouan is Islam's fourth holiest city. Pilgrims come to drink the waters of the holy spring and to visit the Great Mosque.

INSIDE THE PRAYER HALL

Entrance to the **prayer hall** at the southern end of the courtyard is through a set of beautiful, finely carved wooden doors dating from the 19th century. Inside is a rectangular, domed chamber with arched aisles. The *imam* leads the prayers from the **minbar**, a marvelous pulpit sculpted out of wood from Baghdad and thought to be one of the oldest in the Arab world. Behind the *mihrab* (**dome**) at the end of the central aisle are 9th-century tiles, also from Baghdad, surrounding carved marble panels. A carved wooden screen, the *maqsura*, dating from the 11th century, stands nearby and many **Kairouan carpets** cover the floor.

KEY DATES

670	836	Mid-800s	1988
The city of Kairouan is founded by Uqba ibn Nafi, who constructs a small mosque.	The Great Mosque is renovated and enlarged under the Aghlabids and takes the appearance of the building seen today.	The Great Mosque becomes a site for Islamic pilgrimage.	Kairouan is declared a UNESCO World Heritage Site.

Leptis Magna

The location of some of the world's finest Roman remains, Leptis Magna attests to the prosperity and status of the Roman Empire in North Africa. Leptis Magna benefited greatly when Septimius Severus, a native of the city, became Roman emperor in AD 193. During his reign, the population grew to some 70,000 people, and buildings were raised to glorify his name. In the 6th century, attacks by nomadic tribes eventually led to the city's abandonment, at which point sand dunes engulfed it, preserving the site that is still being excavated today.

Column detail, Severan Basilica

THE CITY'S PORT

A promontory protects the harbor at the mouth of the Wadi Lebdah at Leptis Magna, and it is here that the Phoenicians settled in the 7th century BC. They exploited the fertile hinterland and traded olive oil, ivory, and animal skins throughout the Carthaginian empire and around the Mediterranean. During the early 3rd century AD, under the Roman emperor Septimius Severus, the harbor was rebuilt and enlarged. New quays, half-a-mile (1 km) long, were constructed, with warehouses, a temple, and a watchtower, and a **lighthouse** was built on the promontory. The mooring blocks on the quay, which were covered in sand soon after completion, have been well preserved.

EMPEROR SEPTIMIUS SEVERUS

The Roman ruler Lucius Septimius Severus was born in Leptis Magna in Roman North Africa in AD 146. Regarded as an outstanding soldier, Severus rose to the rank of consul and by 190 he was in command of the legions in Pannonia. Soon after the murder of Emperor Pertinax in 193, Severus was proclaimed emperor, but he had to fight off two rivals to secure his position. He was a strong but popular ruler, who was known for his lavish entertaining. His final campaign was to England in 208 to secure the Roman Empire's northern border at Hadrian's Wall. Severus died in York in 211, while preparing to invade Scotland.

THE EMPEROR'S NEW BUILDINGS

Leptis Magna prospered under Roman rule as a major commercial center, but at the beginning of the 3rd century, after the appointment of Septimius Severus as Roman emperor, the city underwent a transformation. Marble was imported from Asia Minor, Greece, and Italy, granite columns from Egypt, and the limestone buildings took on a grand appearance (Classical Style, see p.137). In AD 200, Severus built a fine new **Severan Forum**. At the northeastern end, he constructed the three-aisled **Severan Basilica**. Its marble pilasters were carved with scenes from the lives of Hercules and Dionysus, his family's patron gods. The mighty four-sided **Arch of Septimius Severus**, constructed in white marble, was raised for his visit to the city.

← To Hunters' quarters

Arch of Trajan

⌂ Market

Arch of Tiberius

Arch of Septimius Severus

⌂ **Theater**
Like the market, this vast structure was given to the city by Annobal Rufus. The lower, wider stone steps would have held chairs for distinguished visitors. From the top, the panoramic view of the ancient city is magnificent.

⌂ **Hadrian's Baths**

KEY DATES

600 BC	23 BC	523	1982	1994
A Phoenician trading post is founded on the site of Leptis Magna.	Leptis Magna forms part of the new Roman province of Africa.	The city is sacked by Berber Arabs, and by 650 it has been abandoned.	Leptis Magna becomes a UNESCO World Heritage Site.	A new archeological program begins at Leptis Magna.

HUNTERS' QUARTERS

To the west of the city lies a group of well-preserved, small domed buildings. Wall paintings indicate they belonged to the hunters who supplied the amphitheaters of the Roman Empire with wild animals.

Bust of Emperor Septimius Severus ▼

RECONSTRUCTION OF LEPTIS MAGNA

This shows the many magnificent buildings erected during the reigns of successive emperors, up to and including Septimius Severus.

⊿ Severan Forum

⊿ Severan Basilica
This massive double-apsed building, begun during the reign of Severus to house the law courts, was converted into a church by Justinian I in the 6th century, although part of it appears to have served as a synagogue from the 5th century.

Lighthouse

Harbour

Severan Forum ▼
A series of vast reliefs of the mythological Greek Gorgon Medusa once adorned the arcade of the Severan Forum.

▼ Hadrian's Baths
This baths complex includes an outdoor sports ground (*palaestra*), hot and warm baths (*caldarium* and *tepidarium*), once heated by underfloor fires, and a huge cold bath (*frigidarium*) with two plunge pools, one still containing water.

▲ Market
Once surrounded by arcades and centered on two beautiful kiosks, this grand trading place was endowed by one wealthy citizen, Annobal Rufus, in 9–8 BC.

0 metres   100

0 yards   100

▼ Severan Basilica

▼ Theatre

The Great Pyramid, Giza

The facts and figures about Pharaoh Khufu's pyramid, commonly referred to as the Great Pyramid, are staggering. It was the tallest building in the world until the 19th century, and the precision with which it was built, using simple surveying tools, is remarkable: the greatest difference in length between the four 756-ft (230-m) high sides is just 2 inches (5 cm). The construction methods and exact purpose of some of its chambers and shafts are unknown, but the architectural achievement is clear. The pyramid is estimated to contain over two million blocks of stone weighing on average 2.5 tons, with some weighing as much as 15 tons.

Statue of Khufu (Cheops)

▲ **King's Chamber**
The chamber was probably emptied 600 years after being built, but, despite holding only a lidless sarcophagus, it was often broken into by treasure seekers.

Workers' graffiti

Stress-Relieving Chambers
These were built out of huge blocks of granite weighing up to 80 tons.

Counterbalanced slabs of granite were lowered to seal the tomb

The "air shaft" would have been closed off by the outer casing

King's Chamber

RECONSTRUCTION OF THE KING'S CHAMBER
Built to protect the chamber, the stress-relieving rooms also hold the only reference to Khufu in the Great Pyramid—gangs who built the pyramid left graffiti stating, "How powerful is the great White Crown of Khufu."

Queen's Chamber
This probably held a statue representing the *ka*, or life force, of the king.

"Air Shafts"
These may have been symbolic paths for the king's soul to ascend to the stars.

🔲 **King's Chamber**

Underlying bedrock

🔲 **Great Gallery**

Unfinished underground chamber

Vertical Shaft
This probably served as an escape route for the workers.

KEY DATES			
2589–2566 BC	**2555–2530 BC**	**1400 BC**	**1979**
Pharaoh Khufu builds the Great Pyramid during his reign.	Construction of the pyramids of Khafre and Menkaure on the Giza Plateau.	The Sphinx is restored for the first time; four more conservation phases follow.	The Giza Plateau is inscribed as a UNESCO World Heritage Site.

▲ Queens' Pyramids
These three small pyramids were built for members of the king's family, although the actual identity of their occupants is unknown.

Entrance ➤

SOLAR BOAT MUSEUM

This museum near the Great Pyramid houses a reconstructed solar boat that might have been a funerary barque for Khufu. Discovered in 1954, the boat's 1,200 individual pieces took archeologists 14 years to put back together.

▲ The Sphinx and Pyramid of Khafre viewed from the Giza Plateau

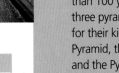

Great Gallery ➤
Soaring nearly 30 ft (9 m) high, this is thought to have been used as a slipway for the huge blocks that sealed the passageway.

⊡ Entrance
The original entrance is blocked, and a lower opening made by the Caliph Maamun in AD 820 is now used.

THE DEVELOPMENT OF PYRAMIDS

It took the ancient Egyptians around 400 years to progress from the mudbrick mastaba to the smooth-sided pyramid. The last stage, from the stepped pyramid to the "true," or smooth-sided, pyramid took just 65 years. During this period, each pyramid was a brave venture into the unknown.

Mastaba
Around 3000 BC, the sandy mounds of the graves of the upper echelons of society were formalized into low, boxlike mastabas.

Stepped Pyramid (c. 2665 BC)
A more impressive memorial was made by putting six stone mastabas on top of each other.

Prototype Pyramid (c. 2605 BC)
The first smooth-sided pyramid was achieved by filling in the steps of a pyramid. This was followed by specially built smooth-sided pyramids.

THE SPHINX

Dating back to 2500 BC and positioned at the entrance to the Pyramid of Khafre, the **Sphinx** is the earliest known ancient Egyptian sculpture. It stands 66 ft (20 m) high, with an elongated body, a royal headdress, and outstretched paws. It is carved from an outcrop of natural rock, augmented by shaped blocks around the base added during one of several renovations. It was once thought that the nose of the Sphinx was shot off by Napoleon's French army, but in reality it was lost before the 15th century.

THE GIZA PLATEAU

During the Egyptian 4th dynasty (2613–2498 BC), the Giza Plateau became the royal burial ground for Memphis, capital of Egypt. In less than 100 years, the ancient Egyptians built three pyramid complexes to serve as tombs for their kings. These consisted of the Great Pyramid, the Pyramid of Khafre (r. 2558–2532), and the Pyramid of Menkaure (r. 2532– 2530). The Sphinx was added to guard the pyramids, while each king's close family and royal court were buried in satellite pyramids and **mastaba** tombs nearby. Of these, one of the most noteworthy is the 6th-dynasty (2345–2181 BC) tomb of Qar, a high-ranking official in charge of maintaining the Giza pyramids. His tomb is decorated with fine reliefs.

KHUFU

The second pharaoh of the 4th dynasty, Khufu (also known as Cheops) probably came to the throne in his 20s and reigned for about 24 years. The Greek historian Herodotus portrayed Khufu as a cruel and oppressive ruler, but this was belied by his posthumous reputation in Egypt as a wise king. Khufu is generally accepted as being the builder of the Great Pyramid—one of the seven wonders of the ancient world. Contrary to popular belief, this massive monument was not built by slaves, but by a conscripted workforce, and its enormous scale is a testament to the pharaoh's skills in harnessing the material and human resources of his country. Khufu's tomb was robbed long before archeologists discovered it, and his only likeness is a small ivory statue (**statue of Khufu**) found at Abydos, to the south of Giza.

Abu Simbel

Hewn out of a solid cliff in the 13th century BC, the Great Temple of Abu Simbel and the smaller Temple of Hathor are a breathtaking sight. Although dedicated to the patron deities of Egypt's great cities—Amun of Thebes, Ptah of Memphis, and Ra-Harakhty of Heliopolis—the Great Temple was built to honor Ramses II. Its 108-ft (33-m) high façade, with four colossal enthroned statues of Ramses II wearing the double crown of Upper and Lower Egypt, was intended to impress and frighten, while the interior revealed the union of gods and king.

Carved baboon on the Great Temple

A NEW LOCATION

When the Aswan Dam proved too small to control the floodwaters of the Nile River, the Egyptian government built the High Dam and created Lake Nasser as a reservoir. But the rising waters of the lake threatened to submerge Abu Simbel. Concern that the temples might be lost led UNESCO to back an international relief program, and in 1964 an ambitious four-year operation began, to move the two monuments to safety. The temples, complete with their artifacts, were cut into 950 blocks and transferred to a higher site against the backdrop of an artificial mountain (**relocated temples**).

THE GREAT STATUES

Three of the four 65-ft (20-m) high statues—the **Ramses II Colossi**—gaze southward to deter even the most determined of the pharaoh's enemies. Their enormous size is thought to represent Ramses' divinity as a supreme god. The gods and Ramses' family feature prominently among the other statues. At the feet of the colossi stand figures of the pharaoh's mother, his wife, Queen Nefertari, and the royal children. Above the entrance to the Great Temple is the falcon-headed statue of the Sun god **Ra-Harakhty**. Hapi, the god of the Nile flood, who is associated with fertility, is featured holding lotus and papyrus, symbols of Upper and Lower Egypt respectively.

WRITING ON THE WALL

Graphic wall paintings and reliefs found in the Great Temple of Abu Simbel and the **Temple of Hathor** glorify Ramses II as a divine ruler. They tell of his victories and show him fighting his enemies. In the Temple of Hathor, Nefertari's consecration as divine queen is illustrated. Surrounding the paintings and reliefs are detailed rows of hieroglyphs. This pictorial script, thought to have developed around 3200 BC, is the world's oldest known form of writing. The word "hieroglyph" means "sacred carved letter" and a complex system of 6,000 symbols was used by the ancient Egyptians to write their names and express their religious beliefs. Stories of the lives of Ramses and Nefertari have been engraved in this way on the walls of Abu Simbel.

TEMPLE OF HATHOR

Dedicated to the goddess Hathor, deity of love, pleasure, and beauty, the smaller temple at Abu Simbel was built by Ramses II to honor his favorite wife, Nefertari. The temple's hypostyle hall has Hathor-headed pillars and is decorated with scenes of Ramses slaying Egypt's enemies, with Nefertari looking on. The vestibule shows the royal couple making offerings to the gods.

Temple of Hathor

▲ Baboons
The façade is topped by a frieze of 22 baboons, their arms raised, supposedly worshiping the rising Sun.

Statue of Ra-Harakhty

◄ Ramses II Colossi
Accompanied by carved images of captives from the north and south, the four colossi on the façade boast of a unified Egypt. Ramses' name adorns the thrones in cartouche form.

Broken Colossus
The second statue on the left lost its head in an earthquake in 27 BC.

Statues of royal family members

▲ Great Temple Façade
Buried in sand for centuries, this façade was discovered in 1813 by the Swiss explorer Johann Ludwig Burckhardt.

Entrance to Great Temple

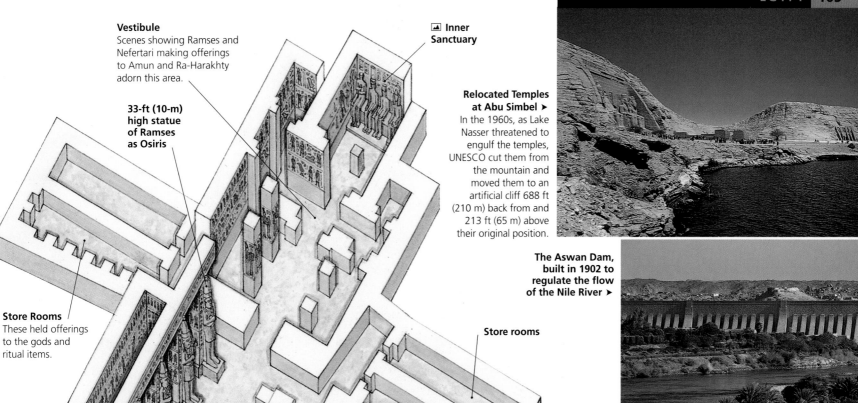

Vestibule
Scenes showing Ramses and Nefertari making offerings to Amun and Ra-Harakhty adorn this area.

☒ Inner Sanctuary

33-ft (10-m) high statue of Ramses as Osiris

Store Rooms
These held offerings to the gods and ritual items.

Store rooms

☒ Hypostyle Hall
The roof of this hall is supported by pillars with colossi in Osiride form—carrying crook and flail. Those on the southern pillars wear the Upper Egypt crown, while the northern ones wear the double crown of Upper and Lower Egypt.

Relocated Temples at Abu Simbel ➤
In the 1960s, as Lake Nasser threatened to engulf the temples, UNESCO cut them from the mountain and moved them to an artificial cliff 688 ft (210 m) back from and 213 ft (65 m) above their original position.

The Aswan Dam, built in 1902 to regulate the flow of the Nile River ➤

Great Temple Façade ▲

Inner Sanctuary ➤
Ramses II sits with the gods Ra-Harakhty, Amun-Ra, and Ptah in the Inner Sanctuary of the Great Temple, which is shrouded in darkness for most of the time. On two days of the year, however, the Sun's rays reach three of these once gold-covered statues.

Battle of Qadesh ➤
Reliefs inside the hypostyle hall show Ramses II defeating Egypt's enemies, including, on the right-hand wall, the defeat of the Hittites in the Battle of Qadesh c. 1275 BC.

Hypostyle Hall ➤

DAYS OF LIGHT

In ancient Egypt, the Sun was considered to be the source of all life and the temple was positioned to allow a shaft of sunlight into the Inner Sanctuary twice a year—possibly at the time of Ramses' birthday in February and his coronation day in October. The rays lit all but the statue of Ptah, god of darkness.

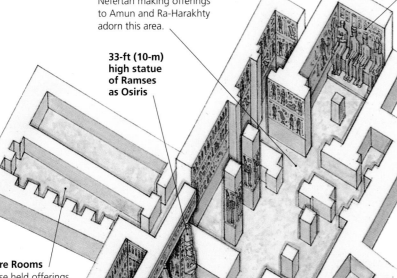

KEY DATES

1257 BC	1817	1822	1968	1979
Ramses II carves out the Great Temple and Temple of Hathor.	The Egyptologist Giovanni Battista Belzoni ventures inside the temples.	Jean-François Champollion cracks the code to decipher Egyptian hieroglyphs.	The work to reposition Abu Simbel is completed.	Abu Simbel is declared a UNESCO World Heritage Site.

Fortress-like exterior of Djenné Mosque, Mali

▲ The mosque's imposing mud-brick façade

▼ Base

Djenné Mosque

With its striking façade and unique architectural style, the Djenné Mosque ranks among the most unusual and beautiful buildings in the world. This large, mud-brick structure is typical of the special African-Islamic "marriage" found on the continent, in which African societies have molded Islam to fit their own traditional beliefs, values, and concerns. A mosque is usually constructed with the finest materials available, but the Djenné Mosque is made with sun-baked mud (also known as adobe or pisé), which, in the skilled hands of the Mali master-masons, has resulted in one of the most remarkable expressions of faith in Africa.

Mosque Interior

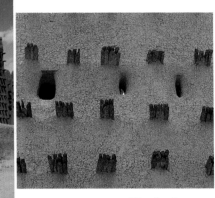

Wooden Beams ▲

Three Sloping Minarets
These are used by the *muezzin* (mosque official) to call the faithful to prayer. Staircases inside each minaret lead directly to the roof.

◄ **Market**
A colorful market is set up in front of the Djenné Mosque every Monday, attracting traders from the surrounding area. Djenné and its region are famous for the mud cloth sold here, known as *bogolan*.

◄ **Pillars and Roof**

🖼 **Wooden Beams**
Giving the mosque its distinctive "spiked" appearance, the palm beams not only support the mud walls, but also serve as a kind of permanent scaffolding for the annual repairs. Visually, they also relieve the solidity of the structure.

KEY DATES

c. 1250–1300	1300–1468	1468	1591	1819	1907	1988
Djenné town is founded on the Bani River and the first mosque is built.	Djenné resists attacks by the Mali empire, remaining an independent city-state.	The Songhay empire, one of the largest in Africa's history, captures and annexes Djenné.	Djenné is taken by Morocco as part of its campaign to drive the Songhay empire out of the region.	Cheikou Amadou abandons the old mosque and builds a new one on a different site.	A third mosque is built on the foundations of the 13th-century original.	Djenné Mosque is declared a UNESCO World Heritage Site.

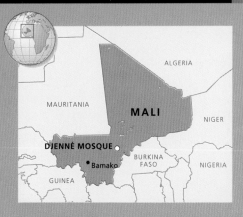

HISTORY OF DJENNÉ MOSQUE

Djenne's first mosque was built in 1280 by Koi Konboro, the 26th king of Djenné, following his conversion to Islam. As a demonstration of his allegiance to his new faith, the king had his royal palace knocked down and the mosque constructed on its site. Konboro's mosque survived until the early 19th century, when the fundamentalist Islamic king, Cheikou Amadou, eager to reinforce local Islamic religious practices, allowed it to fall into disrepair. He built a more austere mosque close by (now the site of an Islamic religious school). In 1907, the French administration in the town arranged for the original mosque to be rebuilt into the mud-brick structure seen today.

MOSQUE DESIGN

With its thick, battlemented walls and towers, and the peculiar "spiked" appearance of the projecting **wooden beams**, the mosque looks more like a fortress than a religious building. Its imposing exterior is made up of **three sloping minarets**, which stand over 33 ft (10 m) high, some **towers**, and a large **base**, accessible via a number of **stepped entrances**. The interior is not accessible to non-Muslims, but views of it can be had from the roofs of nearby houses. The art and skills of the masons have been handed down from generation to generation since the 15th century. The master-masons still mix the mud mortar by foot, and shape the mud bricks by hand. A simple iron trowel is their only tool, and is used for cutting the bricks and levelling the walls.

DJENNÉ TOWN

Founded in 1250 on one of the ancient trans-Saharan trade routes, Djenné quickly grew into a thriving center of commerce, attracting merchants from across Africa. Textiles, brass, ceramics, and copperware were exchanged for Sahel gold, ivory, and precious Saharan salt. By the end of the 13th century, Islam had also arrived, brought to Djenné by Muslim merchants from North Africa, and the first mosque was built. By the 14th century, Djenné had become an important center of Islamic learning, and also one of the wealthiest and most cosmopolitan towns in sub-Saharan Africa.

Spring Renovation ▶
The annual restoration of the mosque is a communal concern, with up to 4,000 townspeople taking part in the work. Specialized masons called *bareys* (a builder-magician caste dating back to the 15th century) carefully oversee the work.

⊡ Pillars and Roof
A forest of 90 wooden pillars supports the roof, which is perforated with small vents to allow light and air to penetrate. In the rainy season, the holes are covered with ceramic caps.

⊡ Base
The large base on which the mosque sits raises it some 10 ft (3 m) above the market area, and separates it both physically and symbolically from the pedestrian and profane activities of the marketplace.

Stepped entrance

Tower

⊡ Mosque Interior
Inside the mosque, the impressive prayer hall, with its sandy floor, is covered by a wooden roof supported by nearly 100 pillars.

WIND, SUN, AND RAIN

The elements cause damage to the Djenné Mosque. Rainwater erodes the walls and damp can weaken the structure. Extreme temperatures and humidity also cause stress to the building. However, a yearly replastering helps keep the mosque in good shape.

Castle of Good Hope, Cape Town

The oldest surviving building in South Africa, the Castle of Good Hope was built by the Dutch East India Company between 1666 and 1679, replacing an earlier clay and timber fort erected by Commander Jan van Riebeeck in 1652. The castle overlooks Cape Town's Grand Parade and is now home to a military museum, an art collection, and a banqueting hall; it is also the headquarters for Cape Army regiments.

Dutch East India Company (VOC) monogram

THE WILLIAM FEHR COLLECTION

The castle houses the famous **William Fehr Collection** of paintings, decorative arts, and furniture. Dr. Fehr (1892–1968) was a local businessman who started collecting colonial pictures and objects at a time when the practice was unusual. His collection now forms an invaluable record of many aspects of social and political life in the Cape, from the early days of the Dutch East India Company (VOC in Dutch) to the end of the 19th century. In addition to landscape paintings by the English artists Thomas Baines and William Huggins, there is 17th-century Japanese porcelain and 18th-century Indonesian furniture.

COMMANDER JAN VAN RIEBEECK

In April 1652, the Dutchman Jan van Riebeeck arrived at the Cape with about 80 men and women to establish a staging post for the Dutch East India Company. This was needed to provision the Dutch ships plying the lucrative trade route between Europe and Asia. Despite setbacks (20 men died during that first winter), the station eventually flourished and began to provide ships with meat, milk, and vegetables. However, rivalry with the indigenous Khoina people over water and grazing soon turned into open hostility and bitter wars followed.

THE CASTLE

The design of the castle was influenced by the work of the French military engineer Vauban, who was employed at the court of King Louis XIV. Pentagonal in shape, it has five defensive bastions from which the outside walls could be defended by cross-fire. The **original entrance** faced the sea, but it was moved to its present position in 1684. From the beginning, the castle was intended as a base for the Dutch East India Company in the Cape. Over the years, buildings were erected inside the courtyard, and a defensive 39-ft (12-m) high **inner wall** was built across it. Today, this area is the site of the William Fehr Collection. The castle also housed facilities to support a community, with living quarters, a church, a bakery, offices, and a jail with a torture chamber. In the 1930s, a new banqueting hall was created from a series of rooms on an upper floor.

▲ **Castle Moat**
Sections of the moat were rebuilt in 1992 as part of an extensive restoration program.

◄ **Dolphin Pool**

◄ **Old Slate**
Slate was taken from a quarry on Robben Island in the 17th century and used as paving material inside the castle.

▼ **Castle Entrance**
The original bell, cast in Amsterdam in 1697, still hangs in the belfry. The coat of arms of the United Netherlands can be seen on the pediment above the gate.

▲ **Leerdam Bastion**

Nassau Bastion

Torture Chamber
Below the Nassau Bastion was the site where prisoners were tortured, in accordance with the Dutch law that required a confession before sentencing.

🖾 **Old slate**

Catzenellenbogen Bastion

▼ **De Kat Balcony**

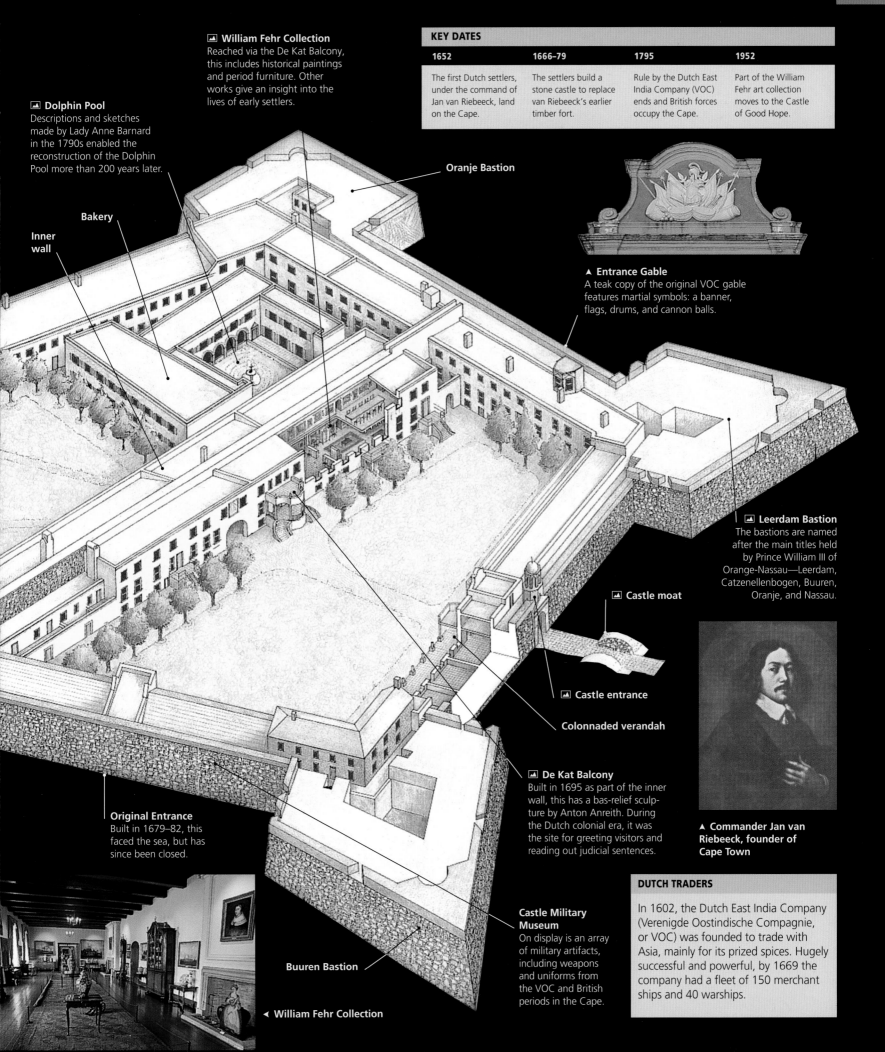

▣ William Fehr Collection
Reached via the De Kat Balcony, this includes historical paintings and period furniture. Other works give an insight into the lives of early settlers.

▣ Dolphin Pool
Descriptions and sketches made by Lady Anne Barnard in the 1790s enabled the reconstruction of the Dolphin Pool more than 200 years later.

Bakery

Inner wall

Oranje Bastion

KEY DATES

1652	1666–79	1795	1952
The first Dutch settlers, under the command of Jan van Riebeeck, land on the Cape.	The settlers build a stone castle to replace van Riebeeck's earlier timber fort.	Rule by the Dutch East India Company (VOC) ends and British forces occupy the Cape.	Part of the William Fehr art collection moves to the Castle of Good Hope.

▲ Entrance Gable
A teak copy of the original VOC gable features martial symbols: a banner, flags, drums, and cannon balls.

▣ Leerdam Bastion
The bastions are named after the main titles held by Prince William III of Orange-Nassau—Leerdam, Catzenellenbogen, Buuren, Oranje, and Nassau.

▣ Castle moat

▣ Castle entrance

Colonnaded verandah

▲ Commander Jan van Riebeeck, founder of Cape Town

▣ De Kat Balcony
Built in 1695 as part of the inner wall, this has a bas-relief sculpture by Anton Anreith. During the Dutch colonial era, it was the site for greeting visitors and reading out judicial sentences.

Original Entrance
Built in 1679–82, this faced the sea, but has since been closed.

Castle Military Museum
On display is an array of military artifacts, including weapons and uniforms from the VOC and British periods in the Cape.

Buuren Bastion

◄ William Fehr Collection

DUTCH TRADERS

In 1602, the Dutch East India Company (Verenigde Oostindische Compagnie, or VOC) was founded to trade with Asia, mainly for its prized spices. Hugely successful and powerful, by 1669 the company had a fleet of 150 merchant ships and 40 warships.

The Taj Mahal, a prime example of
Mughal architecture

ASIA

Krak des Chevaliers

One of the greatest castles in the world, Krak des Chevaliers was built in the middle of the 12th century by the Crusaders. Having captured Jerusalem and the Holy Land from the Muslims, they required strong bases from which to defend their newly won territories. The largest of a string of such fortresses, Krak des Chevaliers withstood countless attacks and sieges, but the Crusaders abandoned it after their defeat at the hands of the Arabs in 1271. Villagers settled within the walls and remained there until the 1930s, when the castle was cleared and restored.

Ruins of a 12th-century Gothic church within Krak des Chevaliers

INSIDE THE CASTLE

Krak des Chevaliers (Castle of the Knights) crowns a 2,133-ft (650-m) high hill at Homs Gap, commanding the route from Antioch to Beirut. The crusading Knights Hospitallers undertook a massive expansion program in the mid-12th century, adding a 100-ft (30-m) thick outer wall, seven guard towers, and **stables** for 500 horses. An inner reservoir, filled with water from an **aqueduct**, supplied the 4,000-strong garrison. Storerooms were stocked with food produced by local villagers, and the castle had its own olive presses and a bakery. The later Muslim occupants converted the Crusaders' **chapel** into a mosque and also added refinements such as **baths** and pools.

THE FINAL CONQUEST

The Crusaders continued their campaigns in the Middle East throughout the 12th and into the 13th centuries, but Krak remained secure. In 1163, the Knights successfully fought off Nuradin, the sultan of Damascus. In 1188, the Muslim leader Saladin attempted to lay siege to the castle, but finding it impenetrable, withdrew his forces. Finally, in 1271, the Mameluk sultan Baibars I, devised a scheme. He forged a letter, purportedly from the Crusader commander in Tripoli, instructing the army at Krak to surrender. Baibars' forces succeeded in taking the Crusaders' bastion without so much as a fight.

TANCRED, PRINCE OF ANTIOCH

In 1096, Tancred of Hauteville (1078–1112) set out with his uncle, Bohemund, and other Norman lords on the First Crusade to the Holy Land. Their objective was to halt the advance of the Seljuk Turks, who were threatening the Byzantine Empire, and to claim Jerusalem for the Christians. Tancred made a name for himself when he captured Tarsus from the Turks. He played a major role in the siege of Antioch and led the march on Jerusalem (1099) and its occupation. A year later, when Bohemund was taken prisoner by the Turks, Tancred took control of the Principality of Antioch. He ruled supreme in northern Syria, mounting attacks on both the Turks and Byzantines. In 1110, he occupied the hilltop fortress that the Crusaders were to transform into Krak des Chevaliers.

RECONSTRUCTION OF KRAK DES CHEVALIERS

This shows how the castle would have looked over 800 years ago. In its heyday, the castle would have housed a garrison of 4,000 men.

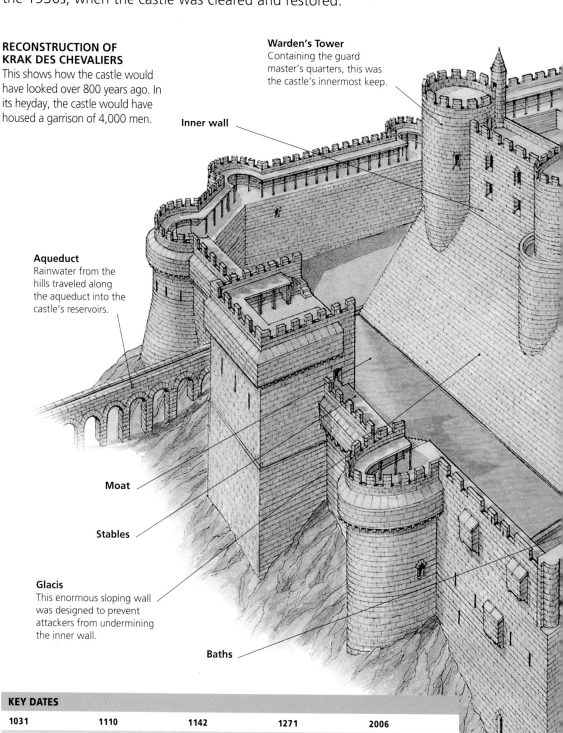

Warden's Tower
Containing the guard master's quarters, this was the castle's innermost keep.

Inner wall

Aqueduct
Rainwater from the hills traveled along the aqueduct into the castle's reservoirs.

Moat

Stables

Glacis
This enormous sloping wall was designed to prevent attackers from undermining the inner wall.

Baths

KEY DATES

1031	1110	1142	1271	2006
The emir of Aleppo builds the original fortress on the site.	Crusaders under Tancred, Prince of Antioch, take the bastion.	The Knights Hospitallers occupy the castle and construct the outer wall.	Baibars I, the Mameluk sultan, captures the castle and adds further fortifications.	The castle is added to UNESCO's World Heritage Site list.

General view of
Krak des Chevaliers ▶

Krak des Chevaliers,
the Crusaders'
magnificent fortress ▶

Inner fortress

◢ Loggia

◢ Tower of the
King's Daughter

Outer wall

Tower of the King's Daughter ▶
The northern face of this tower
has a large projecting gallery from
which rocks could be hurled if the
outer wall was breached. At ground
level, the tower is decorated
with three blind arches.

Chapel
Built by the Crusaders
and converted into
a mosque after the
Muslim conquest, its
Islamic *minbar* (pulpit)
can still be seen.

◢ **Main
entranceway**

Loggia ▶
Running along one side
of Krak's innermost
courtyard, the loggia is
a graceful Gothic arcade
with a vaulted ceiling
(*Gothic Style, see p54*).
It is decorated with
carved floral motifs and
depictions of animals.
Beyond the loggia
is the Great Hall,
which functioned
as a refectory.

Main Entranceway ▶
A long, stepped passage leads
from the site of the former
drawbridge to the upper castle.
Small ceiling apertures throw
light into the corridor, although
they were also intended for
pouring boiling oil over
invaders. The passageways
were high and wide enough to
allow for mounted riders.

Entrance Passage
The passage doubled
back on itself to
confuse any invaders
who managed to get
this far into the castle.

THE PERFECT CASTLE

The British author T. E. Lawrence
("Lawrence of Arabia") described Krak
des Chevaliers as "the most wholly
admirable castle in the world." Indeed,
the castle served as an inspiration for
Edward I, king of England, who passed
by on the Ninth Crusade in 1272 and
returned home to build his own castles
across England and Wales.

A FORTRESS WITHIN A FORTRESS

Krak des Chevaliers has two distinct
parts, separated by a moat—an outer
wall with 13 towers, and an inner
wall and glacis built around a higher,
rocky platform. Anyone attacking
therefore had to, in effect, breach
two castles.

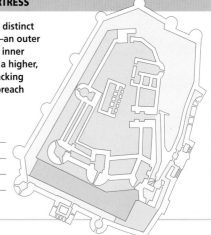

KEY

☐ Baths

☐ Moat

☐ Inner walls

☐ Outer walls

Church of the Holy Sepulcher, Jerusalem

Katholikon **dome**

Built around what is believed to be the site of Christ's crucifixion, burial, and resurrection, this complex church is the most important in Christendom. The first basilica here was built by the Roman emperor Constantine between 326 and 335 at the suggestion of his mother, St. Helena. It was rebuilt on a smaller scale by the Byzantine emperor Constantine Monomachus in the 1040s, following its destruction by Fatimid Sultan Hakim in 1009, but was enlarged again by the Crusaders between 1114 and 1170. A disastrous fire in 1808, and an earthquake in 1927, necessitated extensive repairs.

GOLGOTHA

Inside the church, two staircases lead up to Golgotha, meaning "Place of the Skull" in Hebrew. On the left is a Greek Orthodox chapel, with its altar placed directly over the rocky out-crop on which the cross of Christ's Crucifixion is believed to have stood (**Rock of Golgotha**). The crack in Golgotha, visible from the apse of the **Chapel of Adam** below, is believed to have been caused by the earthquake that followed Christ's death. To the right is a Roman Catholic chapel containing a silver and bronze altar made in 1558 and donated by Cardinal Ferdinand de Medici. In between the two altars is the Stabat Mater, an altar commemorating Mary's sorrow at the foot of the cross.

THE STATUS QUO

No fewer than 17 churches are represented in Jerusalem, a result of many historical schisms. The long, fierce disputes between Christian creeds over ownership of the Church of the Holy Sepulcher were largely resolved by an Ottoman decree issued in 1852. Still in force, and known as the Status Quo, it divides custody of the church among Greeks, Armenians, Copts, Roman Catholics, Ethiopians, and Syrians. Some areas are administered communally. Every day, the church is unlocked by a Muslim keyholder acting as a "neutral" intermediary. This ceremonial task has been performed by a member of the same family for generations.

CHRIST'S TOMB

For the construction of the first church, builders dug away the hillside to leave the alleged **Christ's Tomb** isolated, with enough room to build a church around it. To achieve this, an old temple had to be cleared from the site, and in the process, the **Rock of Golgotha**, believed to be the site where Christ was nailed to the cross, was found. A succession of shrines replaced the original 4th-century one. The present shrine, with two chapels, was rebuilt in 1809–10 after a fire. The outer Chapel of the Angel has a low pilaster with a piece of the stone said to have been rolled from the mouth of Christ's tomb by angels. A low door leads to the inner Chapel of the Holy Sepulcher, which houses the place where Christ's body was said to have been laid.

Rotunda
The most majestic part of the church, this was heavily rebuilt after the 1808 fire.

Crusader Bell Tower
This tower was reduced by two stories in 1719.

▣ **Christ's Tomb**

▣ **Stone of Unction**
This is where the anointing and wrapping of Christ's body after his death has been commemorated since medieval times. The present stone dates from 1810.

Main Entrance
This dates from the early 12th century. The right-hand door was blocked up late in the same century.

▣ **Courtyard**

Chapel of the Franks

THE FIRST CHURCHES

Christianity became the dominant religion in the Holy Land in the 4th century, and impressive churches were built. Before then, Roman suspicion of unauthorized sects meant that Christians were forced to meet and worship in private "house-churches" called *domus ecclesia*.

KEY DATES

326–35	1114–70	1981
Emperor Constantine and St. Helena have the first basilica built.	Crusaders enlarge the building in the Romanesque style and add a bell tower.	The Old City of Jerusalem joins the list of UNESCO World Heritage Sites.

▲ The mosaic of roofs and domes of the Church of the Holy Sepulchre

▲ The Holy Sepulcher seen from the roof of the Chapel of St. Helena

◄ **Courtyard**
The main entrance courtyard is flanked by chapels. The disused steps opposite the bell tower once led to the Chapel of the Franks, the Crusaders' ceremonial entrance to Golgotha.

▼ **Ethiopian Monastery**

⛰ Katholikon Dome
Rebuilt after the 1927 earthquake and decorated with an image of Christ, this dome covers the central nave of the Crusader church. This part of the building is now used for Greek Orthodox services.

Seven Arches of the Virgin
These are the remains of a colonnaded courtyard built in the 11th century.

Center of the World
Jerusalem was once viewed as the spiritual center of the world, as marked by a stone basin in the *katholikon*.

▼ **Stone of Unction**

Christ's Tomb ➤
For Christians, this is the most sacred site of all. Inside the 1810 monument, a marble slab covers the rock on which Christ's body is believed to have been laid.

⛰ Ethiopian Monastery
Living in the cluster of small buildings on the roof of the Chapel of St. Helena is a community of Ethiopian monks.

▲ **Rock of Golgotha**
The outcrop of rock venerated as the site of the Crucifixion can be seen through the glass around the Greek Orthodox altar.

Chapel of Adam

⛰ Rock of Golgotha

Chapel of St. Helena
This chapel is now dedicated to St. Gregory the Illuminator, patron saint of the Armenians.

Stairs to the Inventio Crucis Chapel

THE HOLY FIRE

On the Saturday of Orthodox Easter, all the church's lamps are put out and the faithful stand in the dark—a symbol of the darkness at Christ's Crucifixion. A candle is lit at Christ's Tomb, then another and another, until the entire basilica and courtyard are ablaze with light, symbolizing the Resurrection. Legend says the fire comes from heaven.

The Orthodox Easter ceremony of the Holy Fire

Striking façade of the Dome of the Rock, Jerusalem

Dome of the Rock, Jerusalem

Considered one of the first and greatest achievements of Islamic architecture, the Dome of the Rock is a shrine constructed in AD 688–91 by the Omayyad caliph Abd el-Malik. Built to proclaim the superiority of Islam and provide an Islamic focal point in the Holy City, the majestic structure now dominates Jerusalem and is its symbol. The mathematically harmonious structure echoes elements of Classical and Byzantine architecture (*Classical Style, see p.137* and *Byzantine Style, see p.148*).

▲ **Octagonal arcade of the Dome of the Rock, above which are Koranic verses**

Tile above the south entrance

◄ **View of the Dome of the Rock with the Muslim quarter in the background**

▼ **Freestanding arcades top the eight flights of steps up to the Dome of the Rock**

◄ **Well of Souls**
This staircase leads down to a chamber under the Rock called the Well of Souls. The dead are said to meet here twice a month to pray.

◄ **The Rock**

▼ **Inner Corridor**
The space between the inner and outer arcades forms a corridor around the Rock. The shrine's two corridors recall the ritual circular movement of pilgrims around the Qaaba in Mecca.

◄ **Crescent Finial and Dome**
The dome was originally made of copper but is now covered with gold leaf, thanks to the financial support of the late King Hussein of Jordan.

Drum
The area just below the golden dome is the drum. It is decorated with tiles and verses from the Koran that tell of Mohammed's Night Journey.

Koranic verses

Marble panel

Octagonal Arcade
This is adorned with original mosaics (AD 692) and an inscription inviting Christians to recognize the truth of Islam.

🖾 **Inner corridor**

South entrance

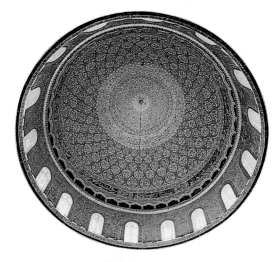

▲ Interior of the Dome
Inside the dazzling golden dome are elaborate floral decorations, as well as various inscriptions. The large text commemorates the Muslim sultan Saladin, who sponsored restoration work on the building.

KEY DATES

691	1500s	1981
Building work on the Dome of the Rock is completed.	Suleyman the Magnificent commissions the dazzling tile work on the exterior.	The Dome of the Rock joins UNESCO's list of World Heritage Sites.

Mosaics
Green and gold mosaics create a scintillating effect on the walls below the dome.

Outer corridor

HOLY SITE

One of the oldest and most beautiful of all Islamic monuments, the Dome of the Rock is the third holiest site of Islam after Mecca and Medina. The shrine is also important in Judaism, since it stands on the site of the two temples of the Jews—the first built by King Soloman and the second by King Herod.

▲ Tile Work
The multicolored tiles that adorn the exterior are faithful copies of Persian tiles that Suleyman the Magnificent added in 1545 to replace the damaged original mosaics.

Stained-glass window

▣ The Rock
The Rock is variously believed to be where Abraham was asked to sacrifice Isaac, where Mohammed left the Earth on his Night Journey, and the site of the Holy of Holies of Herod's Temple.

Outer Wall
Each wall is 67 ft (20.4 m) long. This exactly matches the dome's diameter and its height from the base of the drum.

▣ Well of Souls

MOHAMMED'S NIGHT JOURNEY

The Koran, the holy book of Islam, is regarded as the exact word of Allah. Muslims believe that it can never be truly understood unless read in Arabic; translations into other languages can only ever paraphrase. The Koran is divided into 114 chapters, covering many topics. One of the core episodes recounts the Night Journey of the Prophet Mohammed. In this, he is carried from Mecca to Jerusalem and from there makes the *Miraj*, the ascent through the heavens to God's presence, returning to Mecca in the morning. The story is illustrated with geometric tiling and verses on the exterior of the **drum** of the Dome of the Rock.

HARAM ASH-SHARIF

The Temple Mount, or *Haram ash-Sharif*, is located in the southeastern part of the Old City of Jerusalem. It is a major Islamic religious sanctuary and home to a number of important buildings, including the Dome of the Rock. Traditionally the site of Solomon's Temple, it later housed the Second Temple, enlarged by Herod the Great and destroyed by the Romans. Left in ruins for more than half a century, the *Haram ash-Sharif* became an Islamic shrine in 691 with the construction of the Dome of the Rock.

THE DOME OF THE CHAIN AND THE GOLDEN GATE

Just east of the Dome of the Rock stands the small Dome of the Chain, set at the approximate center of the *Haram ash-Sharif*. The reasons given for its construction are varied. According to one theory, it sits at the site of the Holy of Holies (the most sacred and inaccessible place in Herod's Temple), which is thought of in Jewish tradition as the omphalos, the navel of the universe. The Dome of the Chain is a simple structure with a domed roof supported by 17 columns. It is famous for its marvelous 13th-century interior tiling, which surpasses even that of the Dome of the Rock. Its name derives from the legend that a chain once hung from the roof and whoever told a lie while holding it would be struck dead by lightning. Farther east is the Golden Gate, one of the original Herodian city gates. Jews believe the Messiah will enter Jerusalem through this gate.

INSIDE THE FORTRESS

The cliff-top plateau of Masada is surrounded by two walls, 4,593 ft (1,400 m) long and 13 ft (4 m) wide. Within, King Herod built palaces, barracks, and storehouses. His private retreat, the splendid northern **Hanging Palace**, extended over three terraces, cut into the cliff face and connected by steep staircases. The rooms were lavishly decorated with mosaic floors. Walls and ceilings were painted to resemble stone and marble, and elegant columns surrounded balconies and courtyards. His other residence, the larger **Western Palace**, served as the administrative center and contained Herod's throne room and apartments.

THE ZEALOTS

Around the time of Herod's death in 4 BC, the inhabitants of Masada became embroiled in a rebellion against Rome. The uprising was led by Judas of Galilee, founder of the Zealots, a militant Jewish sect that vehemently opposed the Romans because of their pagan beliefs. The Romans crushed the rebellion and took Masada. In AD 66, at the start of the First Jewish Revolt, the Zealots regained the mountaintop. They lived among the palaces, using the fortress as a base to conduct raids against the Romans. At the time of the **Roman siege of Masada**, there were 1,000 inhabitants.

HEROD THE GREAT

Herod was born in 73 BC, the son of a Jewish father, Antipater, and an Arab mother, Cyprus. Herod, like his father, was a practicing Jew. Antipater was the right-hand man of Hyrcanus, King of Judaea (r. 76–30 BC), and instrumental in Herod's first appointment at the age of 16 as governor of Galilee. With cunning and ruthlessness, Herod moved up the political ladder. He married the king's daughter, found favor with his Roman overlords, and was ultimately crowned king of Judaea himself in 37 BC. He embarked on a massive building program, which included a modern port, Caesarea, fortresses such as Masada, and the grand reconstruction of the Temple in Jerusalem. Orthodox Jews, however, considered him racially impure and were incensed by his tyrannical rule and his excessive taxes.

Masada

This isolated mountaintop fortress, around 1,300 ft (440 m) above the banks of the Dead Sea, is believed to be the location of the oldest synagogue in the world. Masada was fortified as early as the 1st or 2nd century BC and then enlarged and reinforced by Herod the Great, who added two luxurious palace complexes. On Herod's death, the fortress passed into Roman hands, but it was captured in AD 66 during the First Revolt by Jews of the Zealot sect. After the Romans crushed the rebels in Jerusalem, Masada remained the last Jewish stronghold. It was heroically defended for more than two years before the walls were breached by the Romans in AD 73.

▲ Snake Path
As an alternative to the cable car, visitors can reach the fort by hiking up the steep winding path on the mountain's east side.

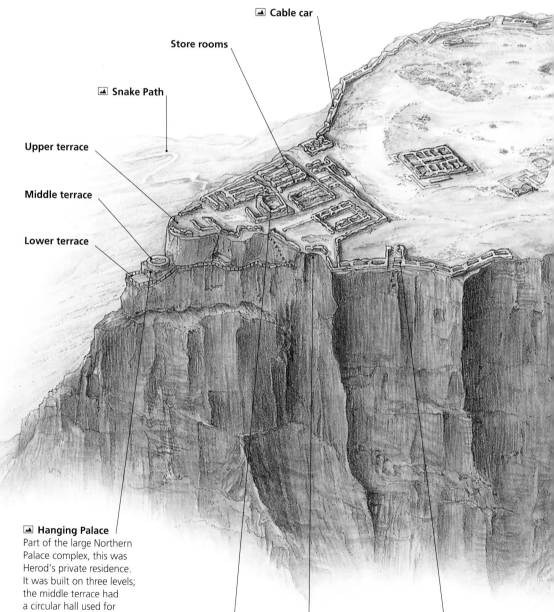

Cable car

Store rooms

Snake Path

Upper terrace

Middle terrace

Lower terrace

▣ Hanging Palace
Part of the large Northern Palace complex, this was Herod's private residence. It was built on three levels; the middle terrace had a circular hall used for entertaining, the lower terrace had a bathhouse.

▣ Calidarium
Masada's hot baths are one of the best-preserved parts of the fortress. The columns on which the original floor was raised, to allow hot air to circulate underneath and heat the room, can still be seen.

Water Gate
This stands at the head of a winding path that leads to the reservoirs below.

▣ Synagogue

THE SURVIVORS

The story of the Roman siege of Masada, and the mass suicide of the Jewish inhabitants, was told by two women survivors. They had escaped the killings and the devastating fire lit by the last man before he, too, took his life, by hiding with their children in a cave.

▲ Cable Car
A large number of pilgrims visit this rocky mountain citadel every year. The cable car was installed to ease their tiring journey.

◲ Columbarium
This is a small building with niches for funerary urns; it is thought the urns held the ashes of non-Jewish members of Herod's court.

◲ Cistern   Southern Citadel

◀ **Cistern**
At the foot of the mountain, Herod built dams and canals that collected the seasonal rainwater to fill cisterns on the northeastern side of the fortress. This water was then carried by donkey to the cisterns on top of the rock, such as this one in the southern part of the plateau.

▼ **Calidarium**

▲ Columbarium

Western Wall

Western Palace
Used for receptions and the accommodation of Herod's guests, the Western Palace was richly decorated, with mosaic floors and frescoes adorning the walls.

▲ Synagogue
Possibly built by Herod, this synagogue is thought to be the oldest in the world. The stone seats were added by the Zealots.

Hanging Palace ▲

West Gate

Roman Ramp
This is now the western entrance to the site.

THE ROMAN SIEGE OF MASADA (AD 70–73)

According to a 1st-century account by Roman historian Flavius Josephus, the Roman legions laying siege to Masada numbered about 10,000 men. To prevent the Jewish rebels from escaping, the Romans surrounded the mountain with a ring of eight camps, linked by walls—an arrangement that can still be seen today. In order to make their attack, the Romans built an enormous earthen ramp up the side of the mountain. Once this had been completed, a tower was constructed against the walls. From the shelter of this tower, the Romans set to work with a battering ram. The defenders hastily erected an inner defensive wall, but this proved little obstacle and Masada fell when it was breached. Rather than submit to capture, slavery, or execution, the Jews inside the fortress chose to commit mass suicide. Josephus relates how each man was responsible for killing his own family.

Remains of one of the Roman base camps, viewed from the top of the fortress

KEY DATES

37–31 BC	1963	2001
King Herod starts his grandiose building project.	Excavations of the Masada stronghold begin.	UNESCO declares Masada a World Heritage Site.

Petra

Set deep in the rock and protected by the walls of a valley is one of the world's most marvelously preserved and impressive archeological sites: Petra. There has been human settlement here since prehistoric times, but before the Nabataeans came, Petra was just another watering hole. Between the 3rd century BC and the 1st century AD, they built a superb city, the center of a vast trading empire. In AD 106, Petra was annexed by Rome. Christianity arrived in the 4th century, the Muslims in the 7th, and the Crusaders in the 12th. Petra then lay forgotten until the early 19th century.

▲ Theater Vaults

THE ARCHITECTURE OF PETRA

The Nabataeans were adventurous architects, always creating a distinctive look. The multiple crowstep is seen as a design of the first settlers, whereas Nabataean Classical buildings reflect a later period. The dating of the façades is very difficult, as many examples of the "early" style appear to have been built during the Classical period, or even later.

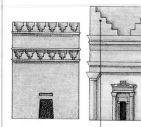

This early design was probably inspired by Assyrian architecture

Single-divide crowstep, lending height

This intermediate style, which is frequently seen at Petra, placed multiple crowsteps with a single-divide crowstep, and added Classical cornices and pillars and Hellenistic doorways.

The stacked look favored by the Nabataeans

Nabataean Classical designs, such as the Bab el-Siq Triclinium here, are complex, possibly experimental fusions of Classical and native styles.

KEY DATES

3rd century BC	1100s	1812	1985
The Nabataeans settle in Petra and make it their capital.	Petra falls into decline after the departure of the Crusaders.	J. L. Burckhardt is the first European to visit Petra.	Petra joins UNESCO's World Heritage list.

The eagle, a Nabataean male deity symbol

"Attic" Burial Chambers
These were a device to protect the dead from animals and tomb robbers.

Single-divide Crowstep
This was a design devised by the Nabataeans to complement the Classical cornice.

▣ **Outer Siq Designs**

Vertical Foothold
This may have been added to aid the sculptors.

▣ **Treasury Tholos**

Mounted Figures
Castor and Pollux, sons of Zeus, flank the portico.

THE OUTER SIQ
The artwork above shows some of the major constructions on the left-hand side of the Outer Siq, leading from the Treasury to the Theater. In reality, of course, the route bends and twists, and on both the left and right sides are a great number of other tombs and features of architectural interest.

▣ **Treasury Interior**
A colossal doorway dominates the outer court and leads to a 129 sq-ft (12 sq-m) inner chamber. At the back of the chamber is a sanctuary with an ablution basin, suggesting that the Treasury was, in fact, a temple.

Stairway to High Place of Sacrifice

▣ **To the Street of Façades**

▲ Treasury Tholos
The central figure may be the Petran fertility goddess El-Uzza. Bullet marks in the tholos and urn have been made over the years by Bedouins attempting to release hidden treasure.

Street of Façades ➤
Carved on four levels, these tightly packed tombs may include some of Petra's oldest façades. Most are crowned with multiple crowsteps.

◄ Outer Siq Designs
A range of intermediate design styles are displayed throughout, including on the Treasury and Theater tombs. One free-standing tomb uniquely combines Classical features with a crowstep used as a battlement.

▼ Treasury interior, door in the outer court

◄ The Palace Tomb, a three-story imitation of a Roman palace

Roman Theater

Tomb Façades
These were cut away when the rear wall of the Theater was being made, leaving just the interiors.

🖼 Theater Vaults
For access, there were tunnels on each side of the stage. Inside, these were dressed with painted plaster or marble.

Stage Wall
This would have hidden the auditorium from the Outer Siq.

IN SEARCH OF PETRA

After the departure of the Crusaders in the 12th century, Petra lay almost forgotten for more than 500 years. In 1812, lured by tales of a lost city, the Swiss explorer Johann Ludwig Burckhardt managed to persuade a guide to lead him to Petra.

THE SIQ
Access to Petra is through a deep ravine called the Siq, which is preceded by a wide valley called the Bab el-Siq. The entrance to the Siq is marked by the remains of a monumental arch and is the start of a gallery of intriguing insights into the Nabataeans. These include rock-cut water channels, graffiti, carved niches with worn outlines of ancient deities, paving stones, and flights of steps leading nowhere. As the Siq descends it becomes almost imperceptibly deeper and narrower (at its narrowest, the walls are only 3 ft/1 m apart). At its deepest, darkest point, the Siq opens out before Petra's most thrilling monument: the **Treasury**. From here, the path leads into the **Outer Siq**.

THE ROYAL TOMBS
Carved into the base of El-Khubtha mountain, where the Outer Siq opens out onto Petra's central plain, are the Corinthian, Palace, and Urn tombs. Together they are known as the Royal Tombs. Their monumental size suggests they were built for wealthy or important people, possibly Petran kings or queens. These tombs and their neighbors are also remarkable for the vivid striations of color rippling through their sandstone walls, an effect heightened in the warm glow of the late afternoon sun. Particularly striking are the Silk Tomb and the ceiling in the Urn Tomb.

THE NABATAEANS
The Nabataeans migrated west from northeast Arabia in the 6th century BC, eventually settling in Petra. As merchants and entrepreneurs, they grasped the lucrative potential of Petra's position on the spice and incense trade routes from East Asia and Arabia to the Mediterranean. By the 1st century BC, they had made Petra the center of a rich and powerful kingdom that extended from Damascus in the north to the Red Sea in the south and had built a city large enough to support 20–30,000 people. Key to their success was their ability to control water. Conduits and terra-cotta piping can be seen along the walls of the Siq—part of an elaborate city water system. Petra continued to thrive under the Romans from AD 106, but changes in trade routes eventually led to its demise.

The Registan, Samarkand

The three buildings surrounding Samarkand's Registan Square comprise one of the world's most spectacular architectural ensembles. In the 15th century, Ulug Beg, grandson of the Turkic conqueror Timur, built a group of mosques, caravanserais (merchants' inns), and the Ulug Beg, a *medresa* (Koranic school), around the city's sandy market square. With the exception of the Ulug Beg, the other buildings were later destroyed and replaced in the 17th century by two more *medresas*, the Sher Dor and Tilla Kari.

Stunning interior of the Tilla Kari Medresa

BUILDING THE REGISTAN

The three *medresas* were built over a period of 230 years. The first was the **Ulug Beg**, begun in 1417. Directly opposite, the **Sher Dor** ("Lion Bearer"), modeled on the Ulug Beg, was added two centuries later. Its unconventional façade depicts live animals and human faces (an interpretation of the Koran forbids this). The combined mosque and *medresa* of **Tilla Kari** ("Gold Decorated") was added in the mid-17th century. Its ceiling appears domed, but is, in fact, flat—an effect created by the decreasing pattern size toward the center. The two later buildings were inspired by the earlier Timurid style.

A CENTER OF SCIENCE AND LEARNING

With room for over 100 students and teachers, lodged in 52 cells around the courtyard, the **Ulug Beg** was effectively a university. Unlike the traditional *medresa*, which was wholly devoted to Islamic studies, students here also received an education in mathematics and the sciences. This was a reflection of Ulug Beg's passions. Known as the "astronomer king," he endowed Samarkand with one of the world's earliest observatories: a two-story structure built on a hill and meant to serve as a giant astronomical instrument pointing at the heavens. Only its circular foundations survive.

GOLDEN SAMARKAND

Until recently, the portion of Central Asia once called Transoxania (roughly modern Uzbekistan, and parts of Kazakhstan and Turkmenistan), was isolated and largely forgotten. But in the Middle Ages, it was the glittering center of the Islamic world, its cities boasting grand palaces and mosques. Most magnificent of all was Samarkand. Already renowned by the time of Alexander the Great, the city owes its legendary reputation to the leader of the Timurid empire, Timur (1336–1405). Brutal and despotic, Timur was responsible for around 17 million deaths as a result of his military campaigns. However, with the riches he accrued, and the artisans he captured and sent back to Samarkand, he built a city that became a political, religious, cultural, and commercial capital whose influence extended across the known world.

Prayer hall

🔲 **Tilla Kari Medresa**
Lavish gold-leaf gilding covers the Mecca-facing *mihrab* (pulpit) beneath the dome chamber.

🔲 **Ulug Beg Medresa**
The façade consists of a central arched *pishtaq* (porch) flanked by two minarets. The elaborate tiling of stars is in keeping with Ulug Beg's passion for astronomy.

Courtyard
This has two arcaded tiers of cells for students and professors.

MATHEMATICS

Ulug Beg employed a mathematical consultant in the building of his *medresa*, Ghiyath ad-Din Jamshid al-Kashi, whose treatise on mathematics and astronomy has survived to the present day.

KEY DATES

c. 1417–20	1619	1647	1932–52	2001
Construction of the Ulug Beg Medresa.	Completion of the Sher Dor Medresa.	The Tilla Kari Medresa is finished.	Restoration of the Ulug Beg Medresa.	The Registan is designated a UNESCO World Heritage Site.

Ornamental Gardens
These have replaced the single-story buildings that once stood in this area.

Registan Square ▲
A vast space at the heart of the city, the Registan, meaning a "sandy place," is the most famous site in Samarkand.

◩ Arched Portals
The Sher Dor Medresa's marvelous courtyard contains large *iwans* (arched portals) that are covered with spectacular tile work.

Bazaar

Sher Dor Medresa ▲
The impressive tile work on the *pishtaq* (porch) depicts two lions stalking gazelles. Behind each lion is a Sun portrayed with a human face.

Minarets
These feature flared tops from which the *muezzin* called the people to prayer.

◩ Sher Dor Medresa

◩ Registan Square

Ablutions pool

▲ Ulug Beg Medresa Tile Work

▼ Ulug Beg Medresa

▼ Tilla Kari Medresa

▼ Arched Portals

◩ Ulug Beg Medresa Tile Work
The brilliant glazed tiles of vine scrolls and flowers in a polychromy of gold leaf and lapis lazuli is typical of Timurid decoration.

Potala Palace, Lhasa

Perched on Lhasa's highest point, the Potala Palace is arguably the greatest monumental structure in Tibet. Thirteen stories high, with more than 1,000 rooms, it was once the residence of Tibet's chief monk and leader, the Dalai Lama, and therefore the center for both spiritual and temporal power. After the 14th Dalai Lama fled to India in 1959, the palace became a museum, serving as a reminder of Tibet's rich and devoutly religious Buddhist culture. The first palace on the site was built by Songtsen Gampo in 641, and this was incorporated into the larger building that stands today. There are two main sections—the White Palace, built by the 5th Dalai Lama in 1645, and the Red Palace, which was completed in 1693.

◄ **Heavenly King Murals**
The east entrance has sumptuous images of the Four Heavenly Kings, Buddhist guardian figures.

◄ **Golden Roofs**
Seemingly floating above the huge structure, the gilded roofs (actually copper) cover the funerary chapels dedicated to previous Dalai Lamas.

◄ **Western Hall**
The largest hall inside the Potala, the Western Hall is located on the first floor of the Red Palace and contains the holy throne of the 6th Dalai Lama.

◄ **Chapel of the 13th Dalai Lama**
This chapel holds the funerary stupa of the 13th Dalai Lama, rising up nearly 43 ft (13 m) in the gloomy interior. The stupa contains the lama's mummified remains and is coated in gold and jewels.

◄ **3D Mandala**

Chapel of the 13th Dalai Lama

Roof of the Chapel of the 5th Dalai Lama

Red Palace

Western Castle or Bastion

Base
Purely structural, this holds the palaces onto the steep hill.

3-D Mandala
This intricate mandala of a palace, covered in precious metals and jewels, embodies aspects of the Buddhist path to enlightenment.

KEY DATES

AD 641	800s	1642	1922	1994
The first Potala Palace is built by Songtsen Gampo, founder of the Tubo kingdom.	The Tubo kingdom collapses and the Potala Palace is almost completely destroyed.	The 5th Dalai Lama becomes spiritual and political leader of Tibet and re-constructs the palace.	The 13th Dalai Lama renovates much of the White Palace and adds two stories to the Red Palace.	UNESCO adds the Potala Palace to its list of World Heritage Sites.

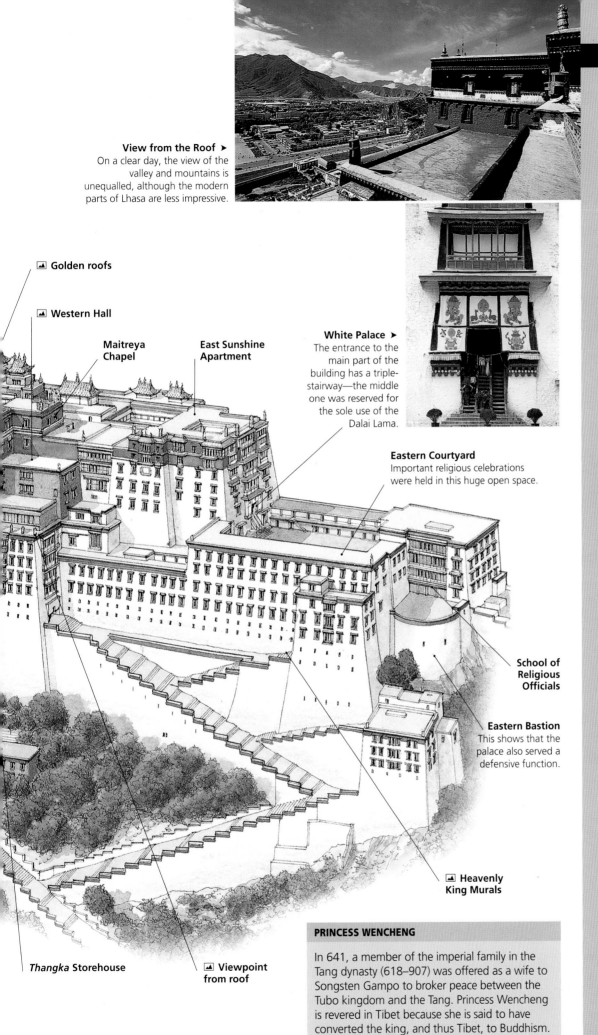

View from the Roof ▸
On a clear day, the view of the valley and mountains is unequalled, although the modern parts of Lhasa are less impressive.

RUSSIAN FEDERATION

MONGOLIA

Beijing

CHINA

POTALA PALACE, LHASA

Shanghai

EAST CHINA SEA

INDIA

Hong Kong

🔺 **Golden roofs**

🔺 **Western Hall**

Maitreya Chapel

East Sunshine Apartment

White Palace ▸
The entrance to the main part of the building has a triple-stairway—the middle one was reserved for the sole use of the Dalai Lama.

Eastern Courtyard
Important religious celebrations were held in this huge open space.

School of Religious Officials

Eastern Bastion
This shows that the palace also served a defensive function.

🔺 **Heavenly King Murals**

Thangka **Storehouse**

🔺 **Viewpoint from roof**

THE WHITE PALACE

The **White Palace** is seven stories high and was used mainly for secular purposes. The top three levels were built around a large central skywell and contained accommodation and offices for senior monks and officials, as well as kitchens and storage areas. The Dalai Lama occupied two rooms on the top floor called the **East and West Sunshine Apartments**. Beneath the top levels lies the Great East Hall, a vast 7,500-sq ft (700-sq m) assembly place for important political ceremonies. The lower levels of the palace are used for storage and provide a frame that supports the main buildings. The first hallway, after the entrance, has several large murals depicting the building of the Potala Palace and the arrival of Princess Wencheng.

THE RED PALACE

At the heart of the Potala complex, the Red Palace was intended for spiritual concerns. It is a complicated structure, with numerous halls of worship as well as the remains of eight Dalai Lamas inside magnificent stupas. Like the **Chapel of the 13th Dalai Lama**, the **Chapel of the 5th Dalai Lama** holds an enormous funerary stupa that rises up over 40 ft (12 m). It is made of sandalwood and reputed to be covered with nearly four tons of gold and almost 20,000 pearls and other gems. Other treasures on display include rare handwritten Buddhist sutras, and a great deal of statuary—one of the best statues is the one of Maitreya in his own chapel on the east side of the top floor.

SONGTSEN GAMPO

The warrior king and founder of the Tubo kingdom, Songtsen Gampo was born in AD 617 and built the original Potala Palace for his wife, Princess Wencheng. Most of it has long since burned down—only the Dharma Cave and the Saints' Chapel remain from the 7th century. They are both in the northern part of the Red Palace. The Dharma Cave is said to be the place where King Songtsen Gampo meditated. Inside, statues of the king, his chief ministers, and Princess Wencheng are venerated. In the Saints' Chapel on the floor above, several important Buddhist figures and the 7th, 8th, and 9th Dalai Lamas are enshrined and worshiped.

PRINCESS WENCHENG

In 641, a member of the imperial family in the Tang dynasty (618–907) was offered as a wife to Songsten Gampo to broker peace between the Tubo kingdom and the Tang. Princess Wencheng is revered in Tibet because she is said to have converted the king, and thus Tibet, to Buddhism. She also instigated the building of many of Tibet's finest temples.

The Great Wall of China

A symbol of China's historical detachment and sense of vulnerability, the Great Wall snakes through the Chinese landscape, over deserts, hills, and plains, for more than 2,500 miles (4,000 km). Yet, despite its seemingly impregnable battlements, the wall was ultimately an ineffective barricade. In the 13th century it was breached by the ferocious onslaught of the Mongols and then in the 17th century by the Manchu, helped by the decline of the Ming dynasty. Today, its dilapidated remains crumble across the rugged terrain of northern China and only select sections have been restored.

Shi Huangdi, the First Emperor

THE EXPANDING WALL

Sections of the bastion called the Great Wall were first built during the Warring States period (475–221 BC) by individual states to thwart incursions by northern tribes and to defend against aggressive neighbors. Simple and unconnected earthen ramparts, they were not joined together until the Qin dynasty (221–207 BC) first unified China under Shi Huangdi, the First Emperor. The maintenance and expansion of the wall reflected each succeeding dynasty's feelings of insecurity. Enlarged under the expansionist Han dynasty (206 BC–AD 220), the wall was neglected by the cosmopolitan Tang dynasty (AD 618–907), only to be heavily fortified by the more inward-looking Ming dynasty (1368–1644).

BUILDING ON SAND

The Qin wall was a simple tamped earth affair, but the later Han dynasty adopted a more advanced technology that enabled them to build walls even in the bleak expanses of the Gobi Desert. They would line wooden frames with a layer of willow reeds and twigs and then fill the frame with a mixture of mud, fine gravel, and water. This would then be pressed firmly into place. When the mixture dried, the frame could be removed, leaving behind a large slab of hard, bricklike mud that could be built upon again in the same manner. This is much like modern construction, when steel rods are use to reinforce concrete.

GENERAL CAI KAI

One of the legends about the wall tells that, during the Ming dynasty, General Cai Kai was put in charge of building the section of wall at Huanghua, 40 miles (55 km) north of Beijing. Word got back to the emperor that the general was taking too long over the task and wasting too much money. The unfortunate general was therefore summarily executed. Later, when the Mongols mounted a concerted attack, General Cai Kai's efforts paid off; Huanghua was the only fortress that successfully warded off the enemy. Realizing his mistake, the emperor exhumed General Cai Kai's body and had it reburied with full honors near the part of the wall that he built.

THE GREAT WALL OF CHINA (MING DYNASTY)

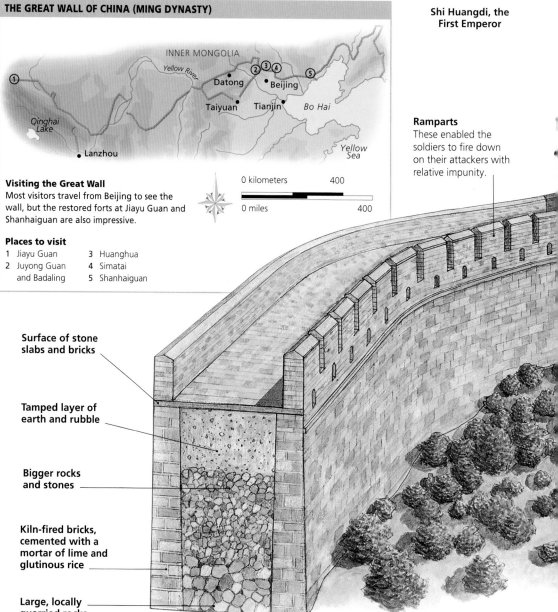

Visiting the Great Wall
Most visitors travel from Beijing to see the wall, but the restored forts at Jiayu Guan and Shanhaiguan are also impressive.

0 kilometers 400

0 miles 400

Places to visit
1 Jiayu Guan
2 Juyong Guan and Badaling
3 Huanghua
4 Simatai
5 Shanhaiguan

Ramparts
These enabled the soldiers to fire down on their attackers with relative impunity.

Surface of stone slabs and bricks

Tamped layer of earth and rubble

Bigger rocks and stones

Kiln-fired bricks, cemented with a mortar of lime and glutinous rice

Large, locally quarried rocks

KEY DATES

5th century BC	119 BC	589	1215	1644	1987
Individual states make defensive walls out of firmly tamped earth.	After driving the Mongols back into the Gobi Desert, the Han dynasty extend the Great Wall.	After centuries of strife, Yang Jian unites China under the Sui dynasty and rebuilds the Great Wall.	The Mongols capture Beijing after being held off for four years by the wall.	The Manchus overrun the wall from the northeast and create the Qing dynasty.	The Great Wall of China is added to UNESCO's World Heritage List.

RECONSTRUCTION OF THE GREAT WALL

This shows a section of the wall as built by the most prolific wall builders of them all: the Ming dynasty. The section at Badaling, some 43 miles (70 km) north of Beijing, was built around 1505 and is similar to this. It was restored during the 1950s and 1980s.

Towers
These were spaced two arrow shots apart to leave no part unprotected.

Carriageway
This averages 26 ft (8 m) in height and 23 ft (7 m) in width.

Cannons
Another Ming addition, cannons were used to defend the wall and warn of attack.

Signal Beacons
Warnings of attack were signaled by the smoke given off by burning dried wolf dung.

Watchtowers ▼

Paved walkway

Cannons ▶

THE SYMBOLIC WALL

The Chinese word for city, "cheng," also means wall. For the Chinese, the wall, as well as serving a practical purpose, symbolized the boundary between home, safety, and civilization inside, and the chaos and barbarism outside.

Panoramic Views ▼
Because the wall took advantage of the natural terrain for defensive purposes, following the highest points and clinging to ridges, it now offers some superb panoramic views.

Watchtowers
A Ming addition, these served as signal towers, forts, living quarters, and storerooms for provisions, gunpowder, and weapons.

Crumbling Ruin ▶
Away from the Beijing area, most of the wall is unrestored and has crumbled away, with only the core remaining.

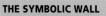

Paved Walkway ▶
In addition to enabling communications via smoke, flares, drums, and bells, the wall acted as a road for the rapid transport of troops over very difficult terrain.

The immense Great Wall of China, snaking over hills near Beijing

Forbidden City, Beijing

Forming the heart of Beijing, the Forbidden City is the world's largest palace complex, with 980 buildings across 1,614,600 sq ft (150,000 sq m). Completed in 1420, it was the Chinese imperial palace for almost 500 years, housing 24 emperors of the Ming and Qing dynasties (1368–1911) and the seat of government. As the symbolic center of the Chinese universe, the compound was the exclusive domain of the imperial court and dignitaries on royal business, but in 1949, it was opened to the public.

Glazed decorative wall relief

DESIGN PRINCIPLES

The harmonious principle of Yin and Yang is central to Chinese design. The Forbidden City is arranged symmetrically on a north-south axis, with hall entrances facing south to avoid the malign Yin effects—cold wind, evil spirits, and barbarian warriors—that come from the north. Odd numbers represent Yang, the masculine element associated with the emperor. Hence the frequent occurrence of three, five, seven, and the highest (and therefore best) single-digit odd number—nine—in architectural details. It is said that the palace has 9,999 rooms, and as nine times nine is especially fortunate, imperial doors usually have 81 golden studs.

SERVING THE EMPEROR

Because of the dual role of the Forbidden City—as the living quarters of the imperial family and the center of administration—eunuchs, the only male servants allowed in the palace, were in a unique position. Allowed access to the emperor's family, a few influential eunuchs wielded great power, siphoning off vast fortunes from the imperial coffers. The fate of the majority, though, was similar to that of a slave. Higher up the social scale, the emperor's concubines lived in a series of palaces beside the **Inner Court**. At night, the emperor would decide which concubine would sleep with him, and the number of times a concubine was chosen determined her social standing.

THE INNER COURT

The structure of the Inner Court mirrors that of the **Outer Court**, but on a smaller scale. There are three main Inner Court palaces—the Palace of Heavenly Purity was originally used as the imperial sleeping quarters, and later for the reception of imperial officials. Beyond this palace lies the Hall of Union, which was used as a throne room by the empress, as well as a depository for the imperial seals used to sign official documents. Still farther on, the Palace of Earthly Tranquillity served as living quarters for the Ming empresses. Behind the Inner Court is the Imperial Garden. On either side of the state apartments were the residences of the imperial family and their attendants—reputed to number as many as 9,000 by the 1700s.

THE LAST EMPEROR

Henry (Aixinjueluo) Puyi ascended the Qing throne in 1908 at the age of three. His brief reign ended on February 12, 1912, when he abdicated in favor of the Republic of China. Puyi remained a virtual prisoner in the palace until 1924, when he fled to the Japanese concession in Tianjin. He never returned to the Forbidden City and died childless and anonymous in 1967 after working for seven years as a gardener at the Beijing Botanical Gardens.

Henry Puyi, the boy emperor

OUTER COURT

Despite its name, this forms the very heart of the complex. The surrounding buildings, originally built to service this series of halls, now house a variety of interesting displays.

◿ Chinese lions

◿ Golden Water
Five marble bridges, symbolizing the five cardinal virtues of Confucianism, cross the Golden Water, which flows from west to east in a course designed to resemble the jade belt worn by officials.

◿ Meridian Gate
From this, the most imposing gate, the emperor would review his armies and issue the calendar for the coming year.

FALL OF THE MING DYNASTY

In 1644, as peasant rebels were storming the capital, the last Ming emperor, Chong Zhen, killed his daughter and concubines before fleeing the Forbidden Palace to hang himself on nearby Coal Hill.

◿ Gate of Supreme Harmony
Originally used for receiving visitors, the 78-ft (24-m) high, double-eaved hall was later used for banquets during the Qing dynasty (1644–1912).

KEY DATES

1406	1664	1925	1987
The Yongle emperor of the Ming dynasty commissions the Forbidden City.	The Manchus (later the Qing dynasty) invade, and burn most of the palace to the ground.	The Forbidden City becomes the Imperial Palace Museum.	The Forbidden City is listed by UNESCO as a World Heritage Site.

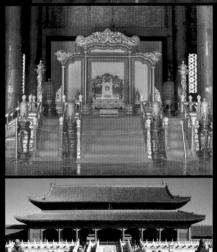

Door in the Forbidden City, with an auspicious number of studs ►

Bronze Cauldrons
Filled with water, these vessels were a practical precaution against fire.

The Hall of Preserving Harmony held the Civil Service Exams

Inner Court

Gate of Heavenly Purity
This led to the Inner Court, which was reserved for the imperial family.

⊿ Marble Carriageway

Hall of Supreme Harmony ►

Gate of Supreme Harmony ►

Hall of Middle Harmony
This building served as a place of preparation for the emperor when on official business.

Chinese Lions ►
The lion symbolized the power of the emperor, and the splendor of the imperial palace. Males are portrayed with a ball under their paw, while females have a lion cub.

⊿ Hall of Supreme Harmony
The largest hall in the palace, this was used for major occasions, such as the enthronement of an emperor. Inside the hall, an ornate throne sits beneath a fabulously colored ceiling.

⊿ Roof Guardians

Roof Guardians ►
These figures, which are associated with water, were supposed to protect the imperial buildings from fire.

▼ Marble Carriageway
The central ramp, carved with dragons chasing pearls among clouds, was reserved for the exclusive use of the emperor.

▼ Meridian Gate

▼ Golden Water

Temple of Heaven, Beijing

Built during the Ming dynasty, Tiantan, commonly called the Temple of Heaven, is one of the largest temple complexes in China and a model of Chinese architectural balance and symbolism. It was here that the emperor, after a ceremonial procession from the Forbidden City, would make sacrifices and pray to heaven at the winter solstice. As the Son of Heaven, the emperor could intercede with the gods on behalf of his people and ensure a good harvest. Off-limits to the common people during the Ming and Qing dynasties, the Temple of Heaven is situated in a large park that now attracts early-morning practitioners of Tai Chi.

Gate to the Round Altar

LAYOUT OF THE TEMPLE OF HEAVEN

The temple is replete with cosmological significance. All the major structures lie on the favored north-south axis. The ancient Chinese saying "sky round, Earth square" is represented by the interplay of squares and circles. Heaven is suggested in the round, conical roofing and the blue tiles of the **Hall of Prayer for Good Harvests** and the **Imperial Vault of Heaven**. The **Round Altar** symbolizes heaven, while Earth is there in its square enclosure. Also important is numerology, with odd numbers being the most fortunate, hence the triple eaves of the Hall of Prayer for Good Harvests and the Round Altar's three tiers.

CEREMONIES AND RITES

The emperor would perform the ceremonies at the Temple of Heaven following natural disasters, which required the appeasement of heaven, or to ensure rain and good harvests. After fasting for three days, he would be conveyed in a spectacular procession from the Forbidden City to spend the night before the sacrifice in the Palace of Abstinence. The next day, before dawn, he would be ceremonially robed. Then, proceeding north to south, with sacred music and dance, he would ascend the Round Altar to burn a freshly killed ox and bundles of silk before an array of wooden spirit tablets (*shenpai*), including those of his ancestors, who were thus also "participating."

THE LAST CEREMONY

Observed by China's emperors since the Zhou dynasty (1100–771 BC), the winter solstice rites at the Temple of Heaven were last performed by the first president of the Republic of China, General Yuan Shikai (1859–1916). Yuan had helped modernize the Chinese army and, as the head of such a force, could easily ask for positions of influence in return for his and the army's support. Once he was made president, he aimed to install himself as emperor and re-establish an imperial dynasty. He performed the ceremony at the Temple of Heaven in 1914, clearly asserting his imperial ambitions. However, despite donning the appropriate robes, he failed to achieve the traditional majesty of the occasion by arriving in an armored car.

TEMPLE OF HEAVEN COMPLEX

The main parts of the complex are all connected by the Red Step Bridge (an elevated ceremonial path) to form the focal point of the park. The doorways at each triple gate are for the emperor (east), the gods (center), and the officials (west). The circular Echo Wall is famous for its supposed ability to carry a whisper from one end of the wall to the other.

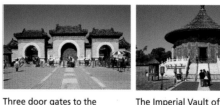

Three door gates to the Imperial Vault of Heaven

The Imperial Vault of Heaven, with the spirit tablets of the gods

The Center of Heaven Stone at the heart of the Round Altar

1 Hall of Prayer for Good Harvests
2 Red Step Bridge
3 Echo Wall
4 Imperial Vault of Heaven
5 Round Altar

KEY

▨ Area illustrated right

Temple of Heaven Complex

HALL OF PRAYER FOR GOOD HARVESTS

The Qinian Dian, or Hall of Prayer for Good Harvests, is the most famous structure at the complex and is often thought to be the "Temple of Heaven." In fact, Tiantan refers not to one building, but to the whole complex.

Name Plaques
These often copied the calligraphy of an emperor.

The circular roof symbolizes the sky

Red is the emperor's color

Dragon and Phoenix Motifs
Used inside and out, these represent the emperor and empress.

Golden Finial
Sitting atop the temple, the finial is 125 ft (38 m) high and prone to lightning strikes.

◩ **Caisson Ceiling**
The splendidly decorated, circular caisson ceiling has a beautiful gilded dragon and phoenix at its center.

▲ **Dragon Well Pillars**
The roofs of the hall are supported on 28 highly decorated pillars. At the center, the four colossal columns known as Dragon Well Pillars represent the seasons, while the outer 12 pillars represent the months of the year. The inner circle of 12 pillars represents the 12 two-hour periods into which the Chinese divided the day.

▲ **Caisson Ceiling**

The Hall of Prayer for Good Harvests was built without the use of a single nail ▶

Blue represents heaven

◩ **Dragon Well Pillars**

Emperor's throne

▲ **Marble Platform**
Three tiers of marble form a circle 300 ft (90 m) in diameter and 20 ft (6 m) high. The balustrades on the upper tier are carved with dragons to signify the imperial nature of the structure.

Symbolic offerings

Central "Dragon and Phoenix Stone"

EMPEROR YONGLE

This Ming emperor ruled from 1403 to 1424 and was responsible not only for moving the capital from Nanjing to Beijing, but also for starting work on the Forbidden City, the Temple of Heaven, and the Ming Tombs.

KEY DATES

1420	1530	1889	1918	1998
Qinian Dian is built. It is originally called the "Temple of Earth and Heaven."	The Round Altar is constructed by Emperor Shizong.	Qinian Dian burns down after a lightning strike.	The Temple of Heaven is opened to the public.	UNESCO inscribes the Temple of Heaven onto the World Heritage List.

Tosho-gu Shrine, Nikko

Nikko was a renowned Buddhist-Shinto religious center, and the warlord Tokugawa Ieyasu (1542–1616) chose this area as the site for his mausoleum. Founded in 1617, Tosho-gu was later enlarged by Ieyasu's grandson, Iemitsu, into the spectacular complex seen today. To create a shrine worthy of a shogun, 15,000 artisans spent two years carving, gilding, painting, and lacquering the 22 buildings. Although a Shinto shrine, Tosho-gu retains many Buddhist elements. The *sugi-namiki* (Japanese cedar avenue) leading to the shrine was planted by a 17th-century lord, in lieu of a more opulent offering.

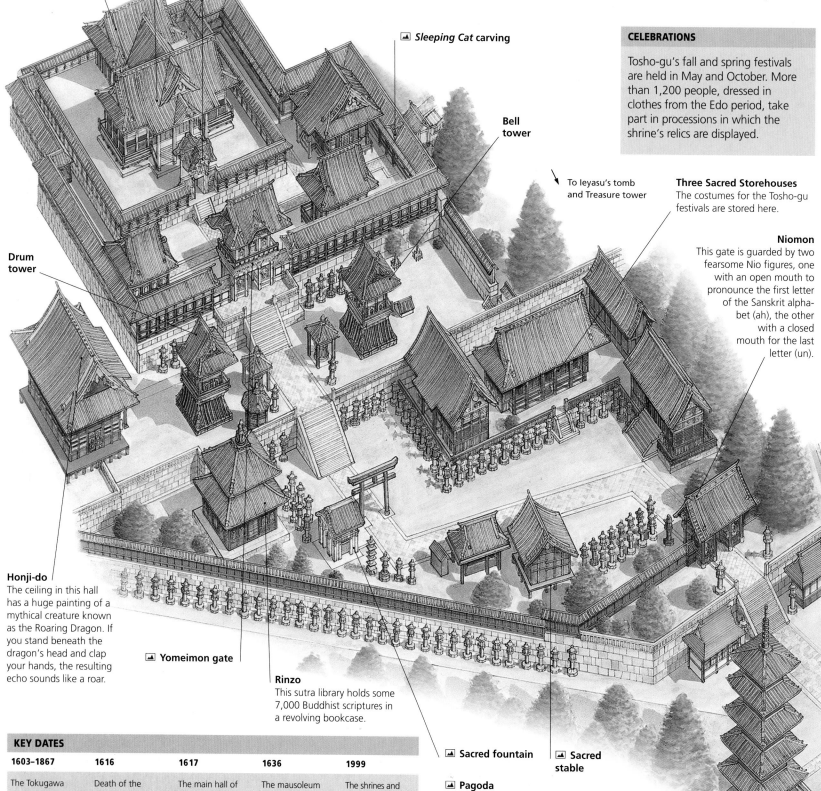

Karamon Gate
This is the smallest gate at Tosho-gu.

Haiden (sanctuary)

Honden (inner sanctuary)

▲ *Sleeping Cat* carving

CELEBRATIONS

Tosho-gu's fall and spring festivals are held in May and October. More than 1,200 people, dressed in clothes from the Edo period, take part in processions in which the shrine's relics are displayed.

Bell tower

To Ieyasu's tomb and Treasure tower

Three Sacred Storehouses
The costumes for the Tosho-gu festivals are stored here.

Niomon
This gate is guarded by two fearsome Nio figures, one with an open mouth to pronounce the first letter of the Sanskrit alphabet (ah), the other with a closed mouth for the last letter (un).

Drum tower

Honji-do
The ceiling in this hall has a huge painting of a mythical creature known as the Roaring Dragon. If you stand beneath the dragon's head and clap your hands, the resulting echo sounds like a roar.

▲ **Yomeimon gate**

Rinzo
This sutra library holds some 7,000 Buddhist scriptures in a revolving bookcase.

▲ **Sacred fountain**

▲ **Sacred stable**

▲ **Pagoda**
Donated by a *daimio* (feudal lord) in 1650, this five-story pagoda was rebuilt in 1818 after a fire. Each story represents an element—earth, water, fire, wind, and heaven—in ascending order.

KEY DATES

1603–1867	1616	1617	1636	1999
The Tokugawa Shogunate brings about a prolonged period of peace.	Death of the shogun Tokugawa Ieyasu; he is later deified.	The main hall of Tosho-gu Shrine is constructed.	The mausoleum and shrine are completed.	The shrines and temple are made a World Heritage Site by UNESCO.

▲ Sacred Stable
A carving of the Three Wise Monkeys decorates this wooden building. A horse, given by the New Zealand government, is kept here for a few hours each day.

▲ Sacred Fountain
This granite basin (1618) for ritual purification is covered with an ornate Chinese-style roof.

Pagoda ►

Extravagant carving by the Yomeimon Gate ►

▲ Yomeimon Gate
Lavishly decorated with beasts and flowers, this gate has one of its 12 columns carved upside down, a deliberate imperfection to keep from angering jealous spirits. Statues of imperial ministers occupy the niches.

▲ Sleeping Cat Carving
Over an entrance in the east corridor, this tiny, exquisite carving of a sleeping cat is attributed to Hidari Jingoro (Hindari the Left-Handed).

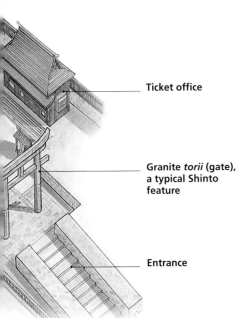

Ticket office

Granite *torii* (gate), a typical Shinto feature

Entrance

Map showing Japan with TOSHO-GU SHRINE, NIKKO, Tokyo, Osaka, and neighboring CHINA, RUSSIAN FEDERATION, NORTH KOREA, SOUTH KOREA, SEA OF JAPAN (EAST SEA), PACIFIC OCEAN

THE SHINTO RELIGION

Shinto, the "way of the gods," is Japan's oldest religion. Its core concept is that deities, *kami*, preside over all things in nature, be they living, dead, or inanimate. The Sun goddess Amaterasu is considered to be Shinto's most important *kami*. From ancient times, the emperor's rule was sanctioned by the authority of the greatest of the gods, said to be his ancestors. Religious rituals in Shintoism are centered around the offering of gifts and food, and the saying of prayers. Although Shinto was the state religion from 1868 to 1946, few Japanese today are purely Shintoists, but most will observe Shinto rituals alongside Buddhist practises.

FEATURES OF TOSHO-GU SHRINE

The shrine's opulence is not at all in keeping with the sense of duty and simplicity that is usually central to Shintoism. This incongruity highlights the transformation that Shintoism underwent following the introduction of Buddhism to Japan in the 6th century. Many of the shrine's buildings have Buddhist architectural elements. The five-story temple (**pagoda**) and the gate guarded by the Nio figures (**Niomon**) are just two examples of how Buddhism and Shintoism coexist at Tosho-gu. The shrine is famous for the ornate carvings that decorate entire buildings, both inside and out. The most exquisite are found at the Twilight Gate (**Yomeimon gate**), whose name implies that it can take all day to view the carvings.

THREE WISE MONKEYS

Introduced to Japan by a Buddhist monk from China in the 8th century, the proverb of the Three Wise Monkeys represents the three truths of Tendai Buddhism. The names of the monkeys are *Mizaru*, meaning "see no evil," *Kikazaru*, meaning "hear no evil," and *Iwazaru*, meaning "speak no evil." In Japan, monkeys are traditionally believed to keep horses healthy, and at Tosho-gu, they are the guardians of the sacred horse, an animal long dedicated to the Shinto gods (**sacred stable**). Their famous gestures of covering their eyes, ears, and mouth are a dramatic representation of the commands of the blue-faced deity Vadjra: if we do not see, hear, or speak evil, we will be spared from all evil.

TOKUGAWA IEYASU

Ieyasu was a wily strategist and master politician who founded the Tokugawa dynasty of shoguns that ruled Japan for over 260 years. Born the son of a minor lord, Ieyasu spent his life attaining power, finally becoming shogun in 1603, when he was 60. He built his capital at the swampy village of Edo (now Tokyo), and his rule saw the start of the flowering of Edo culture. He ensured that, after his death, he would be enshrined as a god and *gongen* (incarnation of the Buddha).

Tomb of Tokugawa Ieyasu

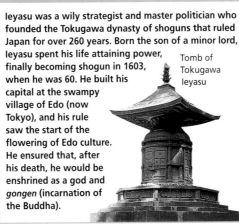

Todai-ji Temple, Nara

There are many reasons to visit the impressive Todai-ji Temple in Nara, but its sheer size must be the main attraction. The temple is only two-thirds of its original size, due to fires and alterations over the centuries, yet it is still the largest wooden building in the world. An enormous and costly project, Todai-ji was ordered by Emperor Shomyo in the mid-8th century to highlight the position of Nara as a powerful Buddhist site and Japan's capital. Inside is a magnificent 53-ft (16-m) high seated bronze statue of the Buddha—the largest in Japan.

Stone lantern at Todai-ji Temple

EMPEROR SHOMYO

The imperial court at Nara embraced Buddhism in the 8th century, during the reign of Emperor Shomyo (r. 724–49). Shomyo built temples in every province and used this vast network to consolidate control of his empire. However, he is best known for commissioning the Todai-ji Temple and its **Great Buddha Vairocana** statue in 743. The statue was a phenomenal endeavor that took seven years to complete, consumed most of Japan's bronze production for several years, and left the country almost bankrupt. When the temple finally opened in 752, Shomyo personally painted the statue's eyes and declared himself the Buddha's servant.

TODAI-JI TEMPLE'S CONSTRUCTION

Japan has extensive forest resources, and wood was a favored building material for centuries, particularly for temples, mainly because of its ability to endure weathering in winter. This has, however, also meant that such structures are highly susceptible to devastating fires. Todai-ji Temple's **Great Buddha Hall** is constructed in the traditional post-and-lintel style. The base of the hall has posts anchored along a rectangular perimeter. This rigid geometric shape marks the boundary between the material and divine worlds. There are 62 pillars supporting the grand, sloping roof. A unique roof construction (**Wooden Hall**) is effective in resisting the many major and minor earthquakes that hit Japan.

BUDDHISM IN JAPAN

Buddhism was founded in India and arrived in Japan via China and Korea in the 6th century. Prince Shotoku (573–621) promoted Buddhism in its early days. Initially, despite incorporating parts of its belief system, Buddhism had an uneasy relationship with Japan's oldest religion, Shinto. Buddhism lost official support after Shinto was declared Japan's national religion in 1868, but it flowered again after World War II. Today, the beliefs and morality of Buddhism permeate modern Japanese life, especially the Zen Buddhist emphasis on simplicity and mental control. Buddhist temples in Japan include a main hall (hondo), with a stark interior, a cemetery, a small Shinto shrine, and, often, a tiered pagoda housing a relic of the Buddha.

OMIZU-TORI FESTIVAL

The Omizu-tori, or water-drawing festival, has been celebrated at Todai-ji Temple since the 8th century to signal the arrival of spring. During the festival, which is held from March 1 to 14, water is ritually drawn from a sacred well in the early hours on the 13th day to the sound of music. Enormous torches are used to purify the water.

Koumokuten
This statue of a "Celestial Guardian" dates from the mid-Edo period (1603–1868).

Kokuzo Bosatsu

Entrance

Great Buddha Vairocana
The casting of this vast statue required hundreds of tons of molten bronze, mercury, and vegetable wax. Fires and earthquakes have destroyed the head several times; the current head dates from 1692.

GREAT BUDDHA HALL

The main hall of Todai-ji was rebuilt several times after natural disasters in the 12th and 16th centuries. The enormous figure inside is a jaw-dropping sight. Occasionally, it is possible to see monks climbing onto the Buddha's raised hand to dust the statue.

▲ The 62-ft (19-m) high Nandaimon (Great Southern Gate) of Todai-ji

▲ **Sacred Site**
Above Nara, the ancient city that was once Japan's capital, sits Todai-ji Temple. The curved roof is almost hidden by the surrounding trees.

◄ Wooden Hall
The unusual bracketing and beam-frame construction of this vast structure, built in 1688–1709, were possibly the work of craftsmen from southern China.

Roofline ►

Ornamental roof decoration

🖻 **Wooden Hall**

🖻 **Roofline**
The striking roofline, with its golden "horns" and curved lintel, was an 18th-century embellishment.

Interior of Daibutsuden (Buddha Hall)

Temple of Kofuku-ji, one of the many temples built by Emperor Shomyo ►

▼ Kokuzo Bosatsu
This statue of Kokuzo—the deity of wisdom and memory—was completed in 1709.

Pillar with Hole
Behind the Buddha is a large wooden pillar with a small hole bored into it. Tradition holds that those who can squeeze through the opening will attain enlightenment.

Tamonten
This figure of a "Celestial Guardian" dates from the same period as Koumokuten in the rear of the hall.

▲ **Great Buddha Vairocana**

Niyorin Kannon Bosatsu
Like the Kokuzo *bosatsu* to the left of the Great Buddha, this "fulfiller of all wishes" is an "Enlightened Being." The statue dates from 1709.

Covered walkway in compound

KEY DATES		
752	**1180, 1567**	**1998**
After enduring fires and earthquakes, Todai-ji Temple is finally completed.	The Great Buddha Vairocana's head melts in raging fires.	The Todai-ji complex at Nara is declared a UNESCO World Heritage Site.

Todai-ji Temple, Nara, which contains Japan's largest bronze Buddha

The Golden Temple, Amritsar

The spiritual center of the Sikh religion, the Golden Temple was built between 1589 and 1601, and is a superb synthesis of Islamic and Hindu styles of architecture. In keeping with the syncretic tradition of those times, its foundation stone was laid by a Muslim saint, Mian Mir. The temple was virtually destroyed in 1761 by an Afghan invader, Ahmed Shah Abdali, but was rebuilt some years later. Maharaja Ranjit Singh, ruler of Punjab, covered the dome in gold and embellished its interiors with lavish decoration during his reign.

Pietra dura detail

THE HOLIEST SHRINE

The Sikhs' holiest shrine, the Golden Temple complex is actually a city within a city, with a maze of lanes protected by 18 fortified gates. The main entrance is through the northern gateway, the Darshani Darwaza, which also houses the Central Sikh Museum and its collections of paintings, manuscripts, and weapons. From here, steps lead down to the Parikrama (marble pathway) encircling the **Amrit Sarovar** ("Pool of Nectar"), after which Amritsar is named, and **Hari Mandir** ("Temple of God"), the golden-domed main shrine. Several holy sites line the Parikrama, including the Dukh Bhanjani Ber, a tree shrine said to have healing powers and the Athsath Tirath, representing 68 pilgrim shrines. The Parikrama continues to the **Akal Takht**. The complex includes the Guru ka Langar—a free kitchen symbolizing the caste-free, egalitarian society the Sikh gurus sought to create.

MAHARAJA RANJIT SINGH

One of North India's most remarkable rulers, Maharaja Ranjit Singh (r. 1790–1839) established Punjab's first Sikh kingdom by persuading rival chieftains to unite. A military genius, his strong army kept both the British forces and Afghan invaders at bay by making Punjab a prosperous center of trade and industry. A devout Sikh, the one-eyed Ranjit Singh was an enlightened ruler who liked to say, "God intended me to look at all religions with one eye."

SIKHISM

With their characteristic turbans and full beards, the Sikhs are easy to identify. Sikhism is a reformist faith, founded in the 15th century by Guru Nanak. It believes in a formless God. It is also called the Gurmat, or the "Guru's Doctrine," and Sikh temples are known as *gurdwaras*, literally, "doors to the guru." Nanak, the first of a series of ten gurus, chose his most devout disciple as his successor. The tenth and last guru, Guru Gobind Singh (1666–1708), reorganized the community as a military order, the Khalsa, to combat religious persecution by the Mughals. He gave the Sikhs their distinctive identity and the Khalsa's five symbols—*kesh* (long hair), *kachha* (underwear), *kirpan* (small sword), *kangha* (comb), and *kara* (bracelet)—that all Sikhs are obligated to wear.

GOLDEN TEMPLE COMPLEX

1 Temple Office
2 Cloakrooms
3 Darshani Darwaza and Clocktower
4 Hari Mandir (Temple of God)
5 Athsath Tirath (68 Shrines)
6 Guru ka Langar (Dining Hall)
7 Baba Karak Singh's Residence
8 Assembly Hall
9 Baba Deep Singh's Shrine
10 Darshani Deorhi (Gateway to Sanctum)
11 Arjun Dev's Tree
12 Akal Takht (Seat of Sikh religious authority)
13 Nishan Sahibs (Flagstaffs)
14 Gobind Singh's Shrine
15 Dukh Bhanjani Ber (Tree Shrine)

KEY

☐ Area illustrated below

Parikrama

Central Sikh Museum

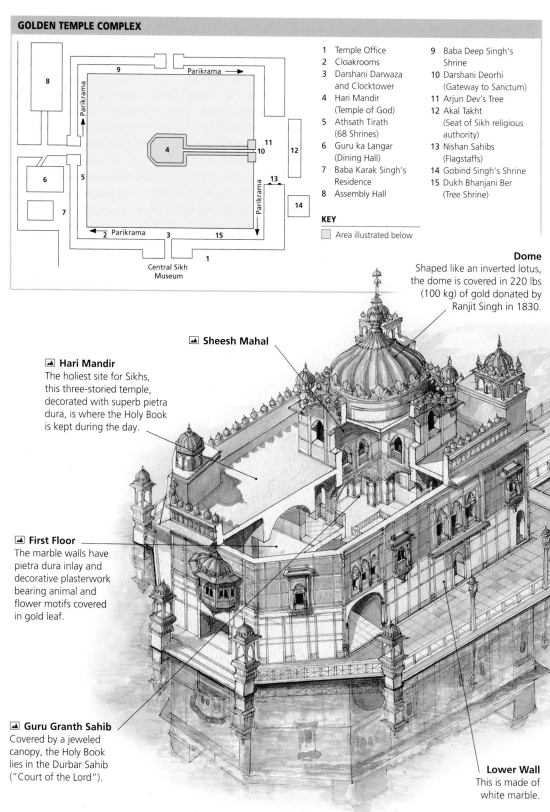

Dome
Shaped like an inverted lotus, the dome is covered in 220 lbs (100 kg) of gold donated by Ranjit Singh in 1830.

▣ Sheesh Mahal

▣ Hari Mandir
The holiest site for Sikhs, this three-storied temple, decorated with superb pietra dura, is where the Holy Book is kept during the day.

▣ First Floor
The marble walls have pietra dura inlay and decorative plasterwork bearing animal and flower motifs covered in gold leaf.

▣ Guru Granth Sahib
Covered by a jeweled canopy, the Holy Book lies in the Durbar Sahib ("Court of the Lord").

Lower Wall
This is made of white marble.

GURU PARAB

The festival of Guru Parab celebrates Guru Nanak's birthday on a full Moon night in late October–early November (date varies). It is particularly spectacular at the Golden Temple, which is illuminated by thousands of lamps.

Hari Mandir ➤

⛰ Akal Takht

⛰ Darshani Deorhi
This gateway provides the first glimpse of the temple's inner sanctum. It has two splendid silver doors and sacred verses carved on its walls.

First floor ➤

Darshani Deorhi ➤

Amrit Sarovar
The pool where Sikhs are baptized was built in 1577 by Ram Das, the 4th guru.

⛰ Causeway
The 200-ft (60-m) long marble causeway is flanked by nine gilded lamps on each side, and leads to the temple across the Amrit Sarovar.

Akal Takht ➤
The seat of the supreme governing body of the Sikhs, this houses the gurus' swords and flagstaffs, as well as the Holy Book at night.

▼ Guru Granth Sahib

Sheesh Mahal ➤
The Hall of Mirrors, on the top floor of the Hari Mandir, has a curved *bangaldar* roof, and its floors are swept with a special broom made of peacock feathers.

KEY DATES

1589–1601	1760s	1776	1830	1984	2003
The Golden Temple is constructed, under the care of the Sikhs' 4th guru, Arjan Dev.	Muslim Afghans attack the Golden Temple and raze it to the ground on several occasions.	The Khalsa (Sikh Commonwealth) rebuild the Golden Temple.	Maharaja Ranjit Singh adorns the temple's dome with gold.	The temple is damaged during Operation Blue Star, undertaken by the army to flush out extremists.	The Punjab government funds an extensive project to beautify the area around the Golden Temple.

Causeway ▲

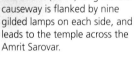

Taj Mahal, Agra

One of the world's most famous buildings, the Taj Mahal was built by the Mughal emperor Shah Jahan in memory of his favorite wife, Mumtaz Mahal, who died in 1631. Its perfect proportions and exquisite craftsmanship have been described as "a vision, a dream, a poem, a wonder." This sublime garden-tomb, an image of the Islamic garden of paradise, cost nearly 41 million rupees and 1,100 lb (500 kg) of gold. About 20,000 workers labored for 12 years to complete it in 1643.

Dome

▲ View of the Taj Mahal
The Taj Mahal complex is bounded on three sides by red sandstone walls. At the far ends of the complex, there are two grand buildings, the western one is the Taj Mahal mosque *(above right)*.

Four Minarets
Each 131 ft (40 m) high and crowned by an open octagonal pavilion, or *chhatri*, the minarets frame the tomb, highlighting the perfect symmetry of the complex.

Main entrance

▣ Dome
The 144-ft (44-m) high double dome is capped with a finial.

Marble Screen
The filigree screen, daintily carved from a single block of marble, was meant to veil the area around the royal tombs.

▣ Pietra Dura
Inspired by the paradise garden, intricately carved floral designs, inlaid with precious stones, embellish the austere white marble surface to give it the look of a jeweled casket.

▣ Tomb Chamber
Mumtaz Mahal's cenotaph, raised on a platform, is placed next to Shah Jahan's. The actual graves, in a dark crypt below, are closed to the public.

Yamuna River

▣ Calligraphic Panels
The size of the Koranic verses increases as the arch gets higher, creating the subtle optical illusion of a uniformly flowing script.

KEY DATES				
1632	**1643**	**1666**	**1983**	**2001**
Work on the Taj begins, following the death of Mumtaz Mahal.	The thousands of artists and craftsmen complete the work on the Taj.	Shah Jahan dies and is laid to rest beside his queen.	The Taj Mahal is declared a UNESCO World Heritage Site.	The Taj Mahal Conservation Collaborative starts to restore the grounds.

▲ **Tomb Chamber**

▲ **Lotus Pool**
Named after its lotus-shaped fountain spouts, the pool reflects the tomb. Almost every visitor is photographed sitting on the marble bench here.

Charbagh
The quadrilateral garden was irrigated with water from the Yamuna River.

PLAN OF THE TAJ MAHAL

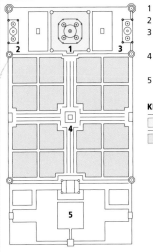

1 Main tomb
2 *Masjid* (mosque)
3 *Mehmankhana* (guesthouse)
4 *Charbagh* (quadrified garden)
5 Gateway

KEY
☐ Area illustrated left
☐ Charbagh

🖼 **Pishtaq (porch)**
Recessed arches provide depth, while their inlaid panels reflect the changing light to give the tomb a mystical aura.

Pishtaq (porch) ▶

Marble inlay above the mosque's central arch ▶

Dome Interior ▶
The dome is actually double-skinned; the interior dome, barely a third of the height of the outer skin, is visible from inside the main chamber, and is separate from the dome visible from outside.

Pietra dura ▶

Calligraphic Panels ▶

MUMTAZ MAHAL

Arjumand Banu (later Mumtaz Mahal) was the emperor's favorite wife. She accompanied him on all his campaigns and died in 1631, while giving birth to their 14th child. They were married for 19 years.

MUGHAL STYLE

Mughal buildings, whether built of marble or red sandstone, assert their exalted, imperial status. The Mughal emperors were great patrons of the arts, literature, and architecture and their rule established a rich, pluralistic culture, blending the best of Islamic and Hindu traditions. Their greatest contribution to architecture was the garden tomb, raised on a high plinth in the centre of a **charbagh** garden. Decorative elements, such as perforated *jalis* (screens)—used extensively for privacy and ventilation—refined inlay work and cusped arches gave Mughal buildings an ethereal grace that offset their massive size. Other features include *chhatris* (domed rooftop pavilions) that were adapted from Rajput architecture, and minarets that gave symmetry to the buildings.

THE PARADISE GARDEN

The hallmark of Mughal landscape design, the paradise garden was introduced by Babur (1483–1530), the first Mughal emperor, who yearned for the beauty of Ferghana, his Central Asian homeland. Based on Islamic geometric and metaphysical concepts of design, the *charbagh* was an enclosed garden divided into four quarters by raised walkways, water channels, and sunken groves. Water, the source of all life, was the central element, and the intersecting channels met at a focal point that contained a pavilion for the emperor, who was seen as a representative of God on Earth.

THE TAJ MAHAL'S DECORATION

It is widely believed that the Taj Mahal was designed to be an earthly replica of one of the houses of paradise. Its impeccable marble facing, embellished by a remarkable use of surface design, is a showcase for the refined aesthetic that reached its zenith during Shah Jahan's reign (1627–1658). The Taj Mahal manifests the richness and wealth of Mughal art, as seen in architecture, garden design, painting, jewelry, calligraphy, and textiles. Decorative elements include ornamental *jalis*, carved panels of flowering plants and **calligraphic panels**, as well as floral motifs in pietra dura, a Florentine mosaic work technique said to have been imported by Emperor Jahangir.

Fatehpur Sikri

Built by Emperor Akbar between 1571 and 1585 in honor of Salim Chishti, a famous Sufi saint of the Chishti order, Fatehpur Sikri was the capital of the Mughal empire for 14 years. One of the best examples of a Mughal walled city, with defined areas and imposing gateways, its architecture is a blend of Hindu and Islamic styles *(Mughal Style, see p.204)*, and reflects Akbar's secular vision as well as his type of governance. The city was abandoned, some say for lack of water, in 1585, and many of its treasures were plundered. It owes its present state of preservation to the efforts of Lord Curzon, Viceroy of India and a great conservationist.

Fretwork *jali*

THE JAMI MASJID AND SALIM CHISHTI

Towering over Fatehpur Sikri is the grand open mosque **Jami Masjid**. Its vast congregational area has monumental gateways to the east and south. The 177-ft (54-m) Buland Darwaza, a triumphal arch, was erected by Akbar to mark his 1573 conquest of Gujarat. The spiritual focus of the complex is the tomb of Sufi mystic Salim Chishti. Ever since Akbar's childlessness was ended after the saint's prediction in 1568, his tomb has attracted thousands, particularly childless women in search of a miracle. Visitors make a wish, tie a thread on the screen around the tomb, and return home confident that their wish will come true.

AKBAR THE GREAT

The greatest emperor of the Muslim Mughal dynasty, Akbar (r.1556–1605) was a brilliant administrator and an enlightened ruler. Just 14 years old when he ascended the throne, his first task was to consolidate and expand his fledgling empire. His most significant move was the political and matrimonial alliances he formed with the Hindu Rajputs. However, it was his policy of religious tolerance that truly set him apart. Akbar was fascinated by the study of comparative religion and built a special "House of Worship" in Fatehpur Sikri, where he often met leaders of other faiths.

LORD CURZON

One of colonial India's most flamboyant viceroys, Lord Curzon (1859–1925) believed British rule was necessary to civilize "backward" India. He introduced sweeping changes in the education system, but he is remembered most for his role as a conservator of Indian monuments. Lord Curzon was responsible for the restoration of a vast number of Hindu, Islamic, and Mughal buildings, among them the gateway to Emperor Akbar's tomb at Sikandra, Agra Fort, the buildings at Fatehpur Sikri, the Jain temples at Mount Abu, and the Taj Mahal. In 1905, due to a difference of opinion with the British military commander-in-chief, Lord Kitchener, Curzon returned to England. By the time he left, he had achieved sufficient legislation to protect India's historic buildings, and set up an organization to conserve them.

PLAN OF FATEHPUR SIKRI

Fatehpur Sikri's royal complex contains the private and public spaces of Akbar's court, including the harem and the treasury. The adjoining sacred area, with the Jami Masjid mosque, Salim Chishti's tomb, and the Buland Darwaza arch are separated from the royal quarters by the Badshahi Darwaza, a royal gateway.

KEY

☐ Area illustrated below

☐ Other buildings

☐ Sacred complex (Jami Masjid)

TANSEN

A musical genius, the legendary composer-musician Tansen was Akbar's Master of Music and one of the "nine jewels" in his court. He developed an exciting new range of melodic modes, or ragas.

Jami Masjid

🔳 **Khwabgah**

Anoop Talao
This pool is associated with Akbar's renowned court musician, Tansen, who, according to legend, could light oil lamps with his magical singing.

🔳 **Turkish Sultana's House**
The fine dado panels and delicately sculpted walls of this ornate sandstone pavilion make the stone seem like wood. It is topped with an unusual stone roof of imitation clay tiles.

🔳 **Diwan-i-Aam**
This large courtyard with an elaborate pavilion was originally draped with rich tapestries and was used for public hearings and celebrations.

KEY DATES

1571	1576	1585	1986
Construction of Emperor Akbar's new capital at Fatehpur Sikri begins.	The 15-story triumphal arch Buland Darwaza is built by Akbar.	Fatehpur Sikri is abandoned by Emperor Akbar.	Fatehpur Sikri becomes a UNESCO World Heritage Site.

Entrance

▲ Pillar in the Diwan-i-Khas
The central axis of Akbar's court, supported by carved brackets, was inspired by Gujarati buildings.

▲ Panch Mahal
This sandstone, five-story open pavilion, overlooking the Pachisi Court, is where Akbar's queens and their attendants savored the cool evening breezes. Its decorative screens were probably stolen after the city was abandoned.

Ankh Michauli ▶
Sometimes identified as the treasury, this building has mythical guardian beasts carved on its stone struts. Its name means "blind man's buff."

◀ Diwan-i-Khas
This hall, used for private audiences and debates, is a unique fusion of different architectural styles and religious motifs.

Diwan-i-Aam ▶

Turkish Sultana's House ▶

Haram Sara Complex

Jodha Bai's Palace

Sunehra Makan

🖼 Panch Mahal

Birbal's House

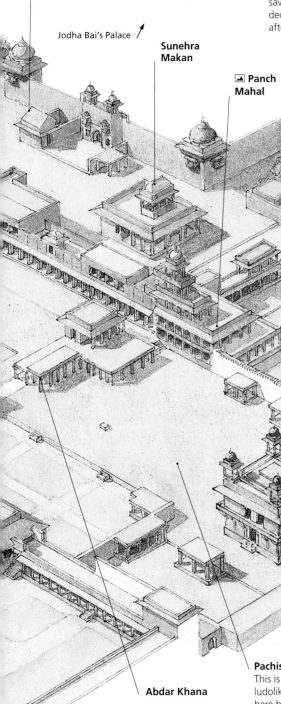

Khwabgah ▲
Akbar's private sleeping quarters, with an ingenious ventilation shaft near his bed, lie within this lavishly decorated "Chamber of Dreams."

🖼 Ankh Michauli

🖼 Diwan-i-Khas

Pachisi Court
This is named after a ludolike game played here by the ladies of the court.

Abdar Khana

The exquisite, white marble tomb of Salim Chishti ▶

The Great Stupa, Sanchi

Dominating the Hill of Sanchi, India's best-preserved and most extensive Buddhist site, is the Great Stupa. Its hemispherical shape is believed to symbolize the upturned alms bowl of a Buddhist monk, or an umbrella of protection for followers of the Buddhist *dharma* (doctrine). The stupa's main glory lies in its four stone *toranas* (gateways), added in the 1st century BC. Their superb sculptures replicate the techniques of wood and ivory carving, and cover a rich variety of Buddhist themes.

Buddha at Sanchi

▲ The Great Stupa and its West Gateway
Enclosing a smaller brick stupa built by Emperor Ashoka in the 3rd century BC, the Great Stupa is capped by a three-tiered stone umbrella symbolizing the layers of heaven.

Vedika (Railings)
These are an impressive re-creation in stone of a typical wooden railing design. They were the inspiration for the stone railings around Sansad Bhavan, or the Parliament House, in New Delhi.

◺ Circumambulatory Paths
The paths have balustrades carved with medallions of flowers, birds, and animals, and the names of the donors who funded them.

◺ Architrave

◺ South Gateway

Four Gateways
These show scenes from the Buddha's life, and episodes from the *Jataka Tales*. The Buddha is not depicted in human form, but only through symbols, such as a Bodhi Tree, footprints, or a wheel.

◺ West Gateway
This animated scene from the *Jataka Tales* shows monkeys scrambling across a bridge to escape from soldiers.

Chattra (Parasol)
The Great Stupa is crowned by a squared-off platform (*harmika*), which encloses a triple "parasol" (*chattra*) atop a mast (*yasti*).

◺ Buddha
Statues of the Buddha meditating, added in the 5th century AD, face each of the gateways.

KEY DATES				
2nd century BC	**1300s**	**1818**	**1912–19**	**1989**
The Great Stupa is built at Sanchi by Emperor Ashoka.	With the decline of Buddhism in India, the Great Stupa falls into disrepair.	The Great Stupa. is "rediscovered" by General Taylor of the Bengal Cavalry.	The Director General of Archeology in India excavates and then restores the site.	The Great Stupa is declared a UNESCO World Heritage Site.

▲ West Gateway

▲ East Gateway

Salabhanjika ➤

South Gateway ➤
The Wheel of Law, seen here being worshiped by devotees, symbolizes the Buddha.

🖼 North Gateway
Here, Sujata, the village chief's daughter, offers the Buddha (represented by the Bodhi Tree) *kheer* (rice pudding), as the demon Mara sends the temptress to seduce him.

THE JATAKA TALES
The Buddha's past lives are retold in this large collection of fables, in which an animal or bird often takes the part of the Buddha. The fables had great religious, moral, social, and cultural significance.

▼ North Gateway

Detail of Architrave ➤
The intricate carving on the architraves is the work of wood and ivory craftsmen hired to carve the stone.

🖼 East Gateway
A scene here shows a royal retinue at the palace of Kapilavastu, the Buddha's home before he renounced his princely life.

🖼 Salabhanjika
Supporting the lowest architrave of the East Gateway is a sensuous, voluptuous tree nymph, gracefully positioned under a mango tree.

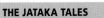

Circumambulatory Paths ➤

BUDDHISM'S ORIGINS AND PHILOSOPHY
The Buddha was born in 566 BC as Siddhartha Gautama, prince of Kapilavastu. Renouncing his princely life, he left his palace at the age of 30 to search for answers to the meaning of human existence and suffering. He spent six years living with hermits, undertaking severe penances and fasts, but found these gave him no answers. Enlightenment finally came at Bodh Gaya, where, after meditating for 49 days under the Bodhi Tree, he discovered that the cause of suffering is desire; and that desire can be conquered by following the Eightfold Path of Righteousness: Right Thought, Understanding, Speech, Action, Livelihood, Effort, Concentration and Contemplation. The essence of the Buddha's teachings is non-violence and peace.

BUDDHIST STYLE
India's earliest Buddhist monuments were stupas, large reliquaries in which the ashes of the Buddha and other great teachers were interred. Solid throughout, the stupa itself is undecorated and designed to stimulate prayer and represent the path to divine understanding. As Indian traditions spread throughout Southeast Asia, the Buddhist stupa reached new heights of complex Buddhist symbolism. Borobodur Temple in Java, with its design and sculpture of the highest order, is probably the greatest monument of this architectural style.

EMPEROR ASHOKA
One of India's greatest rulers, Ashoka (r. 269–232 BC) was the grandson of Chandragupta Maurya, who founded the country's first empire. The carnage and misery brought about by Ashoka's bloody conquest of Kalinga (now Orissa) in 260 BC filled him with remorse. He gave up *digvijaya* (military conquest) for *dharmavijaya* (spiritual conquest), and became a great patron of Buddhism, building many stupas, including the original brick stupa at Sanchi. Ashoka was a humane ruler whose edicts on rocks and pillars all over his vast empire record his ethical code of righteousness and nonviolence (*ahimsa*). He asked his officials to be impartial, just, and compassionate, and his subjects to respect others' religions, give to charity, and avoid the killing of animals.

Grand Palace and Wat Phra Kaeo, Bangkok

This remarkable site was built in the late 18th century to mark the founding of the new capital, to provide a resting place for the sacred Emerald Buddha, and a residence for the king. Surrounded by 1.2 miles (1.9 km) of walls, the complex was once a self-sufficient city within a city. The Thai royal family now lives in Dusit, but Wat Phra Kaeo (shown here), a subcomplex within the Grand Palace complex, is still Thailand's holiest temple and a stunning piece of Buddhist architecture (Buddhist Style, see p.209).

Temple Skyline
Sanam Luang provides a fine view of the decorative spires of Wat Phra Kaeo.

THE EMERALD BUDDHA

In 1434, lightning struck Wat Phra Kaeo temple in Chiang Rai and cracked it open, revealing a simple stucco image that encased a jadeite image: the Emerald Buddha. Chiang Mai's king sent an army of elephants to bring the image to him, but as the animal bearing it refused to take the road to Chiang Mai, it was enshrined at Lampang. After several moves, the Buddha was taken to Laos in 1552, where it remained until King Rama I brought it back to Thailand in 1778. It was kept in Wat Arun before being moved to its current resting place in 1785.

THE RAMAKIEN

The *Ramakien* is an allegory of the triumph of good over evil. Rama, heir to the throne of Ayodhya, is sent into a 14-year exile with his wife Sita and brother Lakshman. Tosakan, the demon-king of Longka, abducts Sita from the forest. Hanuman, the monkey god, helps rescue Sita and defeat Tosakan, and Rama returns triumphantly to Ayodhya. This epic tale was probably established after the Thais took Angkor in the 15th century. All the Chakri kings adopted Rama as one of their names, and the 14th-century kingdom of Ayutthaya was named after the fictional Ayodhya. The legend has also been a great inspiration for Thai painting, classical drama, and puppetry.

EXPLORING WAT PHRA KAEO

When Rama I established his new capital, he envisioned a temple that would surpass its Sukhothai and Ayutthaya predecessors. The result was the splendid Wat Phra Kaeo. The **bot** houses the surprisingly small image of the Emerald Buddha, seated in a glass case high above a gilded altar. Opposite, the **Upper terrace** has several structures, the most striking of which is the **Phra Si Rattana Chedi**, built by King Mongkut (Rama IV) in 1855 to house sacred Buddha relics. The adjacent **Phra Mondop** was initially used as a library. Its exterior has Javanese Buddha images on the four outer corners. To its north is a **model of Cambodia's Angkor Wat**. On the **Northern terrace**, the **Ho Phra Nak** enshrines the ashes of minor royals, while the **Wihan Yot** contains the Nak Buddha rescued from Ayutthaya.

GRAND PALACE AND WAT PHRA KAEO

1 Entrance
2 Wat Phra Kaeo complex
3 Dusit Throne Hall
4 Aphonphimok Pavilion
5 Chakri Throne Hall
6 Inner Palace
7 Phra Maha Monthien buildings
8 Siwalai Gardens
9 Rama IV Chapel
10 Boromphiman Mansion
11 Audience Chamber

KEY
- Wat Phra Kaeo complex
- Buildings
- Lawns

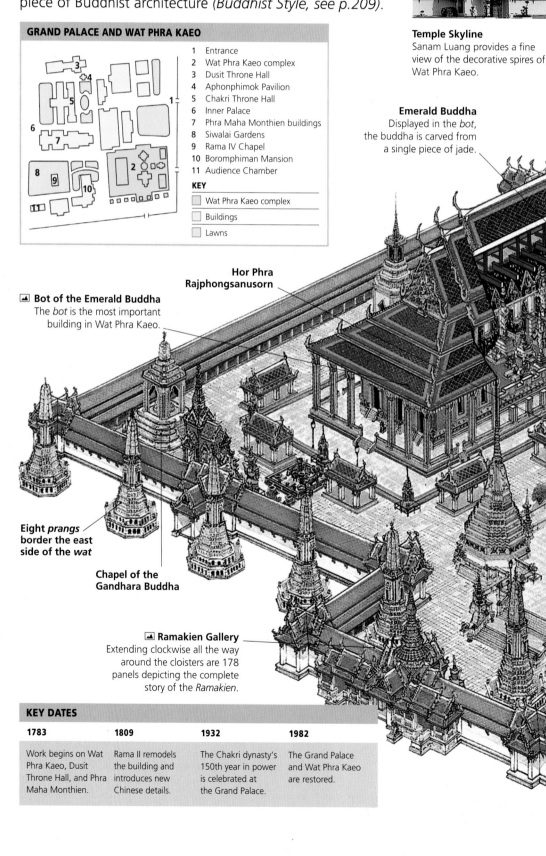

Emerald Buddha
Displayed in the *bot*, the buddha is carved from a single piece of jade.

Hor Phra Rajphongsanusorn

Bot of the Emerald Buddha
The *bot* is the most important building in Wat Phra Kaeo.

Eight *prangs* border the east side of the *wat*

Chapel of the Gandhara Buddha

Ramakien Gallery
Extending clockwise all the way around the cloisters are 178 panels depicting the complete story of the *Ramakien*.

KEY DATES

1783	1809	1932	1982
Work begins on Wat Phra Kaeo, Dusit Throne Hall, and Phra Maha Monthien.	Rama II remodels the building and introduces new Chinese details.	The Chakri dynasty's 150th year in power is celebrated at the Grand Palace.	The Grand Palace and Wat Phra Kaeo are restored.

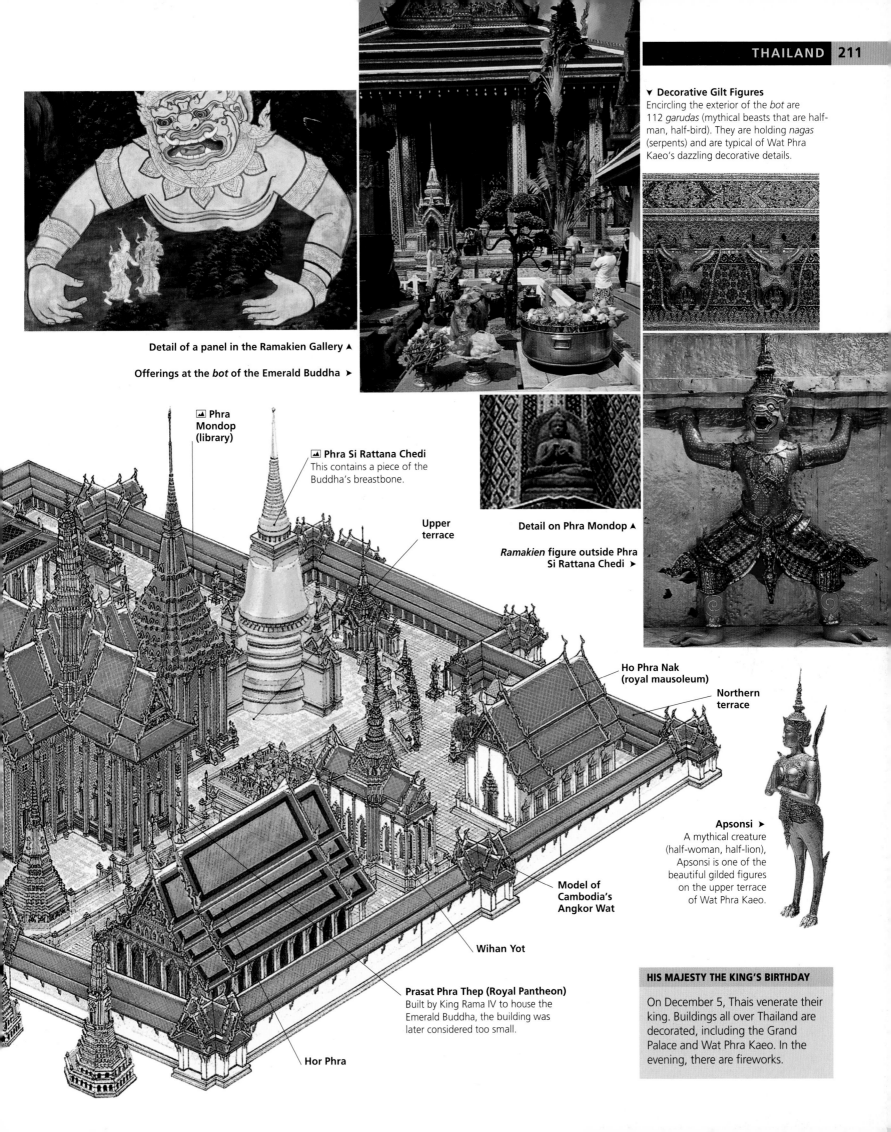

Detail of a panel in the Ramakien Gallery ▲

Offerings at the *bot* of the Emerald Buddha ▶

▼ **Decorative Gilt Figures**
Encircling the exterior of the *bot* are 112 *garudas* (mythical beasts that are half-man, half-bird). They are holding *nagas* (serpents) and are typical of Wat Phra Kaeo's dazzling decorative details.

🔺 **Phra Mondop (library)**

🔺 **Phra Si Rattana Chedi**
This contains a piece of the Buddha's breastbone.

Upper terrace

Detail on Phra Mondop ▲

Ramakien figure outside Phra Si Rattana Chedi ▶

Ho Phra Nak (royal mausoleum)

Northern terrace

Apsonsi ▶
A mythical creature (half-woman, half-lion), Apsonsi is one of the beautiful gilded figures on the upper terrace of Wat Phra Kaeo.

Model of Cambodia's Angkor Wat

Wihan Yot

Prasat Phra Thep (Royal Pantheon)
Built by King Rama IV to house the Emerald Buddha, the building was later considered too small.

Hor Phra

HIS MAJESTY THE KING'S BIRTHDAY

On December 5, Thais venerate their king. Buildings all over Thailand are decorated, including the Grand Palace and Wat Phra Kaeo. In the evening, there are fireworks.

Wat Arun, Bangkok

Named after Aruna, the Indian god of dawn, Wat Arun temple is one of Bangkok's best-known landmarks. Legend says that King Taksin arrived here from the sacked capital, Ayutthaya, in 1767. He enlarged the temple that stood on the site into a royal chapel to house the most revered image of the Buddha in Thailand: the Emerald Buddha. Rama I and Rama II were responsible for the size of the current temple: the central *prang*, or tower, is 260 ft (79 m) high and the circumference of its base is 768 ft (234 m). In the late 19th century, Rama IV added ornamentation created with broken pieces of porcelain. The monument's style is derived mainly from Khmer architecture.

Ceramic flower on the central *prang*

THE CHAKRI DYNASTY

In 1782, Chao Phraya Chakri (later King Rama I) established the Chakri dynasty in Krung Thep (Bangkok). The reigns of Rama I, II and III were a time of stability. Rama II was a literary man, while Rama III was a staunch traditionalist. King Mongkut (Rama IV) modernized Siam (Thailand), and opened it up to foreign trade and influences. His son, King Chulalongkorn, or Rama V (r. 1868–1910), was perhaps the greatest Chakri king. He furthered modernization by introducing financial reforms and abolishing slavery. He was idealized by his subjects, and his funeral was a grand state affair. Even today, he is commemorated on Chulalongkorn Day (October 23).

KHMER ARCHITECTURE

Thailand's stone temple complexes, or *prasats*, were built by the Khmers, who ruled much of Southeast Asia in the 9th–13th centuries. *Prasats* were built to symbolize kingship and the universe. Most have staircases or bridges lined with *nagas* (a seven-headed serpent thought to be the keeper of life's force), leading to a **central monument**. This is usually decorated with carved stone reliefs and topped by a *prang* (tower). *Prangs* symbolize Mount Meru, the abode of the gods in Hindu-Buddhist cosmology. Lintels and pediments over the entrances depict Hindu and Buddhist deities.

ARUNA, INDRA, AND VAYU

Worshiped in India from the early Vedic age (1500 BC), the Hindu deities Aruna, Indra, and Vayu personify nature and the elements. Aruna, the god of dawn, is the charioteer of Surya, the Sun god. Red-skinned, he stands on the chariot in front of the Sun, sheltering the world from its fury with his body. Indra, the god of the sky and the heavens, rides a golden chariot drawn by horses and is armed with a *vajra*, or thunderbolt. Indra sends the rain and rules the weather, and is often depicted sitting on Airavatta, the four-trunked white elephant who represents a rain cloud. Vayu (Phra Pai in Thai) is the god of the winds and messenger of the gods. He is also the regent of the northwest quarter of the heavens and is depicted with white skin, seated on an antelope.

◄ River View of Wat Arun
This popular view of Wat Arun, seen from the Chao Phraya River, appears on the 10-baht coin and in the Tourism Authority of Thailand (TAT) logo.

▲ Ceramic Details

Minor *prangs* at each corner of the *wat*

▲ The Bot
In the temple complex are the usual buildings found in a *wat*. This image of the Buddha in the *bot* (ordination hall) contains the ashes of Rama II.

◄ Stairs on the Central Prang
The steep steps represent the difficulties of reaching higher levels of existence.

◄ Multicolored Tiers
Rows of demons, decorated with pieces of porcelain, line the exterior walls of the central *prang*.

◄ Decoration of the Four Minor *Prangs*

▼ Gold leaf honoring the Buddha

◄ Chinese Guards
Eight sets of steps lead up the first terrace, and each is guarded by Chinese figu[res] that were once used as ball[ast] on Chinese trading ships.

CENTRAL MONUMENT OF WAT ARUN

The monument's design symbolizes Hindu-Buddhist cosmology. The central *prang* is the mythical Mount Meru, and its ornamental tiers are worlds within worlds. The layout of four minor *prangs* around a central one is a symbolic mandala shape.

Top terrace

One of the eight entrances

Indra's weapon, the *vajra*, or thunderbolt, at the *prang*'s crest

SYMBOLIC LEVELS OF THE CENTRAL PRANG

Devaphum
The top represents the peak of Mount Meru, rising above four subsidiary peaks. It denotes six heavens within seven realms of happiness.

Tavatimsa
The central section, where all desires are fulfilled, is guarded at the four cardinal points by the Hindu god Indra.

Traiphum
The base represents 31 realms of existence across the three worlds (Desire, Form, and Formless) of the Buddhist universe.

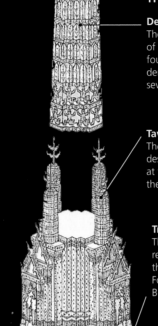

KEY DATES

1700s	Early 1800s	1971
King Taksin remodels Wat Arun temple to house the Emerald Buddha.	Rama II restores the temple and increases the height of the central *prang*.	Wat Arun minor repa lightning s of the spir

Small Cove ►
On the second level of the central *prang* are small coves, inside which are *kinnari*, mythical creatures that are half-bird, half-woman.

🖼 De Four M
Inside t each m are sta Pai, the on hors

Mondops
Between each c *prangs* is a squa *mondop* (altar). a Buddha statue

🖼 Ceramic Details
Around the base of the *prangs* are rows of *yaksha*, or demons, that lend support to the structure. They are decorated with colorful pieces of porcelain donated by the local people

🖼 Stairs on the central *prang*

Vast expanse of the Angkor Wat temple complex, Cambodia

Angkor Wat

One of the largest religious structures in the world, the 12th-century temple of Angkor Wat is covered with exquisite carvings that form the longest bas-relief in existence. It was part of a vast complex of religious and administrative buildings constructed between the 9th and the 15th centuries by the Khmer empire, which ruled most of Southeast Asia at that time. The temple is an earthly representation of the Hindu cosmos. Its five towers, shaped like lotus buds, form a pyramidal structure symbolizing the mythical Mount Meru, home of the gods. The outer walls represent the edge of the world, and the moats, the cosmic ocean. Dedicated to Vishnu, the temple was built for the god-king Suryavarman II (r. 1113–50), probably as a funerary monument. It faces west, toward the setting Sun, a symbol of death.

Central Sanctuary

▲ Meditating Buddhist Monk
Angkor was originally a Hindu site, but it was later converted to Buddhist use. Today, Buddhist monks live in a pagoda by the side of the temple.

▼ The *Battle of Kuruksetra* bas-relief in the West Gallery

East Gallery

Central Sanctuary
Rising 213 ft (65 m) from the heart of Angkor Wat, the Central Sanctuary has four entrances, each facing one of the cardinal directions. Originally dedicated to the Hindu god Vishnu, it now houses four statues of the Buddha.

◄ Gallery of the Bas-Reliefs
The outer side of the gallery comprises 60 columns, while the inner wall is carved with beautiful bas-reliefs of mythological and historical events.

North Gallery

Gallery of the Bas-Reliefs

◄ Causeway
Angkor Wat's majestic façade can be seen from the causeway at its west entrance. Balustrades terminating in the form of the *naga,* the seven-headed serpent, border the causeway on either side and extend all the way around the temple.

View of Angkor Wat ►
The elegance and grace of the temples, and their reflection in the moats that surround them, make Angkor Wat an awe-inspiring sight.

KEY DATES

1113–50	1432	1860	1898	1992	1993
Construction of Angkor Wat during the rule of the Khmer empire.	The Siamese (Thais) sack Angkor Wat and the site is abandoned.	Angkor Wat is "rediscovered" by French naturalist Henri Mouhot.	The French *École Française d'Extrême Orient* starts to clear the site.	Angkor Wat is declared a UNESCO World Heritage Site.	An international conservation project starts the preservation of Angkor Wat's temples.

SPRING EQUINOX

Khmer architects aligned Angkor Wat with the Sun and the Moon. At the spring equinox, it has a spectacular solar alignment with the causeway as the Sun rises over the exact center of the Central Sanctuary.

South Gallery
On the *Judgment of Yama* panel, the souls of the good are being carried on thrones on their way to heaven, while the damned are dragged into hell.

▲ Apsaras
Numerous celestial dancers are carved onto the walls, each slightly different in gesture and detail. The variety of hairstyles and headresses is extraordinary.

⊡ West Gallery
The bas-reliefs here show scenes from the Battle of Kurukshetra, the main subject of the *Mahabharata*.

⊡ Causeway

GALLERY OF THE BAS-RELIEFS

Angkor Wat is covered with 12,917 sq ft (1,200 sq m) of intricately carved scenes that depict Khmer myths, Angkorian warfare, and stories from the great Hindu mythological epics, the *Ramayana* and the *Mahabharata*. Divided into eight sections, some of the most celebrated panels include the **Battle of Kuruksetra** in the **West Gallery**, the *Churning of the Ocean of Milk* in the **East Gallery**, and the *Judgment of Jama* in the **South Gallery**. Angkor Wat also has 1,850 carved **apsaras**, or celestial dancers. These sensuous goddesses, who are naked except for ornate jewelry and elaborate head-dresses, wear enigmatic smiles, known as the "Khmer Smile," and are the glory of Angkor.

THE FALL OF ANGKOR

The last great king of Angkor was Jayavarman VII (1181–1220). He founded the city of Angkor Thom, near Angkor Wat, where he built the Bayon Temple, among many others. This ambitious temple-building program probably depleted the kingdom's coffers, as did wars with neighboring Siam (modern-day Thailand) and Champa (Vietnam). Little is known about the kings that succeeded him, but in 1432, the Siamese sacked Angkor and the last king, Ponhea Yat, was forced to move south toward Phnom Penh, the modern-day capital of Cambodia. Although Angkor Wat remained a holy place, the Khmer empire subsequently went into decline and most of the temples were deserted, gradually becoming covered in jungle.

REDISCOVERY OF ANGKOR

Although the ruins of Angkor Wat had been chronicled by a number of foreigners, their "rediscovery" was attributed to Henri Mouhot, a Frenchman traveling under the auspices of Britain's Royal Geographical Society in 1860. A naturalist and botanist, Mouhot spent three weeks among the ruins, drawing and surveying the temples. He wrote a detailed and lyrical account of his work in his diaries, which were published after his death from malaria in 1861. His descriptions inspired numerous travelers, including the Scottish photographer John Thomson, who took the first black-and-white photographs of Angkor in 1866.

Borobodur Temple, Java

The world's largest Buddhist stupa (*Buddhist Style, see p.209*), Borobodur Temple is made from 1.6 million blocks of volcanic andesite and is constructed over nine levels. Five square terraces are surmounted by three circular ones and another stupa at the top. The structure's powerful image is enhanced further by five levels of sublime carvings depicting the lives of the Buddha, expounding the meaning of his doctrine. These images form the most comprehensive ensemble of Buddhist reliefs ever carved. As pilgrims circumambulate, praying before each image, they ascend from the terrestrial to the divine world. Abandoned in the 10th century, and later buried under ash from a volcanic eruption, the temple was not found again until 1815.

▲ **Temple Roof**

THE BAS-RELIEFS

There are 1,460 superbly carved **bas-reliefs**, extending for 3 miles (5 km), around the five lower levels of Borobodur. As visitors walk clockwise, keeping the monument to the right, the reliefs on the lowest terrace show daily life, earthly pleasures, the punishments of hell, and the laws of cause and effect, or *karma*. This vivid evocation of daily life in ancient Javanese society was later covered with stone to support the temple's weight. The second level depicts the Buddha and his life. These reliefs feature graceful figures with serene expressions wearing jewels and headdresses. Images on the other levels follow texts such as the *Jataka Tales* and *Lalitavistara*, and the Buddha's earlier incarnations and search for enlightenment.

THE SAILENDRA DYNASTY

Between AD 730 and 930, the Sailendra dynasty ruled most of Java in Indonesia. Their name is Sanskrit for "Lords of the Mountain" and they were heavily influenced by the Indian Gupta culture through the maritime trade routes of the region. Java was one of Asia's leading civilizations during this period, enriched by trade and the sale of rice, and the Sailendras created the greatest temples and monuments in Southeast Asia at the time. Borobodur Temple, arguably their finest accomplishment, took 75 years to complete.

THE MEANING OF BOROBODUR

Initially built as a Hindu temple, Borobodur is a re-creation of Mount Meru, the mythical mountain abode of Hindu gods. Symbolically, it is a *mandala*, an aid to meditation, and a meeting place of heaven and Earth. It represents the transition from the lowest manifestations of reality through to the highest spiritual awareness at the summit. The base represents the lowest sphere of consciousness (**Kamadhatu bas-reliefs**). The next level (**Rupadhatu bas-reliefs**) is the intermediate period of consciousness. The upper levels, with 72 small, perforated stupas, each containing a seated **Meditating Buddha**, represent the sphere of formlessness. At the top, the empty central stupa suggests *nirvana*, and symbolizes enlightenment, the ultimate spiritual realm.

▣ Meditating Buddhas
Most of the Buddhas on the temple roof are enclosed in individual stupas, but several are exposed. They are remarkable for their serenity and poise.

▣ Temple Roof
The view from the top of Borobodur Temple is of the volcanic plain with its palm trees and groves.

▣ Rupadhatu Bas-Reliefs

▲ Carved Gateway

▲ One of the Meditating Buddhas

◄ Kamadhatu bas-reliefs of musicians

▼ Seated Buddha
Sitting within an arched niche in the temple, this Buddha is thought to represent a hermit in a mountain cave.

RESTORATION

In 1973, a $21 million restoration project began at Borobodur. The terraces were dismantled, cataloged, cleaned, and reconstructed on a concrete foundation. This Buddhist site is now a national monument in a Muslim country.

🖼 **Carved Gateway**
This archway leading to the roof is guarded by *Kala*, a protective deity and a mythical monster who swallowed his own body.

▲ **Rupadhatu Bas-Reliefs**
These carvings depict the life of Siddhartha Gautama, the Buddha.

View of Borobodur Temple ►
The name of this colossal structure probably came from the Sanskrit *Vihara Buddha Uhr,* meaning High Buddhist Monastery. It is the earthly manifestion of the Buddhist vision of the universe.

CONSTRUCTION

Borobodur is square in plan and 113 ft (34.5 m) high. Originally, five square terraces of diminishing size were built, leading to a sixth from which three circular terraces rose, with a stupa at the summit. The original intention seems to have been to construct a pyramid, but the weight was so great that a stone buttress had to be built around the base to stop it from collapsing.

▲ A graceful, bejewelled king and queen holding court at Borobodur

🖼 **Kamadhatu Bas-Reliefs**
These superb carvings on the first level of the temple illustrate ancient Javanese society.

🖼 **Seated Buddha**

KEY DATES

770–850	c. 928	c. 900	1815	1907–11	1991
Construction of Borobodur Temple under the Sailendra dynasty.	The balance of power shifts to east Java and the temple is abandoned.	Heavy volcanic activity submerges the temple in layers of ash.	Borobodur is rediscovered by British colonial agent Sir Stamford Raffles.	The temple undergoes its first renovation, by the Dutch.	Borobodur is declared a UNESCO World Heritage Site.

Pura Ulun Danu Batur, Bali

One of Bali's most popular and spiritually significant religious complexes, the nine-temple Pura Ulun Danu Batur has a vital association with Danu (Lake) Batur, a volcanic crater lake, but it is uncertain when it was built. It is Bali's guardian temple of water supplies, since it controls the irrigation system of much of the island. From a distance, the temple's silhouette can be seen on the rim of the vast Batur caldera.

TRADITIONAL BELIEFS

Animism, ancestor worship, and a sense of the supernatural permeate Balinese life. The term *sekala niskala* (visible-invisible) sums up the idea that the physical world interacts with a spirit world. Loosely described as "gods" and "demons," the spirits are believed to dwell in natural objects such as stones or trees. Shrines are built for them and they are honored with offerings of flowers and other materials. Ancestors are deified in complex rituals and venerated at temples. Guardian spirits, such as the *Barong,* are invoked in sacred perform-ances to restore a village's cosmic balance.

THE GAMELAN ORCHESTRA

In Bali, and neighboring Lombok, traditional music is performed by a *gamelan* orchestra, a percussion ensemble consisting largely of bronze metallophones (instruments with tuned metal keys), led by drums (*kendang*). Bronze gongs of various sizes form the heart of the orchestra. Struck with mallets, they produce resonant sounds that punctuate the keyed instruments' melodies. There are also a few wind and stringed instruments, including bamboo flutes (*suling*). Most villages own a set of *gamelan* instruments for ritual occasions; some are sacred and played only at religious ceremonies. Temples have a pavilion called a **bale gong** to house the instruments.

BALINESE TEMPLE ARCHITECTURE

A Balinese *pura* (public temple) is a sacred enclosure where Hindu deities are periodically invited to descend into *pratima* (effigies) kept in shrines. Their arrangement follows a consistent pattern, with structures oriented along a mountain-sea axis. The **outer courtyard** and **central courtyard** have secondary shrines and pavilions, including the *kulkul* (watchtower), which houses a drum that is sounded when the deities have descended. The *jeroan* (**inner courtyard**) contains shrines to the temple's core deities, and often to deities of the lakes, sea and mountains, too. The *padmasana*, or lotus throne shrine, in the temple's holiest corner, has an empty seat on top signifying the Supreme God. The *meru* shrine symbolizes the mythical Hindu peak, Mount Meru.

▼ *Canang,* or daily flower offerings, made to the spirits

⊡ Inner Courtyard
The inner courtyard is the most sacred. Three gateways lead from one courtyard to the next.

◄ **Temple Flags**

◄ **Gold-painted Doors**
The great timber doors of the main temple gateway are reserved for the use of priests on important religious occasions.

▼ **Side Gate**

▲ **Inner Courtyard**

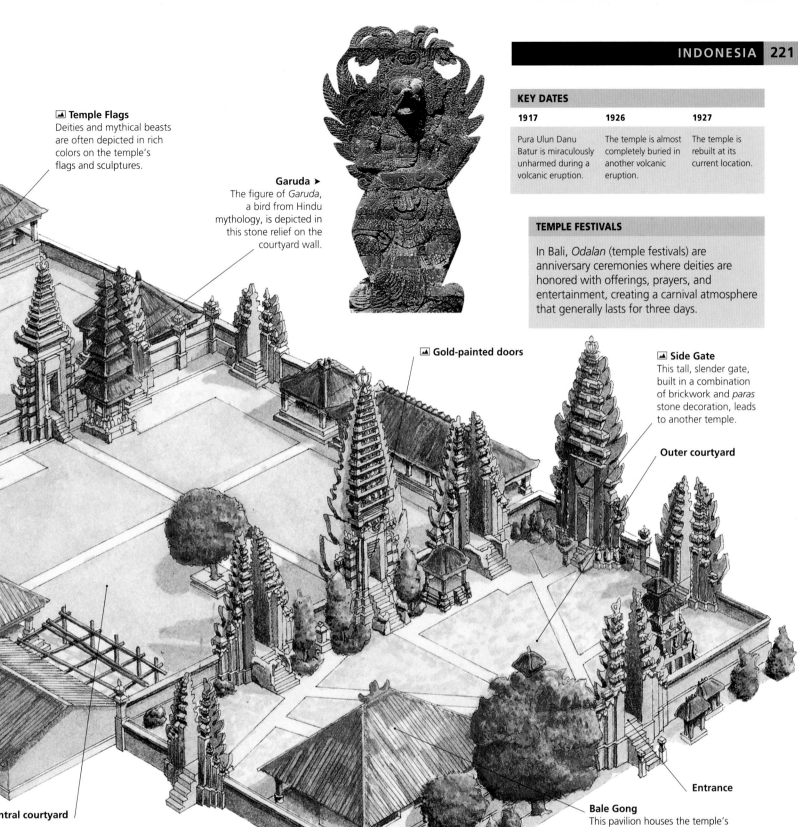

⬙ Temple Flags
Deities and mythical beasts are often depicted in rich colors on the temple's flags and sculptures.

Garuda ➤
The figure of *Garuda*, a bird from Hindu mythology, is depicted in this stone relief on the courtyard wall.

KEY DATES

1917	1926	1927
Pura Ulun Danu Batur is miraculously unharmed during a volcanic eruption.	The temple is almost completely buried in another volcanic eruption.	The temple is rebuilt at its current location.

TEMPLE FESTIVALS

In Bali, *Odalan* (temple festivals) are anniversary ceremonies where deities are honored with offerings, prayers, and entertainment, creating a carnival atmosphere that generally lasts for three days.

⬙ Gold-painted doors

⬙ Side Gate
This tall, slender gate, built in a combination of brickwork and *paras* stone decoration, leads to another temple.

Outer courtyard

Entrance

Bale Gong
This pavilion houses the temple's set of *gamelan* instruments, including a great gong believed to have a magical history.

⬙ Central courtyard

◄ Central Courtyard
The great quadrangle, shown here occupied by a festive structure of bamboo and straw, is the occasional setting for ritual dances.

OFFERINGS TO THE LAKE GODDESS

Devotees present offerings at this temple, which is dedicated to Ida Betari Dewi Ulun Danu, the goddess of Lake Batur. The respect accorded to the goddess is reinforced by events in the temple's history. At its original site, closer to the lake, the temple was saved from destruction in a volcanic eruption in 1917 when the lava flow stopped just short of its walls. After another eruption in 1926, the villagers relocated the temple to its present site.

Offerings of fruits and flowers

Sydney Opera House, with its unique
arched roof design

AUSTRALASIA

Sydney Opera House

No other building on Earth looks like Sydney Opera House. Popularly known as the "Opera House" long before the building had been completed, it is, in fact, a complex of theaters, studios, and music venues linked beneath its famous roofs, or "shells." The building's birth was long and complicated. Many of the construction problems had not been faced before, resulting in an architectural adventure that lasted 14 years. An appeal fund was set up, eventually raising AU$900,000, while the Opera House Lottery raised the balance of the AU$102 million final cost. Today, the Opera House is Sydney's most popular tourist attraction, as well as one of the world's busiest performing arts centers.

Advertising poster

DESIGN AND CONSTRUCTION

In 1957, the Danish architect Jørn Utzon won the international competition to design Sydney Opera House. He envisaged a living sculpture that could be viewed from any angle, on land, air, or sea. It was boldly conceived, posing architectural and engineering problems that Utzon's first sketches did not solve. When construction began in 1959, the intricate design proved impossible to execute and had to be greatly modified. The project remained so controversial that Utzon resigned in 1966 and an Australian design team completed the interior. However, he was reappointed as a consultant, to develop a set of guidelines for any future alterations to the building.

ROLE AND SIGNIFICANCE

Sydney Opera House is instantly recognizable around the world. It is managed by the Sydney Opera House Trust, which is responsible for maintaining its high status as Australia's main cultural landmark and performing arts center. The building is one of the world's most renowned architectural marvels and has won numerous awards, including the prestigious Top Ten Construction Achievements of the 20th Century award in 1999. An estimated 4.4 million people visit the Opera House every year, 75 percent of whom go just to look around the magnificent structure.

THE THEATER AND HALLS

Underneath the ten spectacular, sail-like roofs of varying planes and textures lies a maze of more than 1,000 rooms of all shapes and sizes showcasing different events. The **Concert Hall** is decked out in native white birch and brush box (hardwood timber). The Drama Theater stage is 49 ft (15 m) square, and can be clearly viewed from every seat in the auditorium. Refrigerated aluminum panels in the ceiling control the temperature. Fine Australian art hangs in the **Playhouse** foyer, notably Sidney Nolan's *Little Shark* (1973) and a fresco by Salvatore Zofrea (1992–3). The **Opera Theater** is the second largest venue and hosts lavish opera and dance performances. The theater's proscenium opening is 39 ft (12 m) wide, and the stage extends back 69 ft (21 m).

BACKSTAGE

Artists performing at Sydney Opera House have the use of five rehearsal studios, 60 dressing rooms, suites, and a green room complete with a bar, lounge, and restaurant. The scene-changing machinery works on well-oiled wheels—crucial in the Opera Theater, where there is often a nightly change of performance.

■ Opera Theater

Opera Theater Ceiling and Walls
These are painted black, to focus the audience's attention on the stage.

■ *The Possum Dreaming*

■ Opera House Walkway
Extensive public walkways around the building offer visitors views from many different vantage points.

■ Northern Foyers

▲ Opera Theater
Mainly used for opera and ballet, this 1,547-seat theater is big enough to stage grand operas such as Verdi's *Aïda*.

▲ Concert Hall
This is the largest interior venue in the Opera House, with seating for 2,679 people. It is used for a wide variety of performances, including symphony, choral, jazz, folk, and pop concerts, as well as variety shows.

▲ Northern Foyers
The Reception Hall and the large Northern Foyers of the Opera Theater and Concert Hall have spectacular views over Sydney Harbour.

▼ Detail of The Possum Dreaming (1988)
The mural in the Opera Theater foyer is by Michael Tjakamarra Nelson, an Aboriginal artist from the central Australian desert.

Monumental Steps
These, and the forecourt, are used for outdoor films and free entertainment.

🖾 Concert Hall

KEY DATES

1959–73	1973	2007
The Sydney Opera House is constructed to a design by Jørn Utzon.	Prokofiev's opera *War and Peace* is the first public performance.	The Opera House is inscribed in the UNESCO World Heritage List.

Roofs ➤

🖾 Bennelong Restaurant
This is one of the finest restaurants in Sydney.

Opera House Walkway ➤

Playhouse
Seating almost 400 people, this venue is ideal for intimate productions, yet it is also able to present plays with larger casts.

🖾 Roofs
Although apocryphal, the story that Jørn Utzon's arched roof design came to him while he was peeling an orange is enchanting. The highest point is 221 ft (67 m) above sea level.

Bennelong Restaurant ➤

Detail of Utzon's Tapestry (2004) ▲
TJørn Utzon's original design for this Gobelin-style tapestry, which hangs floor to ceiling in the remodeled Reception Hall, was inspired by the music of 18th-century German composer and musician Carl Philipp Emanuel Bach.

Dunedin Railway Station

Frieze with cherub and foliage

One of New Zealand's finest historic buildings, Dunedin Railway Station is also one of the best examples of railroad architecture in the southern hemisphere. Although not large by international standards, the station's delightful proportions lend it an air of grandeur. It was designed in the Flemish Renaissance style *(Renaissance Style, see p.131)* by New Zealand Railways architect George Troup, whose detailing on the outside of the building earned him the nickname "Gingerbread George."

BEGINNING OF DUNEDIN'S RAILWAY

In the early 1860s, gold was discovered in Dunedin and miners poured into the region. The money gold brought in ensured that, for a time, Dunedin was the commercial capital of New Zealand and railroads were built to transport the growing population. The first rail journey, with the new "Josephine" trains, was from Dunedin to Port Chalmers on September 10, 1872. In 1875, a second station was built in Dunedin to ease the busy first one; a third followed in 1879. The number of passengers continued to grow, so Dunedin Railway Station was commissioned.

AN ARCHITECTURAL CHALLENGE

The construction of Dunedin Railway Station was a great feat of engineering. Built on the foundations of the old harbor, iron-bark piles had to be driven deep into the reclaimed land to prevent flooding. George Troup used a number of railroad staff, whom he had trained in the art of stonemasonry, to help build the station. Machinery, including cranes, was loaned by New Zealand Railways for use during the building work to reduce costs. It is believed that New Zealand's first electrically driven concrete mixer was used in the station's construction. Costing £120,500, the station was seven times larger than its predecessor, Dunedin's third station, built in the late 1800s.

THE DESIGN OF DUNEDIN STATION

George Troup (1863–1941) arrived in New Zealand in 1884, after emigrating from Scotland following an apprenticeship in architectural design. He quickly secured a job with New Zealand Railways in Dunedin, where he was employed to design bridges and stations. He was soon promoted to head of the architectural branch, and while working in this new role he designed Dunedin Railway Station. No expense was spared to create this magnificent building. The **roof** is adorned with red Marseille tiles, while the **exterior stonework** features lavish, ornate detailing—referred to as "Gingerbread style." Inside, the **mosaic floor** is covered with decorative tiles, some of which feature images of railroad engines, wheels, signals, and wagons.

FLOOR RESTORATION

By 1956, the original floor had subsided dramatically. Exact replica mosaics had to be laid on a new concrete foundation in order to alleviate the problem.

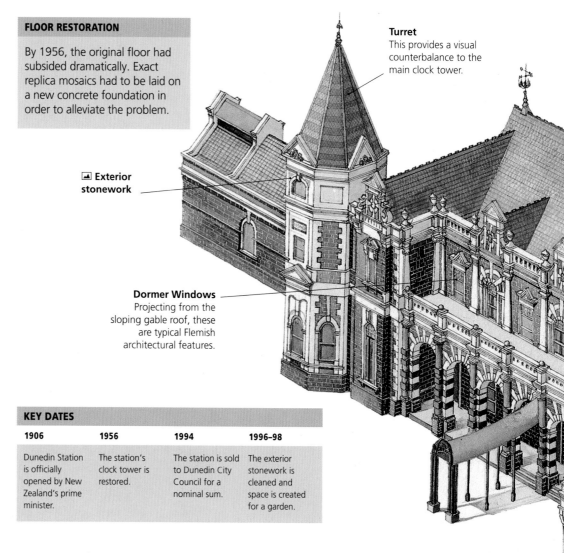

Turret
This provides a visual counterbalance to the main clock tower.

⊿ Exterior stonework

Dormer Windows
Projecting from the sloping gable roof, these are typical Flemish architectural features.

KEY DATES

1906	1956	1994	1996–98
Dunedin Station is officially opened by New Zealand's prime minister.	The station's clock tower is restored.	The station is sold to Dunedin City Council for a nominal sum.	The exterior stonework is cleaned and space is created for a garden.

▼ **Front view of Dunedin Railway Station**

▼ **Exterior Stonework**
Beige Oamaru limestone detailing provides a striking contrast to the darker Central Otago bluestone on the walls and the finely polished Aberdeen granite of the columns.

▲ Stained-glass Windows
Two imposing stained-glass windows on the mezzanine balcony depict two approaching steam engines with lights blazing, facing each other across the ticket hall.

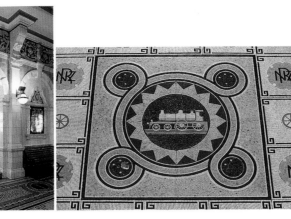

▲ Staircase

▲ Mosaic Floor

Roof
This is covered with clay Marseille tiles from France.

⊡ New Zealand Sports Hall of Fame

⊡ Ticket windows

⊡ Frieze
Cherubs and foliage adorn this frieze from the Royal Doulton factory in England, which encircles the ticket hall below the wrought-iron bordered balcony.

⊡ Stained-glass windows

▲ Ticket Windows
These are ornately decorated with white tiles and a crest featuring the old New Zealand Railways logo.

Clock Tower
This rises 120 ft (37 m) above street level.

Sandstone Lions
These finely carved creatures, one on each corner of the clock tower, guard the cupola behind them.

▲ New Zealand Sports Hall of Fame
This features imaginative displays recounting the exploits and achievements of famous New Zealanders.

Platform
Situated behind the station, the half-a mile (1-km) long platform is still a departure and arrival point for travelers.

Entrance

⊡ Mosaic Floor
More than 725,000 Royal Doulton porcelain squares form images of steam engines, rolling stock, and the New Zealand Railways logo.

⊡ Staircase
Complete with wrought-iron balustrades and mosaic-tiled steps, a staircase sweeps up from the ticket hall to the balcony above.

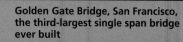

Golden Gate Bridge, San Francisco, the third-largest single span bridge ever built

THE AMERICAS

Sainte-Anne-de-Beaupré

The shrine to St. Anne, mother of the Virgin Mary, is the oldest pilgrimage site in North America. In 1620, a group of sailors who had survived a shipwreck established the shrine and dedicated it to St. Anne. In 1658, a chapel was erected and since then several churches have been built on this site. The fifth and present one, which dates from the 1920s, receives 1.5 million visitors every year, including those who come for the annual pilgrimage on St. Anne's feast day (July 26). The collection of crutches inside the basilica's entrance bears witness to its reputation for miraculous cures. Inside, the dome-vaulted ceiling is decorated with gold mosaics portraying the life of St. Anne. She is also represented in a large gilt statue in the transept, cradling the Virgin Mary.

Great Rose Window

ST. ANNE MUSEUM

The shrine's museum displays works of art that attest to the early Québec settlers' devotion to St. Anne, with wax figures, paintings, and educational artifacts illustrating her life and cult in North America. One of the most important pieces is an 18th-century **sailor painting**, which depicts the French mariners who prayed to St. Anne to save them from a storm; when they survived, they built a shrine in her honor on the banks of the St. Lawrence River.

IN AND AROUND THE BASILICA

There are two chapels on the lower level: the blue-painted **Immaculate Conception Chapel** and the **Blessed Sacrament Chapel**. Also on the lower level is a copy of Michelangelo's **Pietà**, and the tomb of Venerable Father Alfred Pampalon (1867–96), patron saint of alcoholics and drug addicts. The main church is on the upper level, where hundreds of crutches, braces, and artificial limbs attest to miraculous cures. The earliest healing here, in 1658, is said to have been that of Louis Guimond, a crippled man who insisted on carrying stones for the construction of the first church despite his affliction, and who was cured before the other workers' eyes. Pilgrims gather on the wooded hillside beside the shrine to follow the Way of the Cross and to ascend the Santa Scala, or "Holy Stairs," a replica of the staircase that Jesus climbed to meet Pontius Pilate.

THE LIFE OF ST. ANNE

Although the Bible makes no mention of the mother of the Virgin Mary, early Christians had an interest in knowing more about Jesus' family, especially his mother and grandmother. A 3rd-century Greek manuscript called the *Revelation of James* tells the story of Jesus' grandparents, naming them Anne (from Hannah) and Joachim. According to this account, Anne of Bethlehem and Joachim of Nazareth, a shepherd, were childless after 20 years of marriage. Each cried out separately to God, asking why they were childless, and vowing to dedicate any offspring to his work. An angel came to Joachim and Anne, and they learned that they were to have a child, Mary, who became the mother of Christ.

THE BASILICA

In 1876, St. Anne was proclaimed patron saint of Québec, and in 1887 the existing church was granted basilica status. The Redemptorist order became the guardians of the shrine in 1878.

PLAN OF THE SHRINE

KEY
1. Basilica
2. Monastery
3. Church store
4. Museum
5. Blessings Office

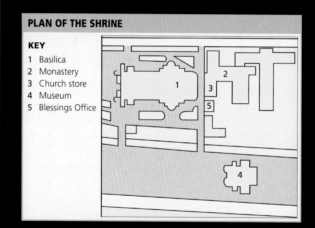

▼ **Façade**
The present basilica was built by the Canadian architect Napoleon Bourassa. He based the design on a mixture of Gothic and Romanesque principles.

▲ **Great Rose Window**
This beautiful stained-glass window was designed by the French artist Auguste Labouret in 1950.

▲ **Façade**

Entrance to the basilica's upper level

▼ **Sailor Painting**
The oil on wood painting *Three Shipwrecked Sailors from Levis* (1754) is one of a collection of marine ex-votos (a votive offering made to a saint) on display in the St. Anne Museum.

Spire

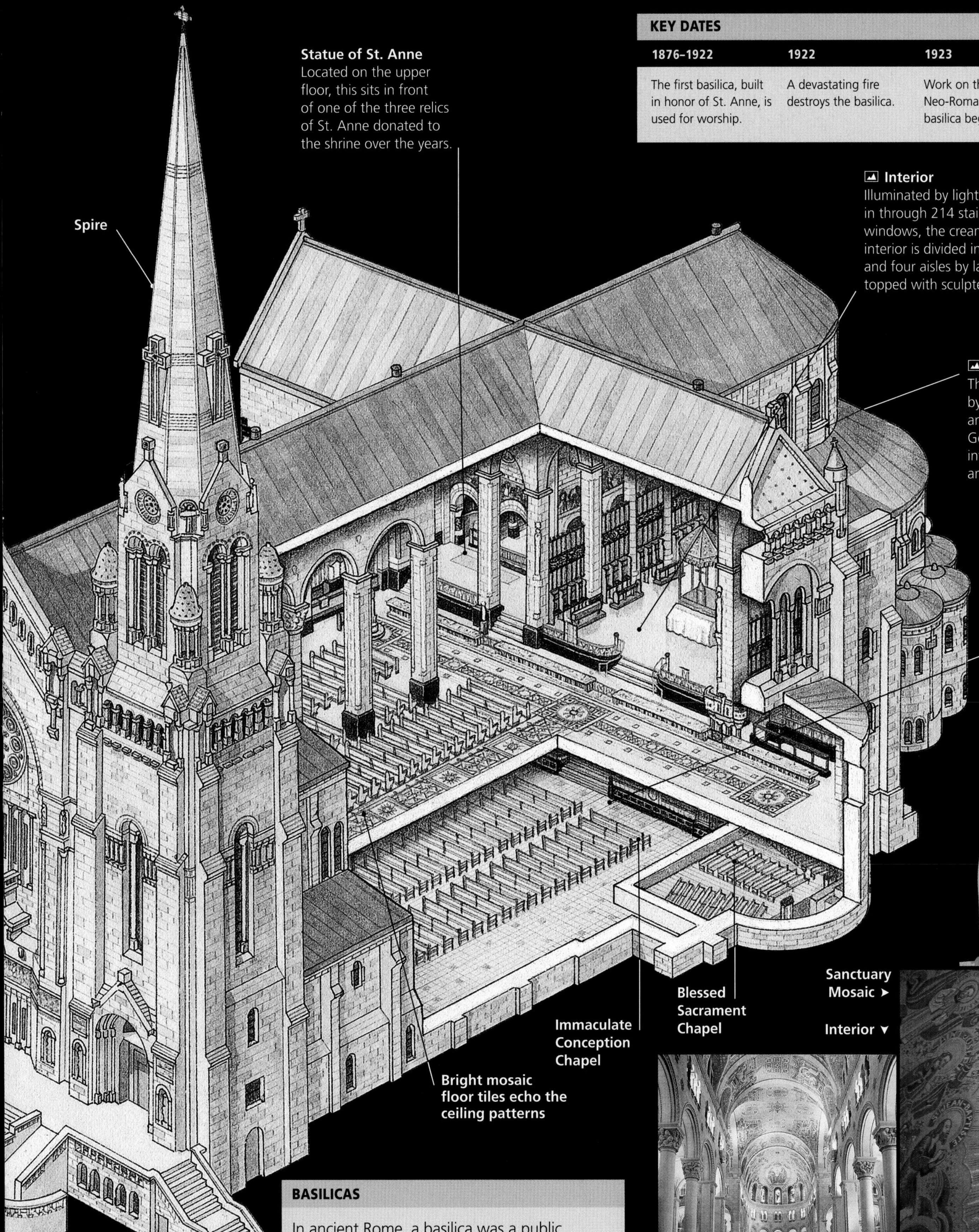

Statue of St. Anne
Located on the upper floor, this sits in front of one of the three relics of St. Anne donated to the shrine over the years.

KEY DATES

1876–1922	1922	1923	1976
The first basilica, built in honor of St. Anne, is used for worship.	A devastating fire destroys the basilica.	Work on the current Neo-Romanesqe basilica begins.	The basilica is consecrated by Cardinal Maurice Roy.

▣ Interior
Illuminated by light streaming in through 214 stained-glass windows, the cream and gold interior is divided into a nave and four aisles by large pillars topped with sculpted capitals.

▣ Sanctuary Mosaic
This splendid mosaic was created by the artists Auguste Labouret and Jean Gaudin in 1940–41. God is shown overlooking an infant Jesus, flanked by Mary and St. Anne.

▼ Pietà
A faithful copy of the original by Michelangelo in St. Peter's Basilica in Rome (see p.130), this depicts Christ at his death being held by a seated Madonna.

Immaculate Conception Chapel

Bright mosaic floor tiles echo the ceiling patterns

Blessed Sacrament Chapel

Sanctuary Mosaic ▶

Interior ▼

BASILICAS

In ancient Rome, a basilica was a public building supported internally by double colonnades and with a semicircular apse at one end. Later, the Catholic Church began to use the the term as a title of honor for important churches, especially those of great age, or an association with a saint. The title gives a church special privileges, principally the right to reserve its high altar for the pope.

CN Tower, Toronto

This 1,815-ft (1,553-m) high engineering marvel has been classified as one of the Seven Wonders of the Modern World. In the 1970s, the railway conglomerate Canadian National Railway (CN), in consultation with local broadcasters, decided to build a new transmission mast to meet Toronto's growing telecommunications needs and to demonstrate its pride in the city. Upon its opening, the tower so impressed visitors that it soon became one of Canada's principal tourist attractions. Its revolving restaurant is renowned for both its food and wine, and its spectacular views.

OBSERVATION DECKS

The **Lookout Level** enables visitors to look out across Toronto. Actually built over several levels, the upper tier has a café and a photo shop. One level below, visitors can feel the wind at 113 stories up, peer straight down through the **glass floor** or dine in the **revolving restaurant**. Thirty-three stories above the lookout, the **Sky Pod** is higher than many of the world's tallest skyscrapers, even though it is not the top of the CN Tower. With an impressive 360-degree view of Toronto and Lake Ontario, on a clear day visitors can see as far as Niagara Falls from this observation deck.

FASCINATING FACTS

Construction of the tower began in 1973, took about 40 months to complete, and cost around CA$63 million. A 75,000 sq-ft (6,968 sq-m) entertainment expansion and renovation was completed in 1998 at a cost of CA$26 million. The tower has six elevators, which travel at 15 mph (24 km/h) and reach the Lookout Level at 1,136 ft (346 m) in 58 seconds; a separate elevator takes visitors 329 ft (101 m) higher to the Sky Pod. The tower is flexible, and in winds of 120 mph (195 km/h), the Sky Pod can sway 18 inches (0.48 m) from the center. Every year, about 2 million people visit the tower.

THE WORLD'S TALLEST BUILDINGS

When assessing a structure for its ranking in the Tallest Buildings in the World list, the international organization the Council on Tall Buildings and Urban Habitat (CTBUH), which sets the criteria for defining and measuring tall buildings, includes only those where at least 50 percent of the height is occupied by useable floor area. It also only measures a building's architectural height and excludes broadcasting aerials and masts. The CN Tower does not meet these criteria, and so it is categorized as a freestanding structure. The tower was the world's tallest freestanding structure from 1975 until 2007, when its height was surpassed by the 2,717-ft (828-m) Burj Khalifa in Dubai, which currently tops the CTBUH's Tallest Buildings in the World list, and the Guangzhou TV & Sightseeing Tower in China, which is 2,000 ft (610 m) high.

The CN Tower at night ▶

▼ The tower from Lake Ontario
The tower's height is emphasized by the lower buildings of Toronto's Harbourfront.

▲ View of the CN Tower from Centre Island's gardens

◀ Revolving Restaurant

▲ Sky Pod

◀ Glass Floor
The ground is more than 1,122 ft (342 m) below this thick layer of re-inforced glass, made from 256 sq ft (24 sq m) of solid glass that is five times stronger than the weight-bearing standard for commercial floors.

▲ Outdoor Observation Level
Open to the elements, this outdoor terrace is secured with steel safety grills. Air temperatures at this height can be up to 50°F (10°C) cooler than at ground level.

◄ View of Toronto from the Lookout Level
At 1,136 ft (346 m) above the city, this level provides panoramas of Toronto, Lake Ontario, and the surrounding area. Visibility can stretch to just under 100 miles (160 km).

Foundations
The single-shaft structure's foundations were sunk around 55 ft (17 m) and required the removal of more than 56,000 tons of soil and shale.

◲ Sky Pod
One of the world's highest obvervation platforms, at 1,465 ft (447 m), the Sky Pod offers fantastic views in every direction. It is reached via its own elevator.

TALLEST SUPPORTED STRUCTURES

There are dozens of television and/or radio broadcast masts that measure more than 2,000 ft (600 m) and all are in the US. Supported by guy wires, these structures do not qualify for inclusion in the Tallest Buildings in the World list. The highest is a 2,063-ft (629-m) television mast near Fargo, North Dakota. Poland's Warsaw Radio Mast was the tallest ever guy-wire-supported mast, at 2,120 ft (647 m), before it collapsed in 1991.

◲ Revolving Restaurant
At a height of 1,148 ft (350 m), 360 The Restaurant at the CN Tower turns a full circle every 72 minutes and boasts the world's highest wine cellar, with more than 500 labels.

◲ Lookout Level

◲ Glass floor

▲ Toronto Islands
These small islands, separated by canals and waterways, can be seen from the lower observation deck of the CN Tower. They are a popular day trip from the Harbourfront.

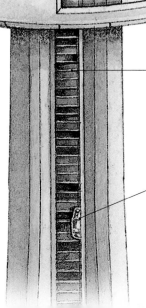

◲ Outdoor Observation Level

Interior Staircase
This is the longest metal staircase in the world, with 1,776 steps. It is opened to the public twice a year—for fundraising stair climbs that attract almost 20,000 climbers.

Exterior Elevators
High-speed and glass-fronted, the elevators shoot visitors up the outside of the building to the upper levels. They reach the Lookout Level in less than a minute.

KEY DATES

1973	1976	1977	1995
Work begins on the the CN Tower, which is to address the city's communication problems.	The CN Tower opens to the public and a time capsule is sealed to mark the event.	The first annual stair climb is held for charity.	The CN Tower is declared a Wonder of the Modern World by the American Society of Civil Engineers.

Old State House, Boston

Dwarfed by the towers of the Financial District, this historic building is typical of the modest and unique architectural style of New England in the 18th century. It was the seat of British colonial government between 1713 and 1776 and a replica royal lion and unicorn decorate each corner of the east façade. After independence, the Massachusetts legislature took possession of the building, and it was used for a variety of purposes, including as a produce market, a merchants' exchange, a Masonic lodge, and a city hall. Its wine cellars now function as a downtown subway station, and it also houses Bostonian Society memorabilia.

Clock face on the east façade

◄ **Old State House amid the skyscrapers of the Financial District**

◄ **East Façade**

Golden Eagle Sculpture
This symbol of America can be seen on the west façade.

THE FREEDOM TRAIL

Sixteen of Boston's most significant historic sights have been linked together as "The Freedom Trail." This 2.5-mile (4-km) long walking route, marked in red on the sidewalk, begins at Boston Common.

🔺 **West Façade**
A Latin inscription, relating to the first Massachusetts Bay colony, runs around the outside of this crest. The relief in the center depicts a local Native American.

◄ **Spire**

◄ **Royal Lion and Unicorn**
A royal symbol of Britain, the original lion and unicorn were pulled down when news of the Declaration of Independence reached Boston in 1776.

◄ **West Façade**

🔺 **Central Staircase**
A fine example of 18th-century workmanship, the central spiral staircase has two beautifully crafted wooden handrails. It is one of the few staircases of its type still in existence in the US.

Council Chamber ►

◄ **Keayne Hall**
This is named after Robert Keayne who, in 1658, gave £300 to the city so that the original Town House of 1657–8 could be built. Exhibits in the room depict events from the Revolutionary War.

KEY DATES

1667	1713	1780–98	1798	1830–40	1840–80	1881	1976
Boston's first Town House is constructed of wood; it burns down in 1711.	The Old State House is built as the site of the provincial government.	The building serves as the Massachusetts State House.	The building is renovated for private retail tenants.	After renovation, the building becomes Boston's city hall.	The building falls into disrepair after being returned to commercial use.	The Old State House is completely restored by the city.	Britain's Queen Elizabeth II addresses Bostonians from the balcony.

Spire

Tower
This is a classic example of Colonial style. In 18th-century paintings and engravings, the tower can clearly be seen above the Boston skyline.

SITE OF THE BOSTON MASSACRE

A circle of cobblestones below the balcony on the east façade marks the site of the Boston Massacre. After the Boston Tea Party of 1773 (where Boston patriots, in protest at taxation, boarded three British East India Company ships and threw their cargoes of tea into Boston Harbor), this was one of the most inflammatory events in the lead-up to the Revolutionary War. On March 5, 1770, an unruly mob of colonists taunted British guardsmen with insults, rocks, and snowballs. The soldiers opened fire, killing five colonists. A number of articles relating to the Boston Massacre are exhibited inside the Old State House.

Cobblestone circle: site of the Boston Massacre

East Façade
This façade has undergone several changes. In 1956, a clock from the 1820s was removed and replaced with a replica of the sundial that once hung here. The clock has now been reinstated.

Council Chamber
Once the chambers for the royal governors, and from 1780, the chambers for the first governor of Massachusetts (John Hancock), this room has hosted many key events. Among them were numerous impassioned speeches made by Boston patriots.

EARLY HISTORY

Constructed in 1713 to replace the first Town House, which had recently burned down, the Old State House is Boston's oldest surviving public building. During its period as the seat of the British colonial government, it was also the Boston center for the political activity that led to the Revolutionary War (1775–81). From the first-floor gallery, Boston's citizens could—for the first time in the English-speaking world—watch their elected legislators debate the issues of the day. The west end housed the county and colony law courts. The wealthy merchant and patriot John Hancock, an active opponent of the Stamp Act (1765), which imposed a tax on all paper goods, and the first signer of the Declaration of Independence, had warehouse space in the basement.

THE BOSTONIAN SOCIETY

The Bostonian Society, which maintains the Old State House, also runs the museum inside the building and a library across the street. Permanent and changing displays and exhibits in the museum recount Boston's history, from its settlement through to the Revolution, and beyond. Permanent exhibitions include "From Colony to Commonwealth," which looks at the role of Boston and the Old State House in the events that led to the American Revolution, and "Treasures from the Bostonian Society's Collections," located in the **Council Chamber**, which features Revolutionary icons and militia equipment. There is also a sound-and-light show on the Boston Massacre of 1770.

LIFE IN COLONIAL BOSTON

First settled by Puritans in 1630, Boston became one of North America's leading colonial cities. Its life and wealth revolved around its role as a busy seaport, but its streets were crooked, dirty, and crowded with people and livestock. Other problems included waste disposal, firefighting, and caring for the numerous poor. Unlike the other major American cities outside of New England, Boston had a "town meeting" form of government. This was unusually democratic for the time and helps to explain why Boston became a center of colonial resistance prior to the Revolutionary War.

Entrance

Central staircase

Balcony
The Declaration of Independence was read from here in 1776. In the 1830s, when the building was the city hall, the balcony was enlarged to two tiers.

Royal Lion and Unicorn

CANADA

SOLOMON R. GUGGENHEIM
MUSEUM, NEW YORK

Washington, D.C.

Los Angeles USA

ATLANTIC
OCEAN

MEXICO GULF OF
MEXICO

GUGGENHEIM AND WRIGHT

Guggenheim amassed his wealth through his family's mining and metal businesses, which he ran from New York. He collected modernist paintings, and in 1942, he asked Frank Lloyd Wright to design a museum to house them. The architect disagreed with the choice of New York as the project's site—he felt the city was over-built, overpopulated and lacking in architectural merit. But he acquiesced, and designed a structure to challenge these shortcomings. Disregarding Manhattan's rectilinear grid system, he brought a fresh notion of museum design to the city by using curving, continuous spaces.

OTHER MUSEUMS

The Solomon R. Guggenheim Foundation runs three other museums. In Bilbao in Spain, a building designed by US architect Frank O. Gehry houses a permanent collection of modern art *(see p.106)*. Solomon's niece, Peggy Guggenheim, donated her large villa in Venice and her collection of post-1910 masterpieces of surrealist and abstract painting and sculpture to the foundation. Opened in 1951, this museum is situated on the Grand Canal in Venice. In cooperation with Deutsche Bank, the Deutsche Guggenheim Berlin has four exhibitions a year, including performance art and music.

THE COLLECTION

Guggenheim started out as a collector of mediocre old masters, but after meeting artist Hilla Rebay, he began to amass a superb stock of works by modernist artists such as Delaunay, Léger, and Kandinsky. The Solomon R. Guggenheim Foundation was founded in 1937 and established the Museum of Non-Objective Art, as the Guggenheim was known until 1959, in a temporary residence. Planning of the new building began in 1943, but it was not until after Guggenheim's death in 1949 that the collection was expanded to include such artists as Picasso, Cézanne, Klee, and Mangold. Thannhauser's collection of Impressionist, Post-Impressionist and early modern art, donated from 1978 to 1991 by collector Justin Thannhauser and his widow, is hung in the **Tower galleries**. The Guggenheim Museum's exhibits change on a regular basis.

Solomon R. Guggenheim Museum, New York

Home to one of the world's finest collections of modern and contemporary art, the building itself is perhaps the museum's greatest masterpiece. Designed by architect Frank Lloyd Wright, the curvaceous, shell-like façade is a New York landmark. Taking its inspiration from nature, the building attempts to render the fluidity of organic forms. Inside, a spiral ramp curves down and inward from a dome, passing works by major 19th- and 20th-century artists. The imaginative layout of the Great Rotunda gives visitors the opportunity to simultaneously view works located on different levels.

Fifth Avenue façade

FRANK LLOYD WRIGHT

Wright (1867–1959) is considered the great innovator of 20th-century US architecture. He spent more than 70 years designing 1,141 works, including houses, offices, churches, schools, and museums. Characteristic of his work are the "Prairie style" homes that became the basis of residential design in the US, and office buildings of concrete, glass bricks, and tubing. Wright received the Guggenheim commission in 1943, and it was completed after his death in 1959; it was his only New York building.

Interior of the Guggenheim's
Great Rotunda

Sculpture terrace

Small Rotunda

THE SOLOMON R. G

Main entrance

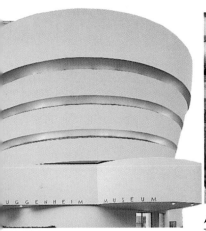

◄ Black Lines (1913)
This is one of the earliest examples of Vasily Kandinsky's "non-objective" art.

▲ The spiral design resembles a nautilus shell, with spaces flowing one into another

▲ Paris Through the Window
The vibrant colors of Marc Chagall's 1913 masterpiece illuminate the canvas, conjuring up images of a magical and mysterious city where nothing is quite what it appears to be.

◄ Woman Holding a Vase
Fernand Léger incorporated elements of Cubism into this work from 1927.

Tower galleries

MUSEUM GUIDE
The Great Rotunda puts on special exhibitions. The Small Rotunda shows some of the museum's celebrated Impressionist and Post-Impressionist holdings. The Tower galleries feature exhibitions of work from the permanent collection, as well as contemporary pieces. A sculpture terrace on the 5th floor overlooks Central Park.

Great Rotunda

Before the Mirror (1876) ►
In trying to capture the flavor of 19th-century French society, Edouard Manet often used the image of the courtesan.

Nude (1917) ►
This sleeping figure is typical of Amedeo Modigliani's stylized work. His simplified faces are reminiscent of African masks.

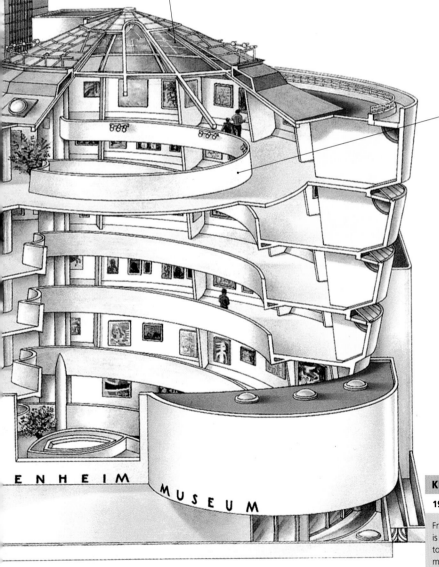

Curving Interior Ramp
Used in place of conventional level floors, this leads to the top of the Great Rotunda.

▲ Woman with Yellow Hair (1931)
Marie-Thérèse Walter, Picasso's mistress, is shown as a gentle, voluptuous figure.

▲ Woman Ironing (1904)
A work from Pablo Picasso's Blue Period, this painting is his quintessential image of hard work and fatigue.

KEY DATES

1942	1949	1959	1992
Frank Lloyd Wright is commissioned to design the museum.	Guggenheim dies and the project is delayed; it finally begins in 1956.	The Solomon R. Guggenheim Museum opens on Fifth Avenue.	The restored and expanded museum, with a new annexe, reopens.

CANADA

EMPIRE STATE BUILDING,
NEW YORK

Washington, D.C.

Los Angeles   USA

ATLANTIC
OCEAN

MEXICO   GULF OF
MEXICO

THE SKYSCRAPER RACE

With the construction of Paris's Eiffel Tower in 1889, US architects were challenged to build ever higher, and at the start of the 20th century the skyscraper race began. By 1929, New York's Bank of Manhattan Building, at 972 ft (283 m), was the city's tallest skyscraper, but Walter Chrysler, the famous car manufacturer, was planning to top that height. John Jakob Raskob, of rival General Motors, decided to join the race and, with Pierre S. Du Pont, was a major investor in the Empire State project. Chrysler kept the height of his building a secret, so Raskob had to be flexible in his planning. He first aimed at building 85 floors but, unsure of Chrysler's goal, he kept going until the building reached 102 floors, and by adding a **tower**, beat Chrysler by 204 ft (62 m).

THE EMPIRE STATE'S DESIGNERS

The Shreve, Lamb & Harmon company had designed some of the most notable skyscrapers in Manhattan. By the time work on the Empire State Building began, they had designed seven buildings, including 40 Wall Street (now the Trump Building), at 70 floors, which was completed in only 11 months. With a team of top engineers and contractors, using up to 3,000 workers, the Empire State Building, too, was completed under budget and in record time.

BUILDING SKYSCRAPERS

The modern skyscraper would not have been possible without several building innovations. Elevators had been in use for some time, but it was not until Elisha Otis's 1854 demonstration of his safety brake that the public began to trust them. The second necessary development was the structural steel skeleton, seen in the world's first skyscraper in 1885. With this construction, the walls became merely a sheathing, not a load-bearing element, and enormously tall, heavy buildings could now rise ever higher. Building in the heart of Manhattan presented a further problem: large amounts of essential construction material could not be kept in the street. To solve this, the aluminum elements were prefabricated and only three days' worth of structural steel was kept on site, creating an extremely complicated organizational job.

Empire State Building, New York

One of the world's most famous buildings, the Empire State broke all height records when it was finished. Construction began in March 1930, not long after the Wall Street Crash, and by the time it opened in 1931, it was so hard to find anyone to fill it that it was nicknamed "the Empty State Building." Only the popularity of its observatories saved it from bankruptcy. However, the building was soon seen as a symbol of New York throughout the world.

◄ **Fifth Avenue Entrance Lobby**
A relief image of the skyscraper is superimposed on a map of New York State in the marble-lined lobby.

▲ **Al Smith, the former governor of New York State, with a model of the Empire State Building**

▲ **Sky Builder**
Suspended high above Fifth Avenue, this steel worker was one of many men whose bravery was well documented in a series of photographs taken during the construction of the building.

▲ **Façade**
The main entrance has a central window with cross-hatched panes that bring natural light into the lobby.

ART DECO DESIGN

The Empire State Building is considered New York's last Art Deco masterpiece. The movement flourished from the 1920s to the 1940s and was noted for its use of crisp, graphic lines, geometric shapes, and vertical setbacks evocative of Aztec pyramid temples.

KEY DATES			
March 1930	**1931**	**1977**	**2002**
Building work begins. By October, 88 floors are completed, and there are 14 to go.	The Empire State Building opens; it is the tallest building in the world.	The first annual Empire State Run-Up takes place.	Donald Trump sells the Empire State Building to a property consortium.

102nd-floor observatory

Views from the Observatory
The 86th floor has outdoor observation decks for bird's-eye views of Manhattan. On a clear day, visitors can see more than 80 miles (125 km) in all directions. The observatory on the 102nd floor closed in 1994.

Lightning Strikes
A natural lightning conductor, the building is struck up to 100 times a year. The observation decks are closed during inclement weather.

International Icon
The Empire State remains as imposing and elegant as when it first opened, although it has been surpassed in height and bulk.

STARRING ROLE
The Empire State Building has been seen in many movies. However, the finale from the 1933 classic *King Kong* is easily its most famous guest appearance, as the giant ape straddles the spire to do battle with army aircraft. In 1945, a real bomber flew too low over Manhattan in fog and struck the building just above the 78th floor. The luckiest escape was that of a young elevator operator whose cabin plunged 79 floors. The emergency brakes saved her life.

CONSTRUCTION
The building was designed to be erected easily and speedily with everything possible prefabricated and slotted into place at a rate of about four stories per week.

Framework
This is made from 60,000 tons of steel and was built in 23 weeks.

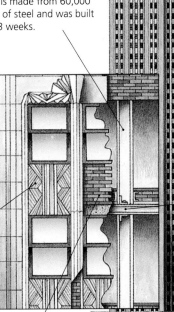

Aluminum Panels
These were used instead of stone around the 6,500 windows. The steel trim masks rough edges on the facing.

Empire State
1,454 ft (443 m),
with mast

Eiffel Tower
1,063 ft (324 m)

Big Ben   Great Pyramid
320 ft   482 ft (147 m)
(97.5 m)

Ten million bricks were used to line the whole building

Pecking Order
New Yorkers are justifiably proud of their city's symbol, which towers above the icons of other countries.

Art Deco Medallions
Displayed throughout the lobby, these depict symbols of the modern age.

Tower
The metal, glass, and aluminum tower on top of the building was designed as a mooring mast for airships, but this soon proved impractical. The tower was later converted into a television mast and now transmits TV and radio to the city and four other US states.

Colored Floodlights
The top 30 floors are floodlit during special and seasonal events.

High-speed elevators travel at up to 1,200 ft (366 m) a minute

The building has 102 floors, but only 85 have office space

Sandwich space between the floors houses the wiring, pipes, and cables

Empire State Run-Up
In this annual event, it takes fit runners just 10 minutes to race up the 1,576 steps from the lobby to the 86th floor.

More than 200 steel and concrete piles support the 365,000-ton building

The world-famous Empire State Building,
New York

Statue of Liberty, New York

A gift of friendship from the French to the American people, the statue was a celebration of a century of independence. The brainchild of French politician Edouard-René Lefebvre de Laboulaye, it has become a potent symbol of freedom and democracy since it was unveiled by US president Grover Cleveland on October 28, 1886. Its spirit is encapsulated in a line from the sonnet engraved on its base: "Give me your tired, your poor, your huddled masses yearning to breathe free." After years of wear and tear, the statue needed restoration—it was given an expensive facelift in time for its 100th anniversary in 1986.

▲ Statue of Liberty National Monument
The statue sits on a 12-acre (5-ha) island at the entrance to New York's harbor. For more than 120 years, it has welcomed the millions of immigrants to the US who have arrived by sea.

Golden Torch
The torch is a 1986 replacement for the original, which became corroded over the years. The replica's flame is coated in 24-carat gold leaf.

🖼 Face of Liberty
The sculptor's mother was the model for Liberty's face. The seven rays of her crown represent the seven seas and seven continents.

THE STATUE
With a height of 305 ft (93 m) from ground to torch, the Statue of Liberty dominates the harbor.

Frame
This was designed by the great engineer Gustave Eiffel, who realized that the copper shell would react to the iron frame and so put a barrier between them.

STRUCTURAL GENIUS

French engineer Gustave Eiffel, creator of Paris's Eiffel Tower, was commissioned to solve the problems of building a large hollow statue that could withstand the forces of wind and weather. His solution was an internal, diagonally braced frame of 1,350 ribs and verticals. This, and his use of steel posts, were seen as structural innovations.

Central Pylon
This anchors the 225-ton statue to its base.

354 Steps
These lead from the entrance to the top.

FRÉDÉRIC AUGUSTE BARTHOLDI

"Liberty Enlightening the World," more commonly known as the Statue of Liberty, was intended by its designer, the French sculptor Frédéric Auguste Bartholdi, as a monument to the freedom he thought was lacking in his own country. He said, "I will try to glorify the Republic and Liberty over there, in the hope that some day I will find it again here." He devoted 21 years of his life to the project, traveling to the US in 1871 to persuade President Ulysses S. Grant and others to help fund the statue's pedestal.

▲ Statue of Liberty Museum
Posters featuring the statue are among the items on display here.

Observation deck and museum

Pedestal
The statue's base is set within the walls of an army fort. At the time, it was the largest concrete mass ever poured.

Original 1886 Torch
This now stands in the main lobby.

Frédéric Auguste Bartholdi (1834–1904)

Face of Liberty ▼

▲ Ferries to Liberty Island
Ferries cross New York's harbor to Liberty Island, which was originally known as Bedloe's Island.

◄ Restoration Celebration
On July 4, 1986, after a $100 million clean-up, the statue was unveiled. The $2 million fireworks display was the largest ever seen in America.

▼ Statue construction workshop in France, c. 1882

▲ From Her Toes to Her Torch
Three hundred molded copper sheets riveted together make up Lady Liberty.

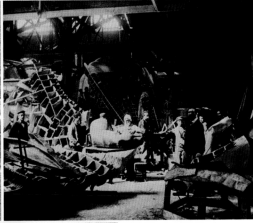

▲ Making the Hand
To create the copper shell, the hand was first made in plaster, then in wood.

▲ A Model Figure
A series of graduated scale models enabled Bartholdi to build the largest metal statue ever constructed.

KEY DATES

1865	1876	1886	1986
Bartholdi has the idea of building a tribute to Liberty in America.	Bartholdi is given the commission to create the Statue of Liberty.	The Statue of Liberty is dedicated; Bartholdi himself unveils the face.	The Statue of Liberty is reopened after extensive restoration.

BUILDING THE LADY

In his Parisian workshop, the sculptor Frédéric Auguste Bartholdi began by creating four scale models, the largest at one-fourth the actual size. This was divided into 300 plaster sections, and each section was then enlarged to full size. A mold of laminated wood was made from each of these sections, and sheets of copper were pounded into the molds to a thickness of just 0.1 inch (2.5 mm). In all, 350 sheets were connected with 2-inch (50-mm) wide iron straps. The straps acted like springs, which allowed the surface to flex in high winds or extremes of temperature. The statue arrived in New York packed in more than 200 crates and was attached to the frame using an estimated 300,000 copper rivets.

FUNDRAISING

Although the French contributed to the cost of the statue, early on in the plan it was decided that funds for the pedestal would come from the US. Since fundraising was going slowly, the media baron Joseph Pulitzer used the editorial clout of his newspaper, *The World,* to criticize the wealthy for withholding their financial support and the middle class for relying on the wealthy. He pointed out that the statue was a gift to the entire US and attacked those who were not supporting it on the grounds that it was a New York project. Soon, the whole nation was involved, and the funds were raised.

THE MUSEUM

The **Statue of Liberty Museum** is located in the base of the structure. The Torch Exhibit in the lobby holds the **original 1886 torch**. The Statue of Liberty Exhibit, on the pedestal's second level, is a biography of Lady Liberty and an examination of the ideals for which she stands. Seven displays, featuring artifacts, photographs, videos, and oral histories, focus on her history. Another area has sections on her symbolism, exploring ideas such as "Mother of Exiles" and "The Statue in Popular Culture." There is also a display of full-scale models of Liberty's face and left foot (**a model figure**). A bronze plaque bearing the text of Emma Lazarus's famous sonnet, *The New Colossus,* was added to the pedestal in the early 1900s.

The White House, Washington, D.C.

The official residence of the president of the United States for more than 200 years, the White House is one of the most distinguished buildings in the United States and was built on a location chosen by George Washington in 1790. Irish-born architect James Hoban designed the original building in a Palladian style *(Neo-Classical Style, see p.57)* and when it was nearing completion, President and Mrs. John Adams became the first occupants. It has survived two fires, in 1814 and 1929, and the interior was completely gutted and renovated during Harry S. Truman's presidency, from 1945 to 1953. In 1901, President Theodore Roosevelt officially gave the White House its current name.

▲ **North Façade**
The Palladian-style façade of the White House is familiar to millions of people around the world.

THE WHITE HOUSE VISITOR CENTER

Interesting exhibits relating to the White House's history, décor, and inhabitants are on display in the White House Visitor Center. Guided tours of the White House are available, but are extremely limited, and can only be booked by special arrangement through a member of Congress or an embassy.

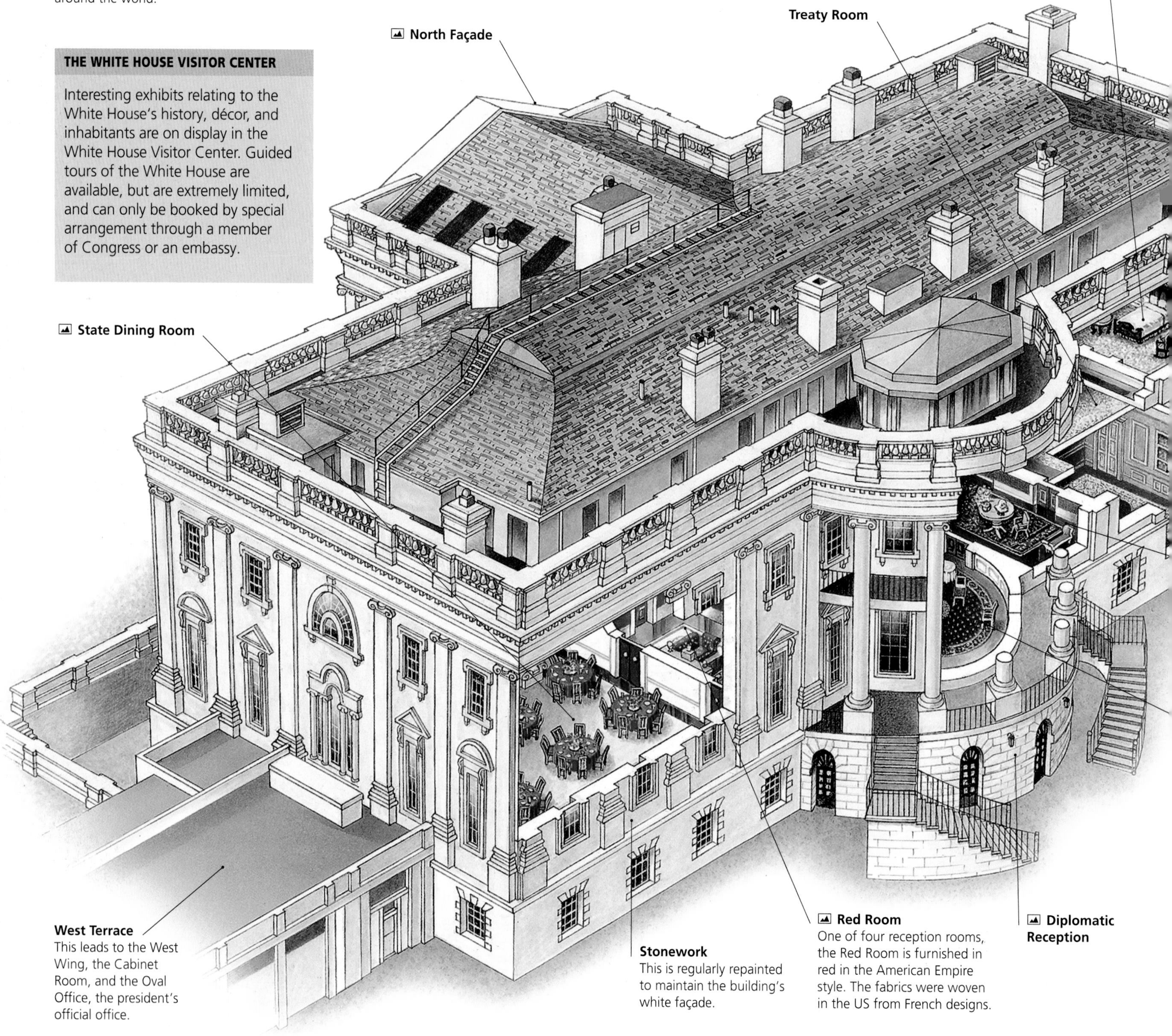

▣ **State Dining Room**

▣ **North Façade**

Treaty Room

▣ **Lincoln Bedroom**

West Terrace
This leads to the West Wing, the Cabinet Room, and the Oval Office, the president's official office.

Stonework
This is regularly repainted to maintain the building's white façade.

▣ **Red Room**
One of four reception rooms, the Red Room is furnished in red in the American Empire style. The fabrics were woven in the US from French designs.

▣ **Diplomatic Reception**

◄ **Vermeil Room**
This yellow room houses seven paintings of first ladies, including this portrait of Eleanor Roosevelt by Douglas Chandor (1949).

▼ **Red Room**

▲ **Lincoln Bedroom**
President Lincoln used this room as his Cabinet Room. It was turned into a bedroom by President Truman, who filled it with furnishings from the Lincoln era.

▲ **Diplomatic Reception**
This room is used to welcome friends and ambassadors. It is elegantly furnished in the Federal Period style (1790–1820).

The East Terrace leads to the East Wing

East Room
This room is used for large gatherings, such as dances and concerts.

State Dining Room ►
Able to seat as many as 140 people, the State Dining Room was enlarged in 1902. A portrait of President Abraham Lincoln, painted by George P. A. Healy in 1869, hangs above the fireplace.

⊡ Vermeil Room

Green Room
Another reception room, this was first used as a guest room before being turned into a dining room by Thomas Jefferson. Today, it is used for small receptions and predinner cocktails for guests at state dinners.

Blue Room

WHITE HOUSE ARCHITECTS

After selecting the site, George Washington held a design competition to find an architect to build the residence where the US president would live. In 1792, James Hoban, an Irish-born architect, was chosen for the task. The White House was built to Hoban's designs and he also reconstructed the building after the British attack in 1814. In 1902, President Theodore Roosevelt hired the New York architectural firm of McKim, Mead, and White to check the structural condition of the building and refurbish areas as necessary. The White House underwent further renovations and refurbishments during the administrations of presidents Truman and Kennedy.

James Hoban, architect of the White House

KEY DATES

1792	1800	1814	1902	1942
Construction begins on the Executive Mansion (renamed the White House in 1901).	President Adams and his wife are the first to move into the White House.	The British set fire to the White House during the War of 1812.	The West Wing is built to house the official offices of the president. Its rooms include the Oval Office.	The East Wing of the White House is added, as instructed by Franklin D. Roosevelt, completing the final structure.

THE WAR OF 1812
Tensions with Britain over restrictions on trade and freedom of the seas began to escalate during President James Madison's administration (1809–17). On June 18, 1812, the US declared war on Britain. In August 1814, British troops reached Washington, D.C., and officers of the Capitol fled, taking the Declaration of Independence and the Constitution with them. On August 24, the British defeated the Americans at Bladensburg, a suburb of Washington. They set fire to the Capitol, the White House, the War Department and the Treasury, but a night of heavy rain prevented the city's destruction. The Treaty of Ghent, which ended the war, was signed on February 17, 1815.

THE WEST WING
In 1902, the West Wing of the White House was built by the architectural firm McKim, Mead, and White for a total cost of $65,196. This wing (the **West Terrace**) houses the Cabinet Room, where government officials convene with the president, and the Oval Office, where the president meets visiting heads of state. Many presidents have personalized the Oval Office in some way: President Clinton chose as his desk a table given to President Rutherford B. Hayes by Britain's Queen Victoria in 1880.

THE WHITE HOUSE INTERIOR
The rooms in the White House are decorated in period styles and filled with valuable antique furniture, china, and silverware. Hanging on the walls are some of America's most treasured paintings, including portraits of past presidents and first ladies. The room that served as the Cabinet Room from 1865 for 10 presidential administrations (**Treaty Room**) was restored in 1961 and contains Victorian pieces bought by President Grant. The most central room on the State Floor (**Blue Room**) was decorated in 1817 in the American Empire style (1810–30) by President Monroe. The same style was later used by first lady Jackie Kennedy to redecorate one of the reception rooms (**Red Room**) in 1962. The Red Room has always been a favorite of first ladies for receiving guests.

United States Capitol, Washington, D.C.

The US Capitol, one of best-known symbols of democracy, has been the center of America's legislative process for 200 years. A fine example of Neo-Classical architecture (*Neo-Classical Style, see p.57*), its interior contains frescoes, murals, and statuary influenced by ancient Greek and Roman designs. George Washington laid the foundation stone in 1793, and by 1800, although unfinished, the Capitol was occupied. Construction resumed under architect Benjamin Latrobe, but the British burned the building in the War of 1812. Restoration began in 1815. Many features, such as Brumidi's murals and the Statue of Freedom, were added later.

▲ **Dome**
Originally made of wood and copper, the 1854 dome was designed by Thomas U. Walter.

🔲 **Rotunda**
Completed in 1865, the 180-ft (55-m) high Rotunda is capped by *The Apotheosis of Washington*, a fresco by Constantino Brumidi.

🔲 **National Statuary Hall**

Hall of Columns
This is lined with statues of notable Americans.

House Chamber

THE DOME

By the 1850s, the original dome was too small for the enlarged Capitol. Moreover, it leaked and was deemed a fire hazard. In 1854, $100,000 was appropriated for architect Thomas U. Walter's new **dome**, which was constructed of cast iron. Walter's double-dome design recalls the Panthéon in Paris. Sculptor Thomas Crawford created a 19.5-ft (6-m) high bronze to crown the dome, and in 1863, during the American Civil War (1861–5), the Statue of Freedom—a Classical female figure standing on a globe with the national motto, *E Pluribus Unum* (Out of many, one)—was raised atop the 287-ft (87.5-m) high dome.

THE ROTUNDA FRIEZE

Thomas U. Walter's 1859 drawings showed a recessed, bas-relief sculpture in the **Rotunda**. The plan changed, and by 1877, a fresco 8 ft 4 in (2.5 m) high and 300 ft (91 m) in circumference was being painted. **The Frieze of American History** has 19 panels, which begin over the west door and move clockwise around the Rotunda. The first panel is the only one to contain allegorical figures, with female personifications of America and History. The rest recount major events in US history, including Columbus's landing, the colonization of New England, the Declaration of Independence, the discovery of gold in California, and the Wright Brothers' first flight in 1903.

STATUARY

In 1864, Congress invited each US state to contribute two statues of notable citizens to stand in the **National Statuary Hall**. Soon, the collection grew too large, and much of it can now be seen in the **Hall of Columns** and in the various corridors of the Capitol. Statues of former US presidents Washington, Jackson, Garfield, and Eisenhower can be seen in the Rotunda. In the Statuary Hall are statues of General Robert E. Lee and President Jefferson Davis; King Kamehameha I, unifier of Hawaii; Robert Fulton, inventor of the first commercially successful steamboat; Huey P. Long, Depression-era demagogue; Sam Houston, president of the Republic of Texas; and Sequoyah, inventor of the Cherokee alphabet.

KEY DATES

1791–92	1829	1851	1983–93
The site is chosen for a new national capital; the city of Washington, D.C., is designed and mapped.	The original Capitol building is completed, after work by three successive architects.	The foundation stones are laid for new wings, which are built by Thomas U. Walter.	The west front and west terrace are restored.

Dome

Rotunda Frieze

Senate Chamber
This has been the home of the US Senate since 1859.

Brumidi Corridors
These are lined with frescoes, bronzework, and paintings by the Italian-American artist Constantino Brumidi (1805–80).

▼ **View of the US Capitol**
The US Capitol marks the precise center of Washington and the city's four quadrants radiate out from the middle of the building.

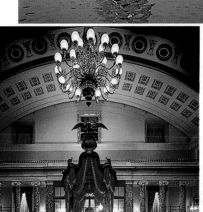

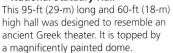 **Old Senate Chamber**

Columbus Doors
Created by Randolph Rogers (1825–92), these doors are made of solid bronze and depict Christopher Columbus's life and his discovery of America—a theme echoed throughout the works of art in the Capitol.

Old Senate Chamber ➤
Occupied by the Senate until 1859, this chamber was then home to the Supreme Court for 75 years. It is used mainly as a museum space today.

Crypt

▼ **East Entrance**
Carved on the pediment are striking Classical female representations of America. These are flanked by figures of Justice and Hope.

▼ **National Statuary Hall**
This 95-ft (29-m) long and 60-ft (18-m) high hall was designed to resemble an ancient Greek theater. It is topped by a magnificently painted dome.

 ▼ **Rotunda**

Golden Gate Bridge, San Francisco

Superlatives flow when describing this world-famous land-mark. It is the third-largest single-span bridge ever built, and, when it was erected, it was the longest and tallest suspension structure. Named after the part of San Francisco Bay dubbed "Golden Gate" in the mid-19th century, the bridge opened in 1937. There are breathtaking views of the bay from this spectacular structure, which has six lanes for vehicles as well as a pathway for pedestrians and cyclists.

One of the builders, in a protective mask

BUILDING THE BRIDGE

The Golden Gate Bridge is a classic suspension bridge of the kind first built in the mid-19th century. Its main elements are anchorages, towers (pylons), cables, and road. Enormous concrete anchorages were poured at either end to hold the cables. The steel for the towers was fabricated in Pennsylvania and shipped through the Panama Canal. Engineer Joseph B. Strauss chose John A. Roebling and Sons, builders of the Brooklyn Bridge, to make the cables. Since no derrick of the time could lift cables as heavy as these, they were spun in place, the machines passing back and forth continuously for six months. For the bridge's paint color, architect Irving Morrow rejected the standard gray, cho-osing instead "International Orange," which he felt blended better with the bridge's setting.

BRIDGE PARTY

The Golden Gate Bridge opened to pedestrian traffic on May 27, 1937, on schedule and under budget. On a typically foggy and windy day, over 18,000 people took part in the grand opening by walking its total length (including the approaches) of 8,981 ft (2,737 m). The next day, President Franklin D. Roosevelt pressed a telegraph key in the White House that opened the bridge to vehicular traffic. Every siren and church bell in San Francisco and Marin County sounded simultaneously. A week-long celebration followed the event.

DESIGNER SQUABBLES

The idea of building a bridge across the Golden Gate was conceived as early as 1872, by railroad tycoon Charles Crocker, but it was not considered feasible until architect Joseph B. Strauss stepped forward with a plan in 1921. Nine years of bureaucratic wrangling passed before Strauss was named chief engineer, but it is actually assistant chief engineer Clifford Paine, and architect Irving F. Morrow, who deserve the credit for the design and building of the bridge that stands today. By all accounts, Strauss seems to have been a difficult man; he fired his first assistant chief engineer, Charles Ellis, for attracting too much publicity. Strauss even kept Ellis's name from appearing on any official documents.

THE FERRIES' RETURN

Although the bridge was built to relieve ferry congestion in San Francisco Bay, in recent years it has become so busy that thousands of car drivers have abandoned their vehicles for reliable water travel—there are now 18 ferries serving the area.

The bridge's length is 1.7 miles (2.7 km), with a center span of 4,200 ft (1,280 m)

THE FOUNDATIONS

The foundations of the twin towers are a remarkable feat of engineering. The south pier, 1,125 ft (345 m) offshore, was sunk 100 ft (30 m) below the surface in open water.

The highway is 220 ft (67 m) above water that is 318 ft (97 m) deep.

65-ft (20-m) thick pier base

155-ft (47-m) high fender

Reinforcing iron frame

The Concrete Fender
During construction, the south pier base was protected from the force of the tides by a fender of concrete. Water was pumped out to create a vast watertight locker.

Divers
TTo reach the bedrock, divers were employed to dynamite 20-ft (6-m) deep holes in the ocean floor.

▼ View from Fort Point, at the south end

▲ Building the Roadway
The steel-supported concrete highway was constructed from the towers in both directions, so that its weight on the cables was evenly distributed.

Bridge Lighting ▲
Sodium vapor lamps were installed to provide nonglare lighting for drivers.

Towers ➤
The hollow, twin steel towers that support the bridge's suspension cables rise to a height of 746 ft (227 m) above the water. Each tower weighs 44,000 tons.

THE BRIDGE IN FIGURES

- Every day, around 118,000 vehicles cross the bridge; this means that every year more than 40 million vehicles use it.
- The original coat of orange paint lasted for 27 years, with occasional touch-ups. In 1965, the paint was removed and a more durable coating was applied. Today, this is touched up by a crew of 38 painters.
- The two great 7,650-ft (2,332-m) cables are more than 3 ft (1 m) thick, and contain 80,000 miles (128,744 km) of steel wire—enough to circle the Earth at the equator three times over.

- The volume of concrete poured into the piers and anchorages during the bridge's construction would be enough to lay a 5-ft (1.5-m) wide sidewalk from New York to San Francisco, a distance of more than 2,500 miles (4,000 km).
- The bridge can stand firm in the face of 100 mph (160 km/h) winds.
- Each of the bridge's piers has to withstand a tidal flow of more than 60 mph (97 km/h), while supporting a huge, heavy tower above.

View north, toward Marin County

Man with a Plan ➤
Chicago engineering titan Joseph Strauss is officially credited as the bridge's designer. He was assisted by Leon Moisseiff, Charles Ellis, and Clifford Paine. Irving F. Morrow acted as consulting architect.

KEY DATES

c. 1872	1923	1933	1937	1985
Earliest discussions about building a bridge across the entrance of San Francisco Bay.	California legislature passes a bill to explore the feasibility of building the bridge.	Construction of the Golden Gate Bridge begins in January.	The bridge opens on time, and under budget, to great celebrations.	The one-billionth car passes over the bridge.

Chaco Culture National Historical Park

One of the most impressive cultural sites in the American Southwest, Chaco Culture National Historical Park at Chaco Canyon reflects the sophistication of the Ancestral Puebloan civilization (also known as the Anasazi) that existed here. With its six "great houses" (pueblos containing hundreds of rooms), and many lesser sites, the canyon was once the political, religious, and cultural center for this people. It is thought that Chaco's population was small; despite the size of the pueblos, the land could not have supported a larger community. Archeologists believe that the city was mainly used as a ceremonial gathering place, with a year-round population of fewer than 3,000 people. The inhabitants sustained themselves largely by growing crops and trading.

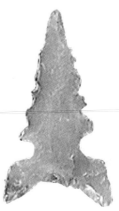

Arrowhead in Chaco Museum

THE KIVAS

Usually, a pueblo had a number of adjoining **kivas** (pit-houses), as well as one great *kiva*. Early smaller *kivas* seem to have been dwellings, but most scholars agree that the great *kivas* were ceremonial places, barred to women and children, not merely community gathering sites. The first Chaco Canyon *kivas* appeared around AD 700, and while most were round, some were D-shaped. *Kivas* were entered through a hole in the roof and there was also a hole in the floor called a *sipapu*, which possibly symbolized the people's connection from birth with Mother Earth. Near the center was a fireplace, and air shafts on the sides of the *kivas* made them more livable.

OTHER ANASAZI SITES

The Aztec Ruins National Monument was built by Puebloans in the 12th century. This important archeological site lies 69 miles (111 km) north of Chaco Canyon. There is a reconstructed great *kiva* here, as well as a pueblo consisting of 450 interconnecting rooms built of stone and mud. Farther to the north is **Mesa Verde**, Spanish for "green table," which was inhabited by Puebloans between 550 and 1300. The Navajo National Monument, located 223 miles (358 km) northwest of Chaco Canyon, was also occupied by the Puebloan people in the late 13th century. Three of their best-preserved cliff dwellings, including the splendid Keet Steel, are here.

THE ANASAZI

Around AD 400, the Chaco Canyon people began to settle in well-defined groups with a common culture known as "Anasazi," a Navajo name said to mean "Ancient Enemy Ancestor." For centuries, their villages stayed small, but a population explosion in the 11th century led to the construction of elaborate cliff dwellings and the building of a road system to connect some 400 settlements. Agriculture thrived—damns and irrigation systems were built and more successful strains of corn (maize) were planted to feed the growing population. However, by 1130 the towns began to empty, perhaps because of drought. People migrated, and by the 13th century the canyon was deserted.

PUEBLO BONITO

Pueblo Bonito is an example of a "great house." It was built in stages over the course of 300 years, from AD 850. This reconstruction shows how it might have looked, with its D-shaped four-story structure that contained more than 650 rooms.

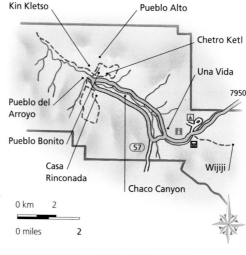

Kivas
These were round, pit-like rooms dug into the ground and roofed with beams and earth.

EXPLORING CHACO

The area around Chaco Canyon is full of hauntingly beautiful ruins left behind by the Ancestral Puebloan people. In addition to the sites described here, they include Una Vida, the fifth-largest great house, with intriguing petroglyphs, Wijiji, Pueblo del Arroyo, and Kin Kletso, a two-story pueblo.

KEY

▰	Highway
⚌	Unpaved road
--	Hiking route
🄰	Camp site/RV
🄿	Picnic area
🄸	Visitor information

Kin Kletso · Pueblo Alto · Chetro Ketl · Una Vida · 7950 · Pueblo del Arroyo · Pueblo Bonito · Casa Rinconada · Chaco Canyon · 57 · Wijiji

0 km   2
0 miles   2

KEY DATES

700–900	850–1250	1896–1900	1920	1987
Domestic and ceremonial *kivas* are built in Chaco Canyon.	Chaco Canyon serves as a religious, trade, and administration center for the Anasazi people.	Archeologist George H. Pepper and his team excavate Pueblo Bonito.	Edgar L. Hewitt excavates the nearby Chetro Ketl.	Chaco Culture National Historical Park is named a UNESCO World Heritage Site.

▲ Stone Doorway

▲ Pueblo Alto

Located on top of the mesa at the junction of several Chacoan roads is Pueblo Alto. In the 1860s, W. H. Jackson discovered an ancient stairway carved into the cliff wall.

▲ Early Astronomers at Fajada Butte

Measurement of time was vital to the Puebloans for crop planting and the timing of ceremonies. A spiral petroglyph carved on Fajada Butte is designed to indicate the changing seasons through the shadows it casts on the rock.

▼ Casa Rinconada

The great *kiva* of Casa Rinconada is the largest religious chamber at Chaco, measuring 62 ft (19 m) in diameter. It was used for spiritual gatherings.

Chetro Ketl ▶

A short trail from Pueblo Bonito leads to another great house, Chetro Ketl. Almost as large as Pueblo Bonito, Chetro Ketl has more than 500 rooms. The masonry used to build the later portions of this structure is among the most sophisticated found in any Puebloan site.

This great house was four stories high

▼ Elaborate cliff dwellings built into the walls of Mesa Verde

Great House Rooms

Hundreds of rooms within Pueblo Bonito show little sign of use and are thought to have been kept for storage, or for guests arriving to take part in ceremonial events.

CHACO POTTERY

Archeologists believe that the inhabitants of Chaco Canyon replaced baskets with ceramics for culinary use between 400 and 750. The ceramic pieces found here to date are decorated with geometric designs and painted using minerals and carbons.

🖼 Stone Doorway

Chaco's skilled builders had only stone tools to work with to create this finely wrought stonework.

Chichén Itzá

The best-preserved Maya site on the Yucatán peninsula, Chichén Itzá continues to confound archeologists. The date of the first settlement in the older, southern part of the site is uncertain, but the northern section was built during a Maya renaissance in the 11th century. Similarities with Tula, the ancient capital of the Toltec empire, and myths of exiled Toltec god-king Quetzalcoatl (Kukulcan) settling at Chichén Itzá, suggest that the renaissance was due to a Toltec invasion. However, other theories hold that Tula was influenced by the Maya, not vice versa. In its heyday as a commercial, religious, and military center, which lasted until about the 13th century, Chichén Itzá supported more than 35,000 people.

▲ Ball Court
At 550 ft (168 m) in length, this is the largest ball court in Mesoamerica. Still in place are the two engraved rings that the ball had to pass through.

Carved figure, Temple of the Warriors

▼ Sacred Cenote

▼ El Castillo

▲ Temple of the Warriors
Set on a small pyramid, this is decorated with sculptures of the rain god Chac and the plumed serpent Kukulcan. A *chacmool* statue and two S-shaped serpent columns guard the entrance.

◄ Nunnery
So called because its small rooms reminded the Spaniards of nuns' cells, this large structure, built in three stages, was probably a palace. This façade of the eastern annexe has particularly beautiful stone fretwork and carvings.

▼ Observatory
Also called El Caracol (The Snail) for its spiral staircase, this building was an astronomical observatory. The various slits in the walls correspond to the positions of certain celestial bodies on key dates in the Maya calendar.

▲ A serpent's head representing the god Kukulcan, El Castillo

◙ Ball court

Main entrance

OFFERINGS

Thousands of objects, including some made of gold and jade, were cast into the Sacred Cenote as offerings to the rain god. If a human sacrificial victim survived, they were thought to possess the power of prophecy.

Tomb of the High Priest

◙ Observatory

◙ Nunnery

La Iglesia
This building is decorated with fretwork, masks of the rain god Chac, and the *bacabs*—four animals who, in Maya myth, held up the sky.

Chichén Viejo

Tzompantli
The "Wall of Skulls" is a low platform whose perimeter is carved with grinning skulls. Archeologists believe that it was used to display the heads of victims of human sacrifice, which was practiced during Chichén Itzá's late period.

Sacred Cenote
A *sacbe* (Maya road) leads to this huge natural well, which is thought to have been revered as the home of the rain god Chac. Archeological evidence indicates that the well was used for human sacrifice.

Platform of the Jaguars and Eagles

El Castillo
Built on top of an older structure that can also be visited, this 79-ft (24-m) high pyramid was dedicated to Kukulcan, the Maya representation of the god Quetzalcoatl. Its height and striking geometric design dominate the whole site.

Temple of the Warriors

Group of a Thousand Columns
Made up of carved stone colonnades on two sides of a huge plaza, this may have been used as a market.

Entrance

KEY DATES

c. 750	c. 900	1904–10	1988
The Sacred Cenote is used for ritual offering to the rain god.	Chichén Itzá becomes the center of Maya culture.	US archeologist Edward Herbert Thompson dredges the Sacred Cenote.	Chichén Itzá is added to UNESCO's World Heritage Site list.

0 meters — 150
0 yards — 150

MAYA DEITIES

A vast array of gods and goddesses were worshiped by the Maya. Some of them were connected to celestial bodies, such as the stars, Sun, and Moon. Others held sway over creation, aspects of daily life, and death. Deities were feared as much as revered and it was essential to appease them as much as possible, often through human sacrifice. Kukulcan, a feathered serpent, was an important deity. Chac, the god of rain and lightning, was venerated, since rainfall was vital to farming communities. Also worshiped was the Sun god Kinich Ahau, who was associated with the jaguar.

EL CASTILLO PYRAMID

Built around 800, the incredible **El Castillo** pyramid has a perfect astronomical design. The four staircases face the cardinal points, with various features corresponding to aspects of the Maya calendar. At the two yearly equinoxes, a fascinating optical illusion occurs whereby a serpent appears to crawl down the north staircase. The temple at the top of the inner pyramid contains a *chacmool*, a carved reclining figure with a stone dish on its stomach thought to have held sacrificial offerings. There is also a beautiful, bright-red throne carved as a jaguar and encrusted with jade. The entrance to the temple is divided by snake-shaped columns.

MAYA CULTURE

Unlike other Mesoamerican peoples, the Maya did not develop a large, centralized empire, living instead in independent city-states. Once thought to have been a peaceful people, they are now known to have shared the lust for war and human sacrifice evident in other ancient civilizations. Immensely talented, the Maya had an understanding of astronomy and developed sophisticated systems of writing, counting, and recording the passing of time (**Observatory**). They predicted the phases of the Moon, equinoxes and solstices, and solar and lunar eclipses. They knew that the Morning and Evening Star were the same planet, Venus, and calculated its "year" to within a fraction of the true figure. Remarkably, they achieved all of this without the use of lenses for observing distant objects, instruments for calculating angles, or clocks.

View of El Castillo pyramid, dominating
the Maya site of Chichén Itzá

Metropolitan Cathedral, Mexico City

The biggest church in Latin America, Mexico City's cathedral is also at the heart of the world's largest Catholic diocese. Its towers rise 220 ft (67 m) above one of the largest public squares in the world, and it took almost three centuries—from 1573 to 1813—to complete. This long period is reflected in the multiple styles of its architecture, ranging from Renaissance (*Renaissance Style, see p.131*) through Baroque (*Baroque Style, see p.81*) to Neo-Classical (*Neo-Classical Style, see p.57*). It has five principal altars and 16 side chapels containing a valuable collection of paintings, sculpture, and church furniture.

▲ **Hymn book on view in the choir**

THE INTERIOR

Like its exterior, the church's interior decoration is a blend of the three prevailing architectural styles of the colonial period. The Baroque altars and side chapels are particularly ornate; a highlight is the richly carved **Altar de los Reyes**. A statue of Christ, the **Señor del Cacao**, which probably dates from the 16th century, is worshiped in the **Capilla de San José**. The statue's name derives from the donations of coffee beans (a common currency in the precolonial era) made by the local people toward the cathedral's construction. An urn containing the remains of Emperor Agustín de Iturbide (1783–1824), the champion of Mexican Independence, is located in the chapel of San Felipe de Jesús.

CONQUISTADORS AND CHRISTIANITY

When the Spanish arrived in the Americas in the 1500s, they encountered flourishing indigenous settlements. In addition to their desire for conquest and their greed for gold, silver, copper, and land, the conquistadors also saw themselves as missionaries and attempted to convert the established Mesoamerican civilizations from paganism to Christianity. Franciscan and Dominican friars preached to, converted, and baptized the indigenous peoples. Although the New World was ultimately conquered by Europeans, elements of the indigenous cultures survived and were absorbed into the developing Christian society.

THE SINKING OF MEXICO CITY

When Spanish conquistador Hernán Cortés led his army into the Aztec capital of Tenochtitlán in 1521, the city stood on an island in Lake Texcoco. After conquering the city, the Spanish razed it to the ground, reused much of the stonework in their own buildings, and gradually filled in the lake. The Metropolitan Cathedral was built on the ruins of the main Aztec temple of worship, whose stones were used in the building's walls. Like so many of Mexico City's buildings, the cathedral has been sinking, almost since its construction, into the ground beneath—the slant is quite visible. Restoration work, mostly carried out underground, has prevented its collapse.

🖼 **Altar de los Reyes**
Carved between 1718 and 1737, the Baroque Altar of the Kings features two oil paintings, the *Adoration of the Kings* and the *Assumption of the Virgin*, both by Juan Rodríguez Juárez.

🖼 **Kings and Queens**
The sculptures adorning the Altar de los Reyes are of kings and queens who have been canonized.

🖼 **Sacristy**
Seventeenth-century paintings and items of carved furniture, including a fine decorated cabinet, can be seen here.

High Altar
This is a block of white marble carved with images of saints.

Side entrance

ALTAR OF PARDON

A figure of the Virgin, by Simón Pereyns, was replaced after the 1967 fire with a black Christ which, legend says, absorbed the poison from a devout man who kissed it on his deathbed.

◄ **Capilla de San José**
This side chapel is one of 16 dedicated to saints and manifestations of the Virgin, all exquisitely decorated with statues and oil paintings.

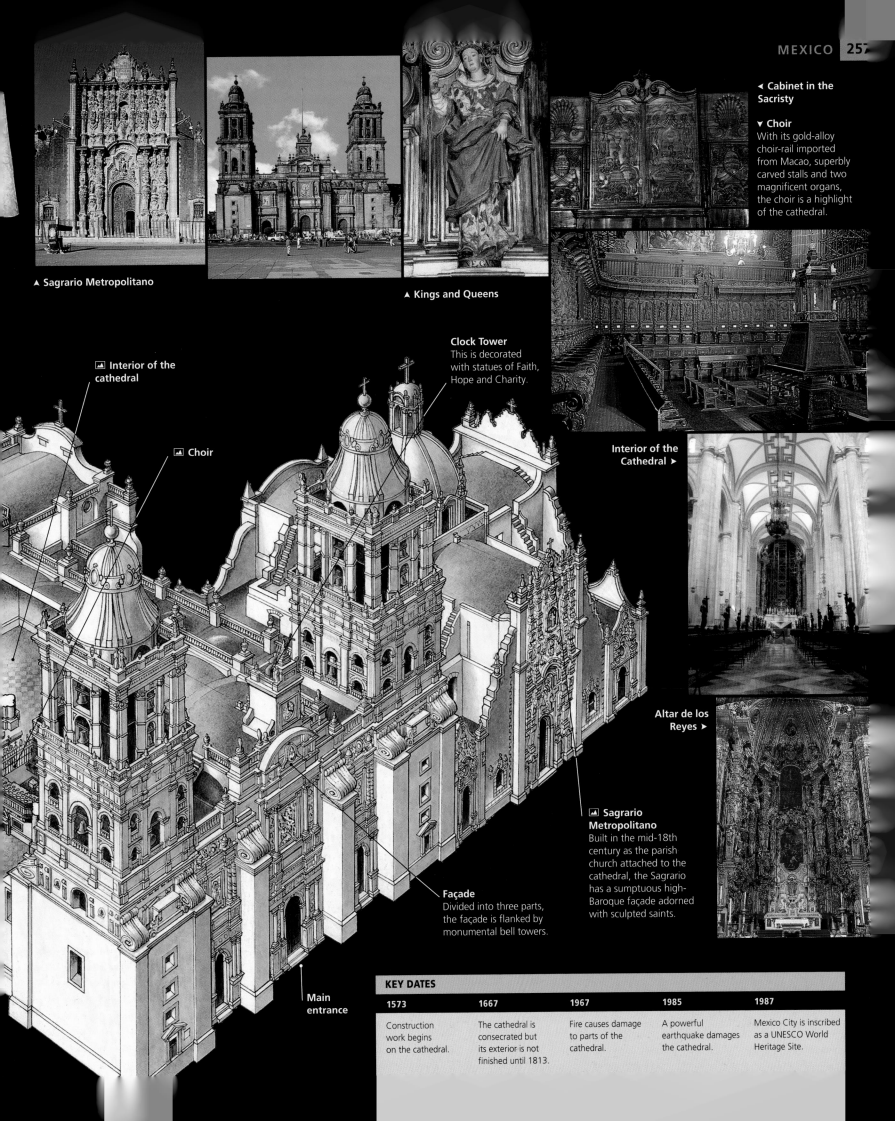

▲ Sagrario Metropolitano

▲ Kings and Queens

◄ Cabinet in the Sacristy

▼ Choir
With its gold-alloy choir-rail imported from Macao, superbly carved stalls and two magnificent organs, the choir is a highlight of the cathedral.

Interior of the Cathedral ►

◢ Interior of the cathedral

◢ Choir

Clock Tower
This is decorated with statues of Faith, Hope and Charity.

Altar de los Reyes ►

◢ Sagrario Metropolitano
Built in the mid-18th century as the parish church attached to the cathedral, the Sagrario has a sumptuous high-Baroque façade adorned with sculpted saints.

Façade
Divided into three parts, the façade is flanked by monumental bell towers.

Main entrance

KEY DATES

1573	1667	1967	1985	1987
Construction work begins on the cathedral.	The cathedral is consecrated but its exterior is not finished until 1813.	Fire causes damage to parts of the cathedral.	A powerful earthquake damages the cathedral.	Mexico City is inscribed as a UNESCO World Heritage Site.

Machu Picchu

The "Lost City of the Inca" is one of the most spectacular archeological sites in the world. Perched high on a saddle between two peaks, surrounded by thick jungle and often shrouded in cloud, it is almost invisible from below. A compact site of just 5 sq miles (13 sq km), it was built in 1460 by the Incan ruler Pachacuti Inca Yupanqui. Although frequently referred to as a city, it was more of a royal retreat for the Inca aristocracy. About 1,000 people inhabited the area and they were completely self-sufficient, being surrounded by agricultural terraces and watered by natural springs. Even at the time, few people outside the closed Inca community were aware of Machu Picchu's existence.

▲ **Llama at Machu Picchu**
The Inca used llamas as pack animals and they were also a source of wool, leather hides, and meat.

INCA ARCHITECTURE

The people who built Machu Picchu possessed incredibly advanced construction skills. Some of the building blocks weigh more than 50 tons, yet they are meticulously designed and fit together so exactly that the thinnest knife cannot be inserted between the mortarless joints. The ruins are roughly divided into two areas: the agricultural sector, consisting of **terraces** for cultivation; and the **urban sector**, with structures of varying size, canals, and steps. The design of the site reveals the creativity of the builders. The enormous walls, delicate terracing, and steep ramps could almost have been sculpted out of the rock by the elements.

HIRAM BINGHAM

The discovery of this major Incan site in 1911 was one of the most significant archeological finds of the 20th century. American explorer Hiram Bingham had set out to find Vilcabamba, the legendary last refuge of the defeated Inca empire, but instead he came across Machu Picchu. It took Bingham and his team several years to clear the thick vegetation that had covered the ruins. Underneath were houses, temples, canals, and thousands of steps and terraces. What made the discovery so exciting was the fact that the Spanish conquistadors had not found and plundered the site, and that it was also untouched by treasure hunters.

INCA CULTURE

The Inca founded their capital, Cusco, in the 13th century and began a period of conquest. By the early 16th century, the Inca empire reached from Chile to Colombia and controlled around 12 million people. This well-organized civilization had a sophisticated economy and a road network of 20,000 miles (32,200 km). They ruled with fierce military might and had a strict social hierarchy, yet they also learned from the cultures they conquered. The Inca worshiped the natural world, seeing the Sun as the ultimate giver of life and their leader as its direct descendant. Mountain peaks, home of the spirits, were used for human sacrifice. Celestial events were monitored so they knew when to plant and harvest crops, and when to hold religious ceremonies.

▲ **Intihuatana**

Preserved Brick Work ▶

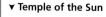

▼ **Temple of the Sun**

Agricultural terraces and irrigation channels prevented soil erosion ▶

THE INCA TRAIL

The legendary Inca Trail climbs and descends a number of steep valleys and crosses three mountain passes of more than 12,000 ft (3,658 m). The breathtaking scenery includes snow-capped mountains, dense cloud forest, and delicate flowers. Cobblestones laid by the Inca, as well as the tunnels that they constructed, can still be seen. It takes about four or five days before hikers are rewarded with the unforgettable sight of Machu Picchu through the Sun gate (Intipunku).

Majestic view of Machu Picchu at the end of the Inca Trail

▲ **Sacred Plaza**
With huge windows, the Temple of the Three Windows adjoins the Sacred Plaza, along with the Main Temple, which contains an almost flawlessly constructed wall.

KEY DATES

c. 1200	1460	Mid-1500s	1911	1983
The Inca found their capital at Cusco, Peru, and begin their far-reaching expansion.	Machu Picchu is built, 7,970 ft (2,430 m) above sea level.	Machu Picchu is abandoned, possibly due to civil war over succession.	The site is uncovered by US explorer Hiram Bingham.	Machu Picchu is delcared a World Heritage Site by UNESCO.

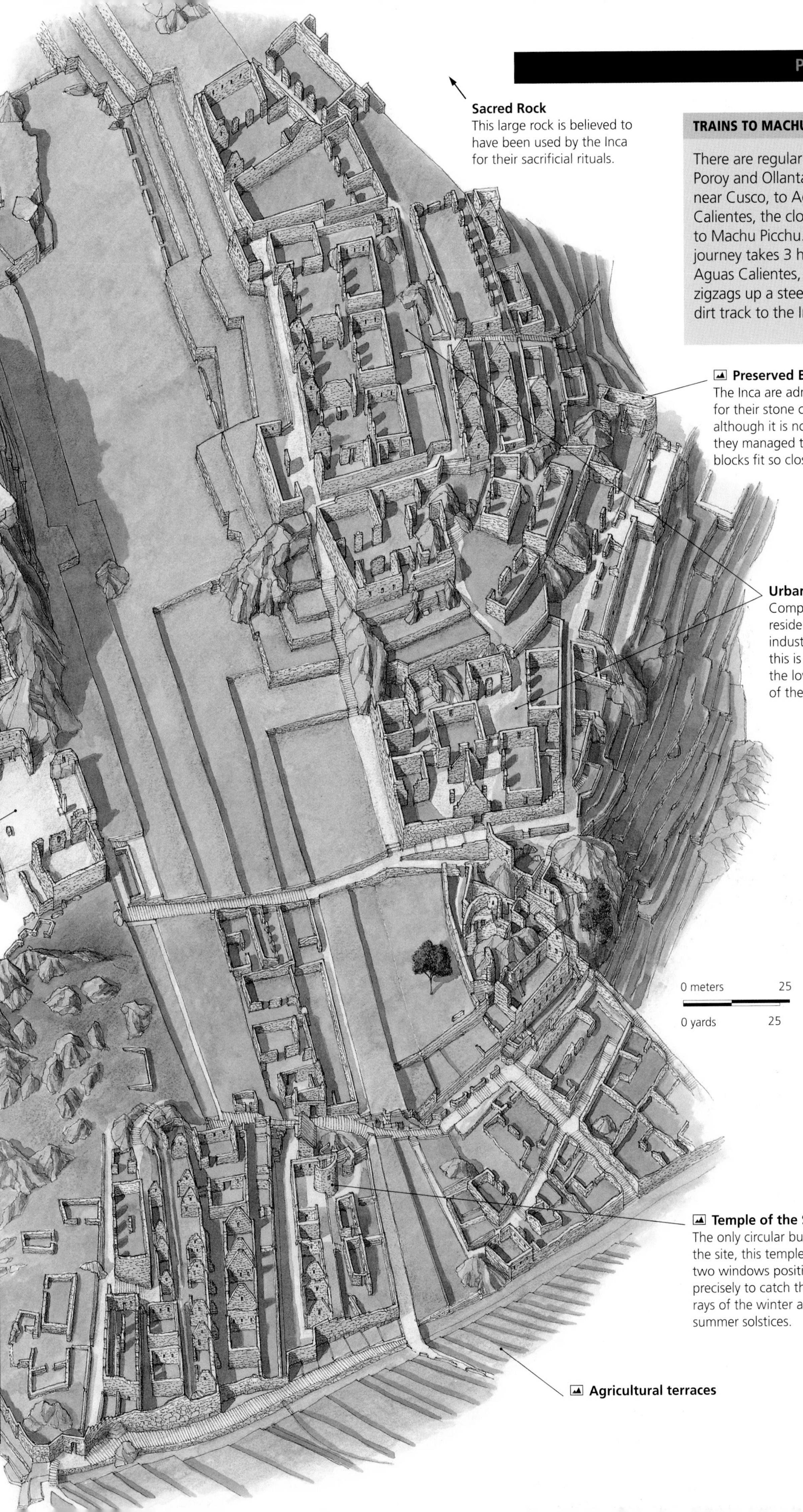

⊿ Intihuatana
This sundial, the size of a
grand piano, was extremely
sacred and one of the most
important features of the
whole site. Winter solstice
festivals took place here.

Sacred Rock
This large rock is believed to
have been used by the Inca
for their sacrificial rituals.

TRAINS TO MACHU PICCHU

There are regular trains from
Poroy and Ollantaytambo,
near Cusco, to Aguas
Calientes, the closest town
to Machu Picchu. The scenic
journey takes 3 hours. From
Aguas Calientes, a local bus
zigzags up a steep, narrow
dirt track to the Inca site.

⊿ Preserved Brick Work
The Inca are admired today
for their stone constructions,
although it is not known how
they managed to make the
blocks fit so closely together.

Urban Sector
Comprising the
residential and
industrial areas,
this is located in
the lower section
of the site.

⊿ Sacred Plaza

▼ View of Machu Picchu
Made up of around 200
buildings and connected by
more than 100 stairways, the
ruined palaces, temples, and
residences were built around
large central squares.

0 meters   25

0 yards   25

⊿ Temple of the Sun
The only circular building on
the site, this temple contains
two windows positioned
precisely to catch the first
rays of the winter and
summer solstices.

⊿ Agricultural terraces

Brasília

A 20th-century city of pure invention, Brasília is the realization of a seemingly impossible dream. President Juscelino Kubitschek de Oliveira (1956–60) was elected partly on the basis of his highly ambitious pledge to move the capital of Brazil 746 miles (1,200 km) inland, from Rio de Janeiro into the country's empty center, before the end of his first term. This was miraculously achieved by the tens of thousands of workers who created the specially built city from an area of scrubland. The principal public buildings, which include a cathedral, are strikingly designed. Brasília fulfilled Kubitschek's ambition to develop the country's interior and create a monument both to modern architecture and Brazil's economic potential.

THE CITY'S LAYOUT

Brasília's unique design is referred to as the **Pilot Plan**. Urban planner Lúcio Costa said he simply used a shape that followed the lie of the land. He wanted to form a centralized, geometric plan to create an ideal city, and therefore an ideal society. The design is based on two axes: a **Monumental Axis** and a **Residential Axis**. Six wide avenues are intended to provide the grandeur of a capital city, with the **Supreme Court**, **Congress Complex**, and Presidential Palace (**Planalto Palace**) representing the balance of the three powers. The residential area is made up of "superblocks"—six-story apartment buildings, grouped to form neighborhood units.

THE COMPETITION

In 1957, Lúcio Costa and Oscar Niemeyer were announced as the winners of the competition launched to choose the urban design of Brasília. Costa was responsible for the general design of Brasília, but Niemeyer created the main buildings. Both were students of the modernist architect Le Corbusier, the father of functional, boxlike buildings. Costa has been criticized for not providing for public transportation, and for designing a city for 500,000 people that today houses two million residents, many living in slums. However, it is generally agreed that Niemeyer achieved his goal of creating a city with "harmony and a sense of occasion" with his powerful public buildings.

OSCAR NIEMEYER

The vision of Oscar Niemeyer has become synonymous with the rise of modern Brazil. Born in 1907, Niemeyer graduated from Rio de Janeiro's National School of Fine Arts in 1934 and collaborated with Lúcio Costa and Le Corbusier on the new Ministry of Education and Health in Rio. His style became more daring as he incorporated reinforced concrete into his buildings. He is probably best known for his designs for the main public buildings in Brasília, such as the concave and convex domes of the **National Congress**, the simple yet evocative **cathedral** and the spectacular **Palace of Justice**. A pioneer of modern architecture, he has won numerous prizes.

BRASÍLIA CATHEDRAL

The striking yet simple form of the cathedral provides Brasília with a recognizable identity. An illusion of space is created in the interior by the circular floor being set below ground level and therefore lower than the entrance.

Baptistry
This unusual, egg-shaped building is said to be a representation of the host (sacramental bread). It is connected to the cathedral by a tunnel.

← Cathedral entrance

A PRIESTLY VISION

In 1883, an Italian priest named Dom Bosco had a vision about the future site of Brazil's new capital. Each year, on the last Sunday in August, a procession in Brasília celebrates the anniversary of his dream.

Pulpit ▶
This contains a huge crucifix carved from a single piece of tropical cedarwood.

KEY DATES

1956	1957	1958	1960	1987
Kubitschek is inaugurated as president of Brazil. A competition is launched for the design of Brasília.	Construction of the city begins, based on Lúcio Costa's Pilot Plan.	The foundation stone of the cathedral is laid; the building is consecrated in 1970.	Brasília is inaugurated on April 21 and becomes the capital city of Brazil.	Brasília is designated a World Heritage Site by UNESCO.

Cathedral Design
Oscar Niemeyer's design symbolizes a crown of thorns, and consists of sixteen 131-ft (40-m) high concrete columns that suggest arms reaching toward the sky.

◢ Nave
This is decorated with stained glass made from 16 pieces of painted fiberglass. Suspended from its ceiling are three floating angels by the Brazilian sculptor Alfredo Ceschiatti.

THE PILOT PLAN

Brasília's design, the Pilot Plan, is based on the shape of an airplane: the Monumental Axis (the fuselage) intersects with the Residential Axis (the wings). Two main traffic arteries divide the city, while the infrastructure is strictly divided into sectors.

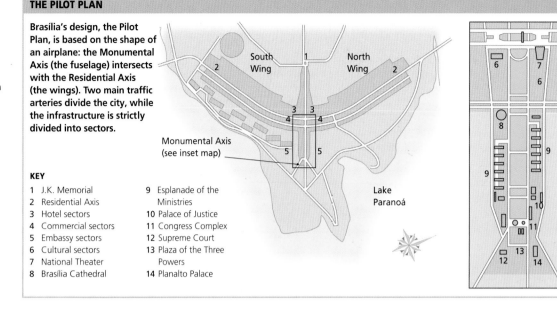

South Wing

North Wing

Monumental Axis
(see inset map)

Lake Paranoá

KEY
1 J.K. Memorial
2 Residential Axis
3 Hotel sectors
4 Commercial sectors
5 Embassy sectors
6 Cultural sectors
7 National Theater
8 Brasília Cathedral
9 Esplanade of the Ministries
10 Palace of Justice
11 Congress Complex
12 Supreme Court
13 Plaza of the Three Powers
14 Planalto Palace

▾ Alfredo Ceschiatti's sculpture *The Four Evangelists* stands outside the cathedral

Water—a recurring theme in Brasília— surrounds the cathedral

Nave ▸

▾ JK Memorial
Inaugurated in 1981, this monument was built to honor the former Brazilian president Juscelino Kubitschek, whose tomb is housed here.

◢ Pulpit

▾ National Congress
The juxtaposition of the dishes and twin towers provides the dramatic, space-age silhouette that is a symbol of the city.

▾ Palace of Justice
This low-rise, unimposing building features water cascading between its delicate white arches. Nearby is a stone sculpture of the head of Juscelino Kubitschek.

Monumental Axis ▴
Light gilds the row of rectangular buildings standing sentrylike along the Esplanade of the Ministries. Each one is home to a different government department. In the distance is the Congress Complex.

INDEX

ACKNOWLEDGMENTS

The Publishers would like to thank the following people whose contributions and assistance have made the preparation of this book possible:

Additional Contributors
Jane Egginton, Frances Linzee Gordon, Denise Heywood, Andrew Humphries, Roger Williams.

Editorial and Design Assistance
Louise Buckley, Tracy Smith, Stuti Tiwari Bhatia and Neha Dhingra.

Illustrators Richard Almazan, Studios Arcana, Modi Artistici, Robert Ashby, William Band, Gilles Beauchemin, Dipankar Bhattacarga, Anuar Bin Abdul Rahim, Richard Bonson, François Brosse, Michal Burkiewicz, Cabezas/Acanto Arquitectura y Urbanismo S.L., Jo Cameron, Danny Cherian, Yeapkok Chien, ChrisOrr.com, Stephen Conlin, Garry Cross, Bruno de Robillard, Brian Delf, Donati Giudici Associati srl, Richard Draper, Dean Entwhistle, Steven Felmore, Marta Fincato, Eugene Fleury, Chris Forsey, Martin Gagnon, Vincent Gagnon, Nick Gibbard, Isidoro González-Adalid, Kevin Goold, Paul Guest, Stephen Gyapay, Toni Hargreaves, Trevor Hill, Chang Huai-Yan, Roger Hutchins, Kamalahasan R, Kevin Jones Assocs., John Lawrence, Wai Leong Koon, Yoke Ling Lee, Nick Lipscombe, Ian Lusted, Andrew MacDonald, Maltings Partnership, Lena Maminajszwili, Kumar Mantoo Stuart, Pawel Marczak, Lee Ming Poo, Pawel Mistewicz, John Mullaney, Jill Mumford, Gillie Newman, Luc Normandin, Arun P, Lee Peters, Otakar Pok, Robbie Polley, David Pulvermacher, Avinash Ramscurrun, Kevin Robinson, Peter Ross, Simon Roulstone, Suman Saha, Fook San Choong, Ajay Sethi, Derrick Slone, Jaroslav Staněk, Thomas Sui, Ashok Sukumaran, Peggy Tan, Pat Thorne, Gautam Trivedi, Frank Urban, Mark Warner, Paul Weston, Andrzej Wielgosz, Ann Winterbotham, Martin Woodward, Bohdan Wróblewski, Hong Yew Tan, Kah Yune Denis Chai, Magdalena Zmadzinska, Piotr Zubrzycki.

Indexers Hilary Bird, Jane Henley.

Special Assistance Maire ní Bhain at Trinity College, Dublin; Chartres Cathedral, Procurate di San Marco (Basilica San Marco); Campo dei Miracoli, Pisa; Hayley Smith and Romaine Werblow from DK Picture Library; Mrs Marjorie Weeke at St Peter's Basilica; Le Soprintendenze Archeologiche di Agrigento di Pompei; Topkapı Palace, Istanbul; M Oulhaj (Mosque of Hassan II); The Castle of Good Hope.

Additional Photography Shaen Adey, Max Alexander, Fredrik & Laurence Arvidsson, Gábor Barka, Philip Blenkinsop, Maciej Bronarski, Demetrio Carrasco, Tina Chambers, Kate Clow, Joe Cornish, Andy Crawford, Ian Cumming, Tim Daly, Geoff Dann, Robert O'Dea, Barbara Deer, Vladimír Dobrovodský, Jiří Doležal, Alistair Duncan, Mike Dunning, Christopher and Sally Gable, Philippe Giraud, Heidi Grassley, Paul Harris, Adam Hajder, John Heseltine, Nigel Hicks, Ed Ironside, Stuart Isett, Dorota & Mariusz Jarymowicz, Alan Keohane, Dinesh Khanna, Dave King, Paul Kenward, Vladimir Kozlik, Andrew McKinney, Jiří Kopřiva, Neil Lukas, Paweł Marczac, Eric Meacher, Katarzyna and Wojciech Mędrzak, Michael Moran, Roger Moss, Hanna and Maciej Musiał, Tomasz Myśluk, Stephen Oliver, Vincent Oliver, Gary Ombler, Lloyd Park, John Parker, Amit Pasricha, Aditya Patankar, Artur Pawłowski, František Přeučil, Ram Rahman, Bharath Ramamrutham, Rob Reichenfeld, Magnes Rew, Alistair Richardson, Terry Richardson, Alex Robinson, Lucio Rossi, Rough Guides/Tim Draper, Rough Guides/Michelle Grant, Rough Guides/Nelson Hancock, Rough Guides/Suzanne Porter, Rough Guides/Dylan Reisenberger, Rough Guides/Mark Thomas, Jean-Michel Ruiz, Kim Sayer, Jürgen Scheunemann, Colin Sinclair, Toby Sinclair, Frits Solvang, Tony Souter, Jon Spaull, James Stevenson, Eric Svensson, Cécile Tréal, Lübbe Verlag, Cylla Von Tiedemann, BPS Walia, Mathew Ward, Richard Watson, Stephen Whitehorn, Dominic Whiting, Linda Whitwam, Jeppe Wikström, Alan Williams, Peter Wilson, Paweł Wójcik, Stephen Wooster, Francesca Yorke.

Photography Permissions Dorling Kindersley would like to thank all the churches, temples, mosques, castles, museums, and other sights too numerous to list individually for their assistance and kind permission to photograph their establishments.

Picture Credits Key: a-above; b-below/bottom; c-center; f-far; l-left; r-right; t-top

DORLING KINDERSLEY would like to thank the following for their assistance: National Archaeological Museum, Naples: 132ca; © Patrimonio Nacional 112-3; Private Collection 169crb; Etablissement public du musée et du domaine nationale de Versailles 58tl, 58ca, 58c, 58cb, 58crb, 59bl.

Works of art have been reproduced with the permission of the following copyright holders: *Paris through the Window (*1913), Marc Chagall © ADAGP, Paris, 2011 237tl; *Black Lines* (1913) Vasily Kandinsky © ADAGP, Paris, 2011 237tr; *Woman Holding a Vase* (1927), Fernand Léger © ADAGP, Paris, 2011 237tc; *Woman Ironing* (1904) Pablo Picasso © Succession Picasso/DACS 2011 237crb; *Woman with Yellow Hair* (1931) Pablo Picasso © Succession Picasso/DACS 2011 237cb; *Snake* (1996) Richard Serra © ARS, NY and DACS London 2011 107tl.

The Publishers thank the following individuals, companies, and picture libraries for permission to reproduce their photographs:

A1 PIX: Mati 185bl.
ACCADEMIA ITALIANA: Sue Bond 132tr.
ARCHIVO ICONOGRAFICO S.A. (AISA) : 144tr.
AKG: 89tl, 89tc, 173tc, 175crb.
ALAMY IMAGES: Walter Bibikow 118–9; Robert Harding World Imagery 185cra; Dallas and John Heaton 176–7; David Jones 164–5; Steve Murray 254–5.
ANCIENT ART & ARCHITECTURE COLLECTION: 161ca.
ARCAID: Paul Rafferty 107crb.
ARCHIVIO DELL'ARTE: Luciano Pedicini 132c.
FABRIZIO ARDITO: 183tc.
THE ART ARCHIVE: 163br; Devizes Musem/Eileen Tweedy 39cra.
ART DIRECTORS: Eric Smith 185br.
AXIOM: Heidi Grassley 163bc; James Morris 163crb.
TAHSIN AYDOGMUS: 148tc.
JAUME BALAYNA: 111cra.
OSVALDO BöHM:116bc.
BORD FÁILTE/IRISH TOURIST BOARD: Brian Lynch 16tc, 17cra.
GERARD BOULLAY: 55tc; 55tr.
BRAZIL STOCK PHOTOS: Fabio Pili 261fbl.
BRIDGEMAN ART LIBRARY, LONDON/NEW YORK: Private Collection 43tc; Royal Holloway & Bedford New College, *The Princes Edward and Richard in the Tower* by Sir John Everett Millais 34br; Basilica San Francesco, Assisi 127tc; Smith Art Gallery & Museum, Stirling 22tl; Stapleton Collection 160tl, 163cr.
DEMETRIO CARRASCO: 97cra, 97cr.
CHINAPIX: Zhang Chaoyin 186bl, 186bc.
PHOTOS EDITIONS COMBIER, MACON: 48fcr.
CORBIS: Archivo Iconografico, S.A. 211tl; Yann Arthus-Bertrand 261br; Bettmann Archive 238cl, 238c, 243cl; Dave Bartruff 69cra, 151clb; Marilyn Bridges 39bl; Chromo Sohm Inc./Jospeh Sohm 189cra; Elio Ciol 4bc, 173crb; Dean Conger 193br; Eye Ubiquitous/Thelma Sanders 166clb; Owen Franken 64–5; Todd Gipstein 243tc; Lowell Georgia 192tr; Farrell Grehan 90–1; John and Dallas Heaton 8t, 8bc; John Heseltine 52–3, Angelo Hornak 29tc, 43cb; Wolfgang Kaehler 166tl, 185crb; Kelly-Mooney Photography 195tr; Charles Lenars 188tr; Jean-Pierre Lescourret 2–3; Craig Lovell 186tl; David Samuel Robbins 186clb; Sakamoto Photo Research Lab 199tr; Kevin Schafer 39bc; James Sparshatt 1; Paul A Souders 5br; Sandro Vannini 166cla; Vanni Archive 140ca; Nik Wheeler 166cl; Adam Woolfitt 146–7; CRESCENT PRESS AGENCY: David Henley 211crb. GERALD CUBITT: 211tr. CULVER PICTURES INC: 239tl, 242cl, 242br, 243clb. DAS FOTOARCHIV: Henning Christoph 166tr. DEUTSCHE APOTHEKENMUSEUM: 75tc. DIATOTALE: Château de Chenonceau 63c. ASHOK DILWALI: 206tr.
DOMBAUVERWALTUNG DES METROPOLITANKAPITELS KÖLN: Brigit Lambert 70cla, 70clb, 70c, 70cra, 70cr, 70cb, 71tl, 71tc.
D.N. DUBE: 207tl, 207tc.
EKDOTIKE ATHENON S.A: 140cb, 143cla.
MARY EVANS PICTURE LIBRARY: 38tr, 42cr, 56bl, 102c, 129bc.
EYE UBIQUITOUS: Julia Waterlow 261crb.
FORTIDSMINNEFORENINGEN: Kjersheim/Lindstad, NIKU 13cra.
MICHAEL FREEMAN: 247bc, 247crb.
CHRISTINA GAMBARO: 175cra.
GEHRY PARTNERS LLP: 106tr.
EVA GERUM: 72ca, 72c, 72cr, 72crb, 72fcrb, 73bc.
GETTY IMAGES: Altrendo Images 138–9; Robert Harding World Imagery/Gavin Heller 214–5; Hulton-Deutsch 19crb, 192ca; Image Bank/Anthony Edwards 40–1/Mitchell Funk 240–1/Peter Hendrie 210tr, Frans Lemmens 170–1/A Setterwhite 243ca; National Geographic/Raymond K Gehman 190–1; Photodisc/Life File/David Kampfner 100–1; Photographer's Choice/John Warden 189crb; Stone/Jerry Alexander 258cra, /Stephen Studd 152–3; Taxi/Gary Randall 228–9, /Chris Rawlings 222–3.
EVA GLEASON: 256–7t, 256bc, 257tr, 257cra, 257crb.
LA GOÉLETTE: *The Three Graces* Charles-André Van Loo photo J J Derennes 62tr.
GOLDEN GATE BRIDGE, HIGHWAY & TRANSPORT ATION DISTRICT (GGBHTD): 248tr, 248bc, 248br, 249tl, 249cra, 249crb.
GUGGENHEIM BILBAO MUSEO: 107tl, 107tc, 107tr, 107cra.
SONIA HALLIDAY: Laura Lushington 60bc.
ROBERT HARDING PICTURE LIBRARY: 66ca, 130tl, R Francis 54c; R Frerck 258clb; Sylvain Grandadam 261cr; Michael Jenner 145bc; Christopher Rennie 200–1; Eitan Simmnor 173cra; James Strachan 185bc; Explorer/P Tetrel 59tr.
DENISE HEYWOOD: 216tl, 216tr, 216cla, 216cl, 216clb, 216bc, 217ca, 218tr, 219tl, 219tr, 219ca, 219cr, 219cra, 219crb.
JULIET HIGHET: 219tc.
HISTORIC ROYAL PALACES (Crown Copyright): 35clb, 36tc, 36ca, 36fcra, 36cb, 36crb, 36bc, 36br, 37tr.
HISTORIC SCOTLAND (Crown Copyright): 23tc, 24ca, 25cra, 25crb.
ANGELO HORNAK LIBRARY: 28tl, 29cr.
IMAGES OF AFRICA: Shaen Adey 168cb; Hein von Horsten 168ca; Lanz von Horsten 169bl.
IMAGINECHINA: 193cra, 195tc.
IMPACT PHOTOS: Y Goldstein 184ca.
INDEX: 114tr.
INSIGHT GUIDES: APA/Jim Holmes 97tc.
HANAN ISACHAR: 150ca, 174tc, 175ca, 181tl.
PAUL JACKSON: 182tr.
JARROLD COLOUR PUBLICATIONS: 19tl.
MICHAEL JENNER PHOTOGRAPHY: 150br, 173tl.
KEA PUBLISHING SERVICES LTD: Francesco Venturi 97ftl, 97tl, 97tr.
IZZET KERIBAR: 150cra.
KOSTOS KONTOS: 140tr.
KUNSTHISTORISCHES MUSEUM, VIENNA: *Italienische Berglandschaft mit Hirt und Herde* (GG 7465) (*Italian Landscape with Shepherd and Herd*), Joseph Rosa 84tl.
BERND LASDIN: 69crb, 69bc, 69br.
HÅKON LI: 12ca, 12cb, 12cr.
JÜRGEN LIEPE: 160tr.
LÜBBE VERLAG: 84tr.
MAGNUM: Topkapı Palace Museum/Ara Guler 145tc.
NATIONAL PARK SERVICE (CHACO CULTURE NATIONAL HISTORICAL PARK): Dave Six 250tr.
NATIONAL PARK SERVICE (STATUE OF LIBERTY NATIONAL MONUMENT): 243c, 243cb.
JÜRGEN NOGAI: 69tc, 69cr.
RICHARD NOWITZ: 175tr, 175cr, 175br, 179tl, 181cb, 181br, 183ca.
© THE OFFICE OF PUBLIC WORKS, IRELAND: 17tc, 17tr, 17ca.
ORLETA AGENCY: Jerzy Bronarski 86tl, 86cla, 86cl, 86clb, 87ca.
PALACIO DA PENA: 103bc.
PALEIS HET LOO: 47ca, 47cra, 47cb, 47crb, 47br.
PANOS PICTURES: Christien Jaspars 167tc.
PHOTOS 12: Panorama Stock 189br.
PHOTOBANK: Peter Baker 150bc, 151cr.
ANDREA PISTOLESI: 247br.
POWERSTOCK: Superstock 78–9.
PRAGUE CITY ARCHIVES (ARCHIV HLAVNIKO MESTA PRAHA): 93tr.
FABIO RATTI: 179c.
GEORGE RIHA: 83tr.
ROCAMADOUR: 66tl.
THE ROYAL COLLECTION © 2004, Her Majesty Queen Elizabeth II: 34tl, 34tr, 34cla, 36fbr.
ROYAL GEOGRAPHICAL SOCIETY PICTURE LIBRARY: Chris Caldicott 166ca, 258cr; Eric Lawrie 4br, 259bl; Sassoom 258crb.
SHALINI SARAN: 209ftl, 209tl, 209tc, 209ca, 209c, 209bc.
ST PAUL'S CATHEDRAL: Peter Smith 32tl, 32cl, 32bl.
SCALA GROUP SPA: 122bc, 123bc, 124cb, 126clb, 126bc, 127bc, 128clb, 130tr.
SCHLÖSSERVERWALTUNG: 77cla, 77ca, 77cl, 77c.
SCHLOSS SCHÖNBRUNN: 84cla, 84clb, 84bl, 84bc, 85tc, 85cb.
SHRINE OF SAINTE-ANNE-DE BEAUPRÉ: 230tr, 230br, 231crb, 231bc, 231br.
SKYSCAN: 39br.
SOLOMON R GUGGENHEIM MUSEUM: photo by D Heald 237tl, 237tc, 237tr, 237cra, 237cr, 237cb, 237crb.
SOUTH AMERICAN PICTURES: Tony Morrison 261bl.
STATE RUSSIAN MUSEUM: 96tr.
SUPERSTOCK LTD: 212ca.
COURTESY OF SYDNEY OPERA HOUSE TRUST: 225tl, 225tc, 225cra, 225br, 225ftr.
SUZIE THOMAS PUBLICITY: 225tr.
TRAVEL INK: Allan Hatley 212crb; Pauline Thorton 212fbr.
TRIZECHAHN TOWER LIMITED PARTNERSHIP: 232cra, 232cb, 233tl.
TRINITY COLLEGE, Dublin: 18bc.
TURNER ENTERTAINMENT CO: 239c
UNIVERSITY MUSEUM OF CULTURAL HERITAGE – UNIVERSITY OF OSLO, NORWAY: 13tl.
VASAMUSEET: Hans Hammarskiöld 14tl, 14ca, 14cl, 14c, 14clb, 14bl, 14bc, 15tc.
MIREILLE VAUTIER: 258cla, 258ca, 261bc.
ROGER VIOLLET: 57tc.
ViSIONS OF THE LAND: Garo Nalbandian 178cl, 178bl, 178cra, 183tl, 183cra; Basilio Rodella 175tl, 178cla, 178clb, 181tc, 181ca, 181cra, 181crb.
B.P.S. WALIA: 203cb.
Reproduced by kind permission of the DEAN AND CHAPTER, WESTMINSTER: 31br.
WHITE HOUSE HISTORICAL ASSOCIATION: 245tl, 245tc, 245cla, 245ca, 245c, 245cb.
PETER WILSON: 136ca.
WOODMANSTERNE: Jeremy Marks 32clb.
WORLD PICTURES: 185tr.
Reproduced by kind permission of the DEAN AND CHAPTER OF YORK: 29ftl; Alan Curtis 29tr; Jim Korshaw 29tl; Newbury Smith Photography 28c.
ZEFA: age fotostock 108–9; Masterfile/Gail Mooney 10–11.
FRONT JACKET: GETTY IMAGES: Travel Ink/Gallo Images; BACK JACKET: ALAMY IMAGES: John Warburton-Lee Photography/Christian Kober tl; GETTY IMAGES: Photodisc/Glen Allison tc, Photographer's Choice/Peter Gridley tr.

All other images © Dorling Kindersley.
For further information see: www.dkimages.com